JULINE

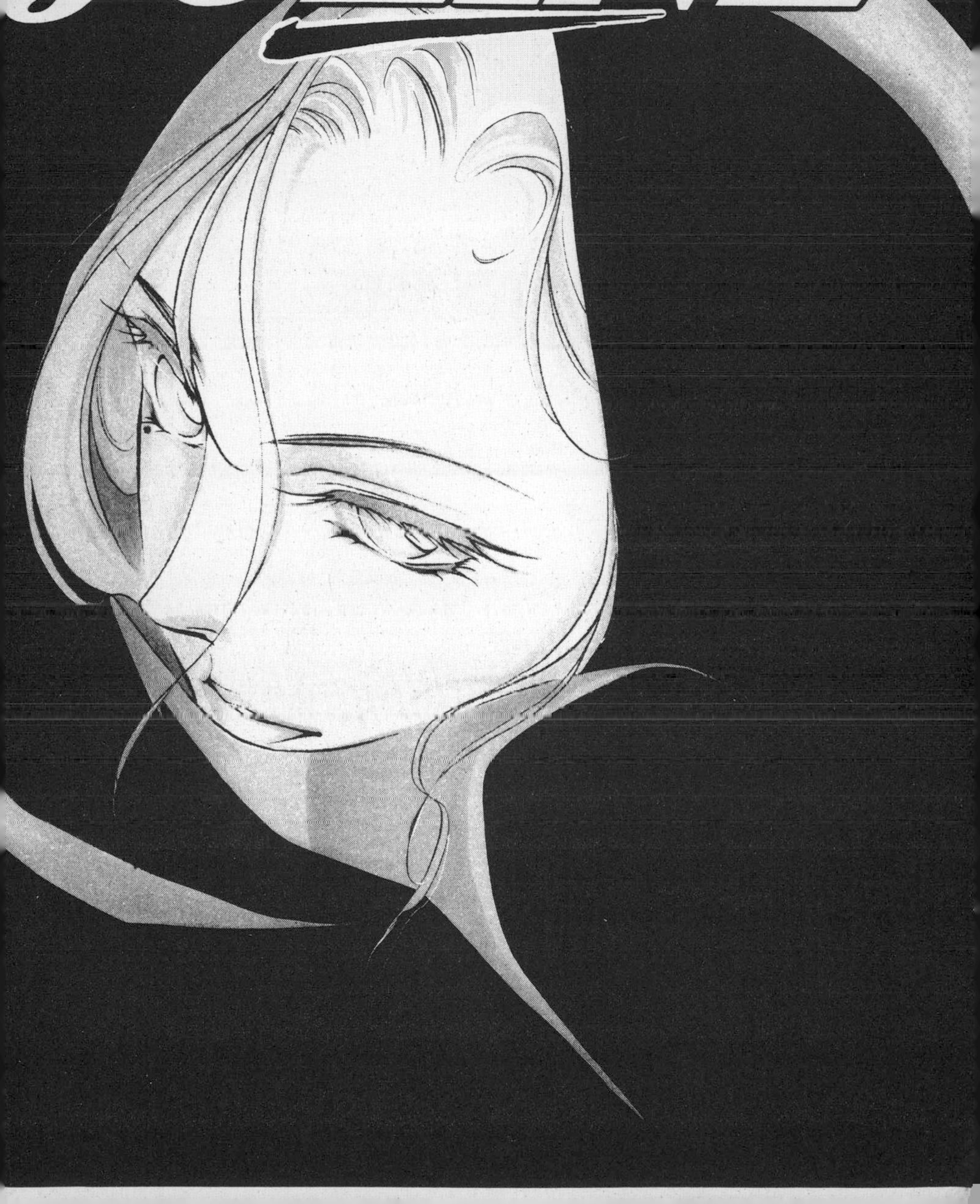

TOKYOPOP® Presents Juline 5 by Narumi Kakinouchi
TOKYOPOP is a registered trademark
of Mixx Entertainment, Inc.
ISBN: 1-931514-05-4
First Printing April 2002

10   9   8   7   6   5   4   3   2   1

Translator – Dan Papia. Retouch Artist – Jinky De Leon.
Production Assistant – Dolly Chan. Graphic Designer – Akemi Imafuku.
Copy Editors – Eric Althoff and Trisha Kunimoto.
Editor – Robert Coyner. Associate Editor – Paul Morrissey.
Senior Editor – Jake Forbes. Production Manager – Fred Lui. Art Director – Matt Alford.
Brand Manager – Joel Baral. VP of Production – Ron Klamert. Publisher – Stuart Levy.

Email: editor@TOKYOPOP.com
Come visit us at www.TOKYOPOP.com

TOKYOPOP®
Los Angeles – Tokyo

JULINE

Vol. 5

By Narumi Kakinouchi

Juline ◉ Character Guide

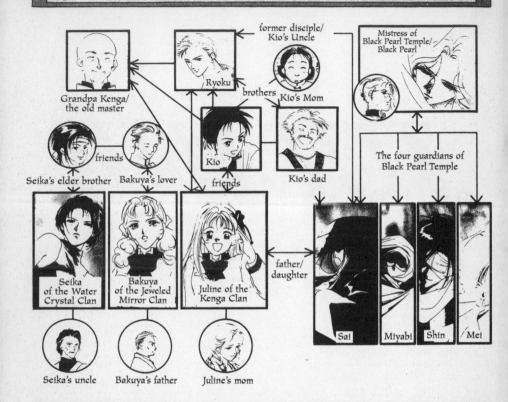

former disciple/
Kio's Uncle
Mistress of
Black Pearl Temple/
Black Pearl
Ryoku
brothers
Kio's Mom
Grandpa Kenga/
the old master
friends
Kio
The four guardians of
Black Pearl Temple
Seika's elder brother
Bakuya's lover
friends
Kio's dad
father/
daughter
Seika
of the Water
Crystal Clan
Bakuya
of the Jeweled
Mirror Clan
Juline of the
Kenga Clan
Sai
Miyabi
Shin
Mei
Seika's uncle
Bakuya's father
Juline's mom

BACKSTORY

A new kung fu temple has appeared in the shadow of Sleeping Dragon Mountain, the House of the Black Pearl. The ruler of the clan, Black Pearl, has captured three sacred relics she plans to use to awaken the long hibernating dragon and find the ultimate power.

Now possessing the Jeweled Mirror of the Houkyo Clan, the Water Crystal of the Suisho Clan and the Ivory Sword of the Kenga Clan, Black Pearl has assembled everything she needs - or has she? One of the items is a fake, and now the princesses of the clans, Juline, Seika and Bakuya, along with the young warrior Kio, have a chance to stop Black Pearl and take their clans' sacred relics back. But the path is treacherous, and if these young warriors want to take down Black Pearl, they may be forced to sacrifice the lives of their loved ones.

Take care of your mother and grandfather while I'm away.

But where are you going, Father?

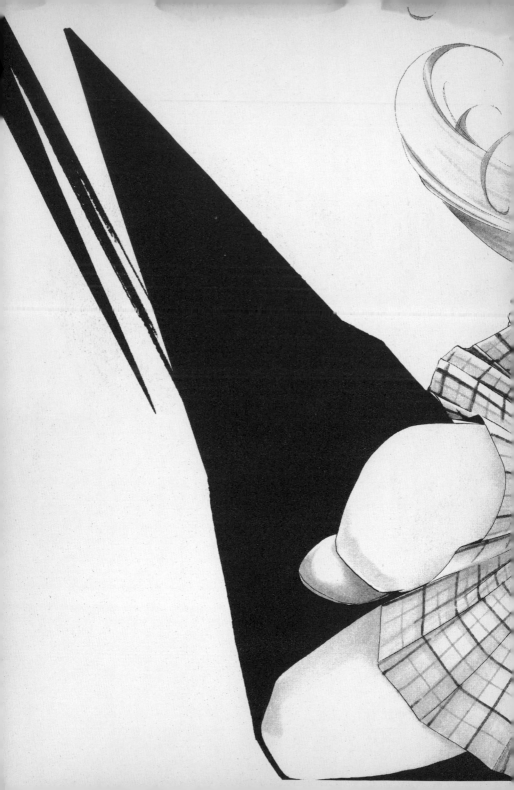

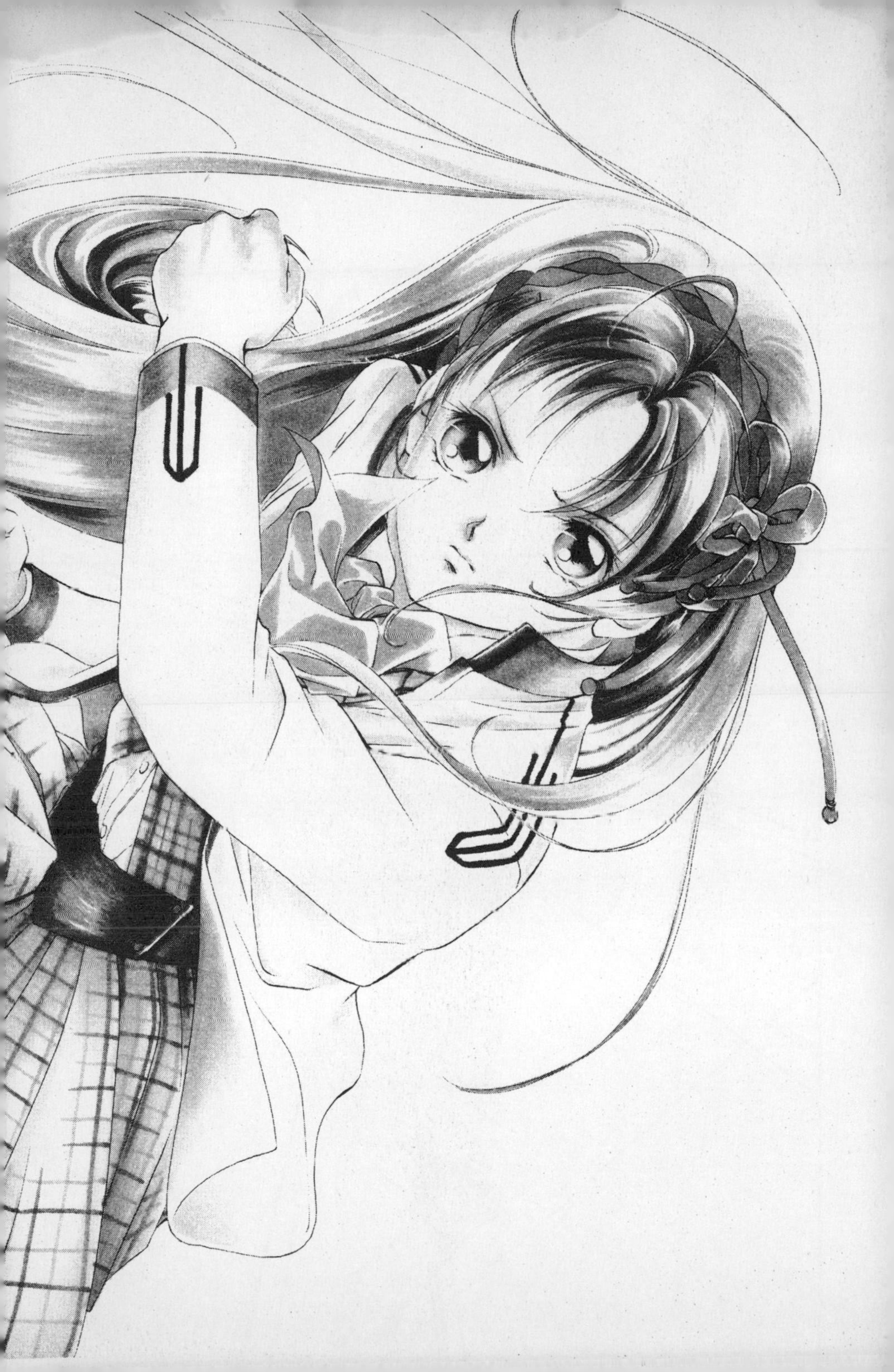

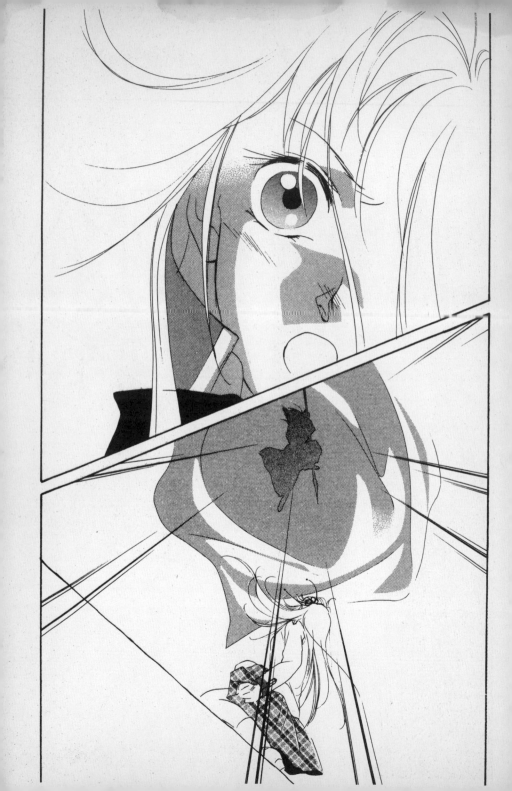

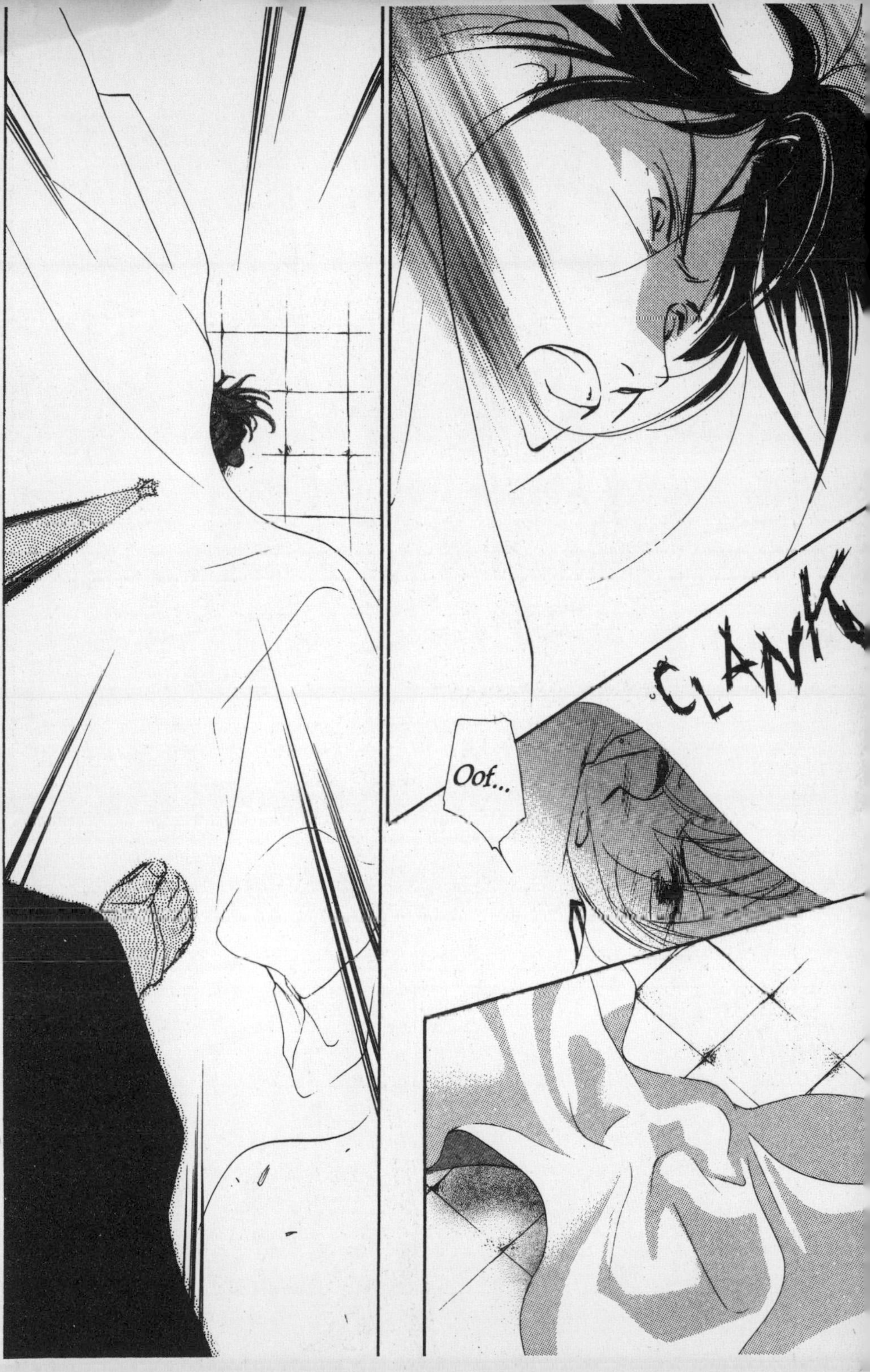
CLANK
Oof...

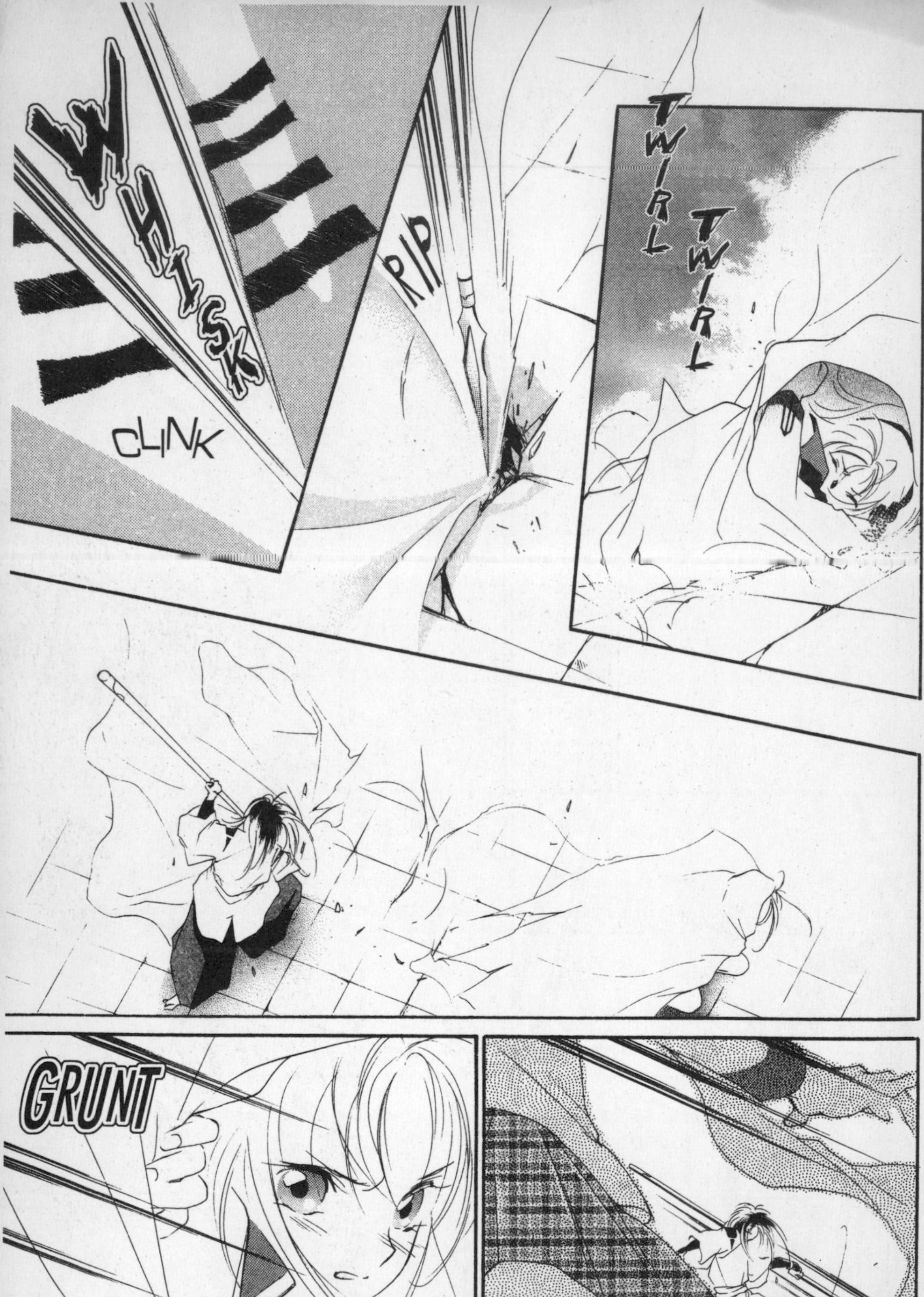
WHISK
CLINK
RIP
TWIRL TWIRL
GRUNT

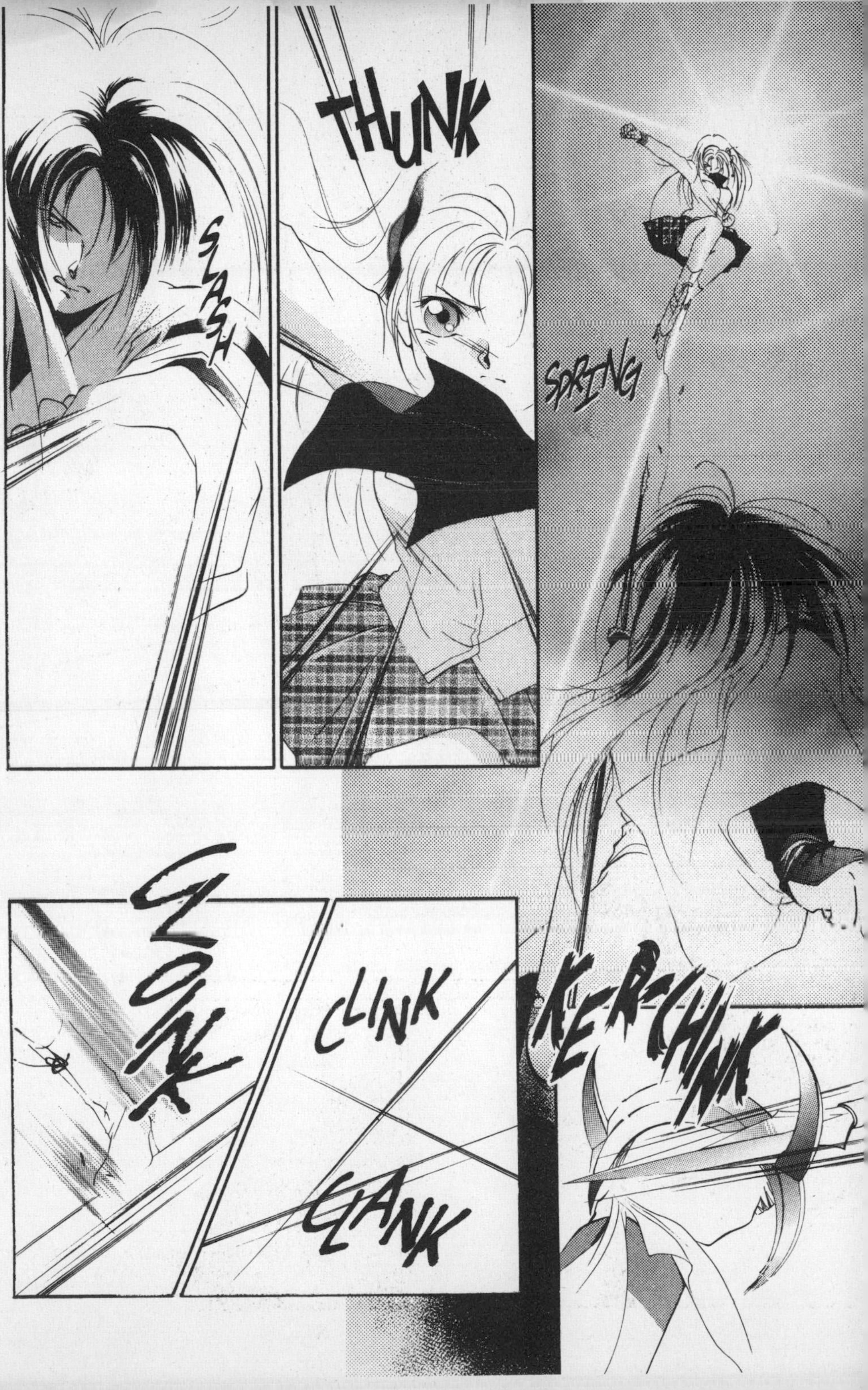
SLASH
THUNK
SPRING
CLONK
CLINK
CLANK
KER-CHINK

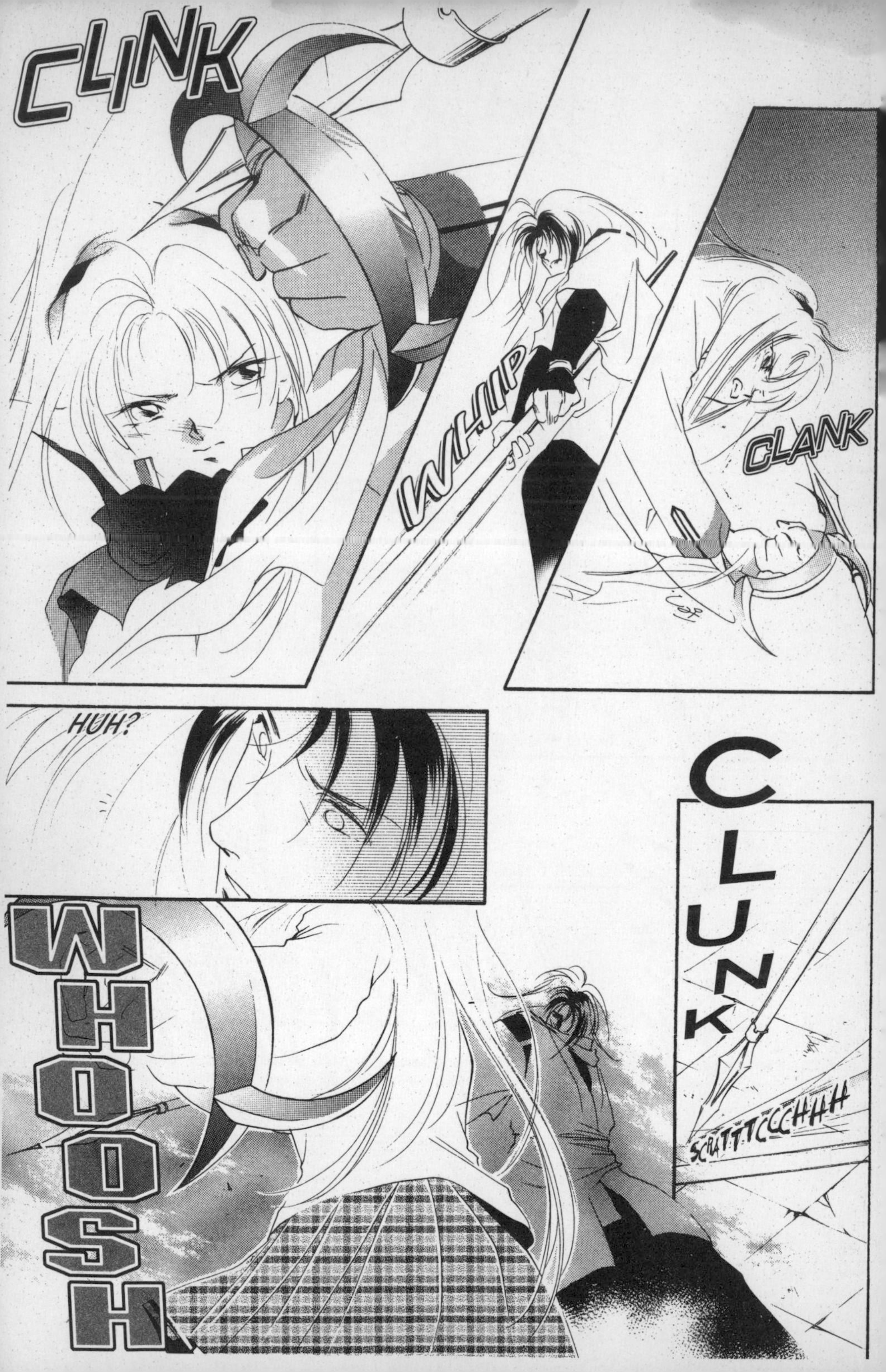
CLINK
WHIP
CLANK
HUH?
WHOOSH
CLUNK
SCRATTTCCCHHH

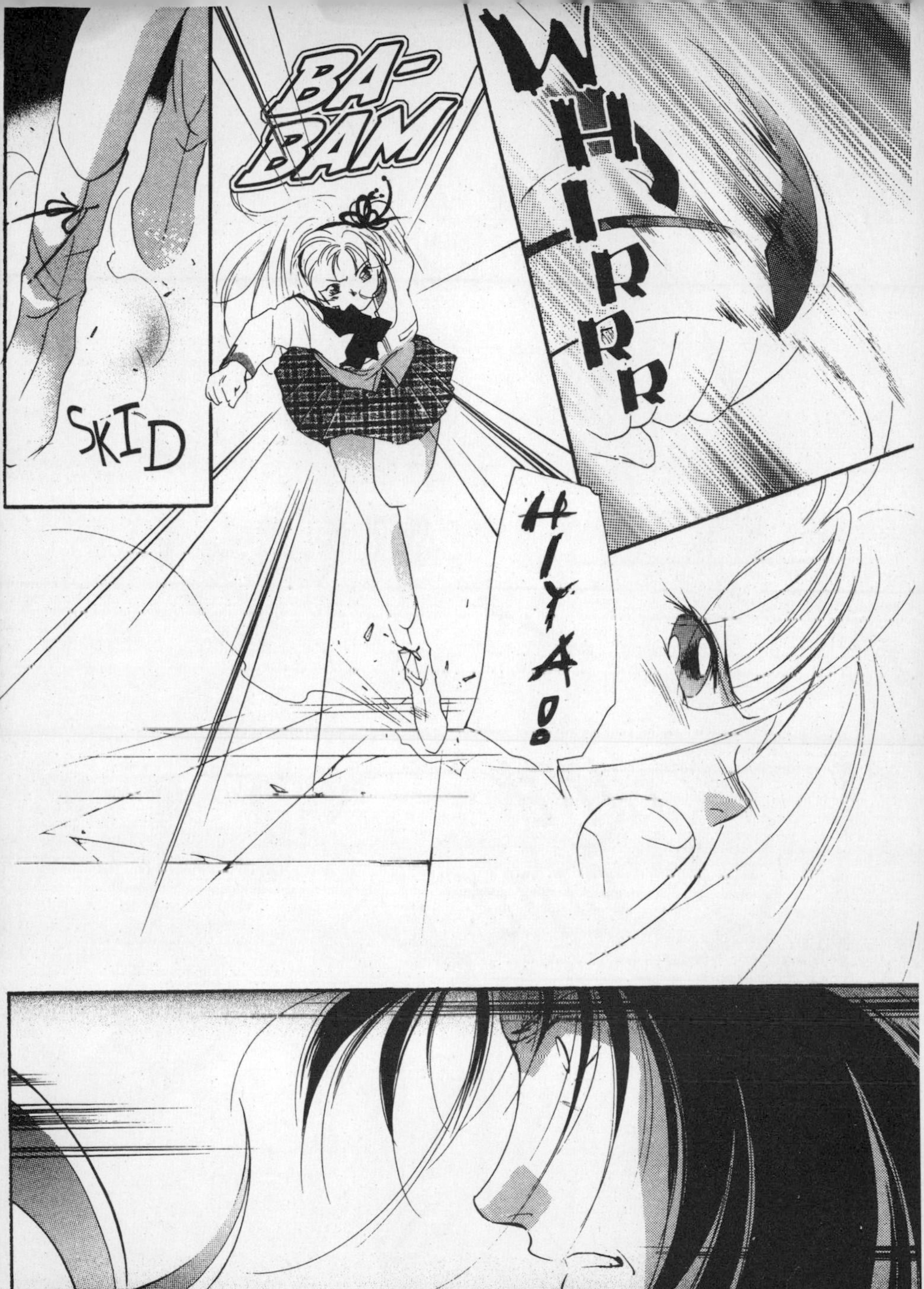
SKID
BA-BAM
WHIRRR
HIYA!

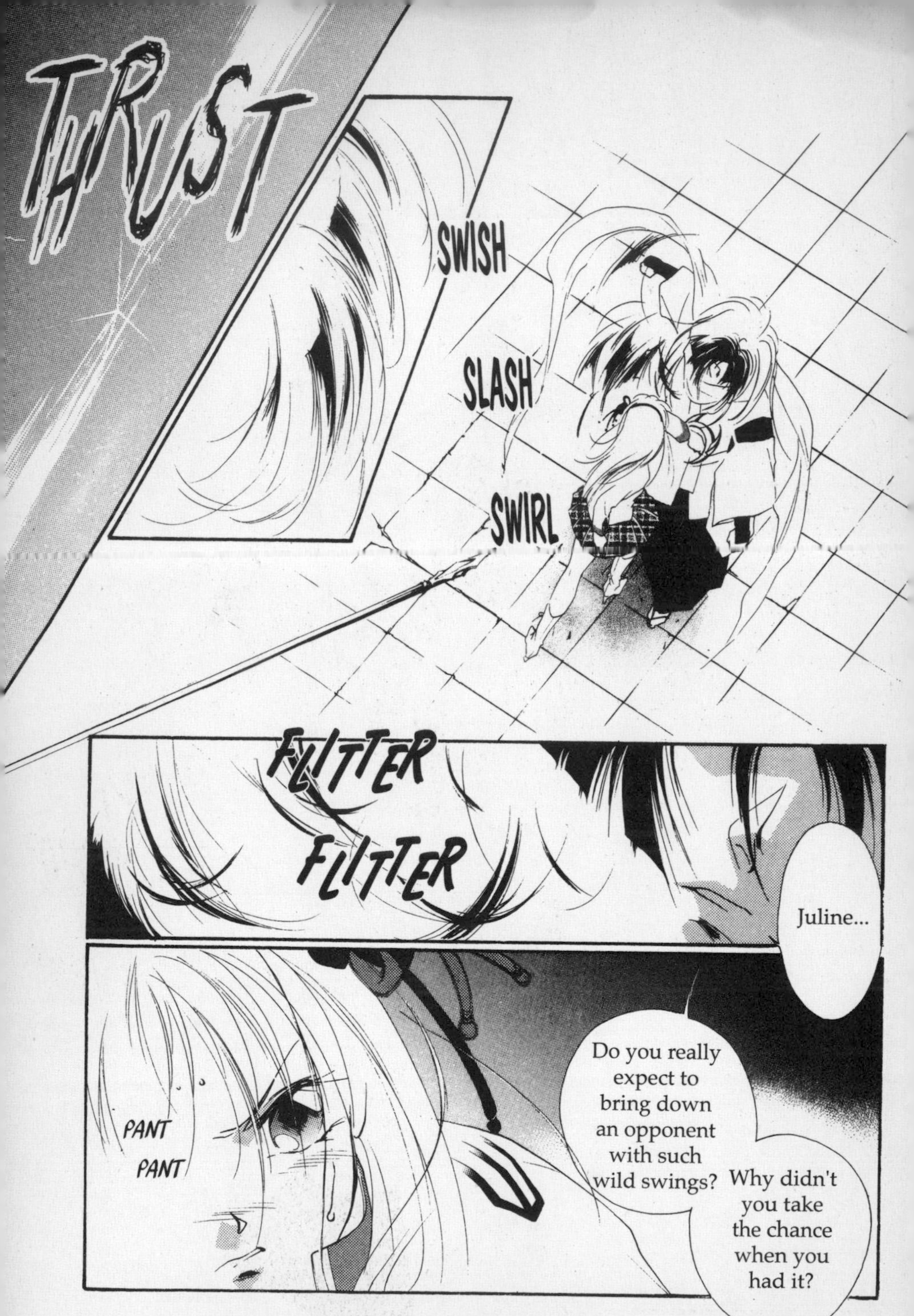
THRUST
SWISH
SLASH
SWIRL
FLITTER
FLITTER
Juline...
PANT
PANT
Do you really expect to bring down an opponent with such wild swings?
Why didn't you take the chance when you had it?

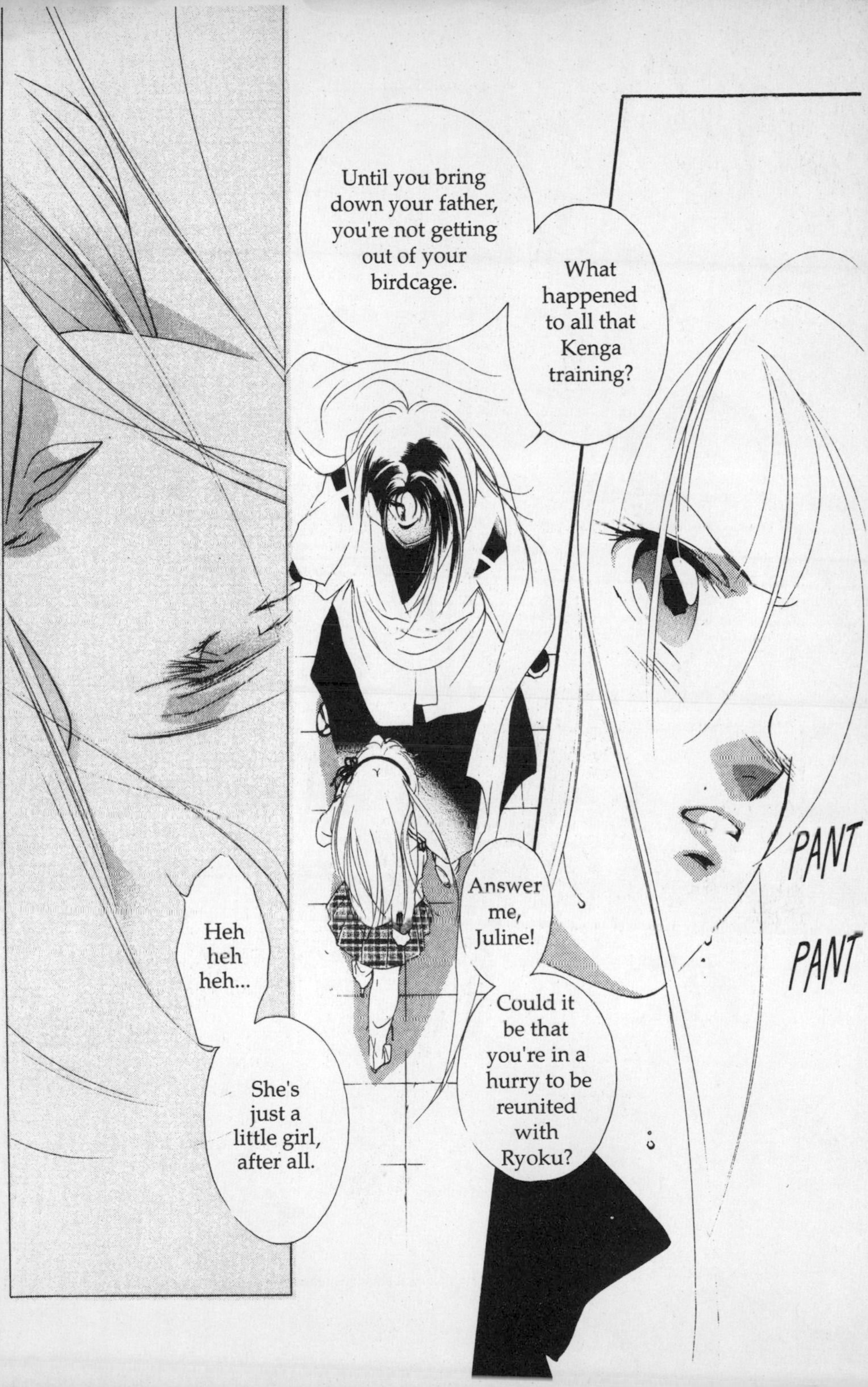
Heh heh heh...
She's just a little girl, after all.
Until you bring down your father, you're not getting out of your birdcage.
What happened to all that Kenga training?
Answer me, Juline!
Could it be that you're in a hurry to be reunited with Ryoku?
PANT
PANT

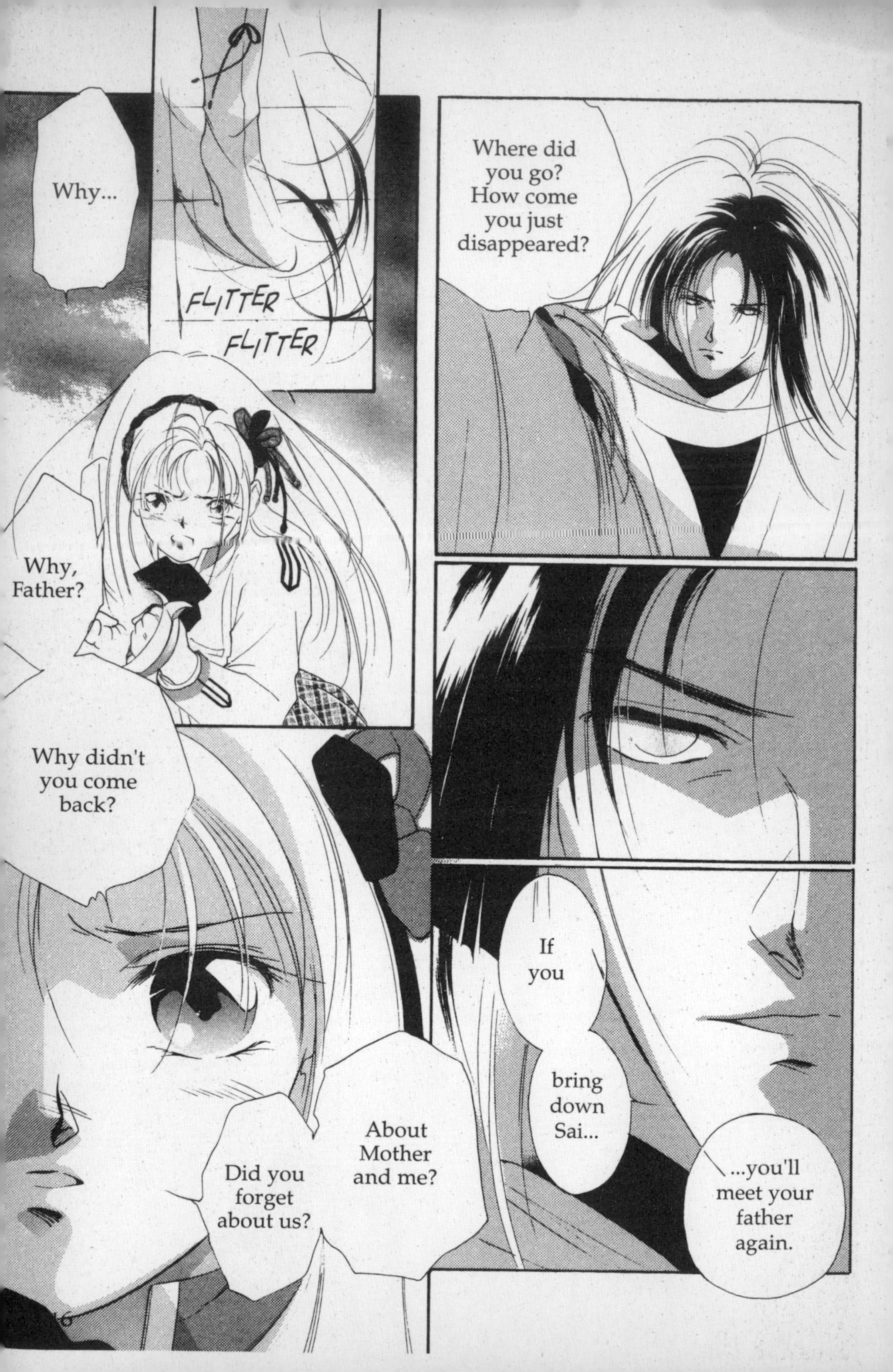
Why...
FLITTER
FLITTER
Where did you go? How come you just disappeared?
Why, Father?
Why didn't you come back?
Did you forget about us?
About Mother and me?
If you
bring down Sai...
...you'll meet your father again.

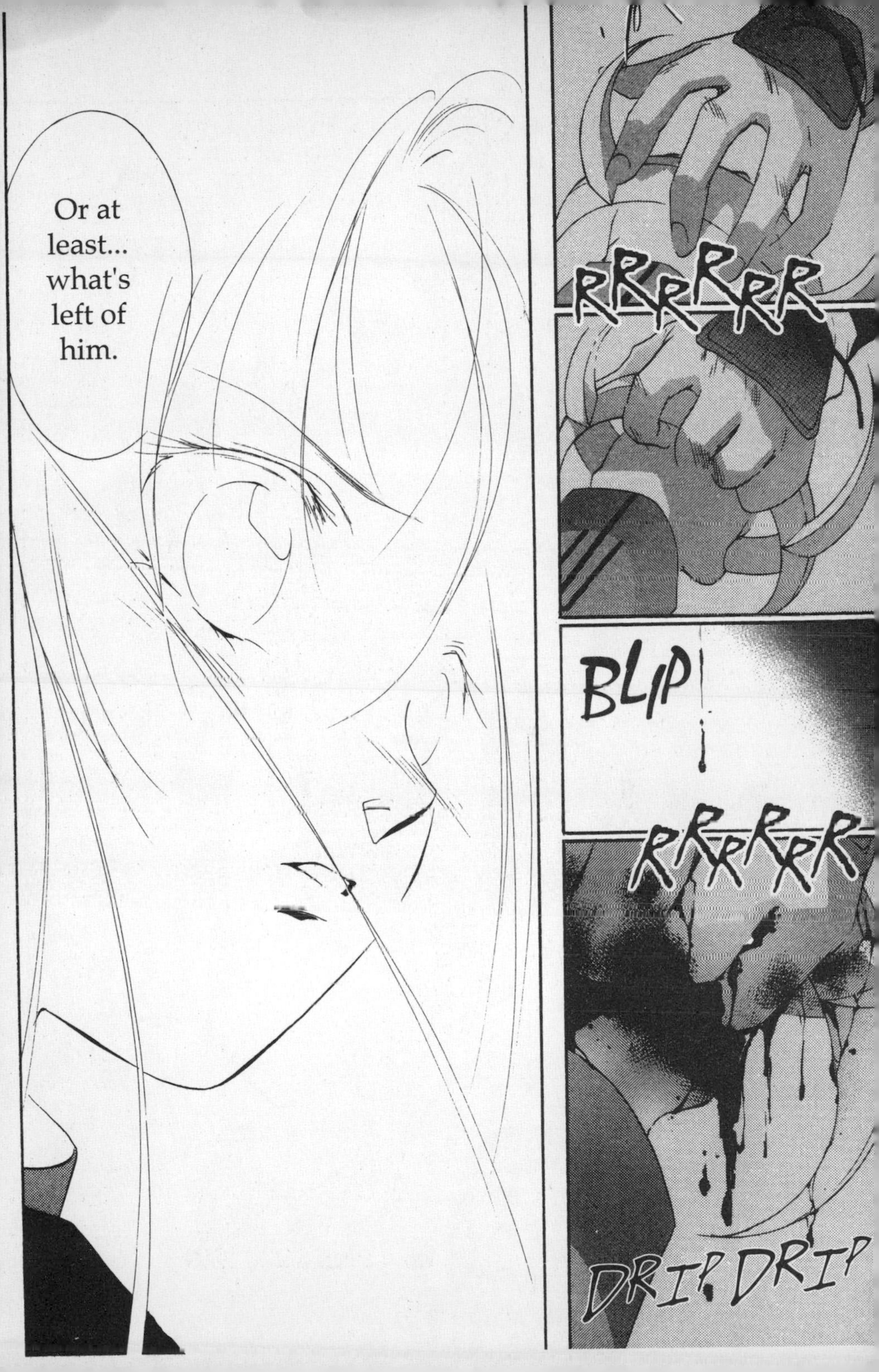
Or at least... what's left of him.
RRRRRR
BLIP
RRRRRR
DRIP DRIP

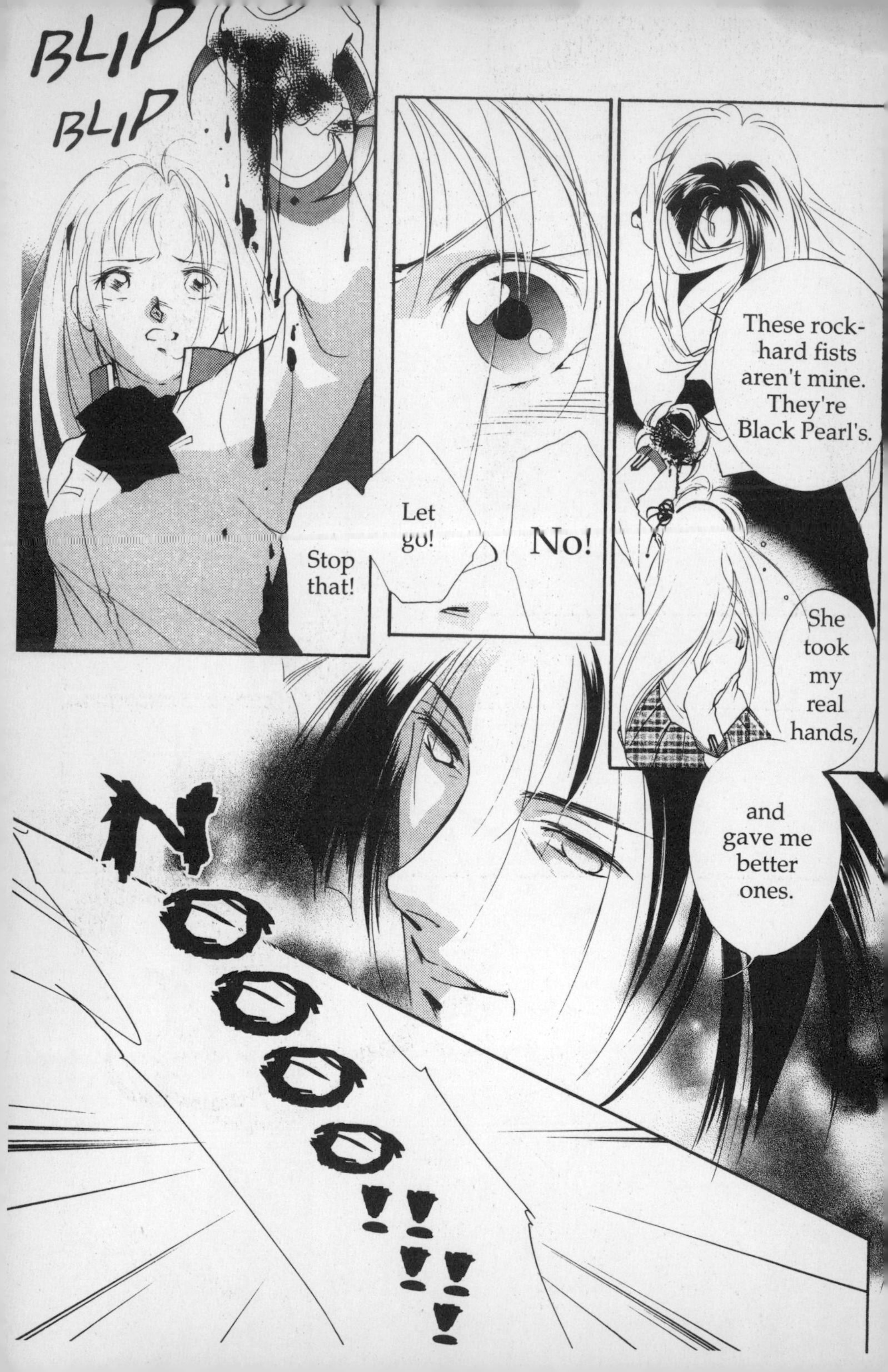
BLIP
BLIP
Stop that!
Let go!
No!
These rock-hard fists aren't mine. They're Black Pearl's.
She took my real hands,
and gave me better ones.
NOOOO!!!

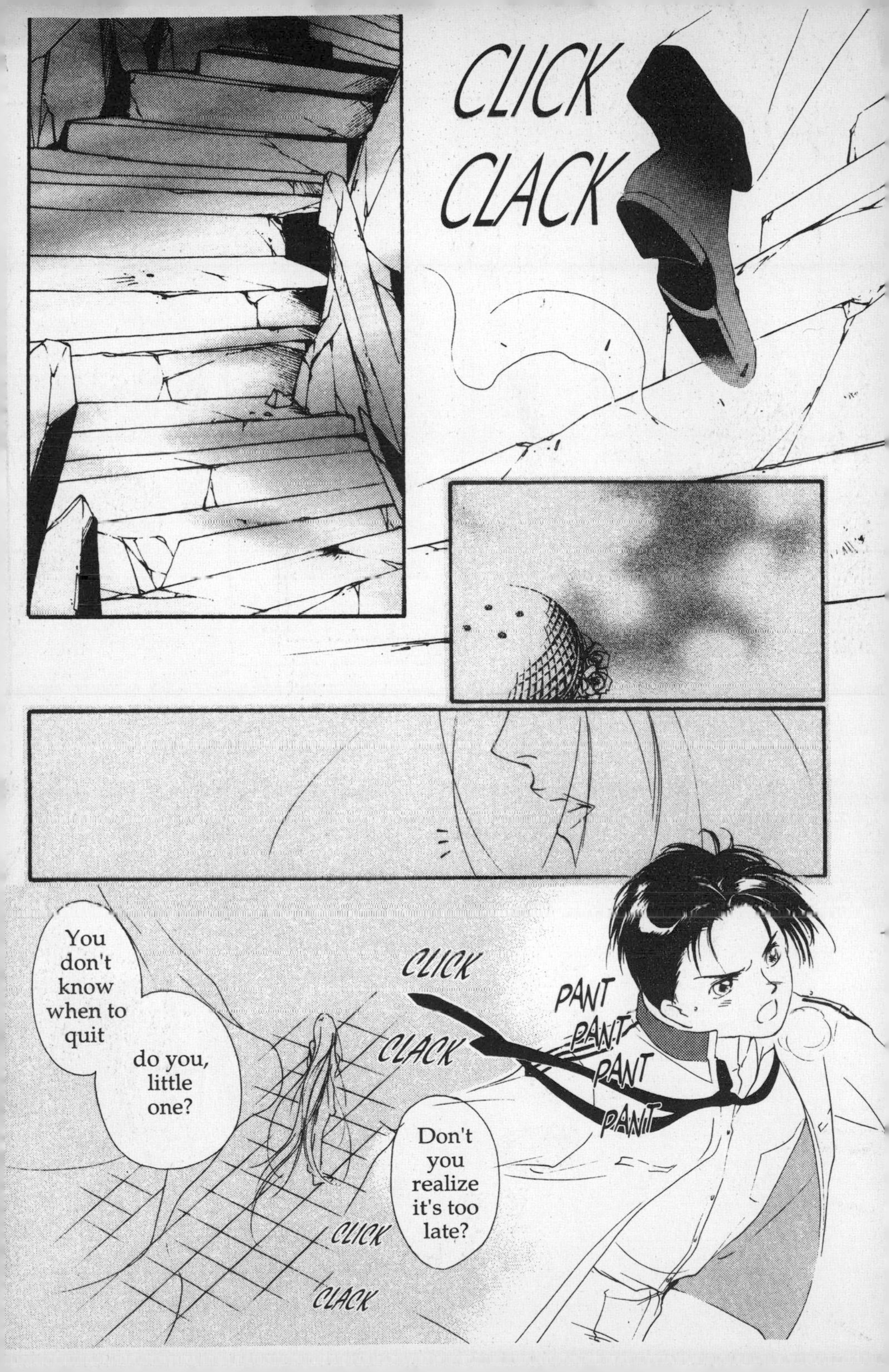
CLICK
CLACK
You don't know when to quit
do you, little one?
CLICK
CLACK
PANT
PANT
PANT
PANT
Don't you realize it's too late?
CLICK
CLACK

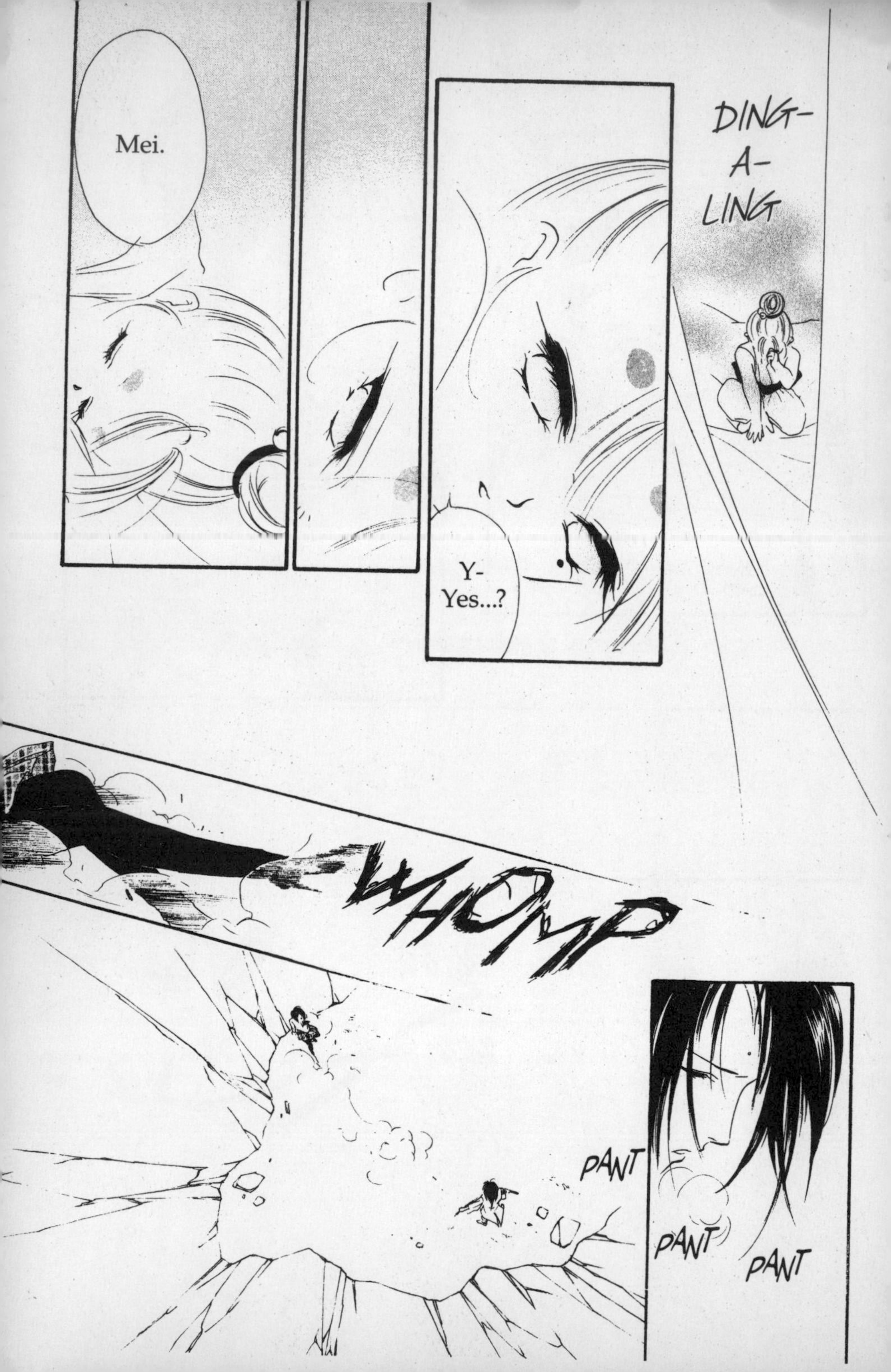

Mei.
Y-
Yes...?
DING-
A-
LING
WHOMP
PANT
PANT
PANT

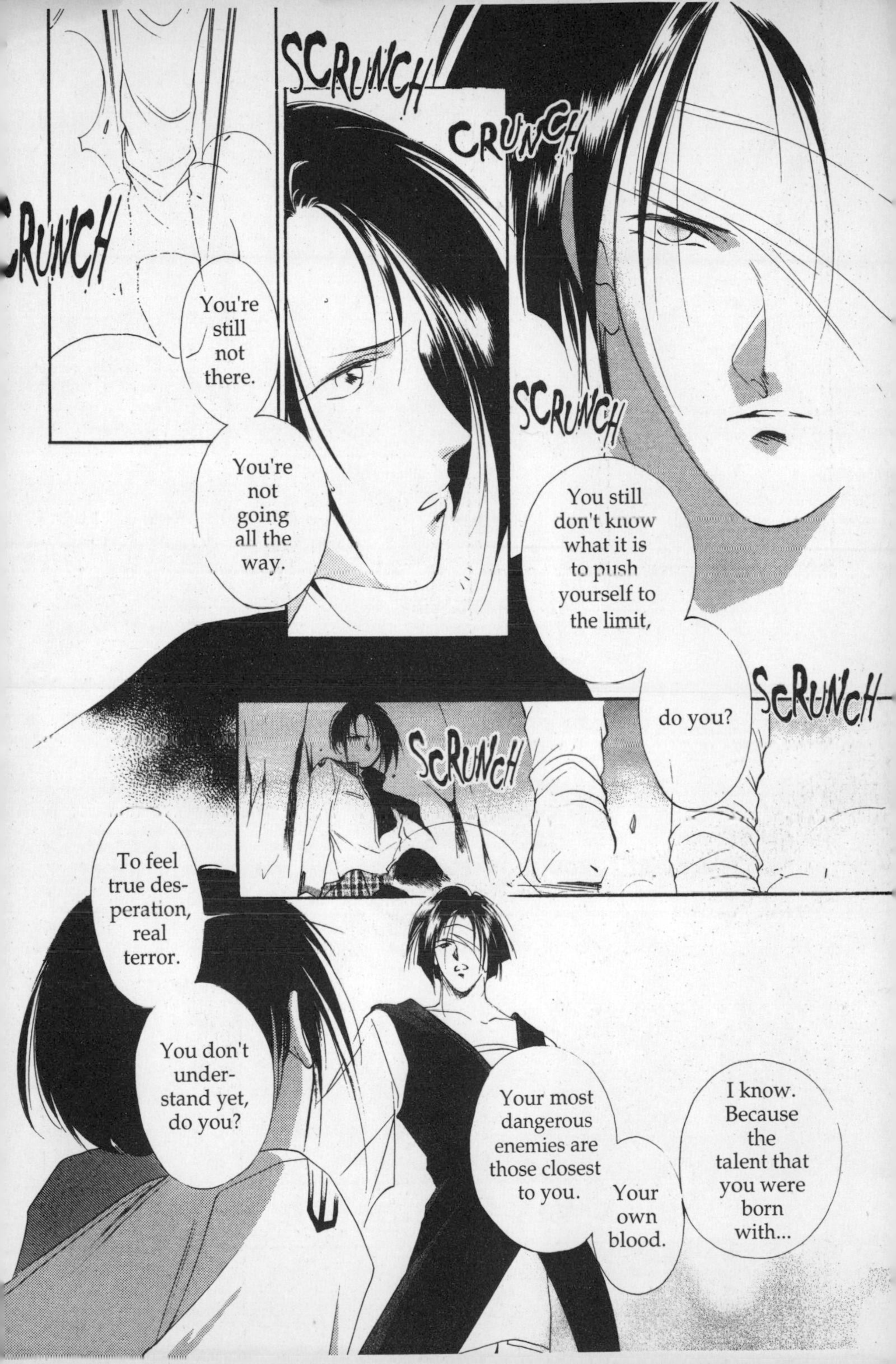
CRUNCH
SCRUNCH
CRUNCH
You're still not there.
You're not going all the way.
SCRUNCH
You still don't know what it is to push yourself to the limit,
do you?
SCRUNCH
SCRUNCH
To feel true des-peration, real terror.
You don't under-stand yet, do you?
Your most dangerous enemies are those closest to you.
Your own blood.
I know. Because the talent that you were born with...

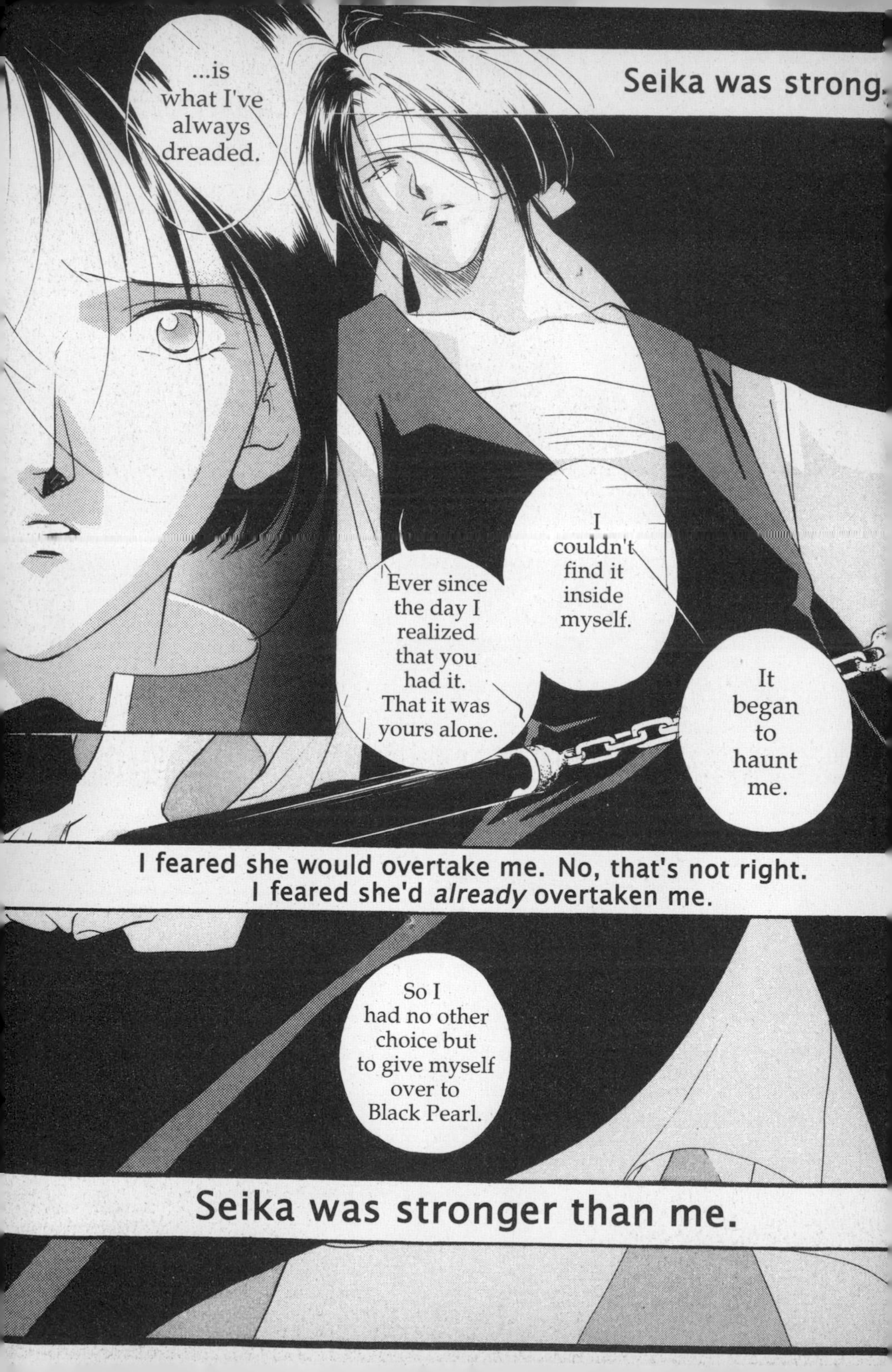

...is what I've always dreaded.
Seika was strong.
Ever since the day I realized that you had it. That it was yours alone.
I couldn't find it inside myself.
It began to haunt me.
I feared she would overtake me. No, that's not right.
I feared she'd *already* overtaken me.
So I had no other choice but to give myself over to Black Pearl.
Seika was stronger than me.

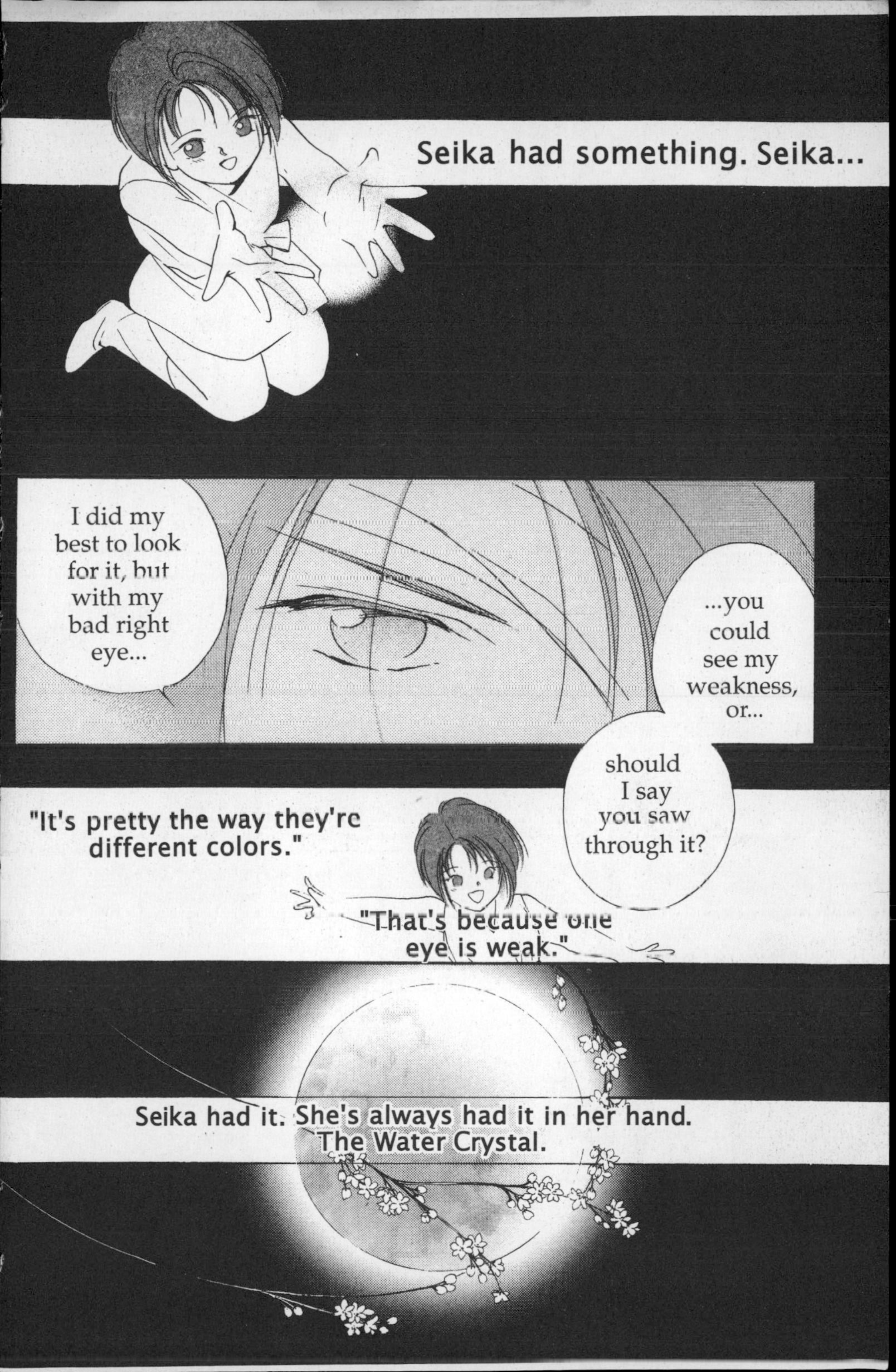
Seika had something. Seika...
I did my best to look for it, but with my bad right eye...
...you could see my weakness, or...
should I say you saw through it?
"It's pretty the way they're different colors."
"That's because one eye is weak."
Seika had it. She's always had it in her hand. The Water Crystal.

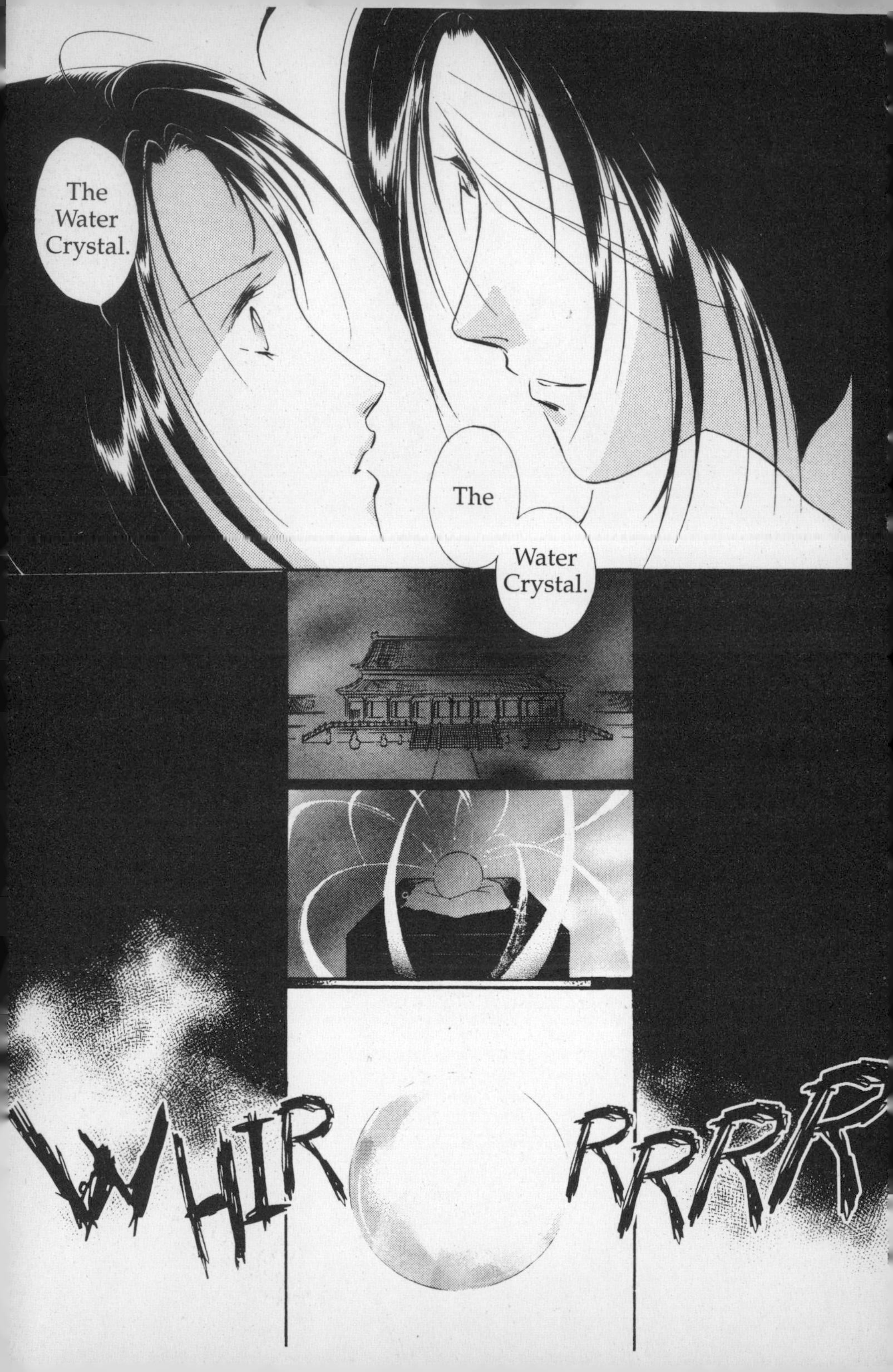
The Water Crystal.
The Water Crystal.
WHIRRRRRR

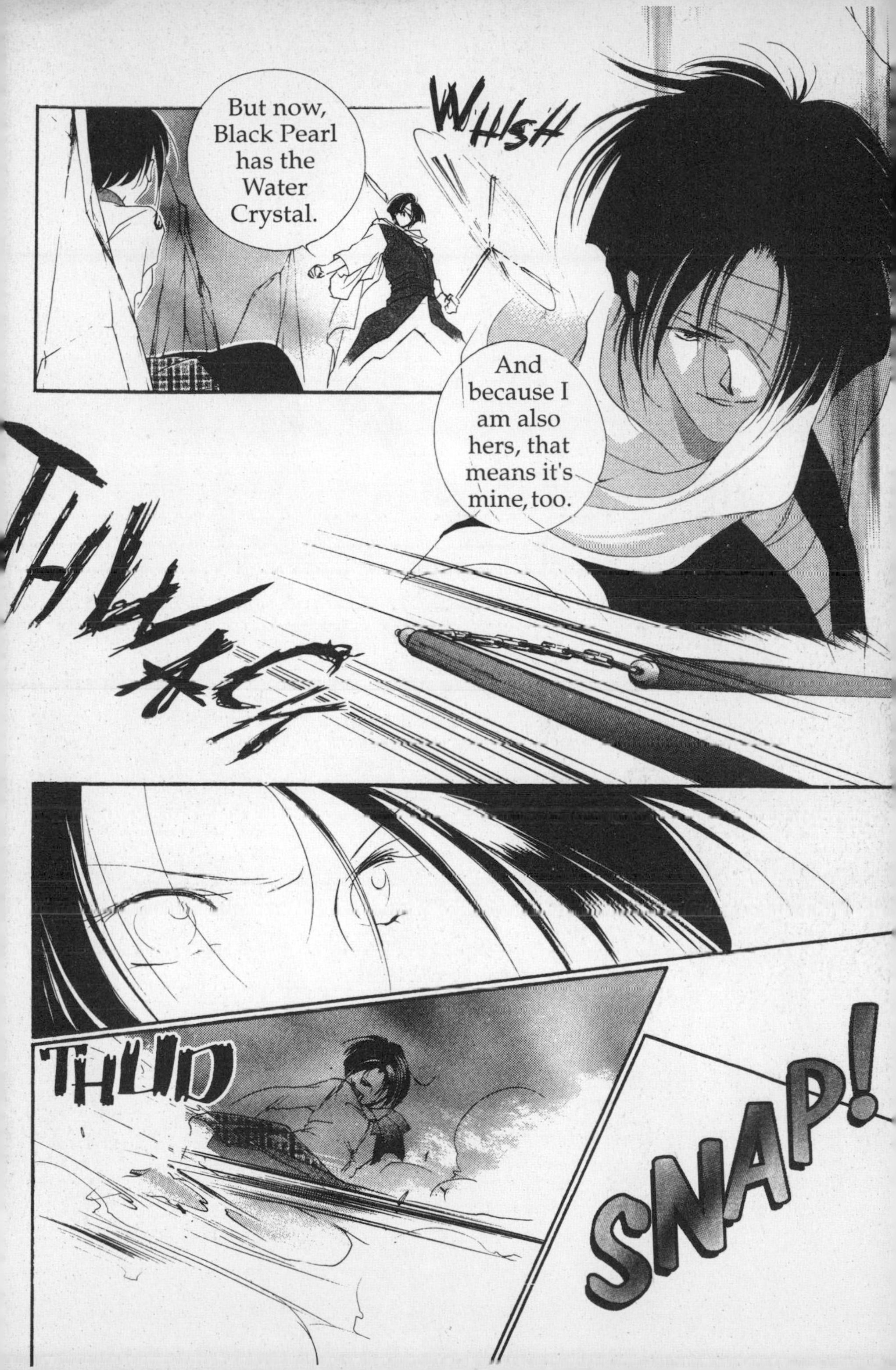
But now, Black Pearl has the Water Crystal.
WHISH
And because I am also hers, that means it's mine, too.
THWACK
THUD
SNAP!

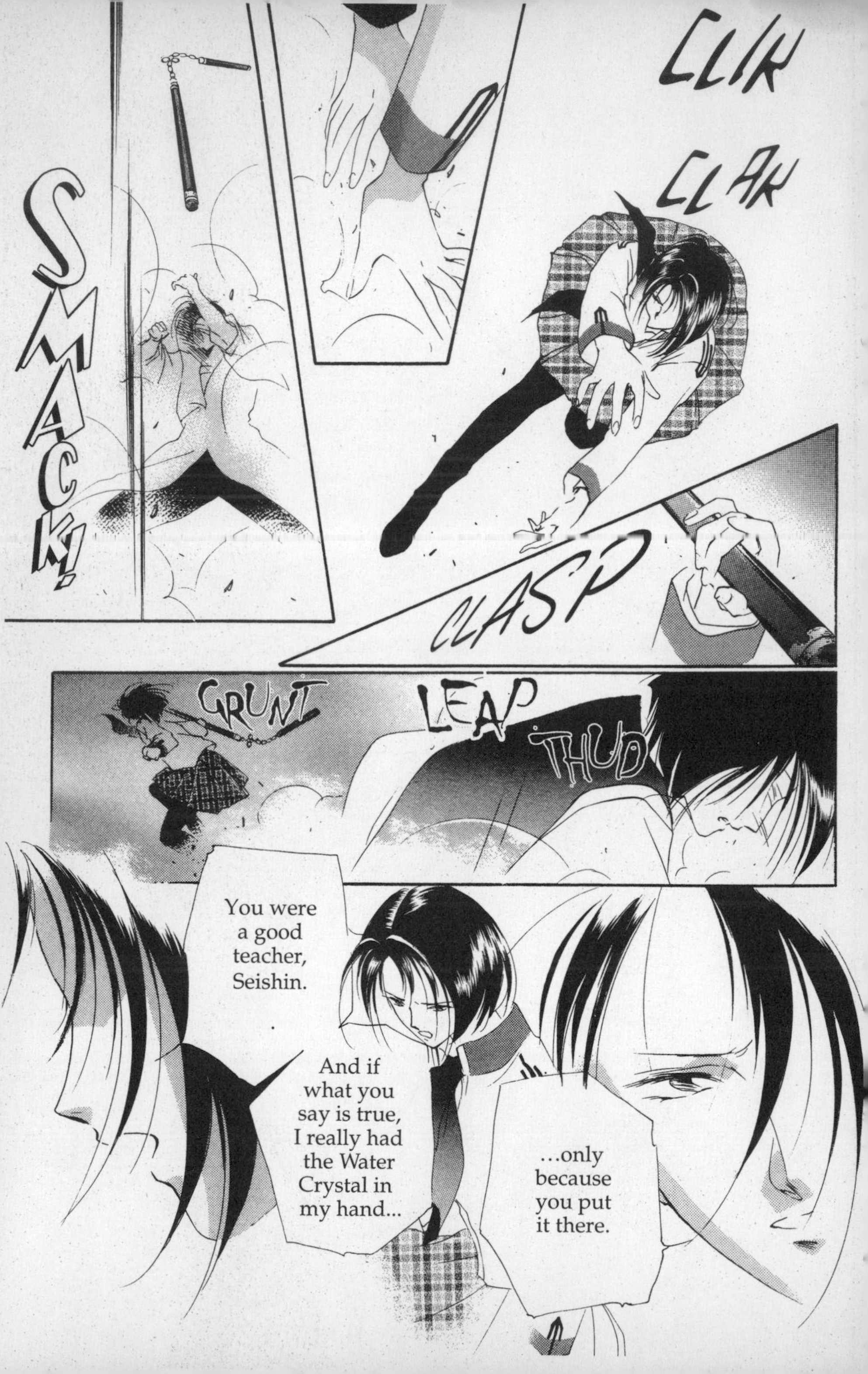
SMACK!
CLIK
CLAK
CLASP
GRUNT
LEAP
THUD
You were a good teacher, Seishin.
And if what you say is true, I really had the Water Crystal in my hand...
...only because you put it there.

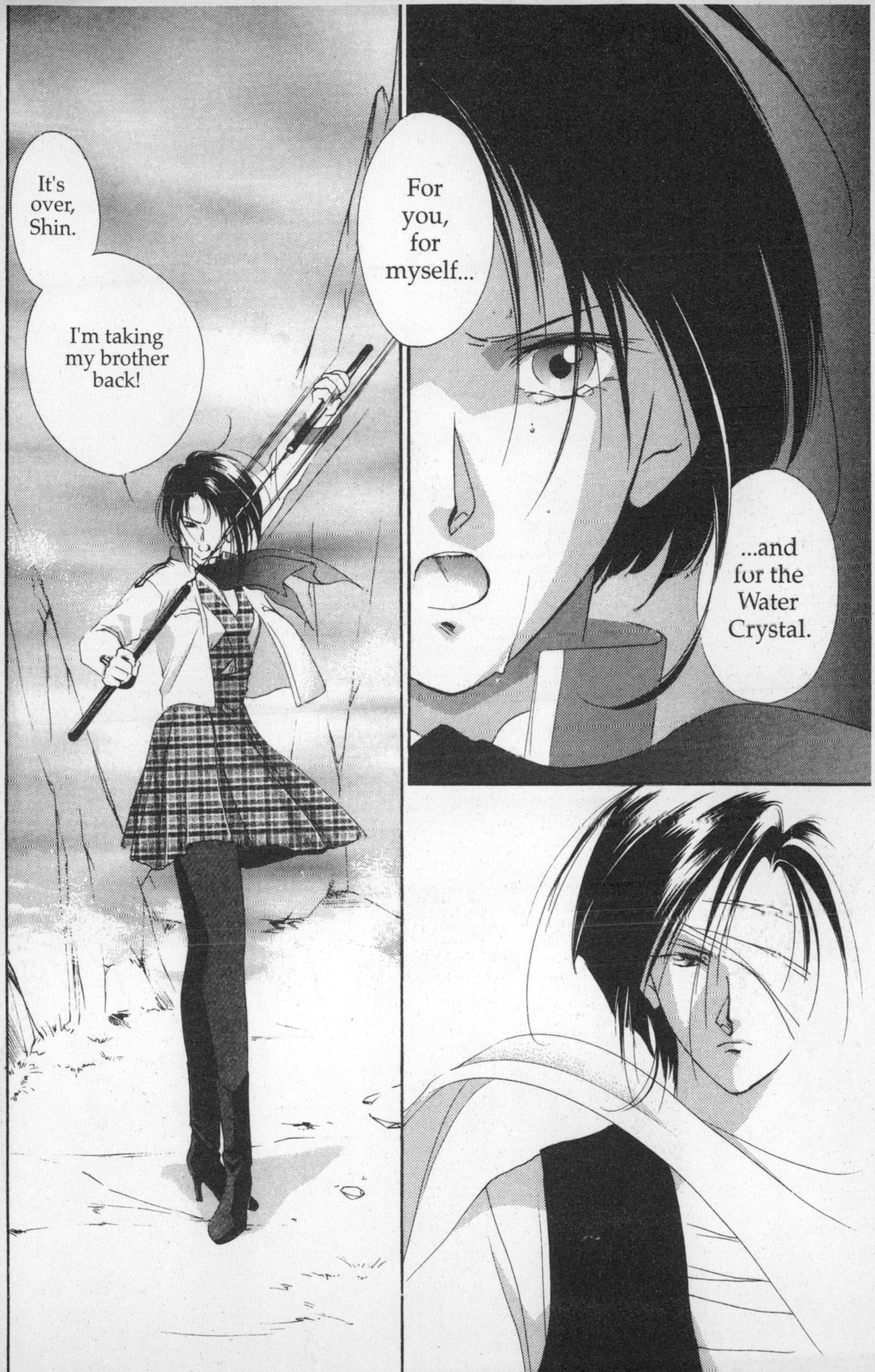
It's over, Shin.
I'm taking my brother back!
For you, for myself...
...and for the Water Crystal.

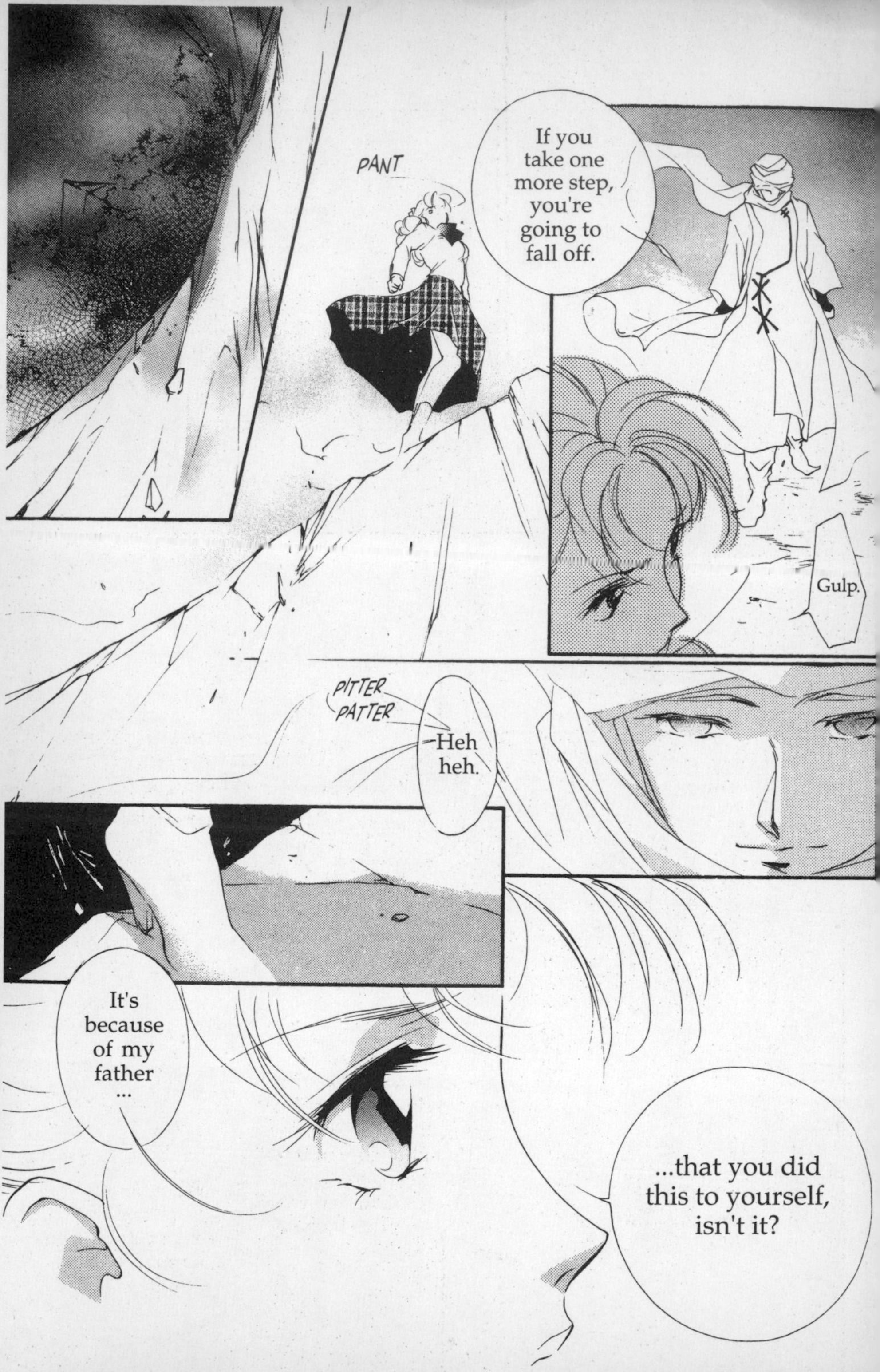
PANT
If you take one more step, you're going to fall off.
Gulp.
PITTER PATTER
Heh heh.
It's because of my father ...
...that you did this to yourself, isn't it?

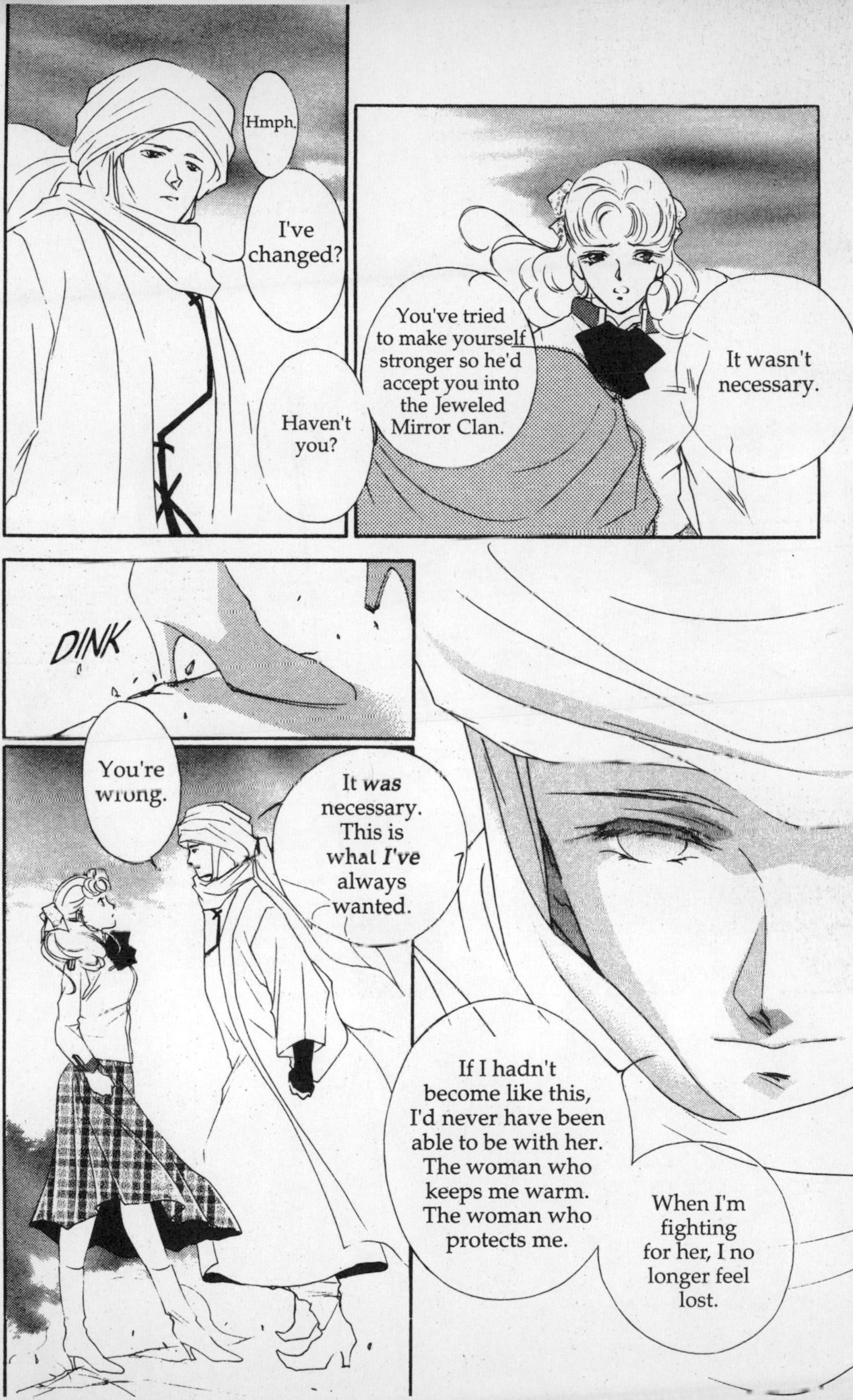
Hmph.
I've changed?
Haven't you?
You've tried to make yourself stronger so he'd accept you into the Jeweled Mirror Clan.
It wasn't necessary.
DINK
You're wrong.
It was necessary. This is what I've always wanted.
If I hadn't become like this, I'd never have been able to be with her. The woman who keeps me warm. The woman who protects me.
When I'm fighting for her, I no longer feel lost.

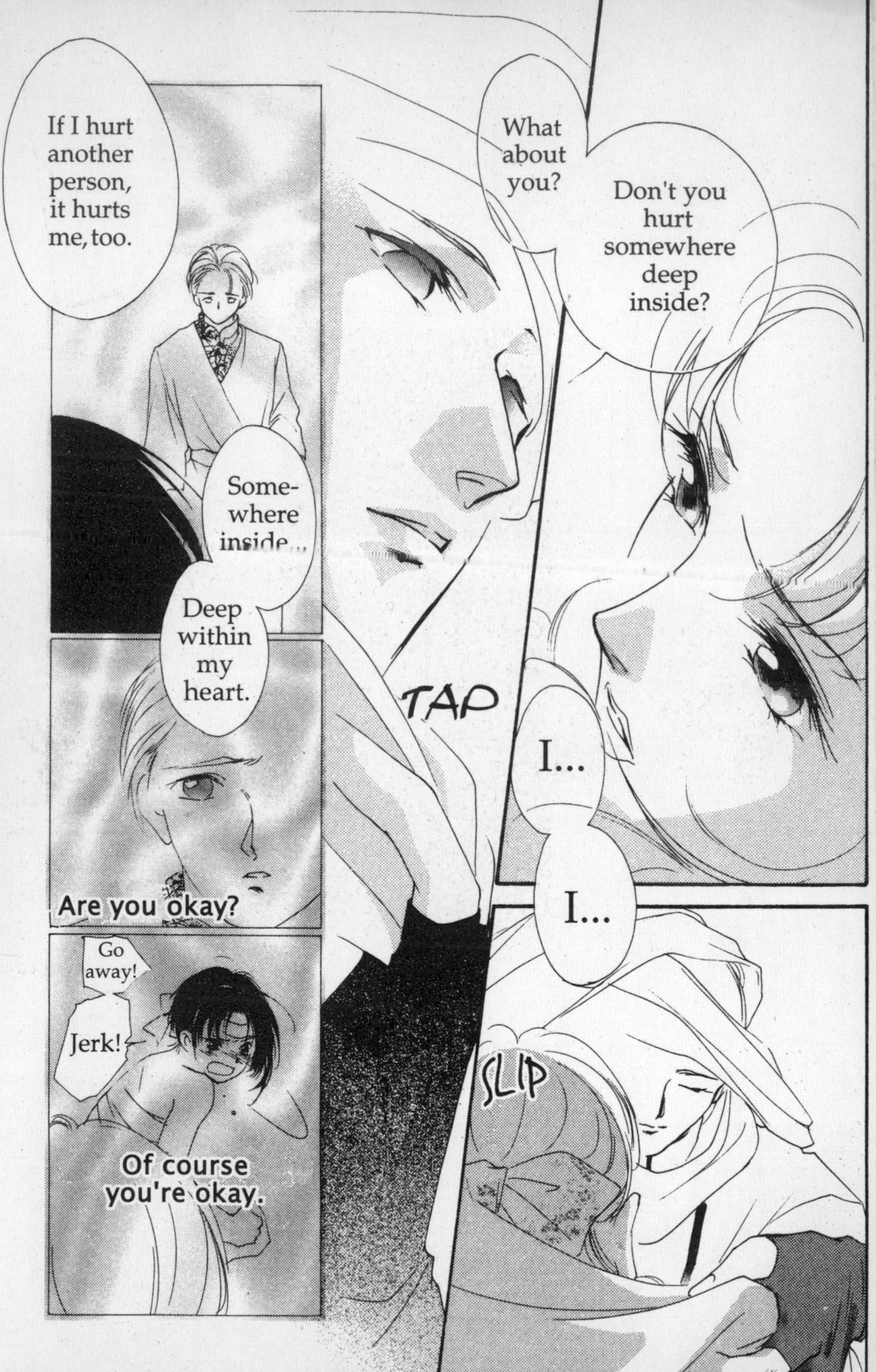
If I hurt another person, it hurts me, too.
Some-where inside...
Deep within my heart.
Are you okay?
Go away!
Jerk!
Of course you're okay.
What about you?
Don't you hurt somewhere deep inside?
TAP
I...
I...
SLIP

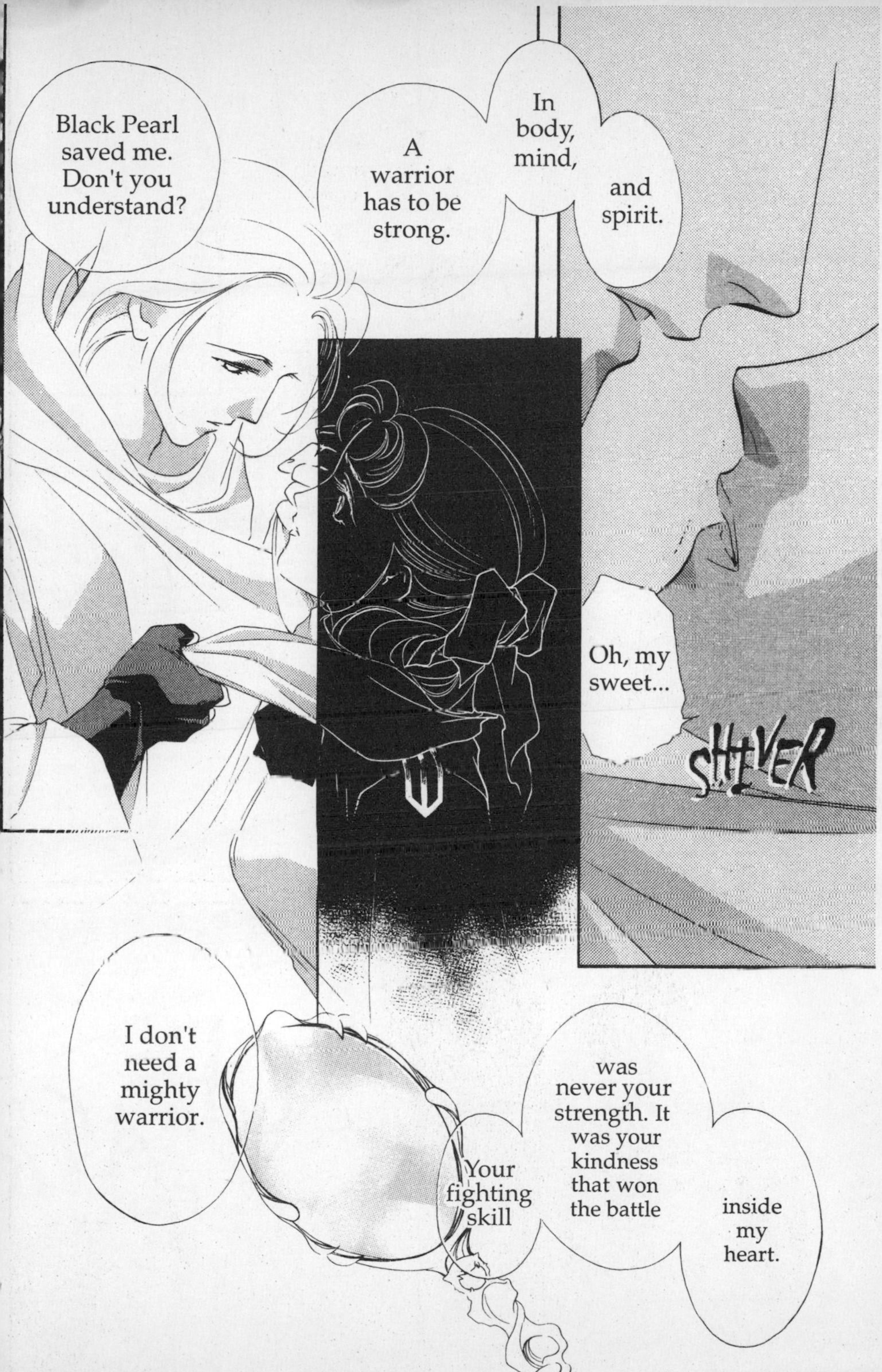
Black Pearl saved me. Don't you understand?
A warrior has to be strong.
In body, mind,
and spirit.
Oh, my sweet...
SHIVER
I don't need a mighty warrior.
Your fighting skill
was never your strength. It was your kindness that won the battle
inside my heart.

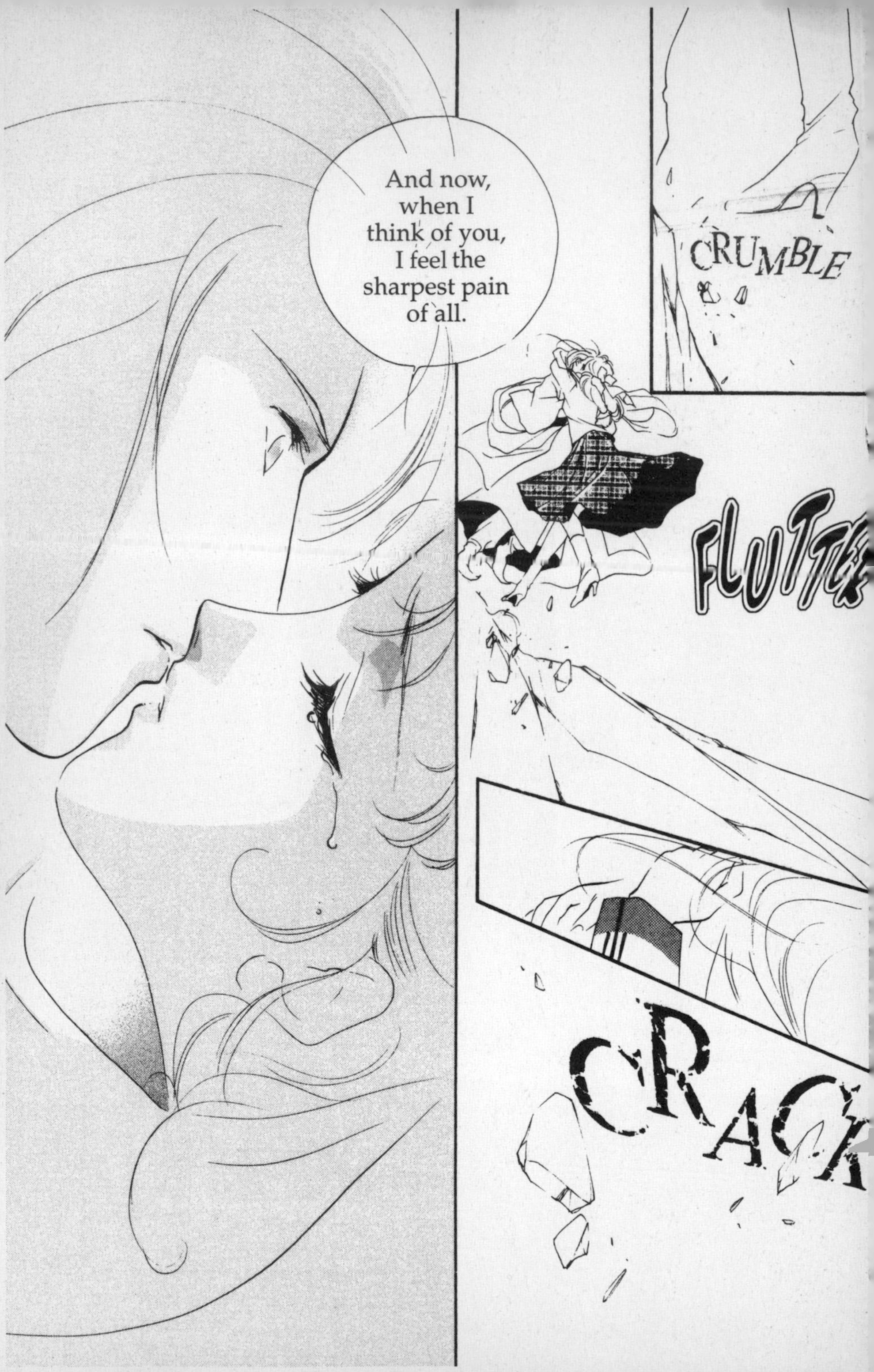
And now, when I think of you, I feel the sharpest pain of all.
CRUMBLE
FLUTTER
CRACK

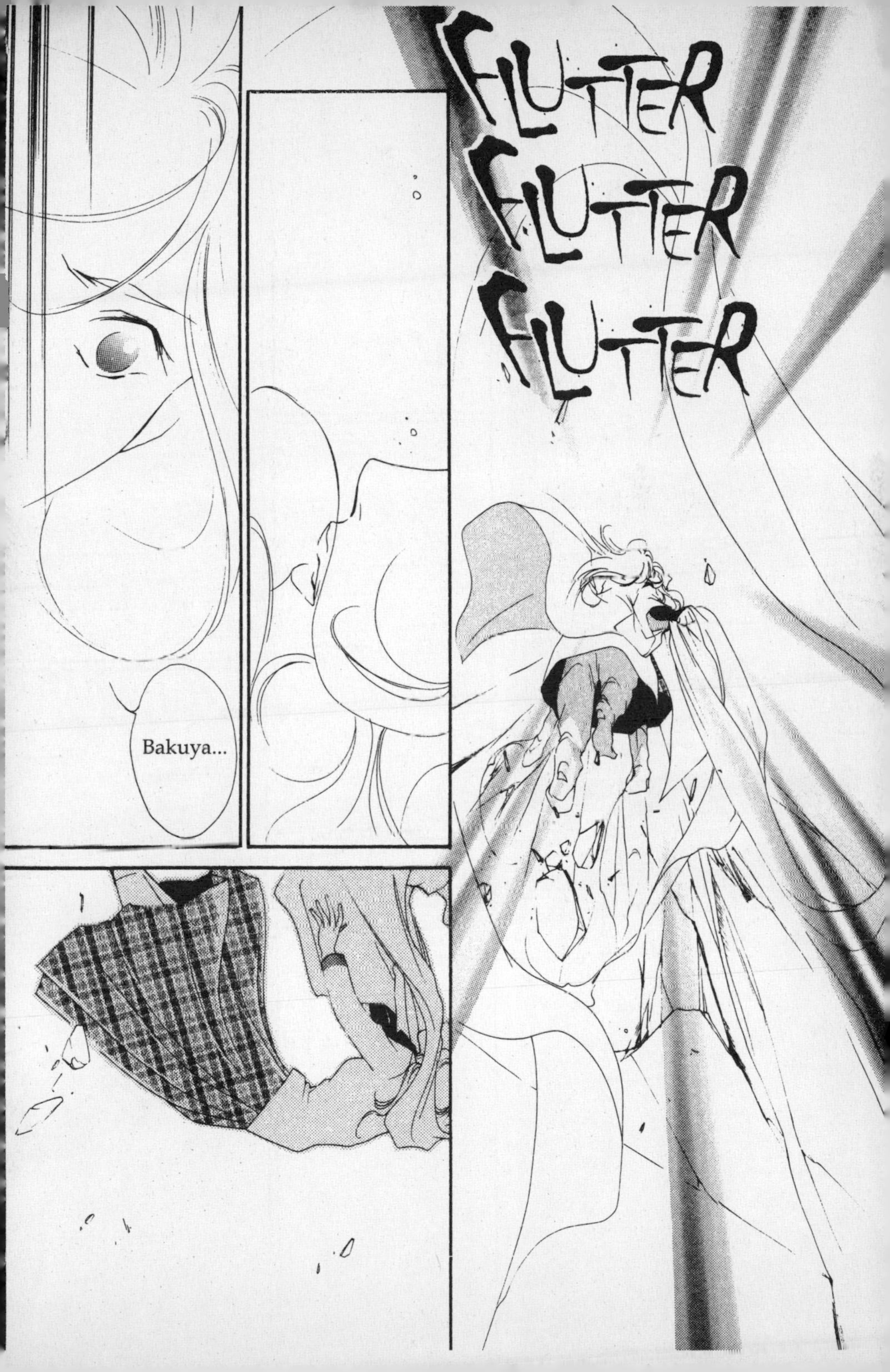
Bakuya...
FLUTTER FLUTTER FLUTTER

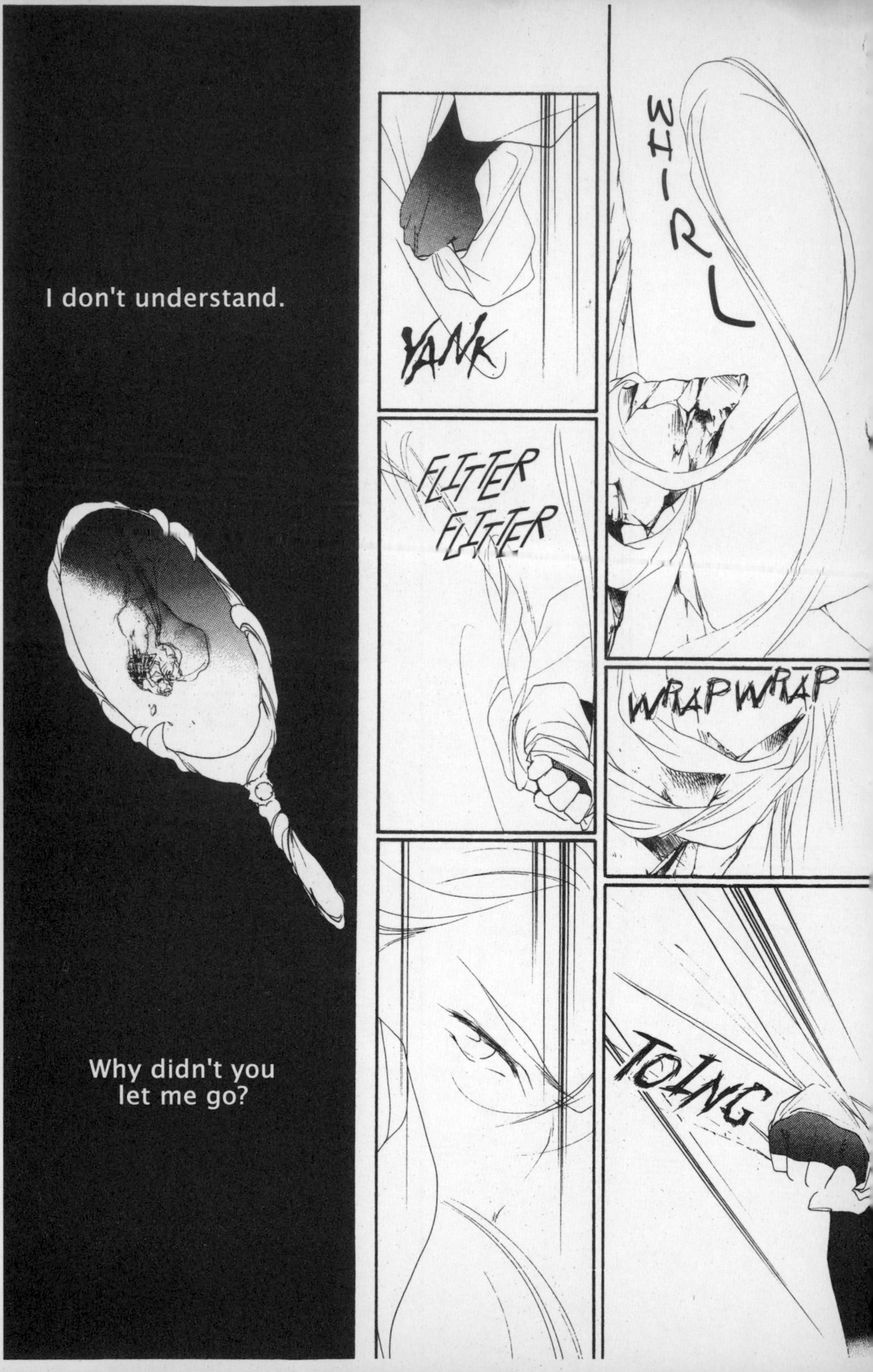
I don't understand.
Why didn't you let me go?
YANK
FLITTER FLITTER
WHIRL
WRAPWRAP
TOING

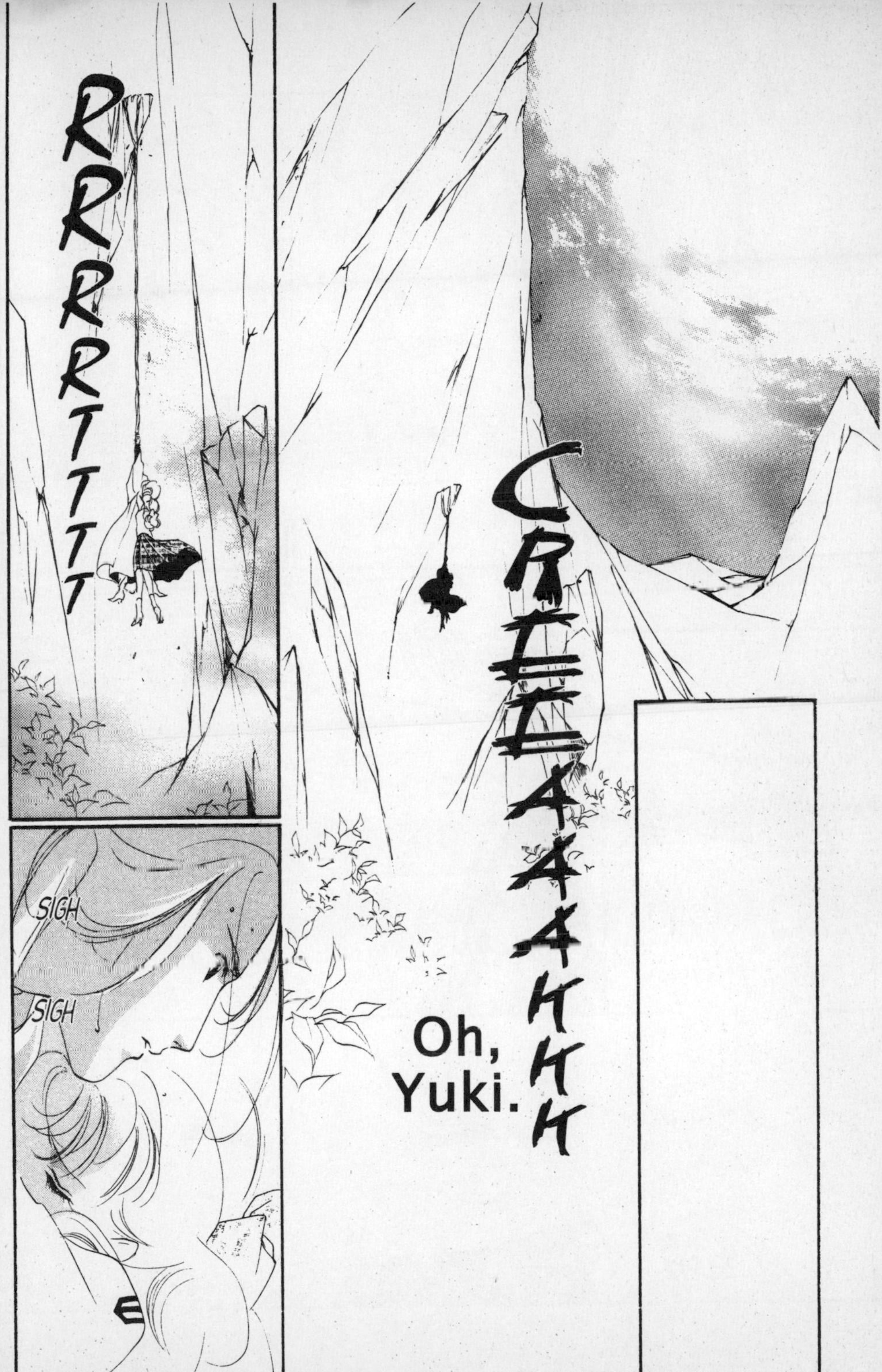
RRRRRTTTTT
SIGH
SIGH
CREEAAAKKKK
Oh, Yuki.

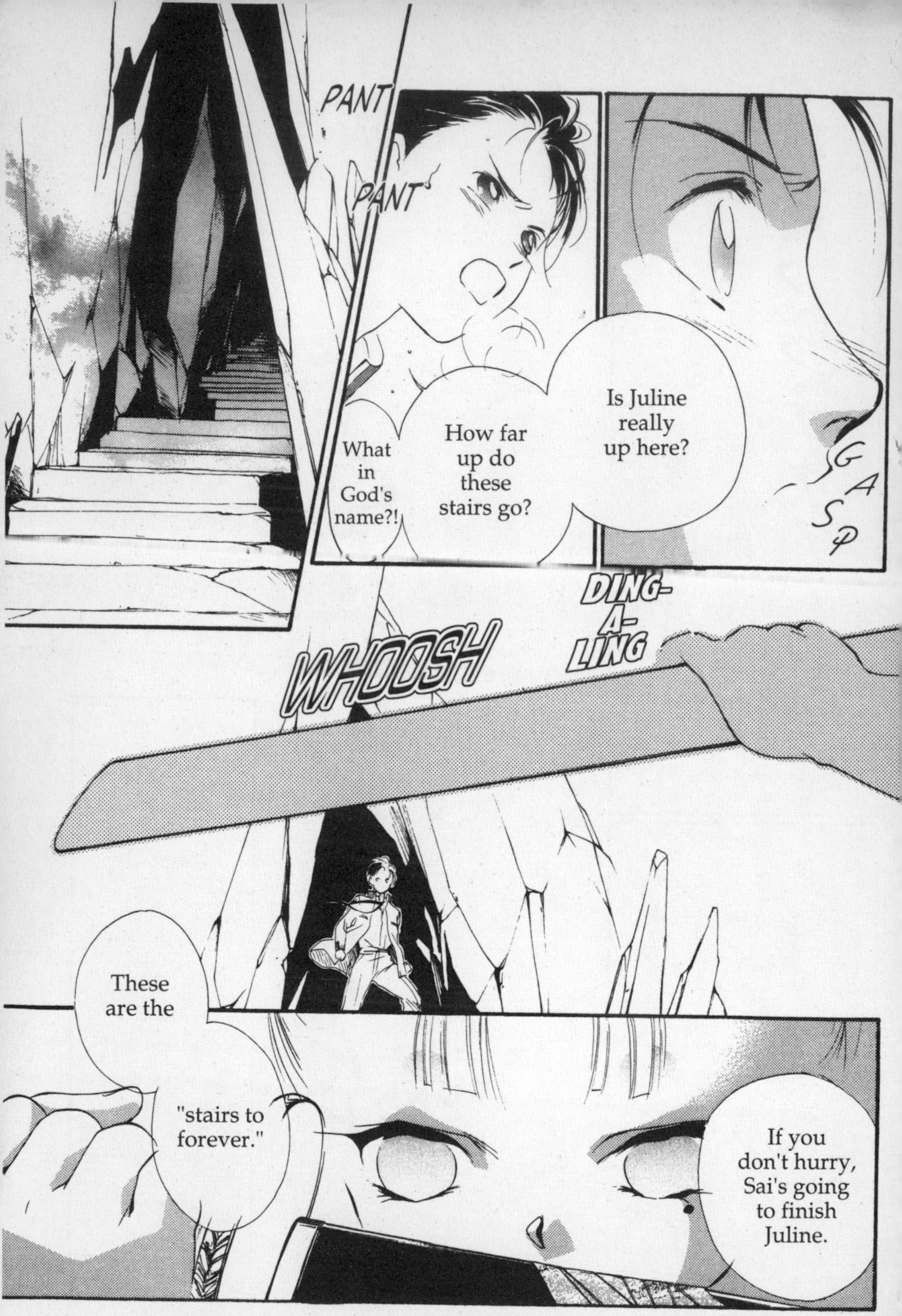
PANT
PANT
What in God's name?!
How far up do these stairs go?
Is Juline really up here?
GASP
WHOOSH
DING-A-LING
These are the
"stairs to forever."
If you don't hurry, Sai's going to finish Juline.

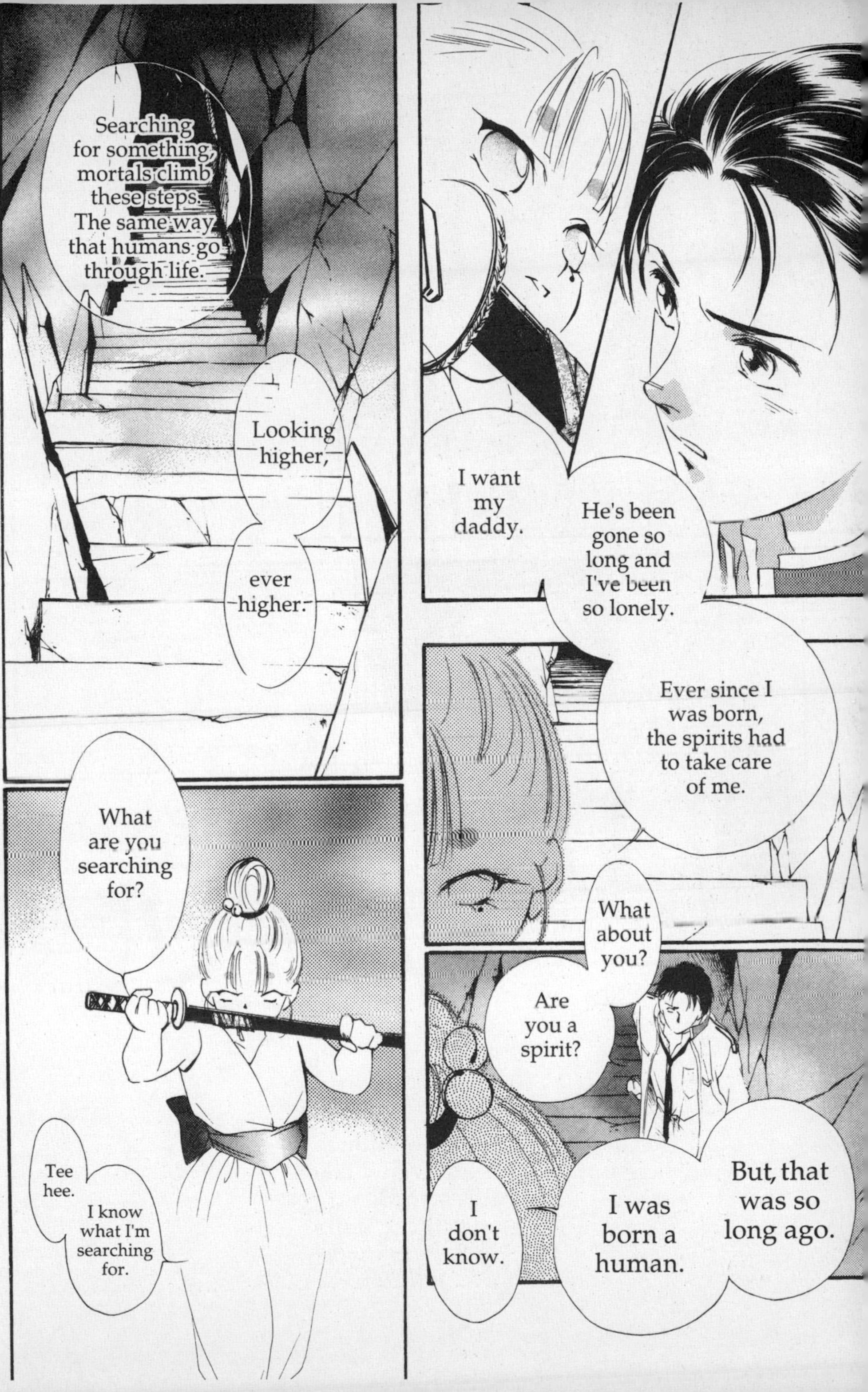
Searching for something, mortals climb these steps. The same way that humans go through life.
Looking higher,
ever higher.
What are you searching for?
Tee hee.
I know what I'm searching for.
I want my daddy.
He's been gone so long and I've been so lonely.
Ever since I was born, the spirits had to take care of me.
What about you?
Are you a spirit?
I don't know.
I was born a human.
But, that was so long ago.

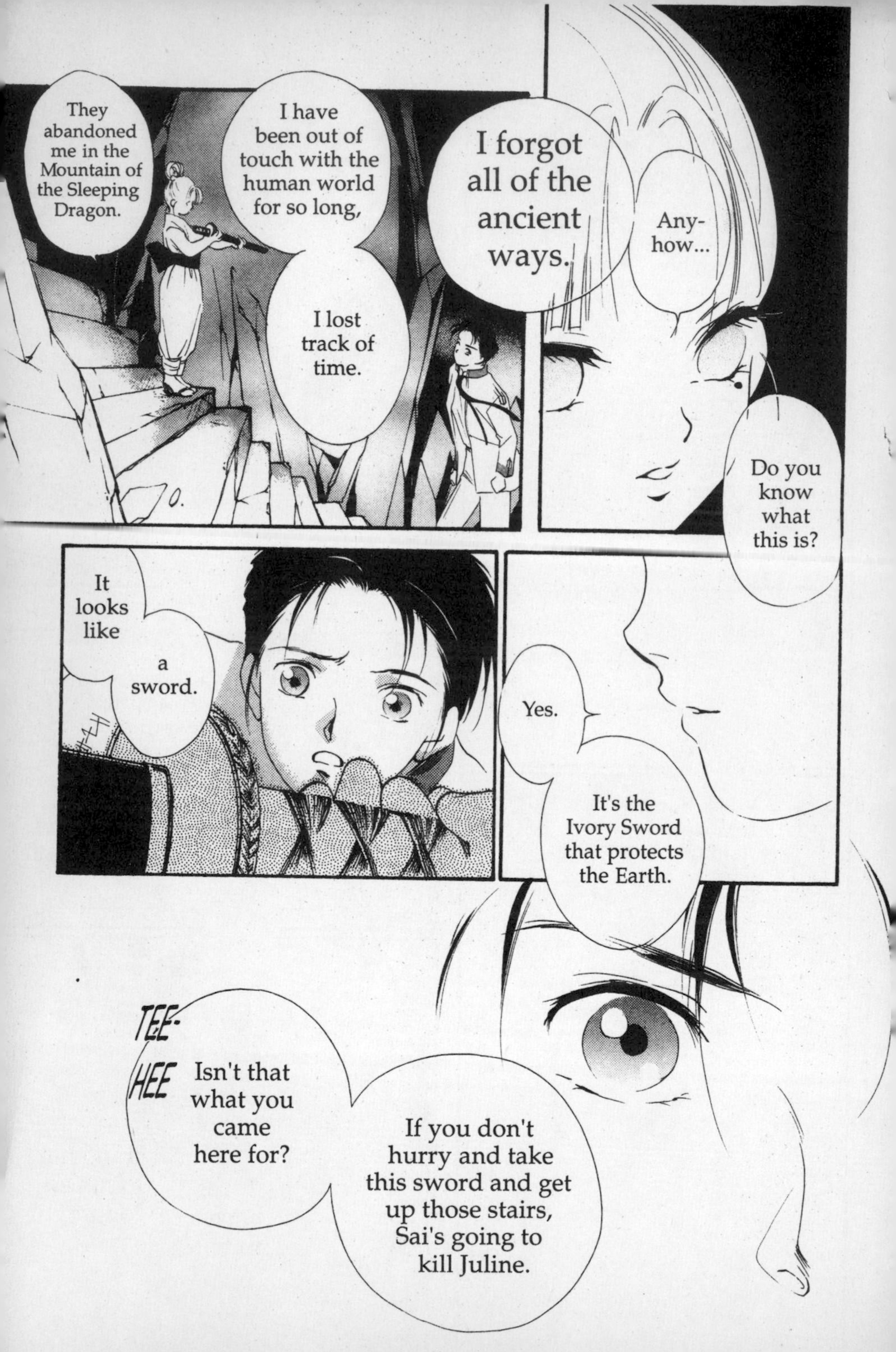

They abandoned me in the Mountain of the Sleeping Dragon.
I have been out of touch with the human world for so long,
I lost track of time.
I forgot all of the ancient ways.
Any-how...
Do you know what this is?
It looks like
a sword.
Yes.
It's the Ivory Sword that protects the Earth.
TEE-HEE
Isn't that what you came here for?
If you don't hurry and take this sword and get up those stairs, Sai's going to kill Juline.

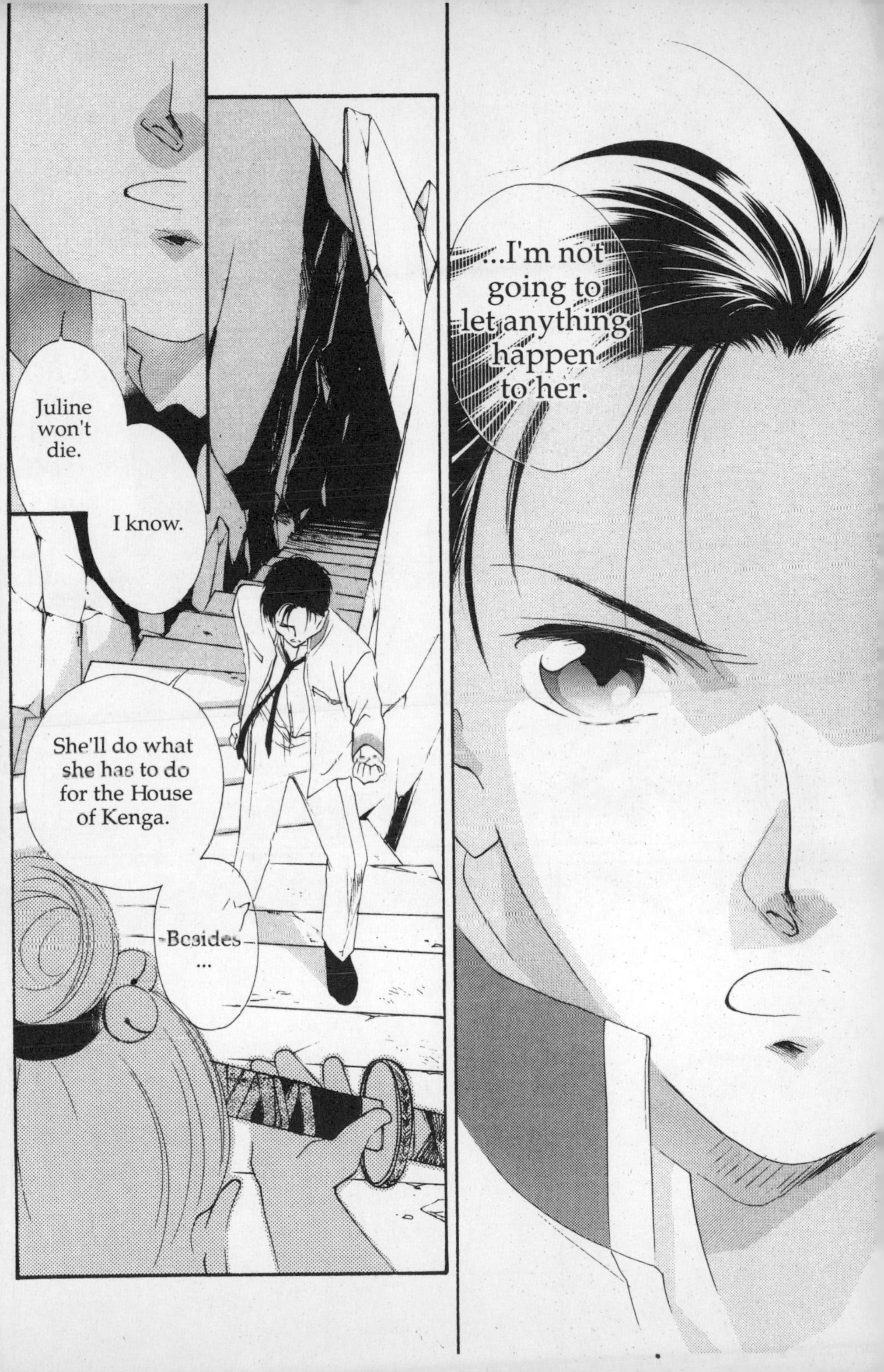

Juline won't die.
I know.
She'll do what she has to do for the House of Kenga.
Besides...
...I'm not going to let anything happen to her.

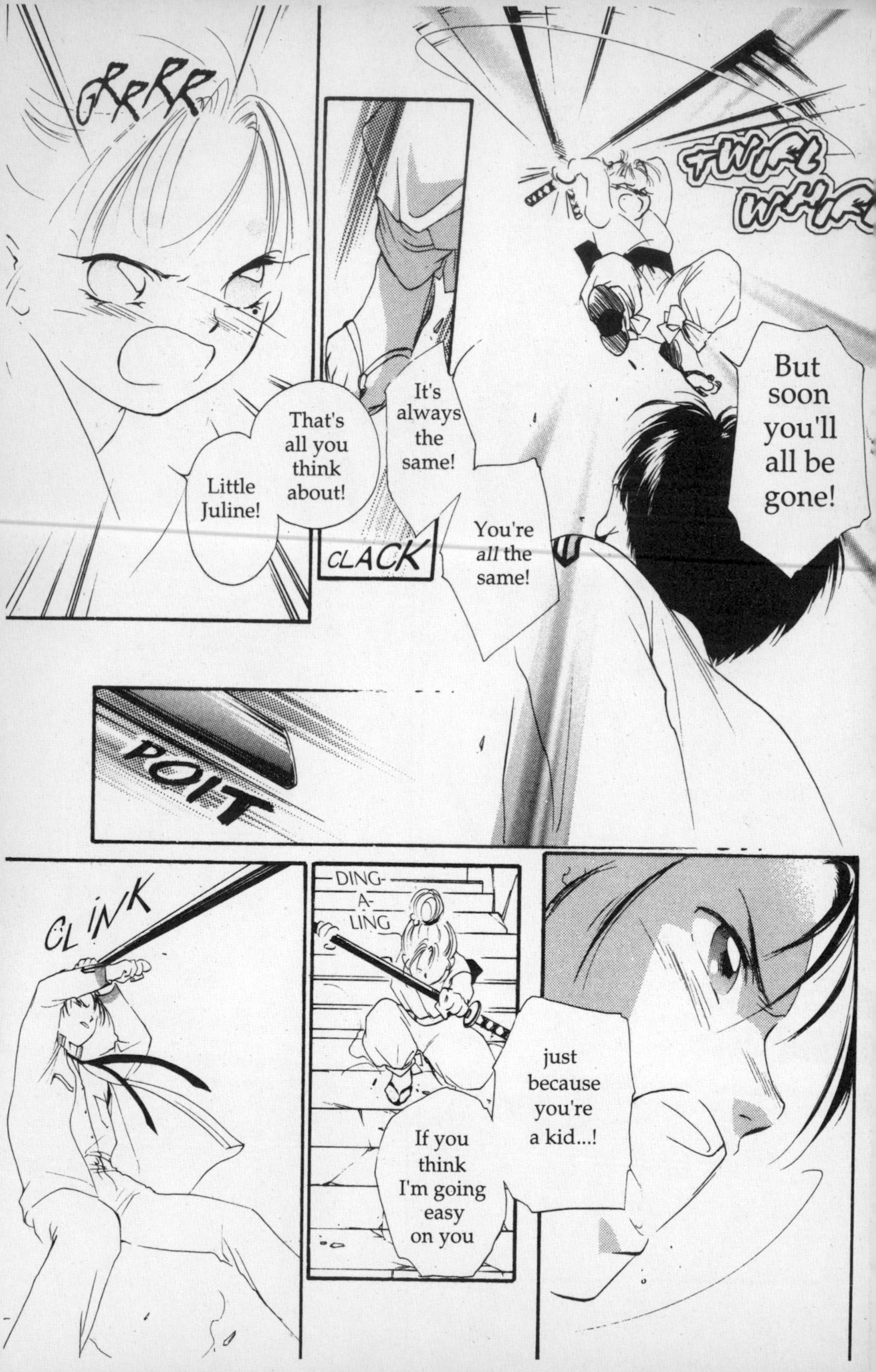
GRRRR
Little Juline!
That's all you think about!
CLACK
It's always the same!
You're *all* the same!
TWIFF
WHIF
But soon you'll all be gone!
POIT
CLINK
DING-A-LING
If you think I'm going easy on you
just because you're a kid...!

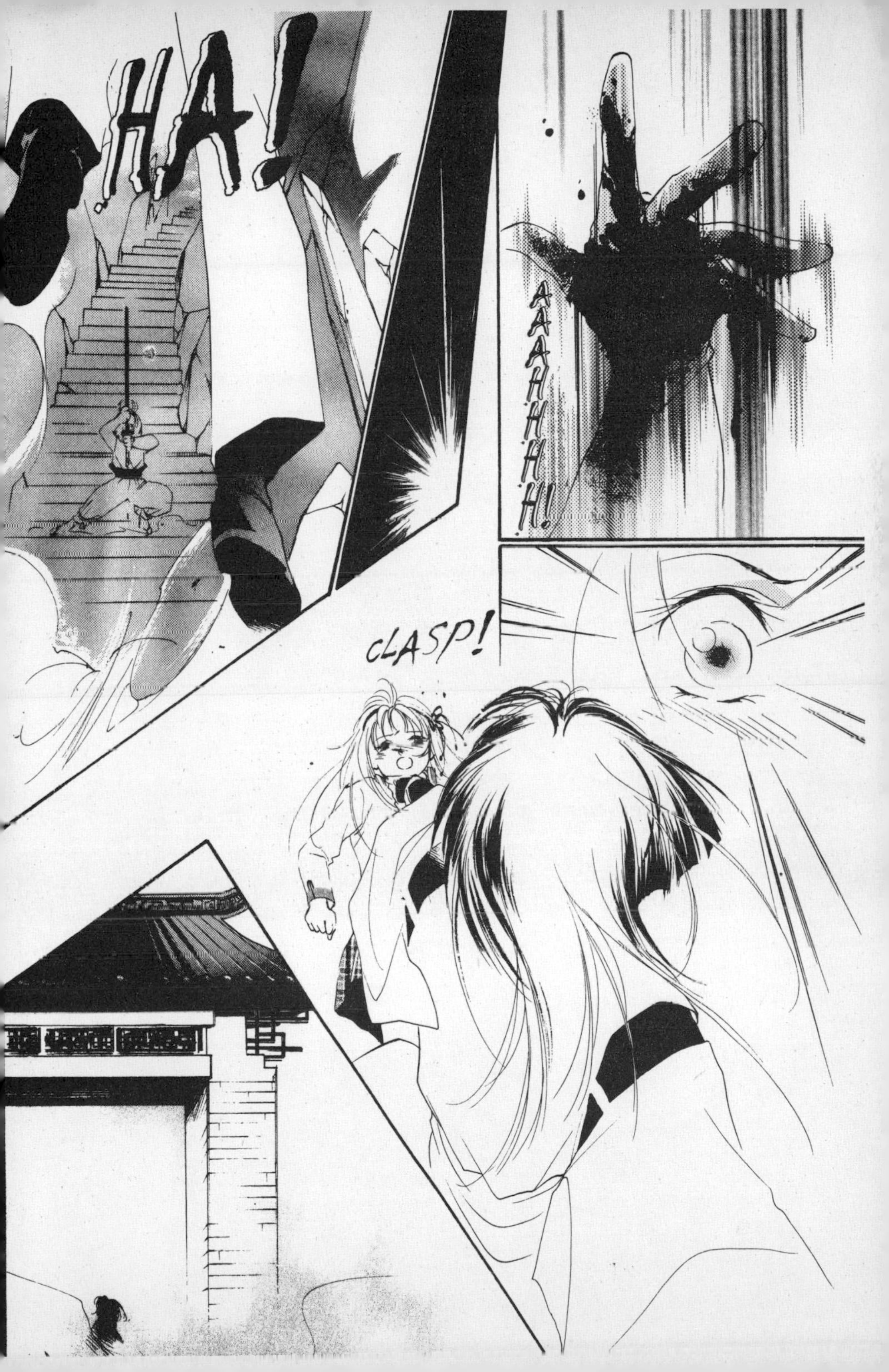

HA!
AAAAHHHHH!
CLASP!

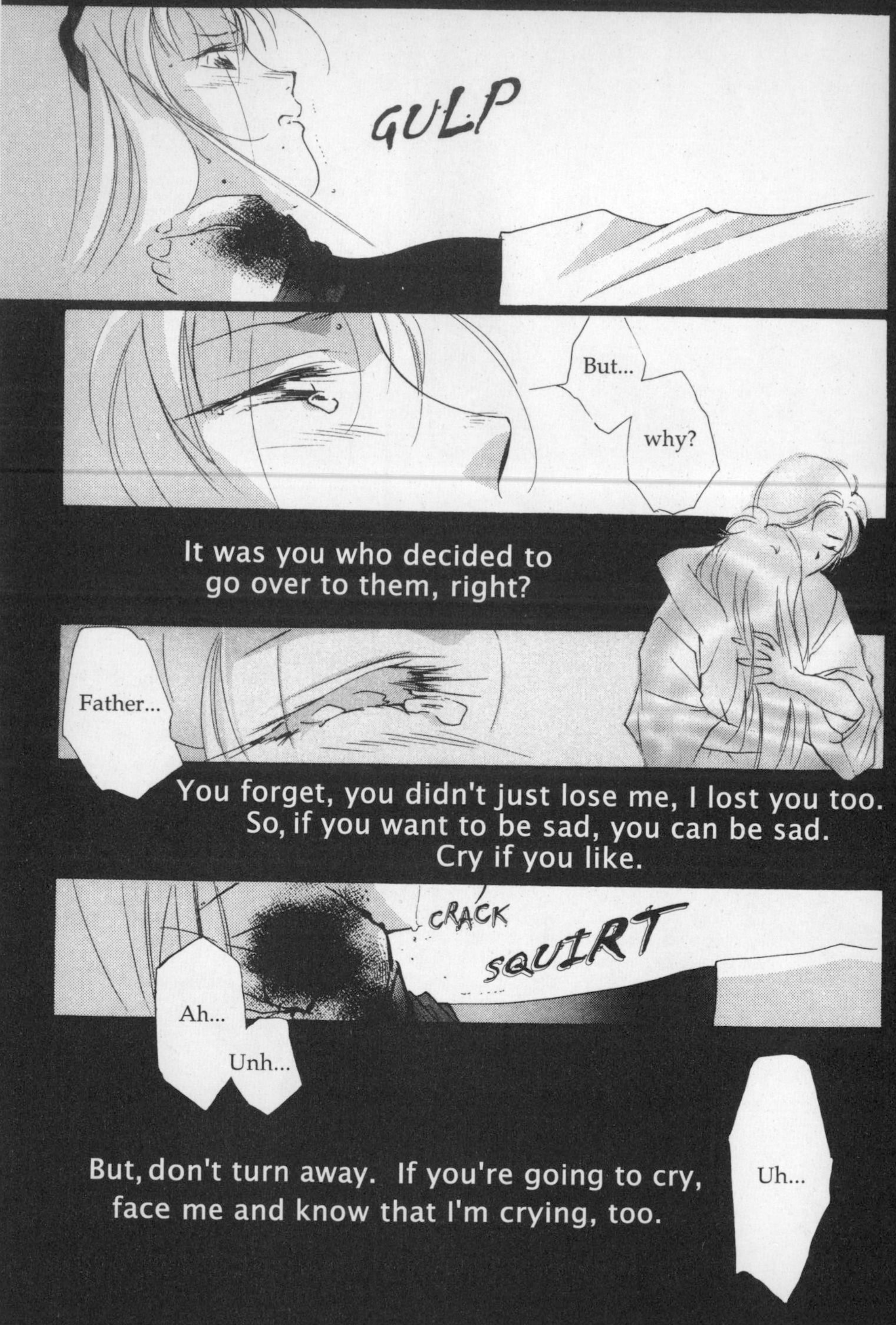
GULP
But...
why?
It was you who decided to go over to them, right?
Father...
You forget, you didn't just lose me, I lost you too. So, if you want to be sad, you can be sad. Cry if you like.
CRACK
SQUIRT
Ah...
Unh...
But, don't turn away. If you're going to cry, face me and know that I'm crying, too.
Uh...

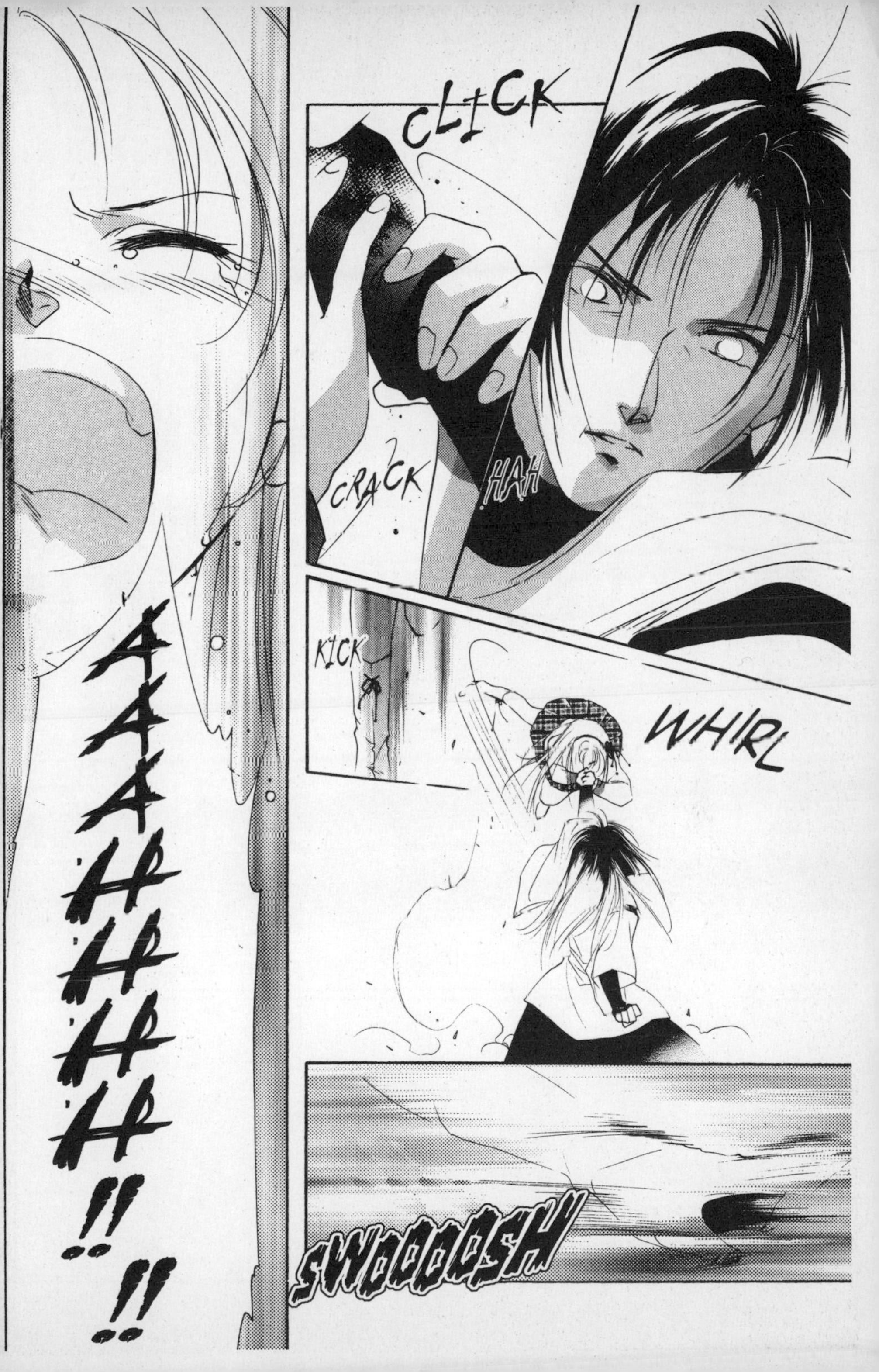

AAAHHHH!!!!
CLICK
CRACK
HAH
KICK
WHIRL
SWOOOOSH

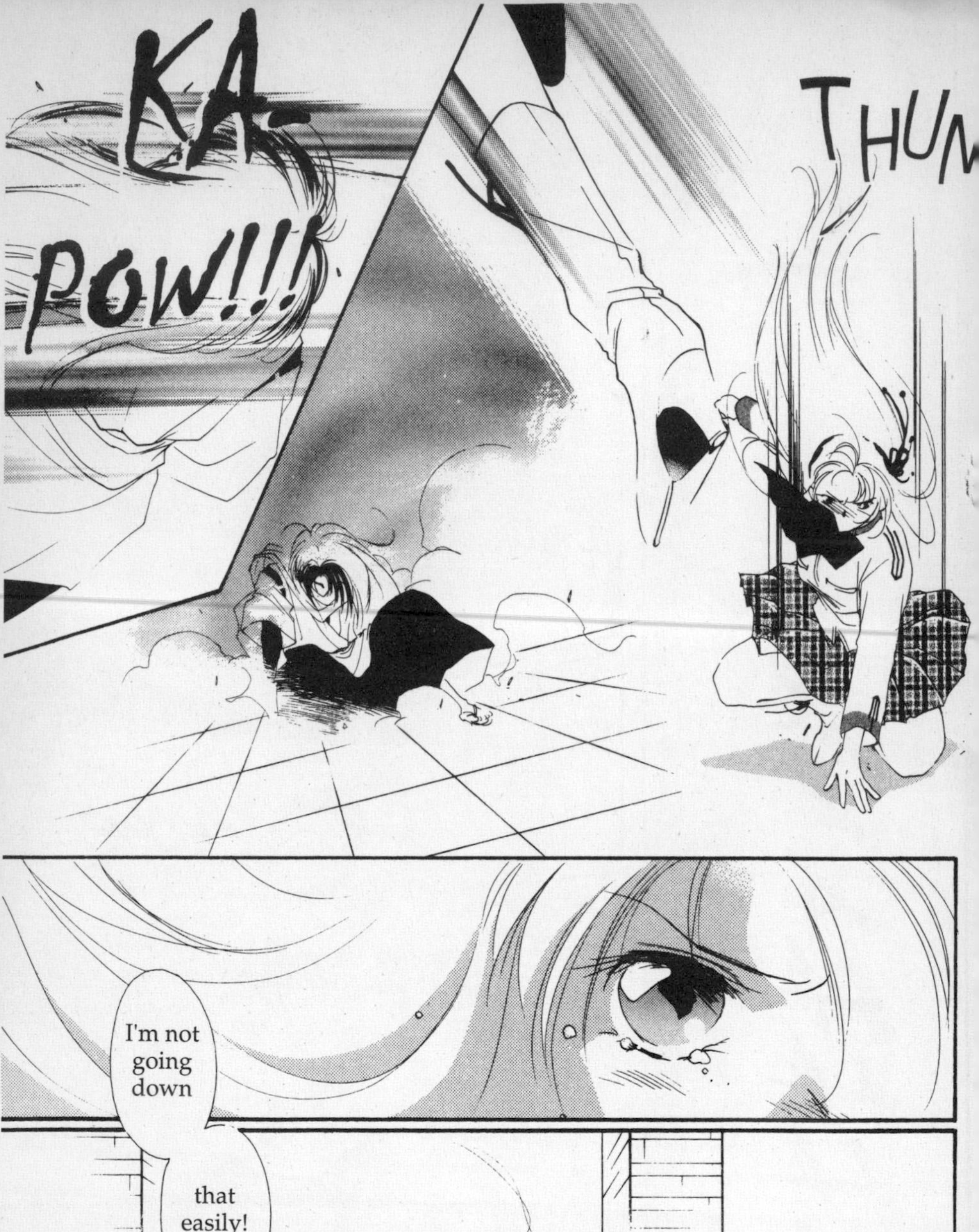
KA-POW!!!
THUM
I'm not going down
that easily!
CLICK CLACK

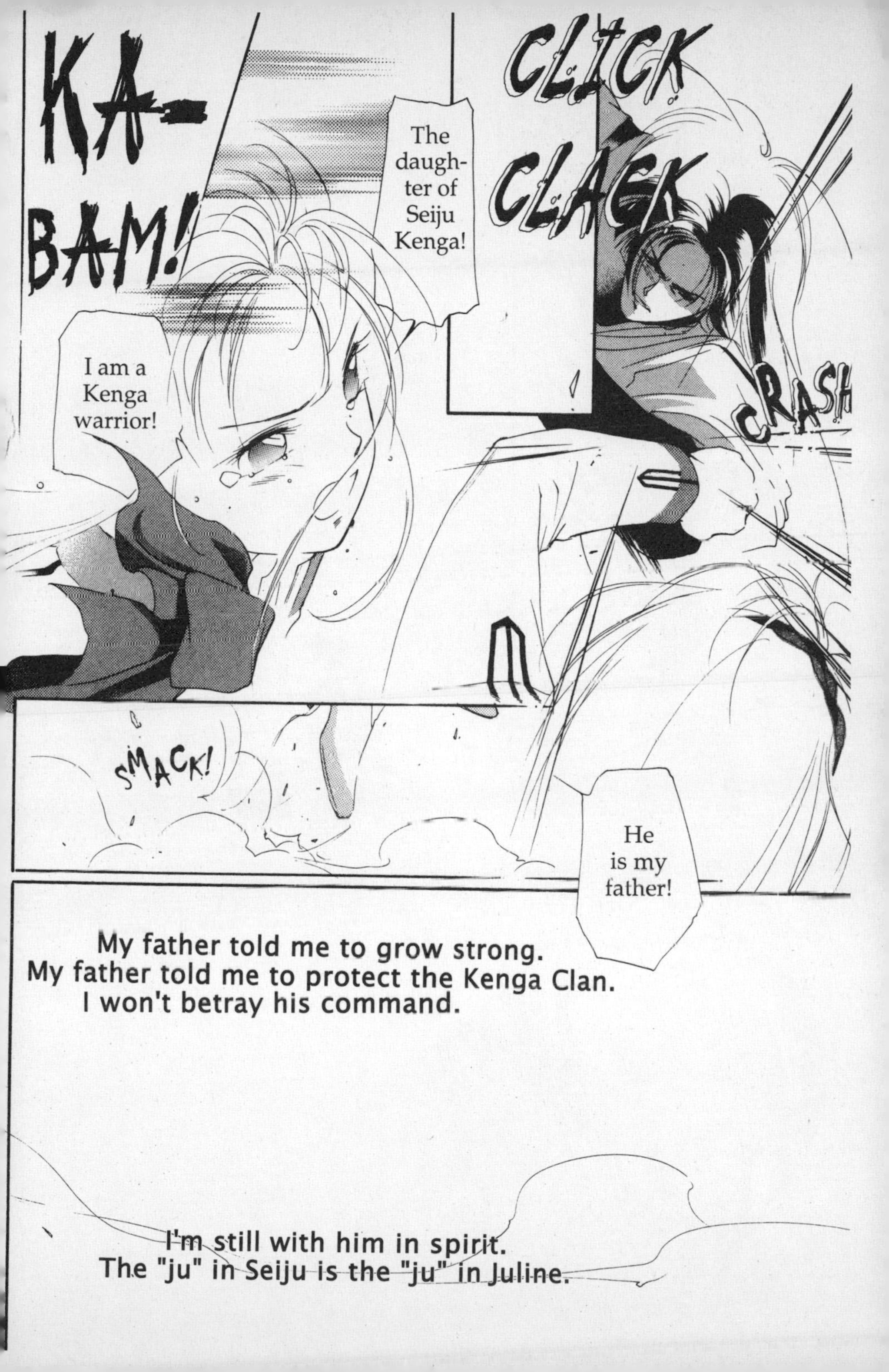
KA-BAM!
I am a Kenga warrior!
The daughter of Seiju Kenga!
CLICK CLACK
CRASH
SMACK!
He is my father!
My father told me to grow strong.
My father told me to protect the Kenga Clan.
I won't betray his command.
I'm still with him in spirit.
The "ju" in Seiju is the "ju" in Juline.

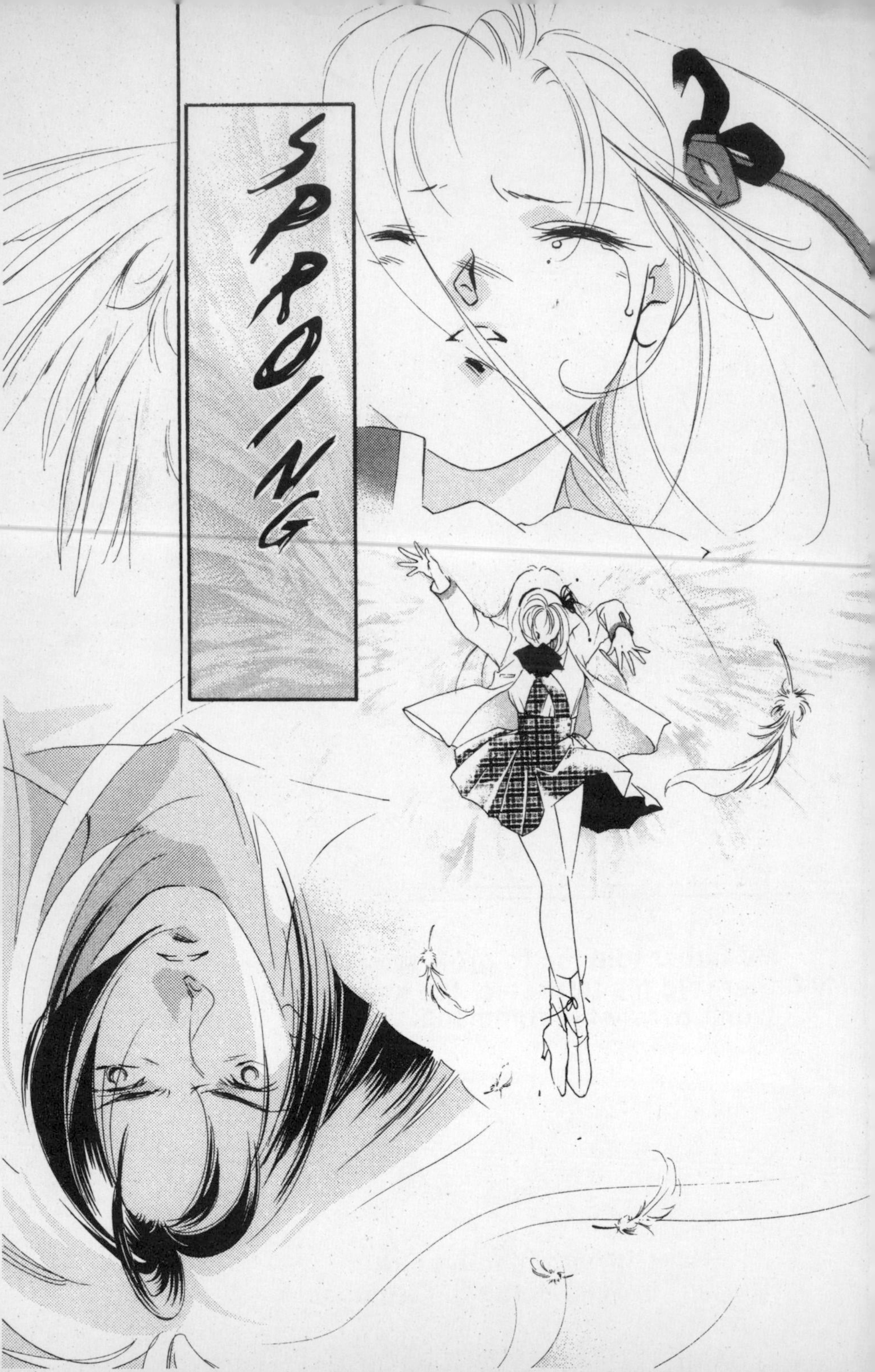
SPROING

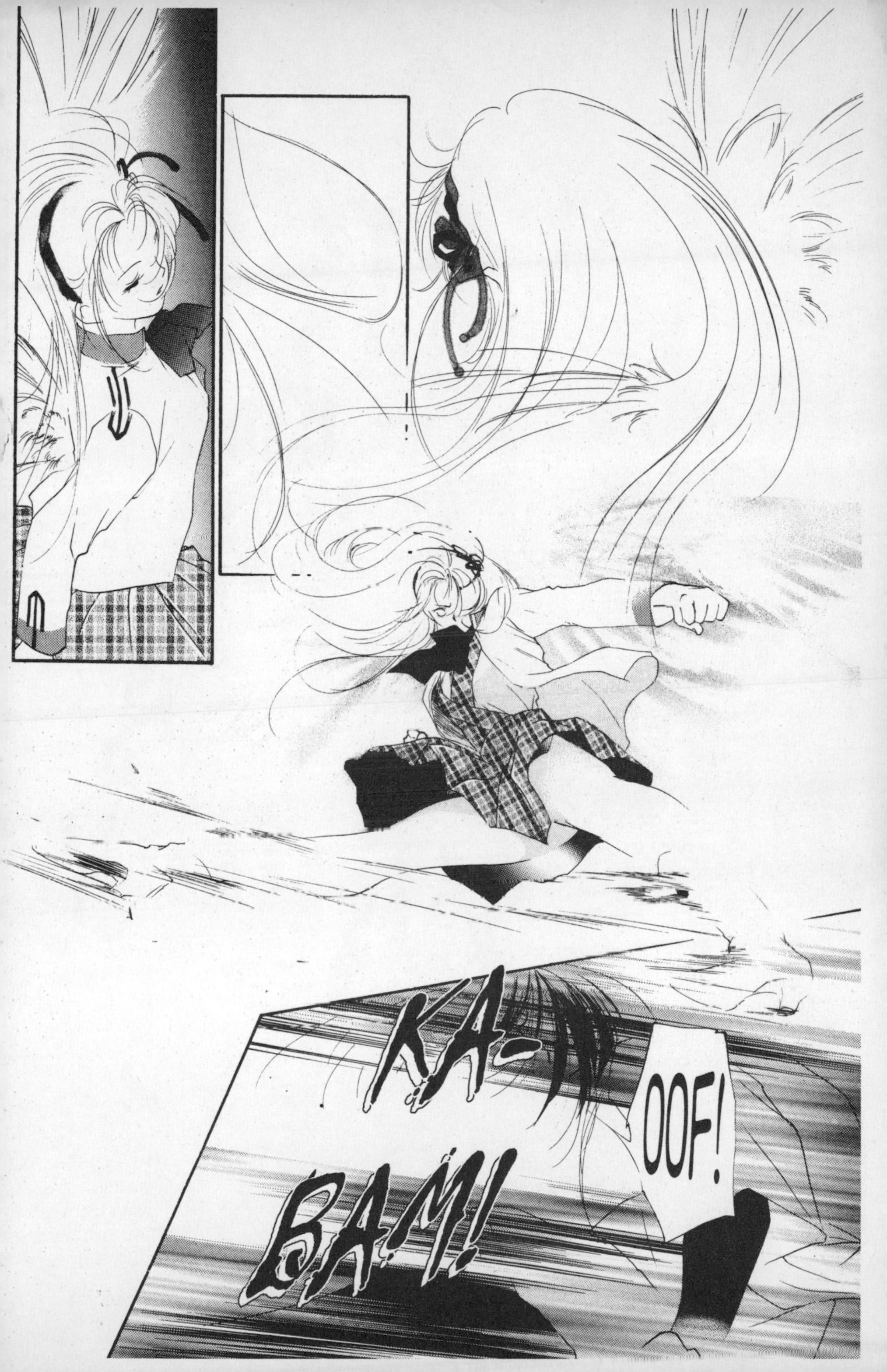
KA-BAM!
OOF!

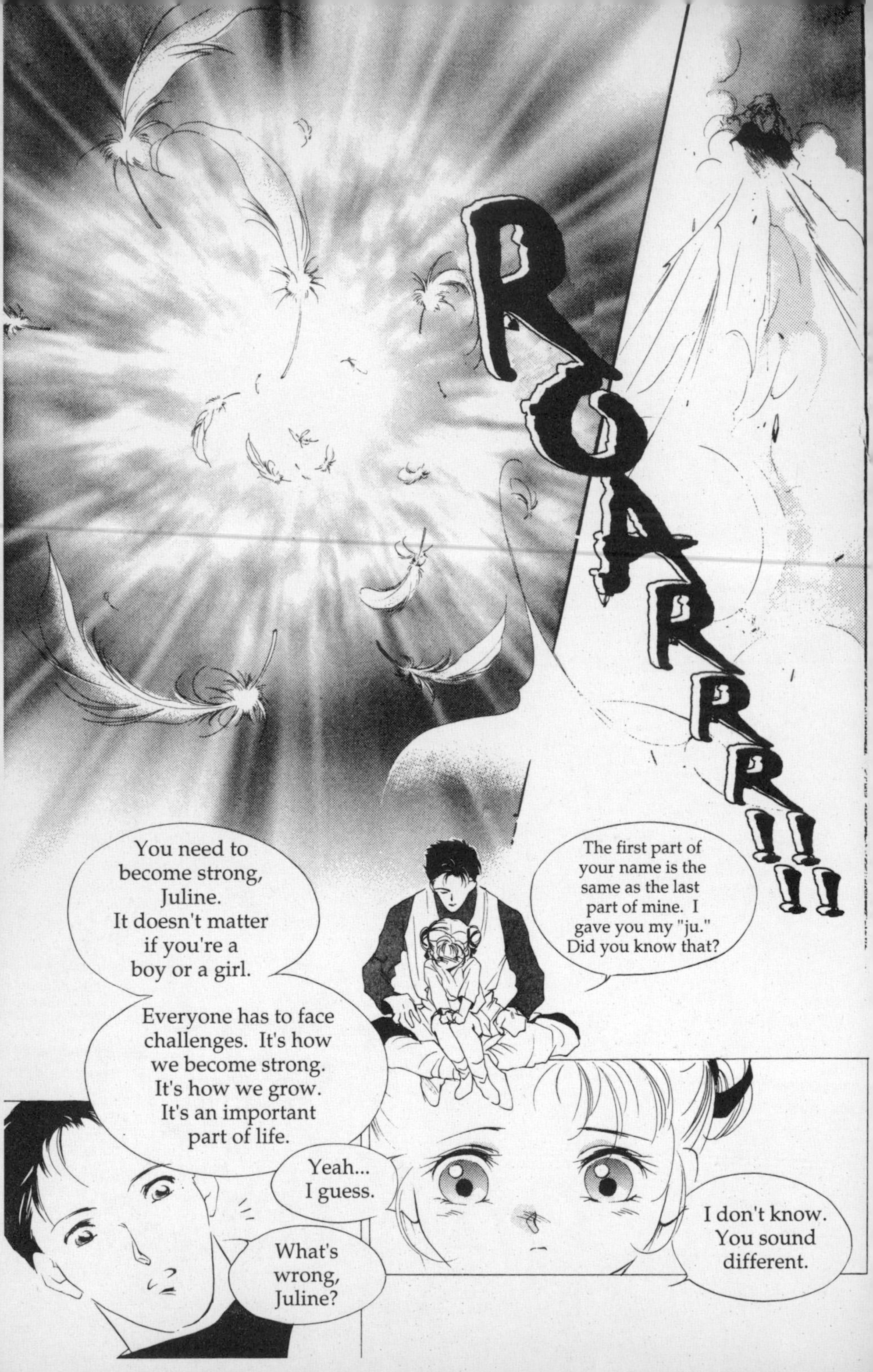
ROARRR!!
You need to become strong, Juline. It doesn't matter if you're a boy or a girl.
The first part of your name is the same as the last part of mine. I gave you my "ju." Did you know that?
Everyone has to face challenges. It's how we become strong. It's how we grow. It's an important part of life.
Yeah... I guess.
What's wrong, Juline?
I don't know. You sound different.

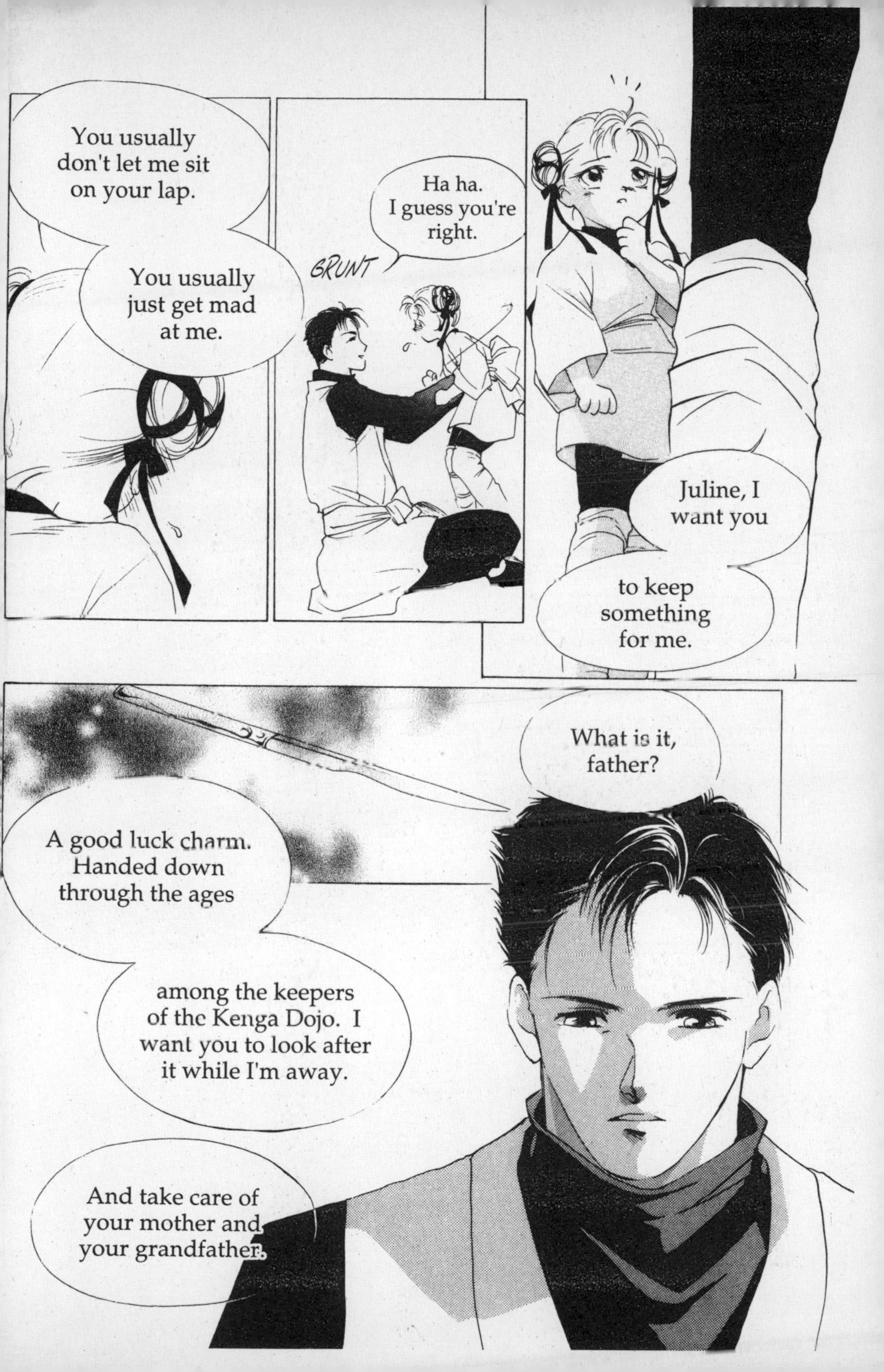
You usually don't let me sit on your lap.
You usually just get mad at me.
Ha ha. I guess you're right.
GRUNT
Juline, I want you
to keep something for me.
What is it, father?
A good luck charm. Handed down through the ages
among the keepers of the Kenga Dojo. I want you to look after it while I'm away.
And take care of your mother and your grandfather.

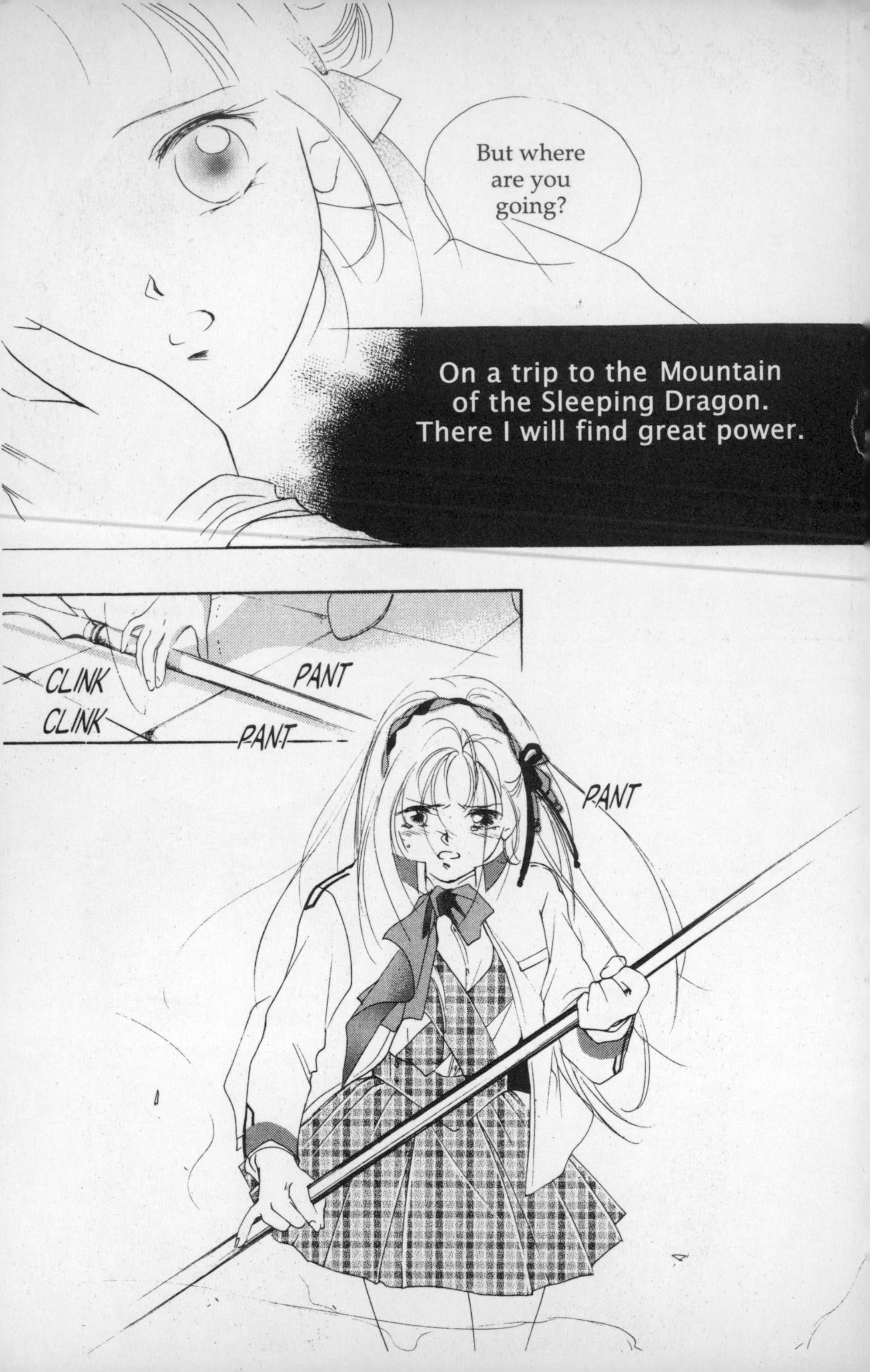
But where are you going?
On a trip to the Mountain of the Sleeping Dragon. There I will find great power.
CLINK
CLINK
PANT
PANT
PANT

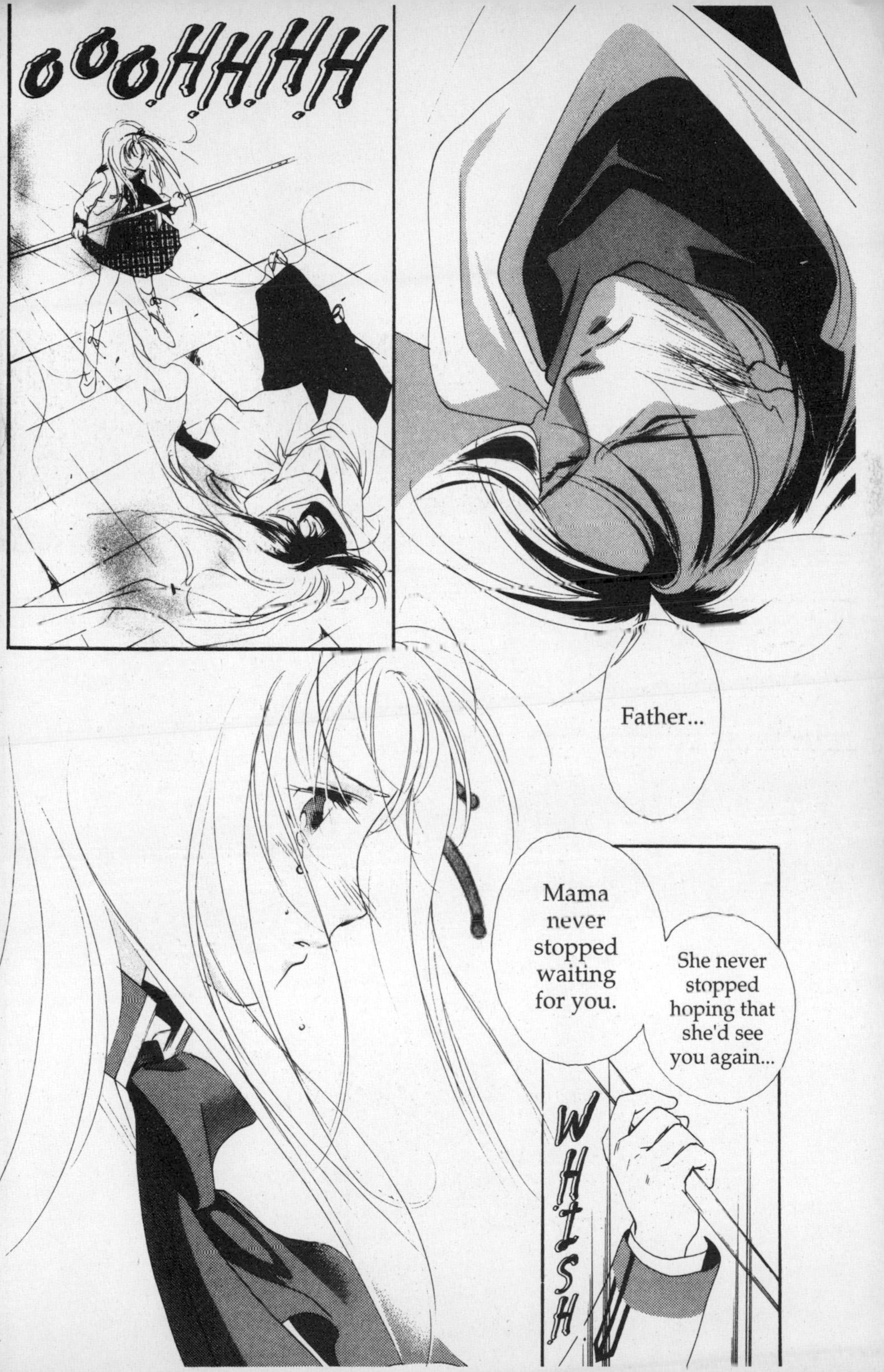
OOOHHHH
Father...
Mama never stopped waiting for you.
She never stopped hoping that she'd see you again...
WHISH

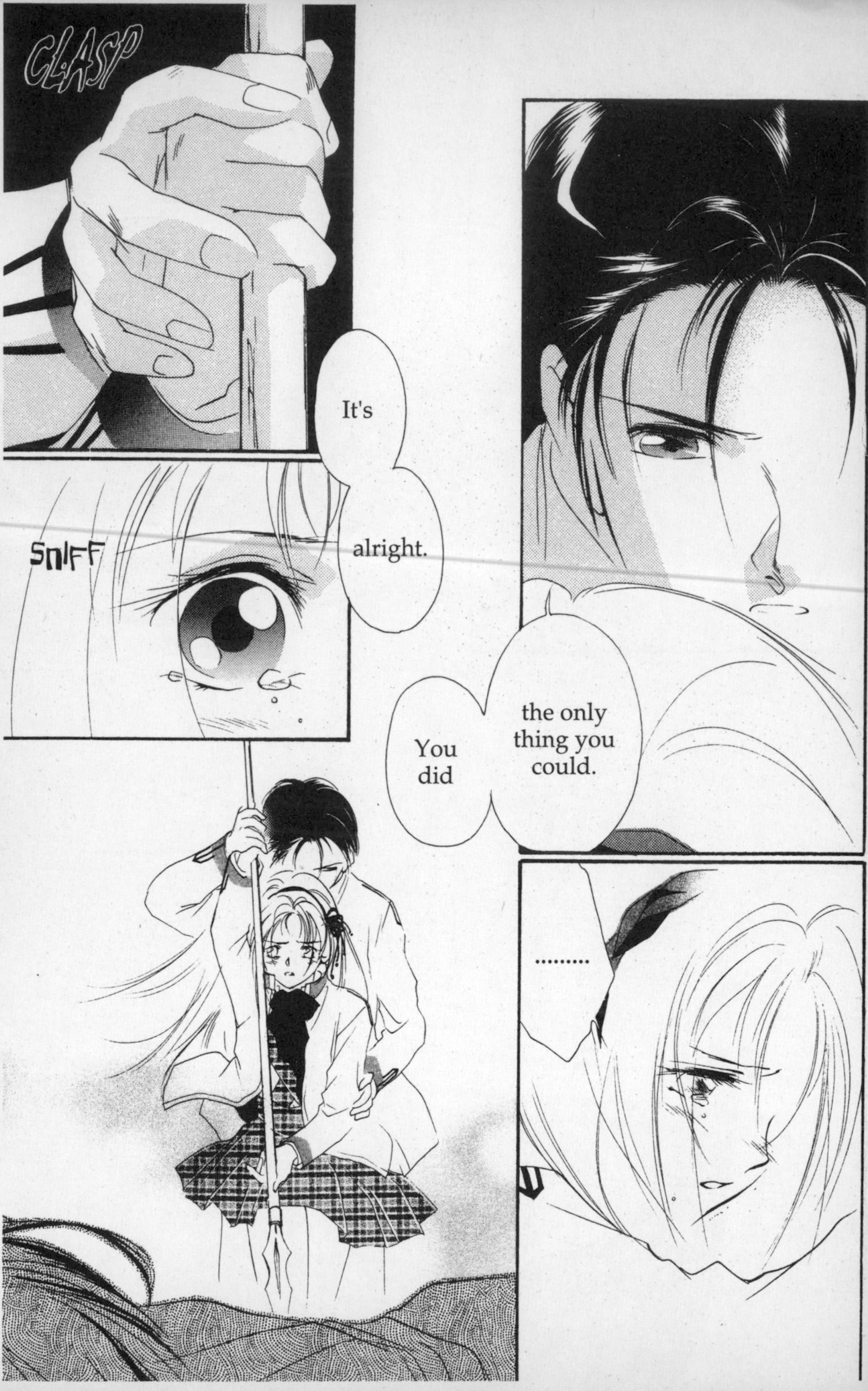
CLASP
SNIFF
It's alright.
You did the only thing you could.
....

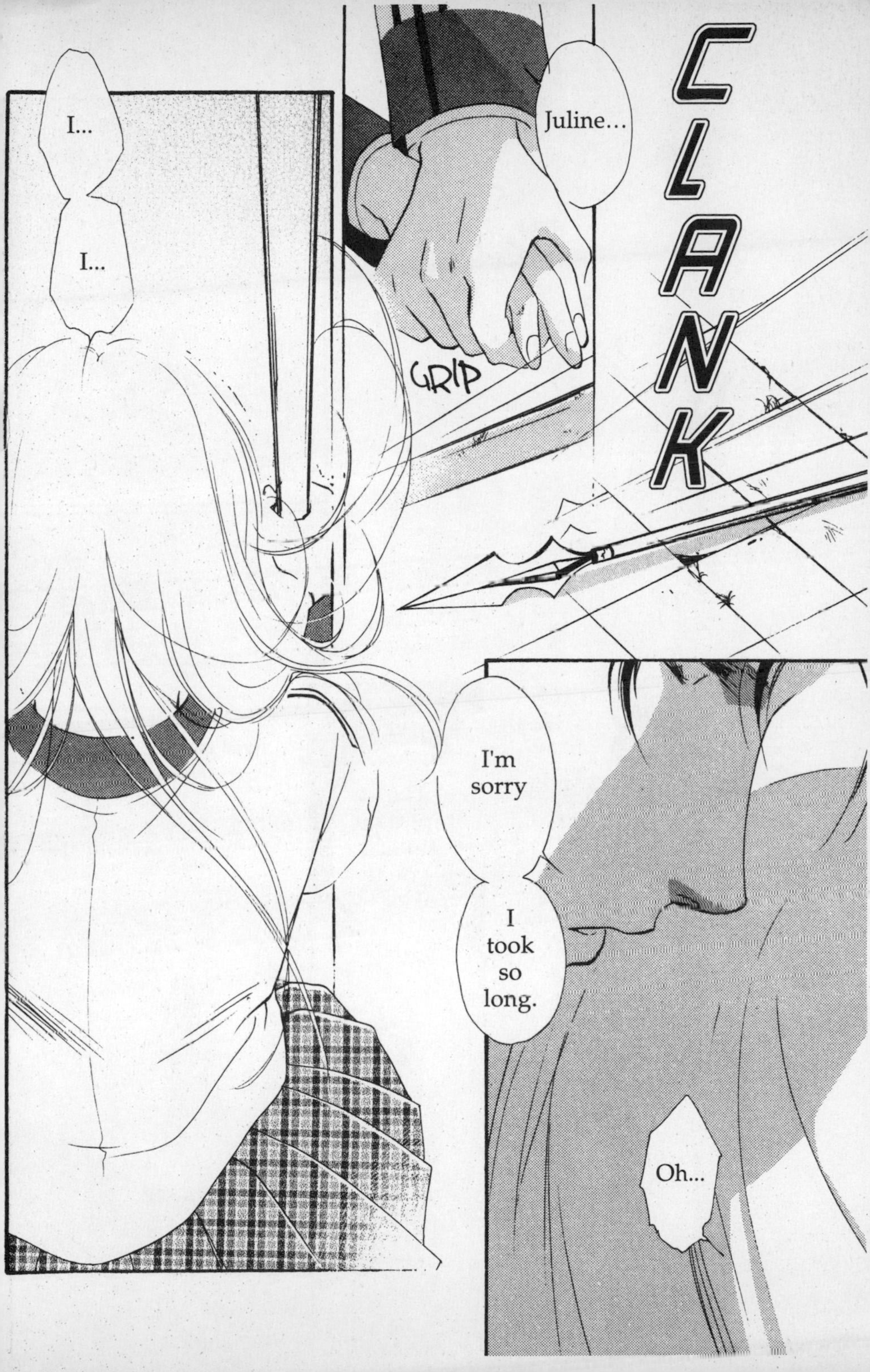

I...
I...
Juline...
GRIP
CLANK
I'm sorry
I took so long.
Oh...

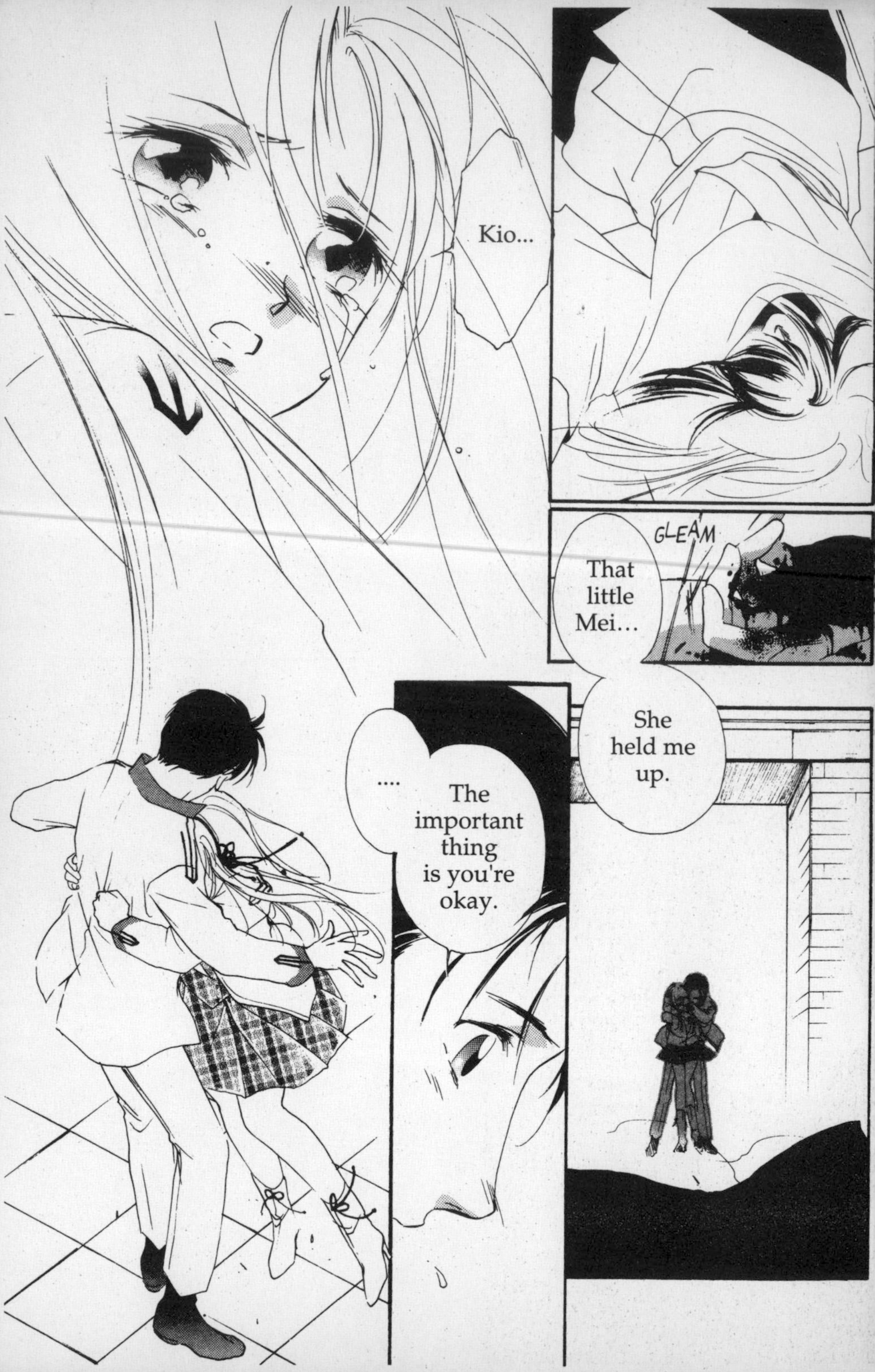
GLEAM
That little Mei…
She held me up.
....
The important thing is you're okay.
Kio...

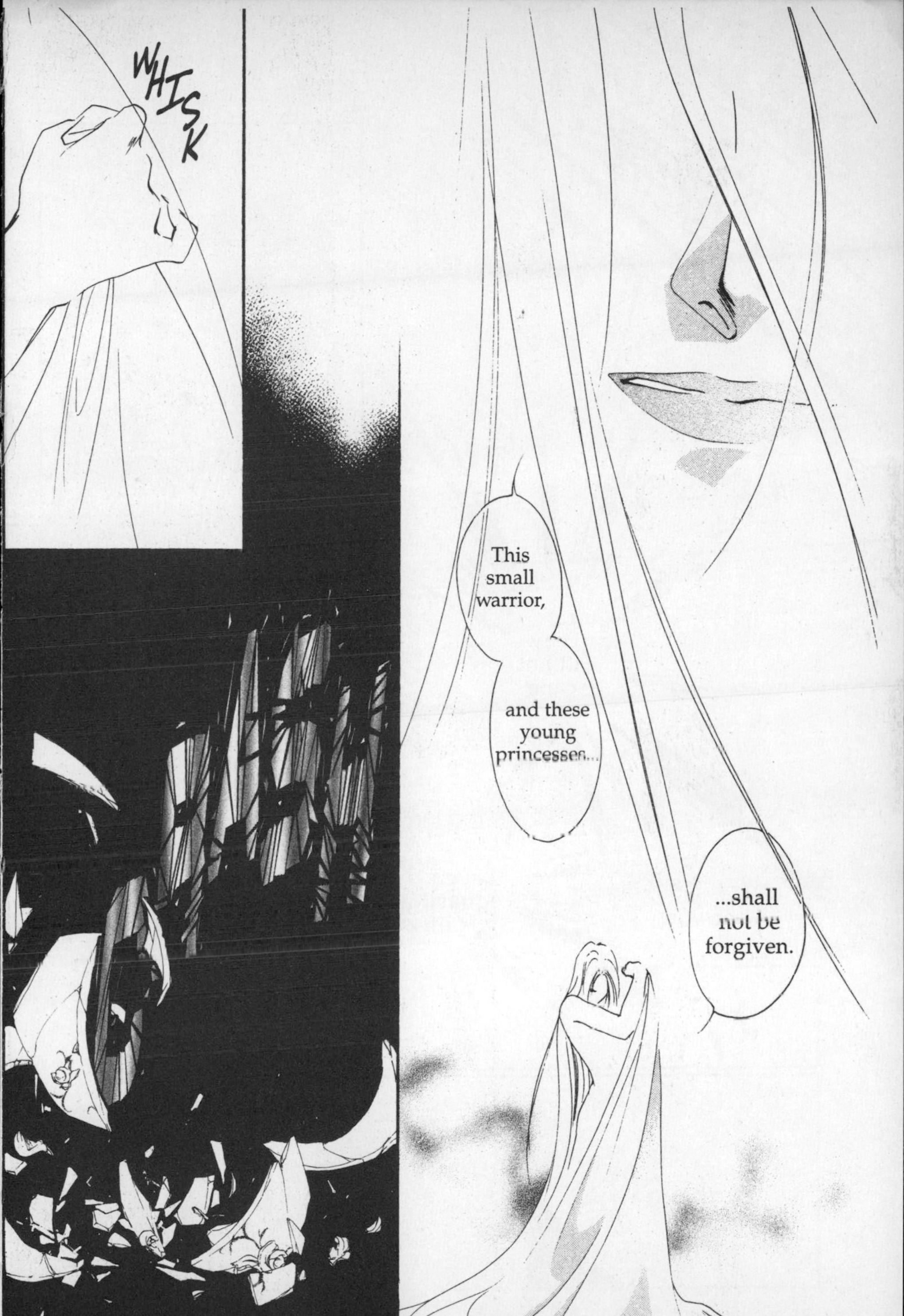
WHISK
This small warrior,
and these young princesses...
...shall not be forgiven.

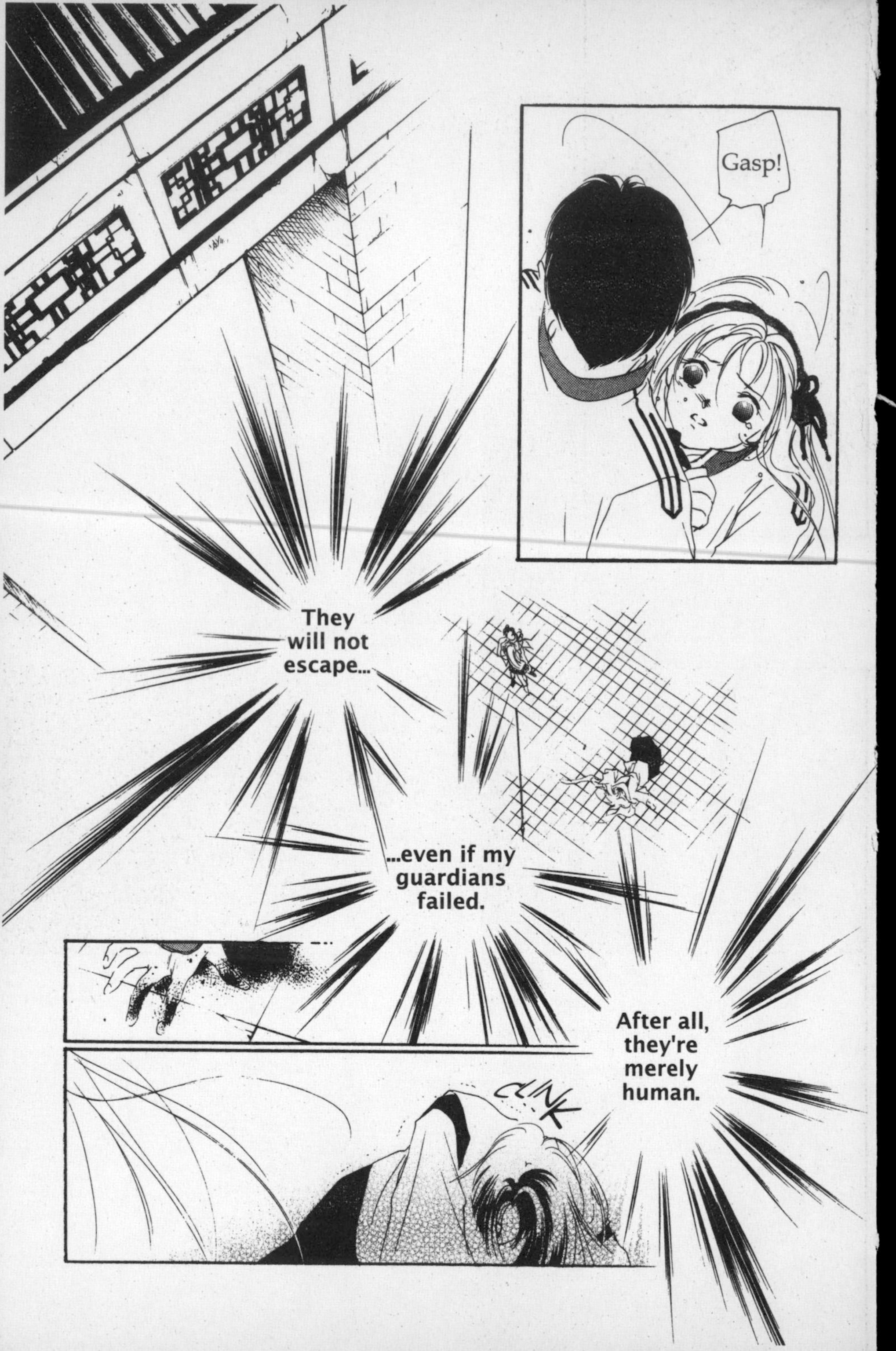
Gasp!
They will not escape...
...even if my guardians failed.
After all, they're merely human.
CLINK

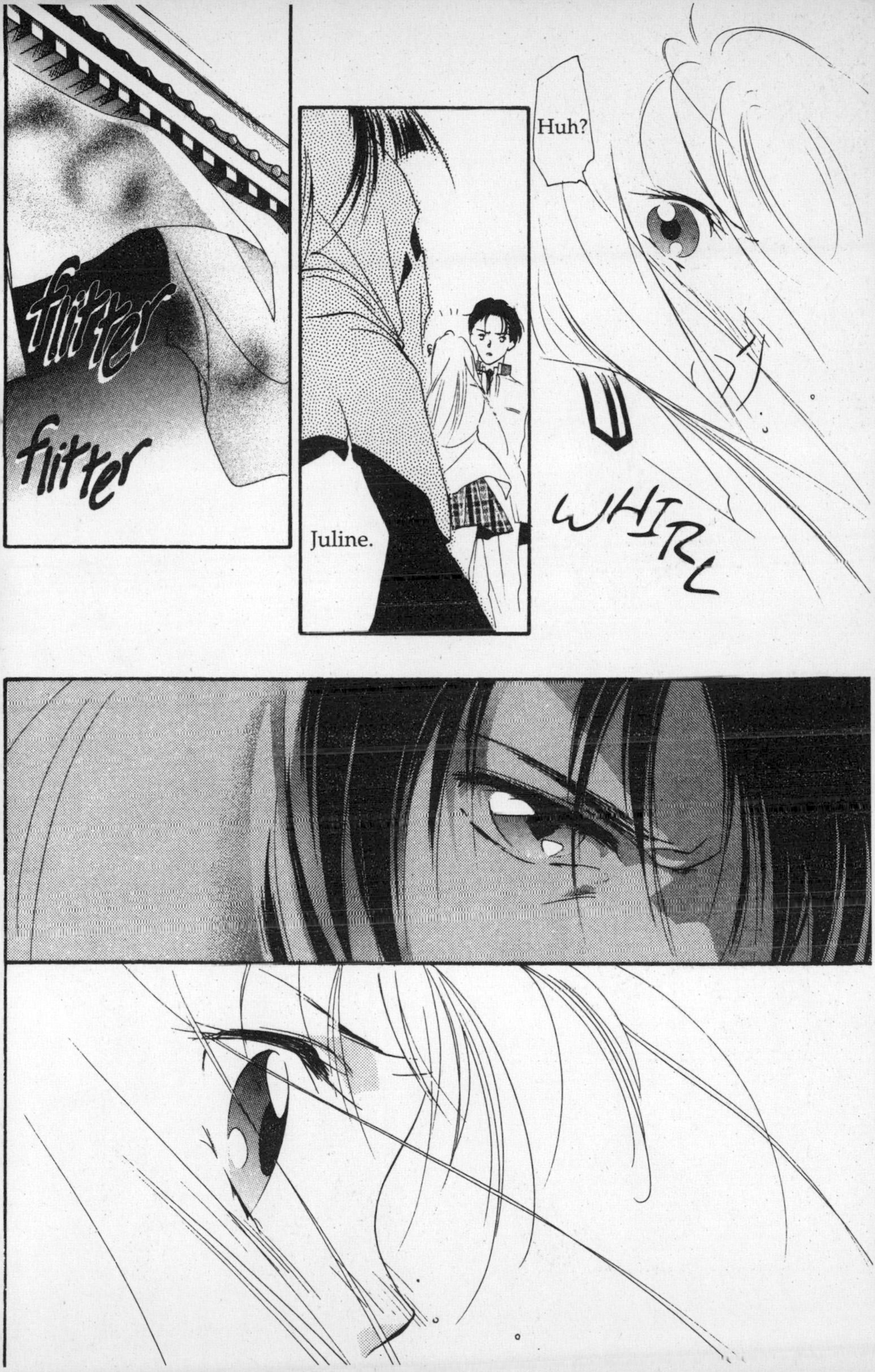
flitter
flitter
Juline.
Huh?
WHIRL

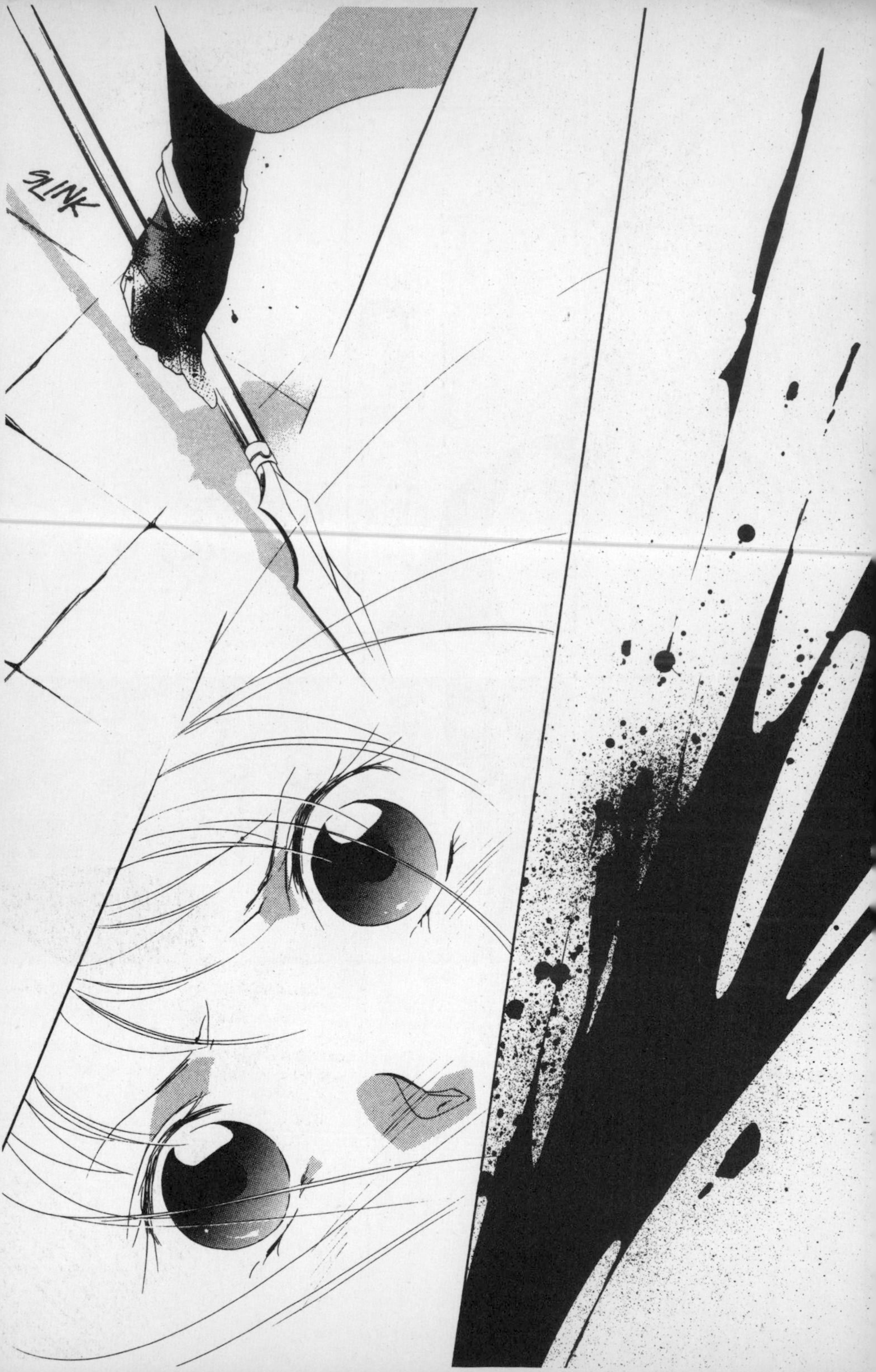
SLINK

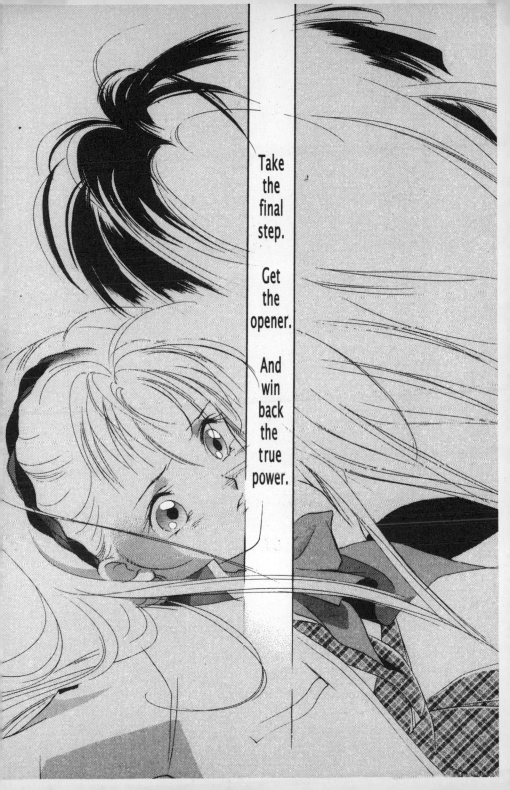

Take the final step.

Get the opener.

And win back the true power.

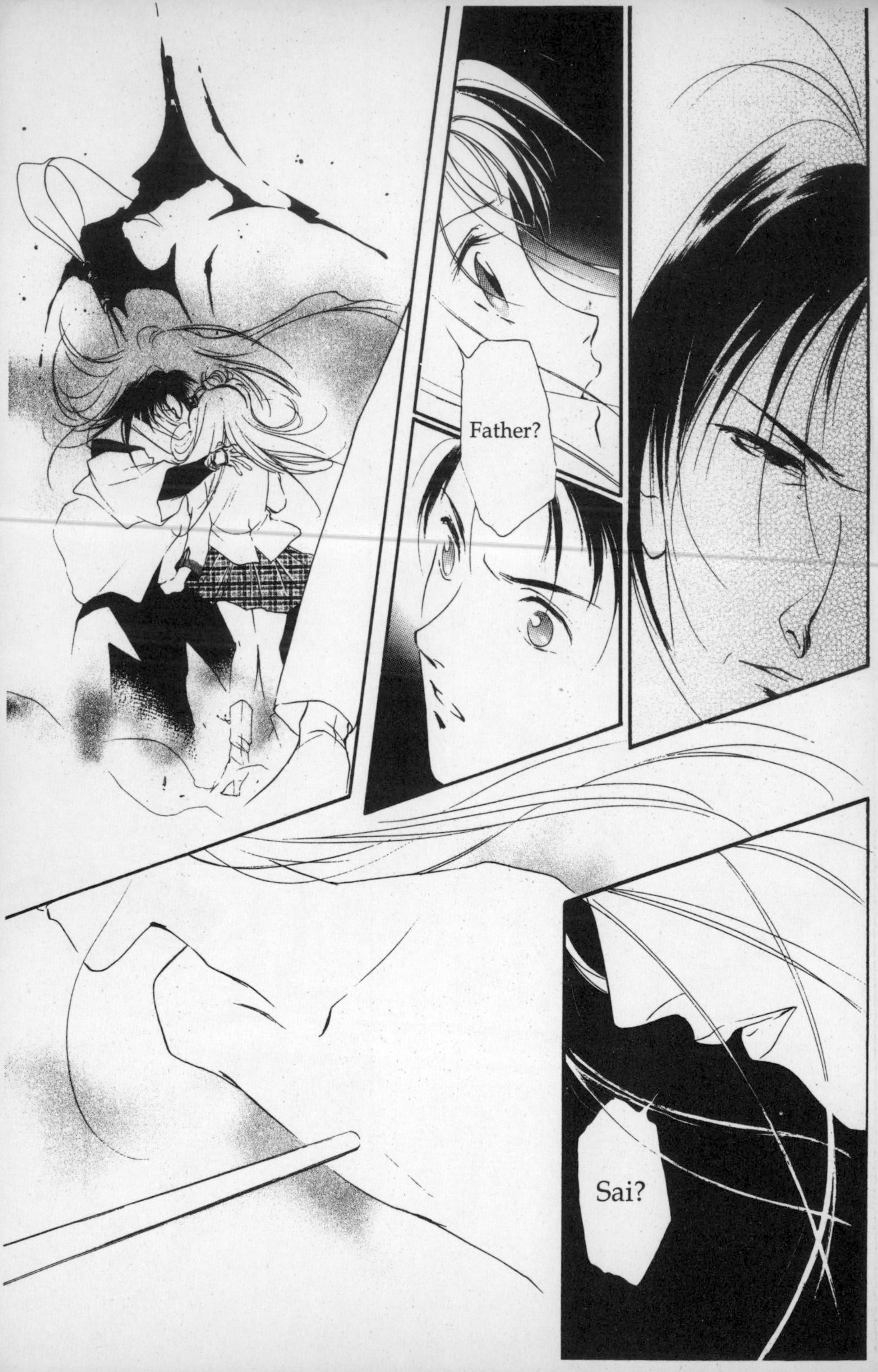
Father?
Sai?

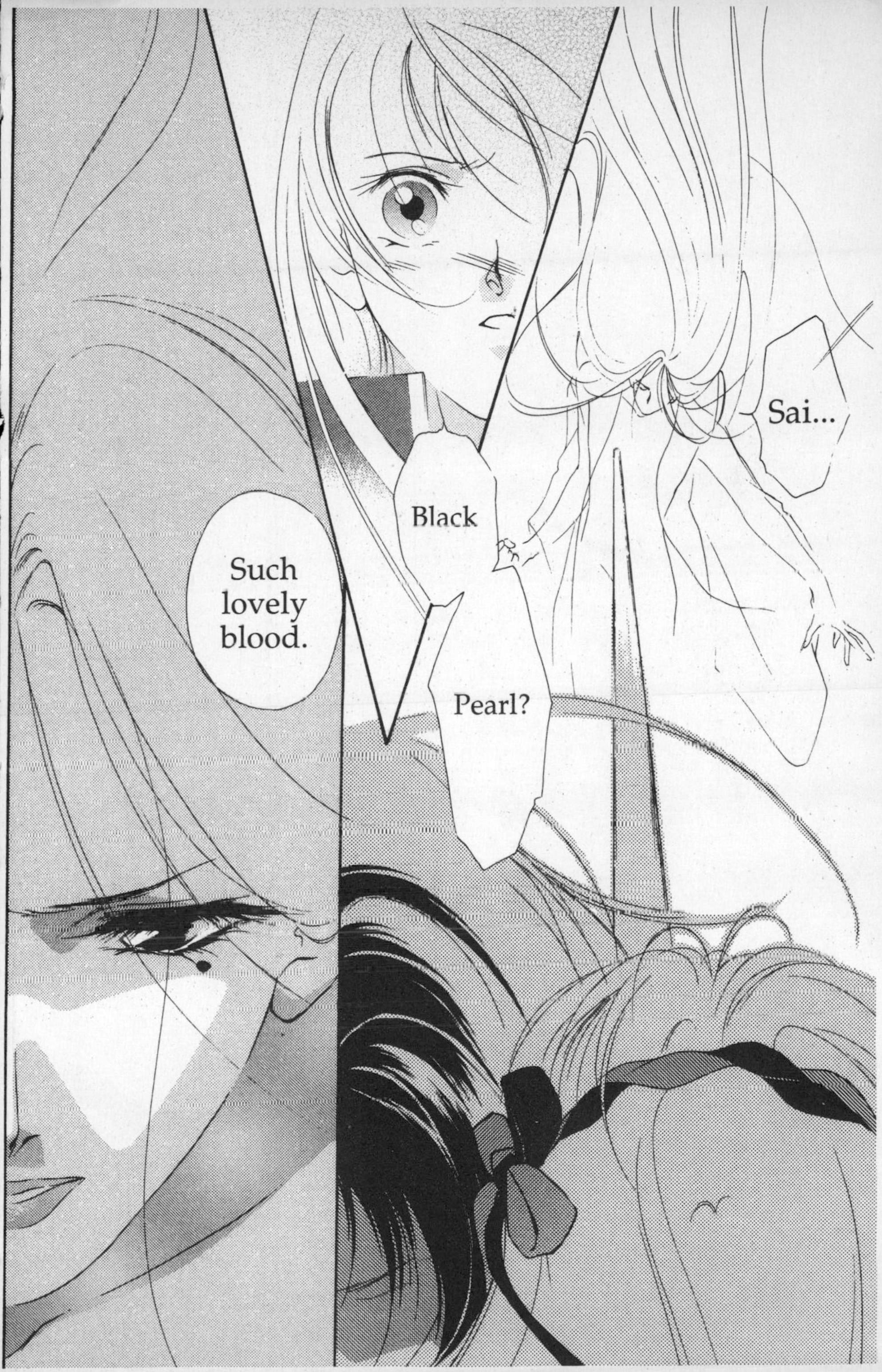
Such lovely blood.
Black
Pearl?
Sai...

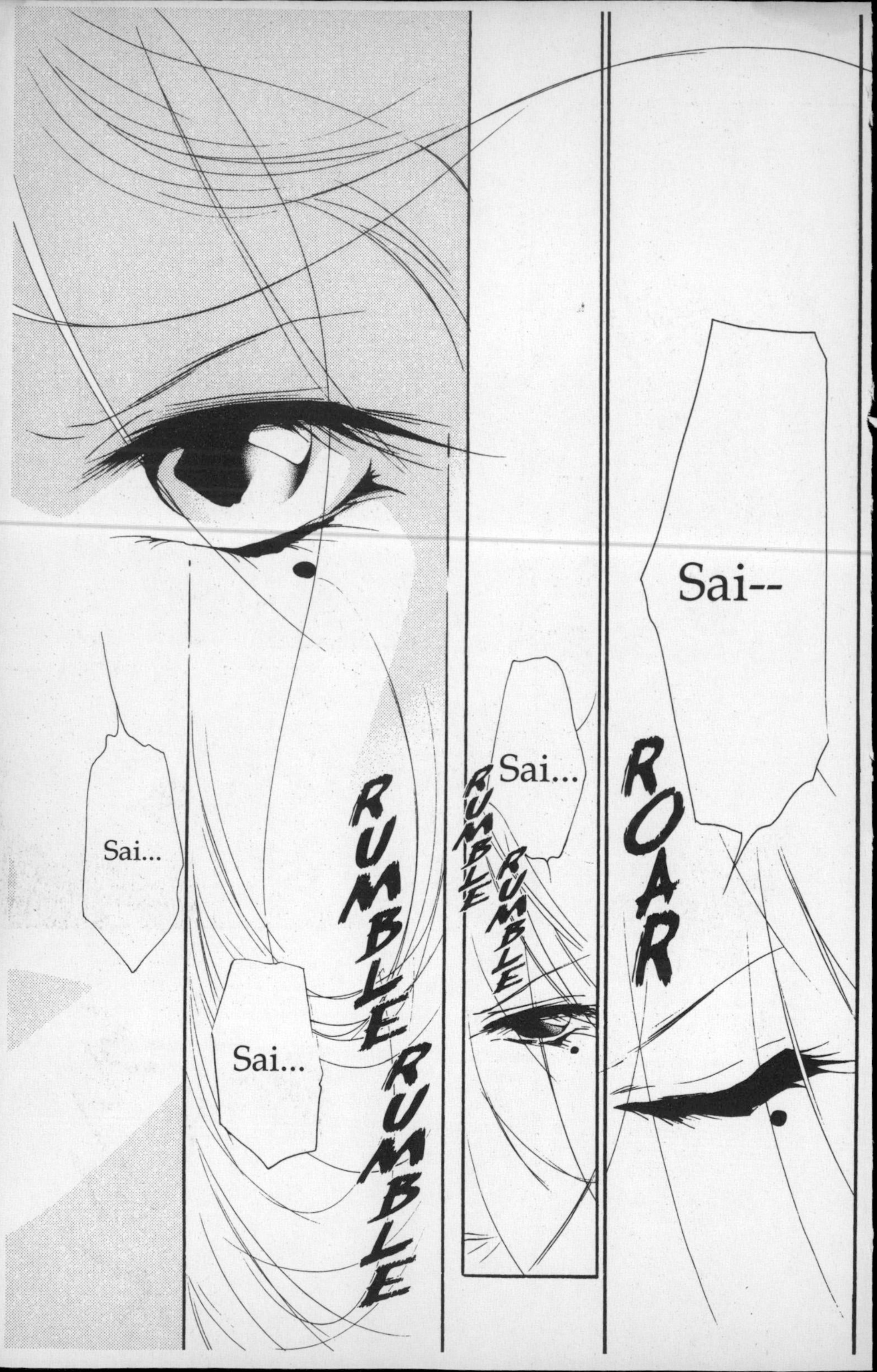
Sai...
Sai...
RUMBLE RUMBLE
Sai...
RUMBLE RUMBLE
Sai--
ROAR

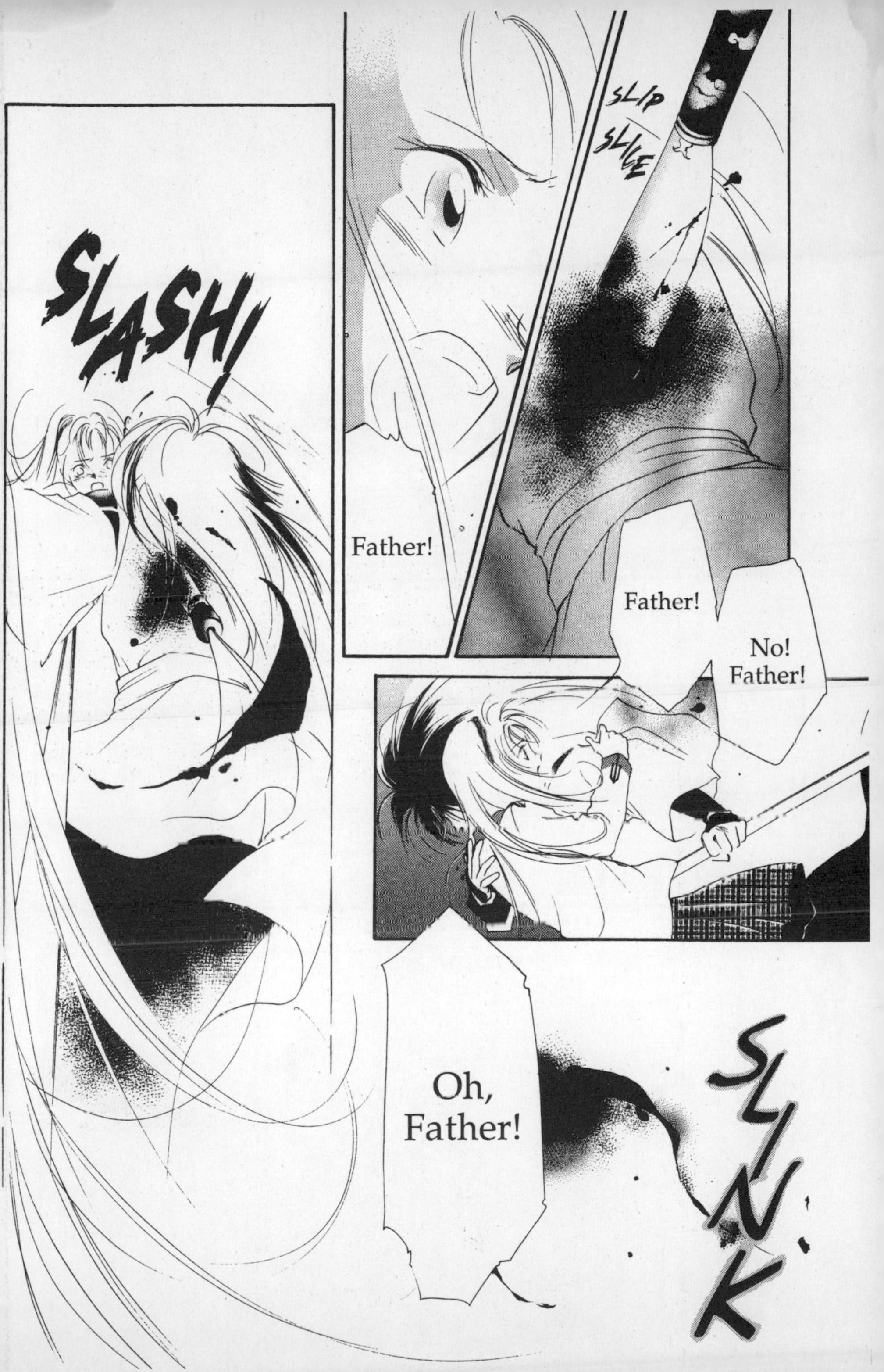
SLASH!
Father!
SLIP
SLICE
Father!
No! Father!
Oh, Father!
SLINK

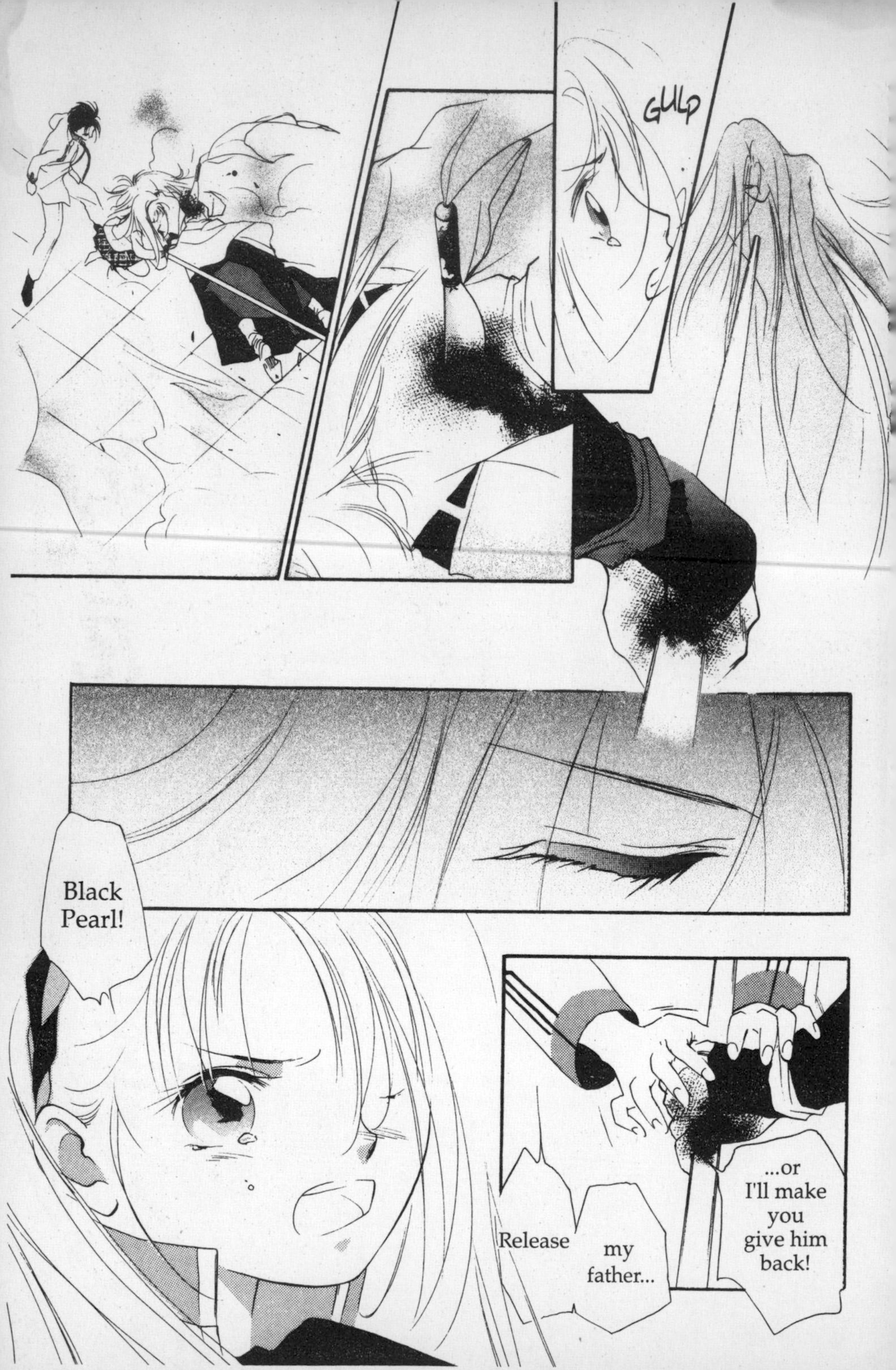
GULP
Black Pearl!
Release
my father...
...or I'll make you give him back!

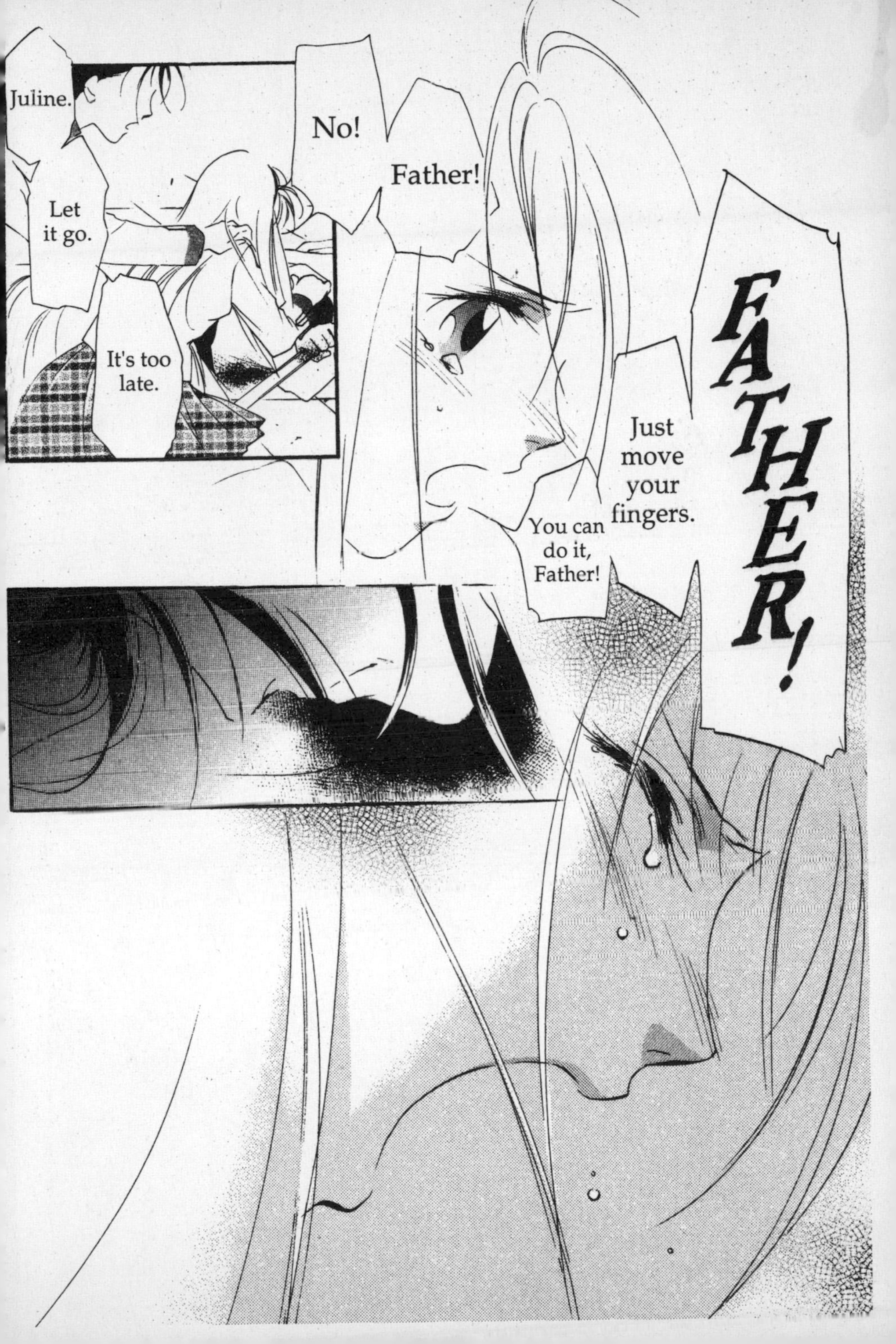
Juline.
Let it go.
It's too late.
No!
Father!
Just move your fingers.
You can do it, Father!
FATHER!

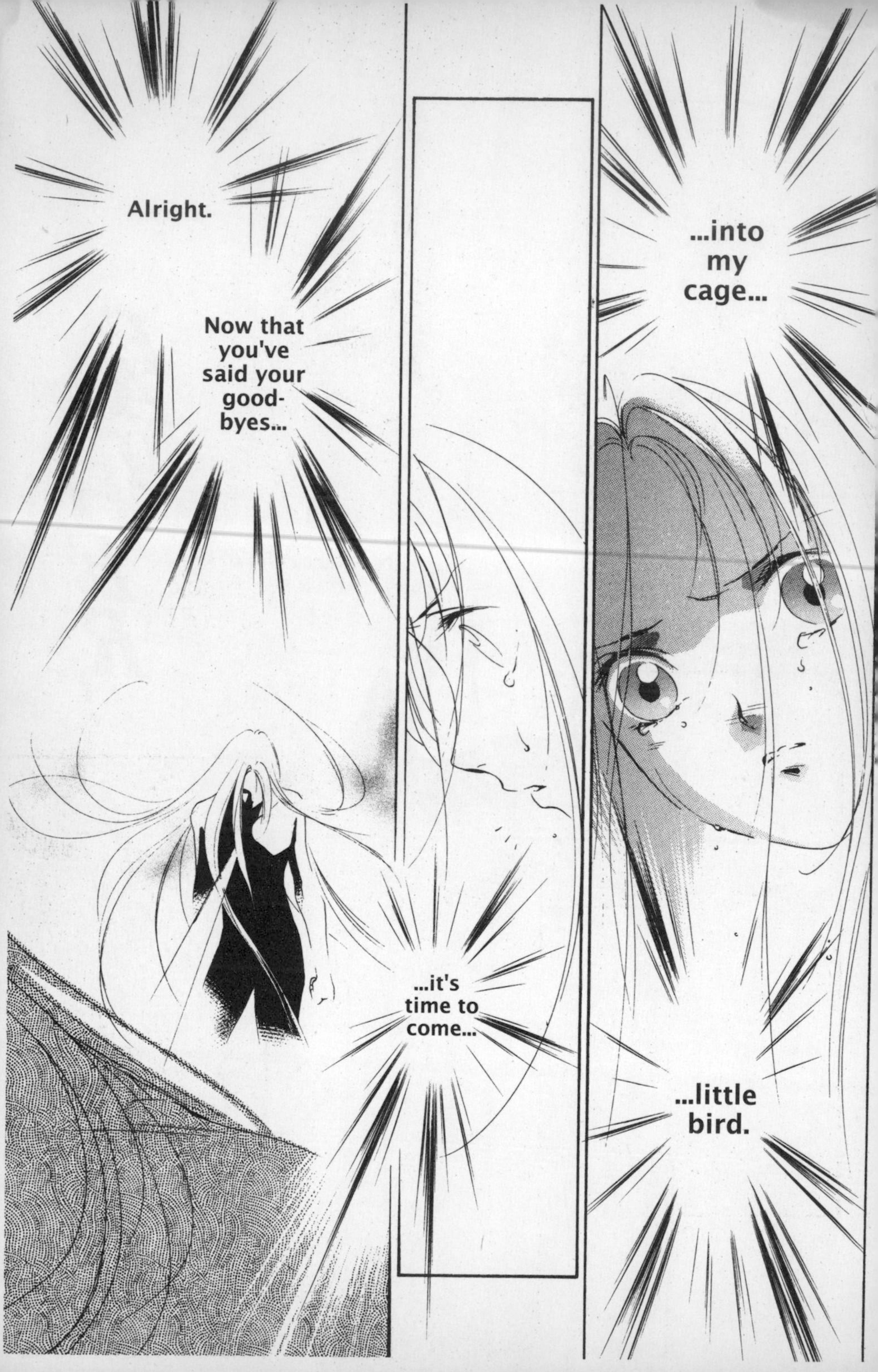
Alright.
Now that you've said your good-byes...
...it's time to come...
...into my cage...
...little bird.

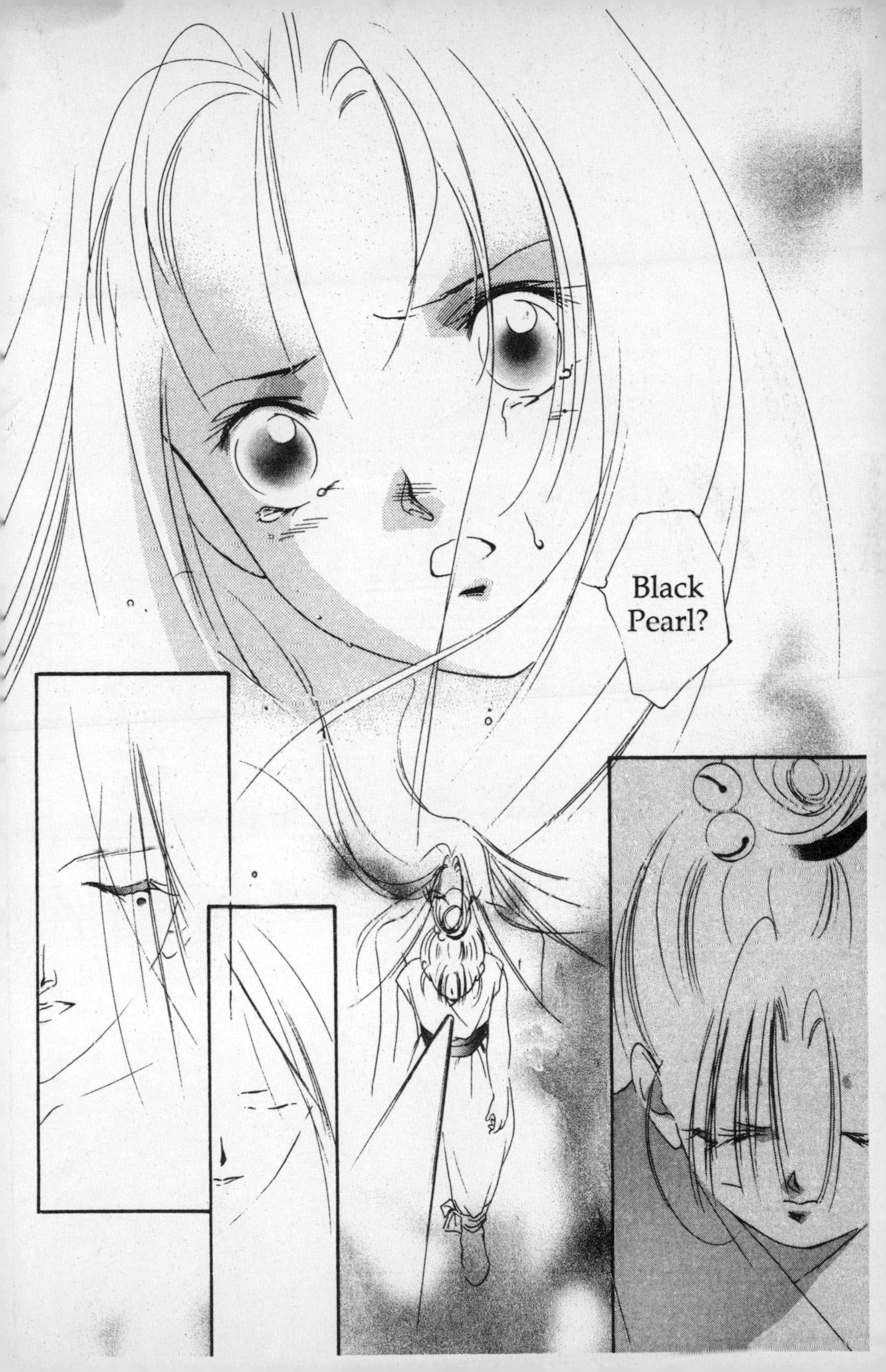
Black Pearl?

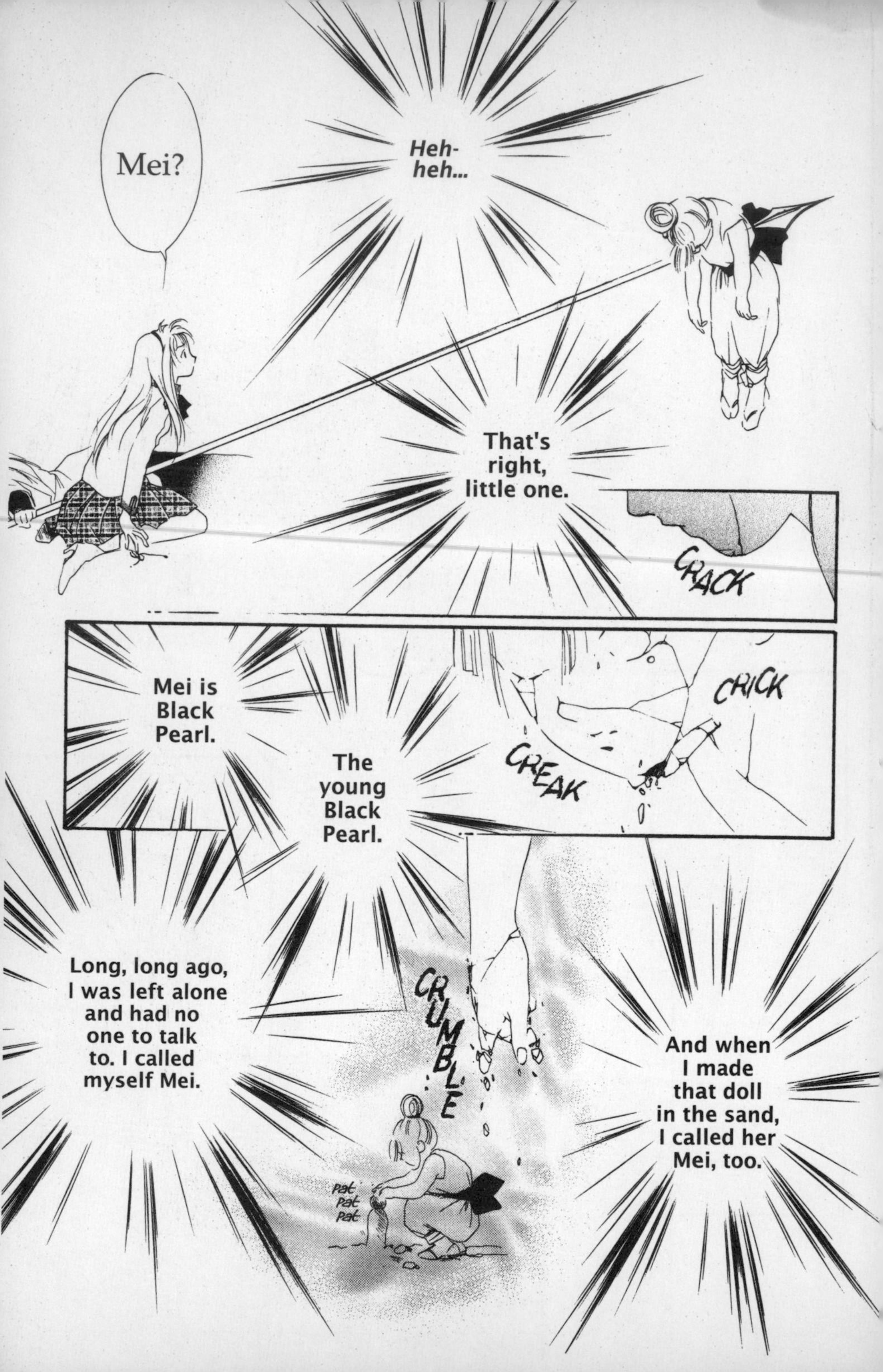
Mei?
Heh-heh...
That's right, little one.
CRACK
Mei is Black Pearl.
The young Black Pearl.
CRICK
CREAK
Long, long ago, I was left alone and had no one to talk to. I called myself Mei.
CRUMBLE
Pat pat pat
And when I made that doll in the sand, I called her Mei, too.

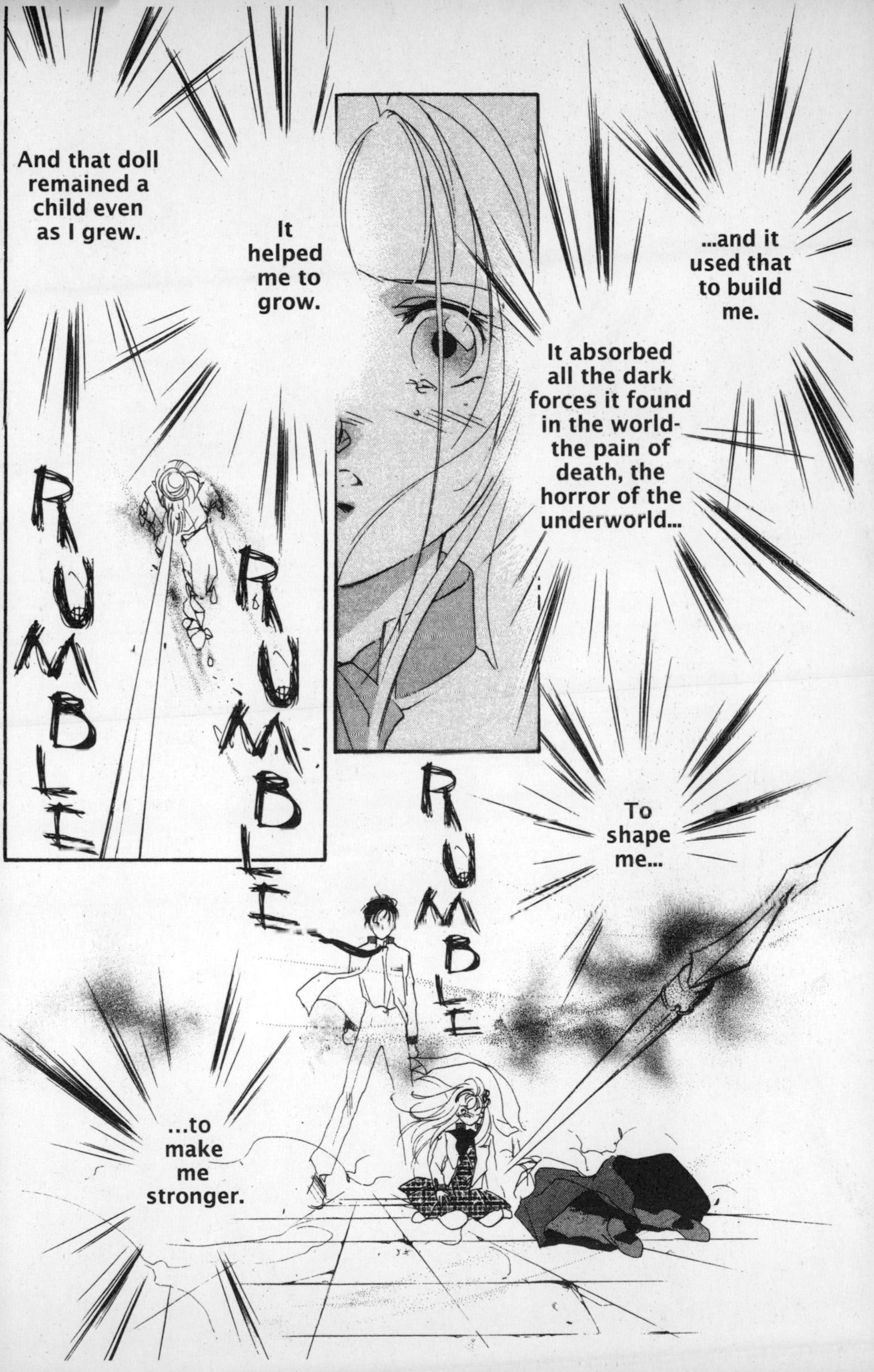

And that doll remained a child even as I grew.
RUMBLE
RUMBLE
It helped me to grow.
It absorbed all the dark forces it found in the world- the pain of death, the horror of the underworld...
...and it used that to build me.
RUMBLE
To shape me...
...to make me stronger.

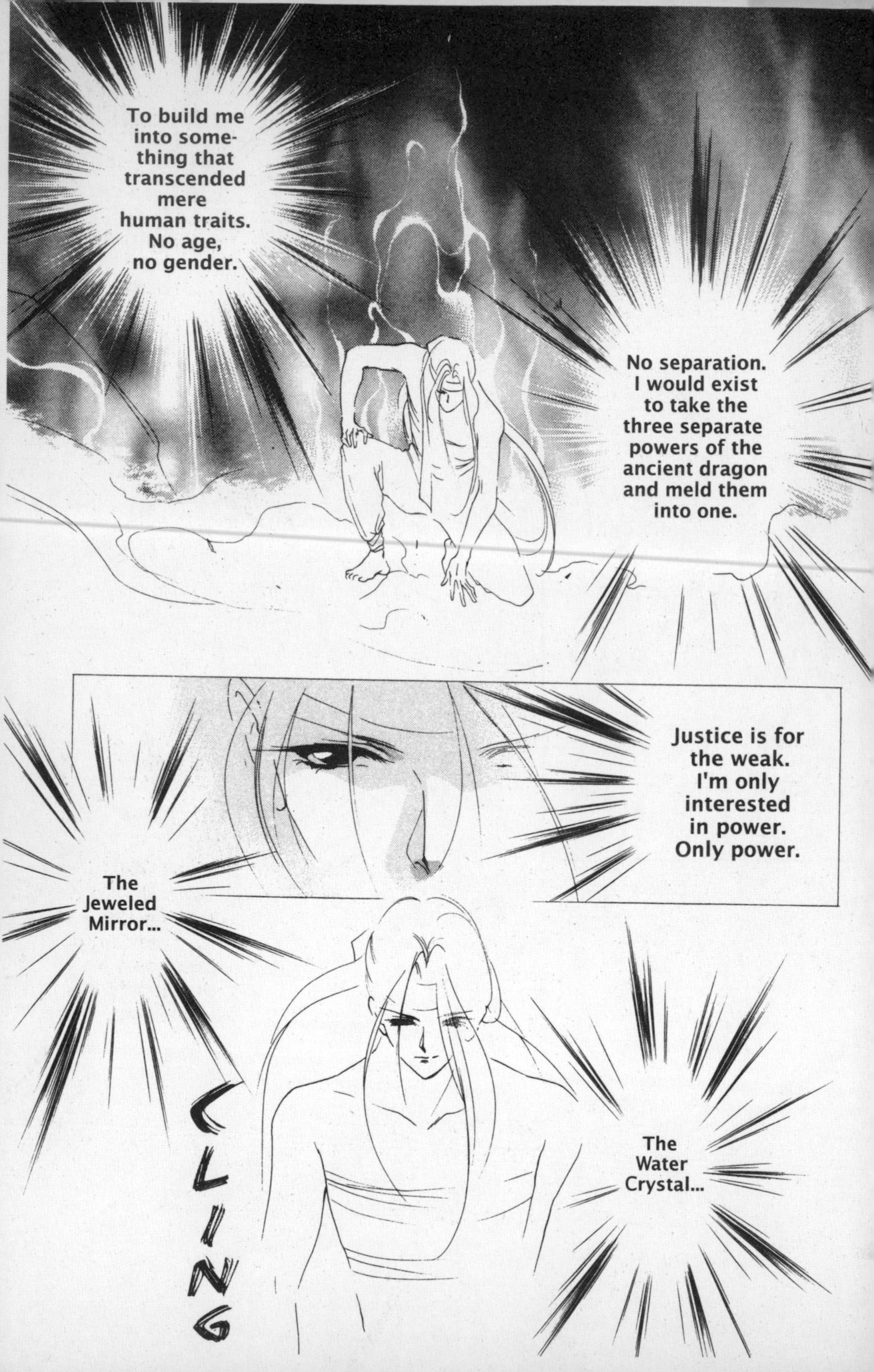
To build me into something that transcended mere human traits. No age, no gender.
No separation. I would exist to take the three separate powers of the ancient dragon and meld them into one.
Justice is for the weak. I'm only interested in power. Only power.
The Jeweled Mirror...
CLING
The Water Crystal...

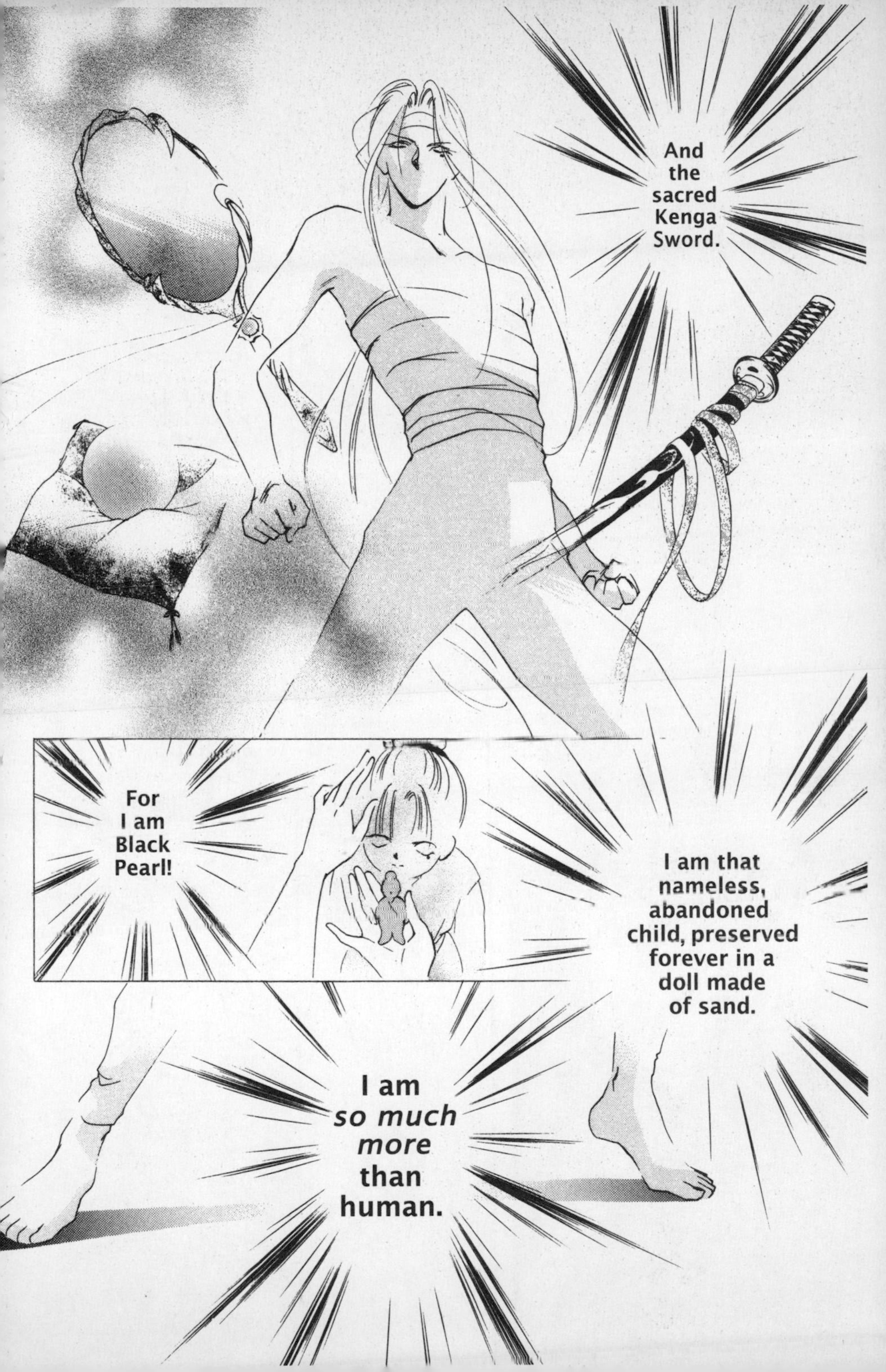
And the sacred Kenga Sword.
For I am Black Pearl!
I am that nameless, abandoned child, preserved forever in a doll made of sand.
I am *so much more* than human.

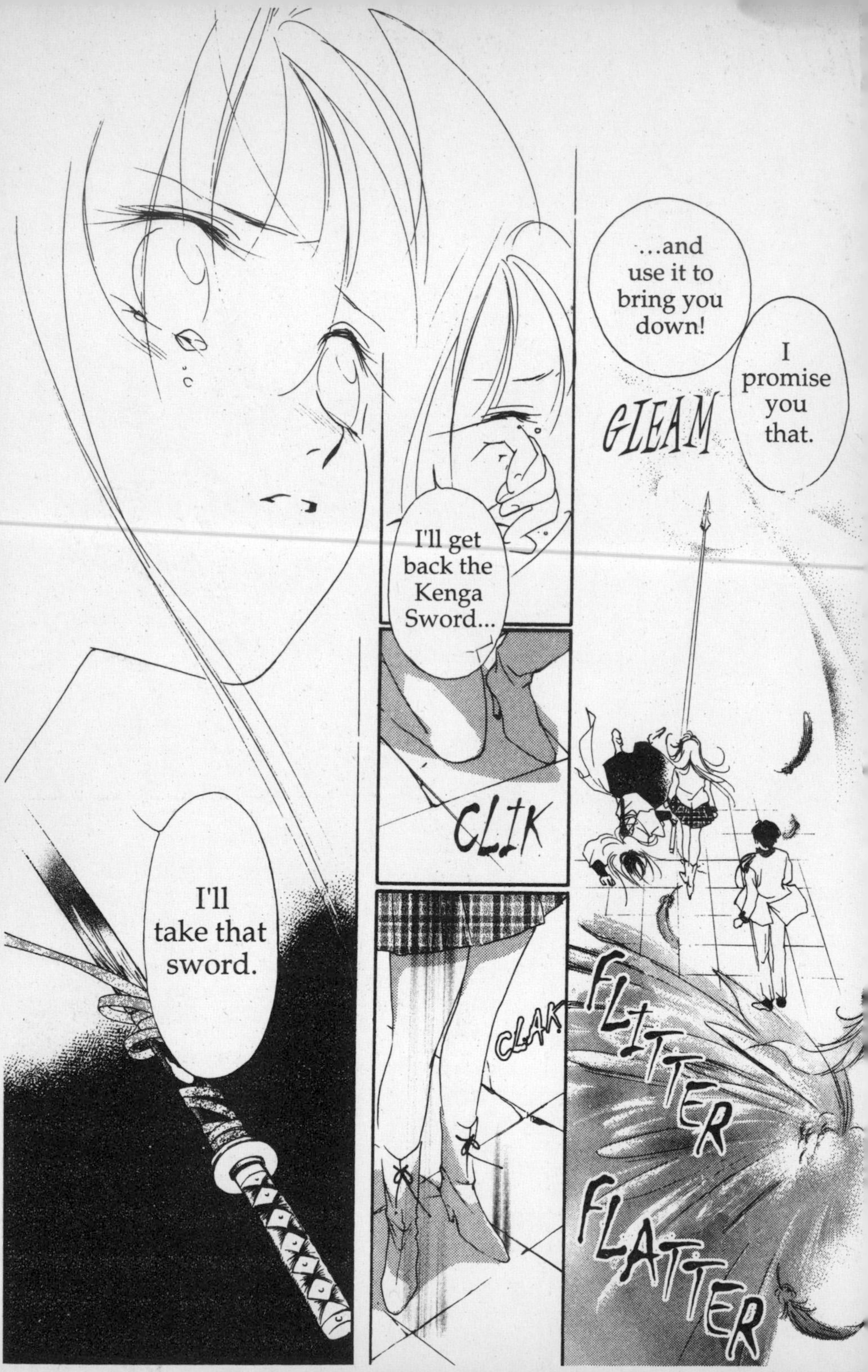
I'll take that sword.
I'll get back the Kenga Sword...
CLIK
CLAK
...and use it to bring you down!
I promise you that.
GLEAM
FLITTER FLATTER

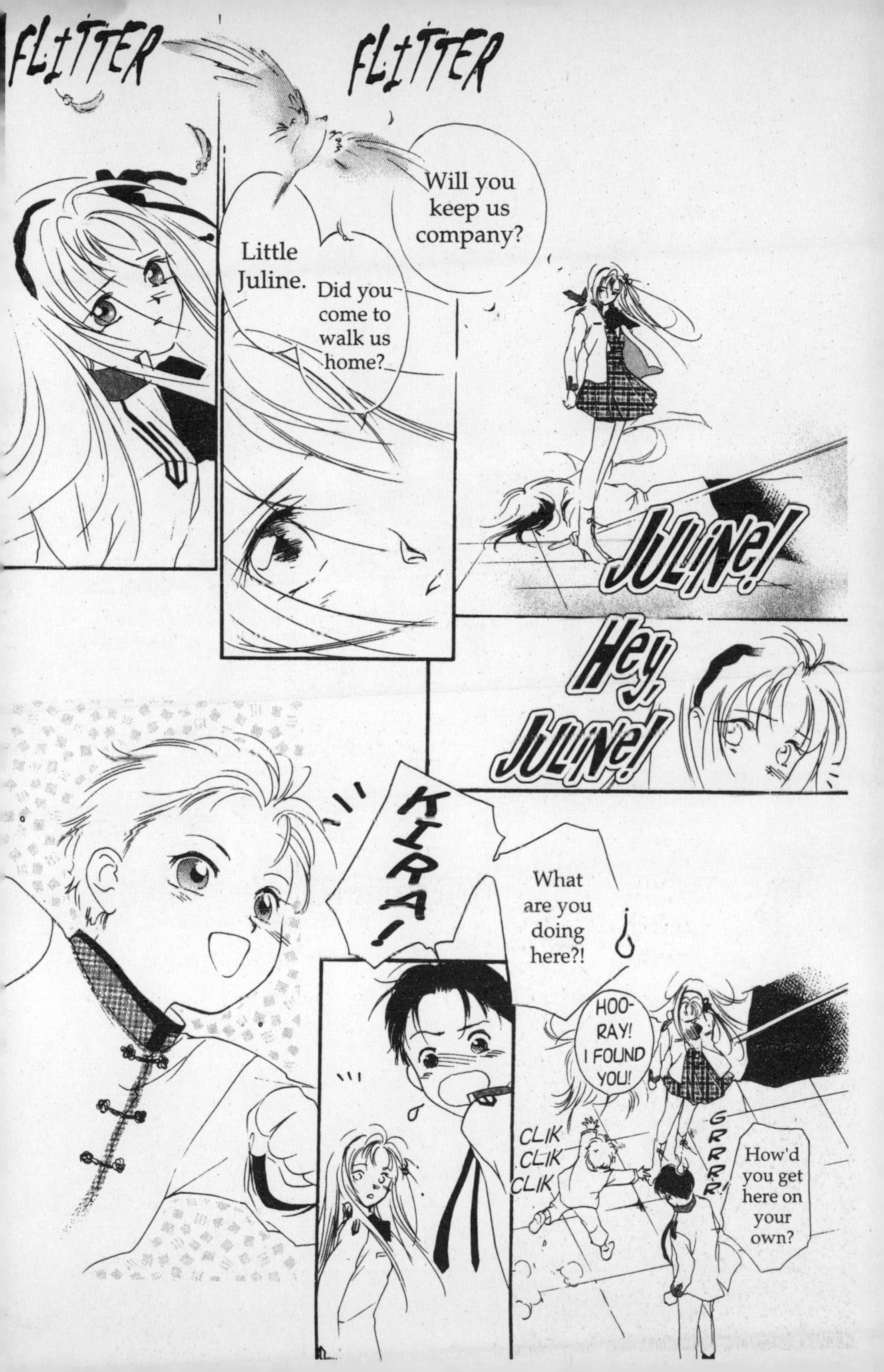
FLITTER
FLITTER
Little Juline.
Did you come to walk us home?
Will you keep us company?
JULINE!
Hey, JULINE!
KIRA!
What are you doing here?!
HOO-RAY! I FOUND YOU!
CLIK CLIK CLIK
GRRRR!
How'd you get here on your own?

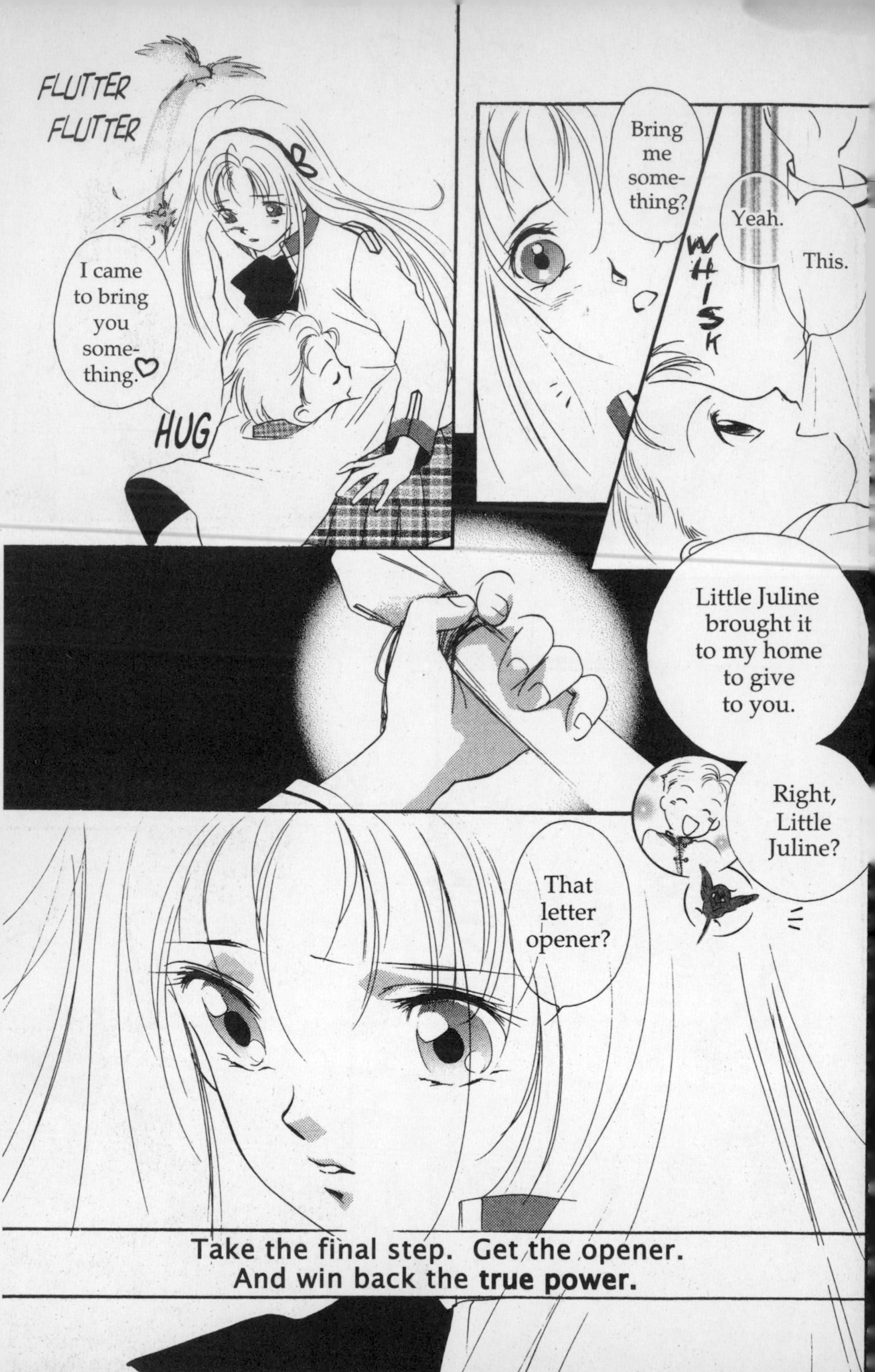
FLUTTER
FLUTTER
I came to bring you something.♡
HUG
Bring me something?
WHISK
Yeah.
This.
Little Juline brought it to my home to give to you.
Right, Little Juline?
That letter opener?
Take the final step. Get the opener.
And win back the **true power.**

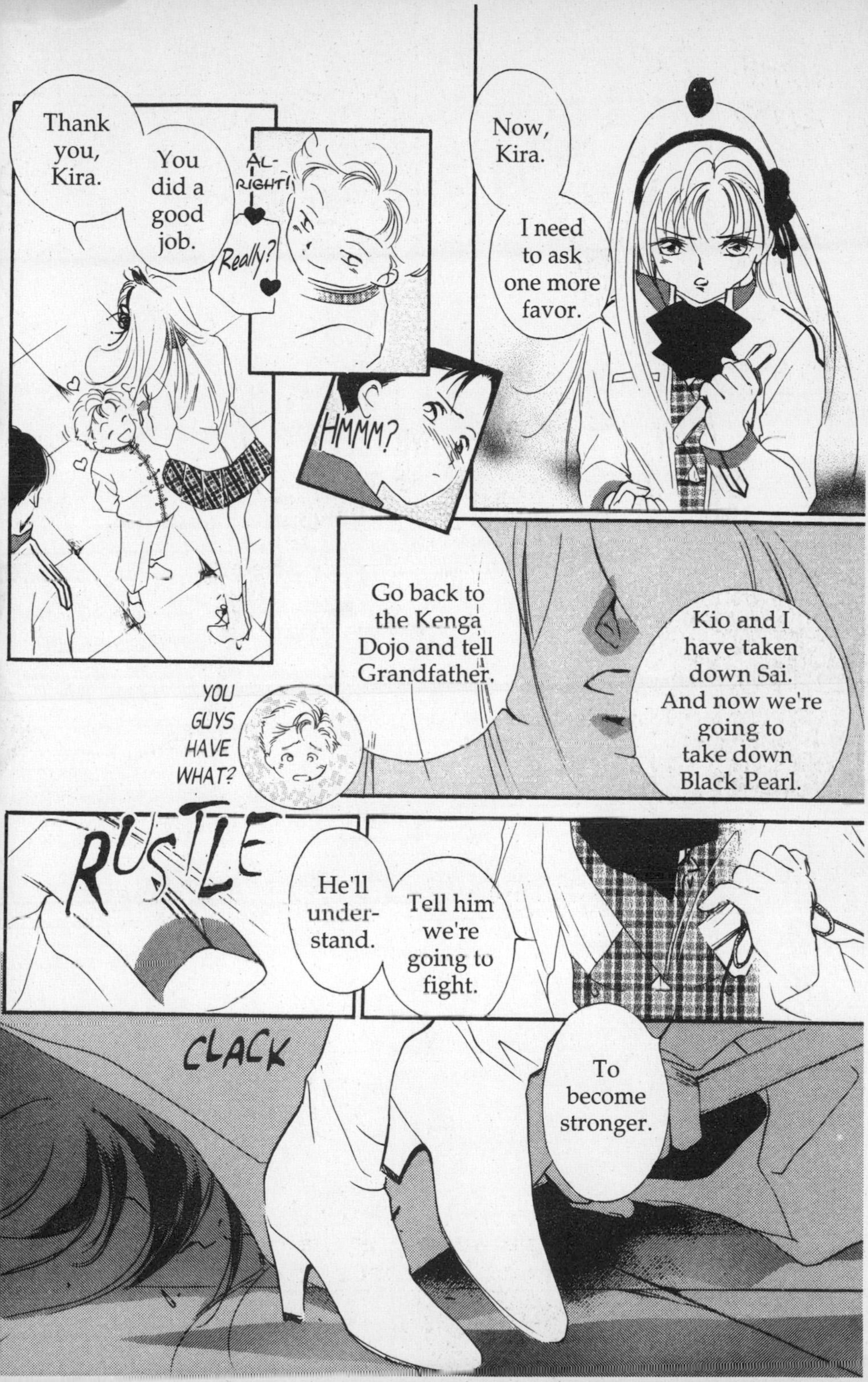
Thank you, Kira.
You did a good job.
AL-RIGHT!
Really?
HMMM?
Now, Kira.
I need to ask one more favor.
Go back to the Kenga Dojo and tell Grandfather.
Kio and I have taken down Sai. And now we're going to take down Black Pearl.
YOU GUYS HAVE WHAT?
RUSTLE
He'll under-stand.
Tell him we're going to fight.
CLACK
To become stronger.

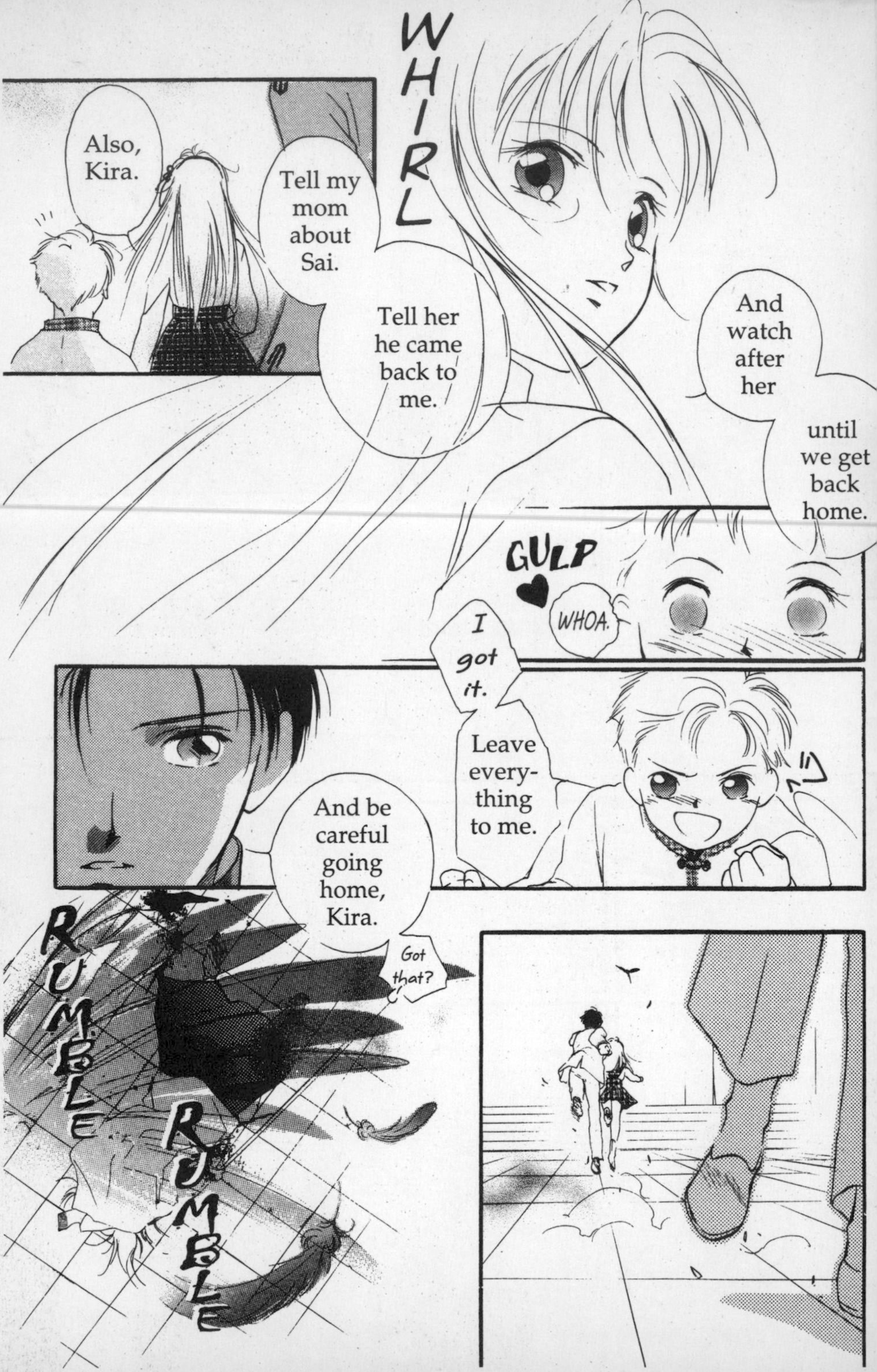
Also, Kira.
Tell my mom about Sai.
WHIRL
Tell her he came back to me.
And watch after her
until we get back home.
GULP
WHOA.
And be careful going home, Kira.
Got that?
I got it.
Leave every-thing to me.
RUMBLE RUMBLE

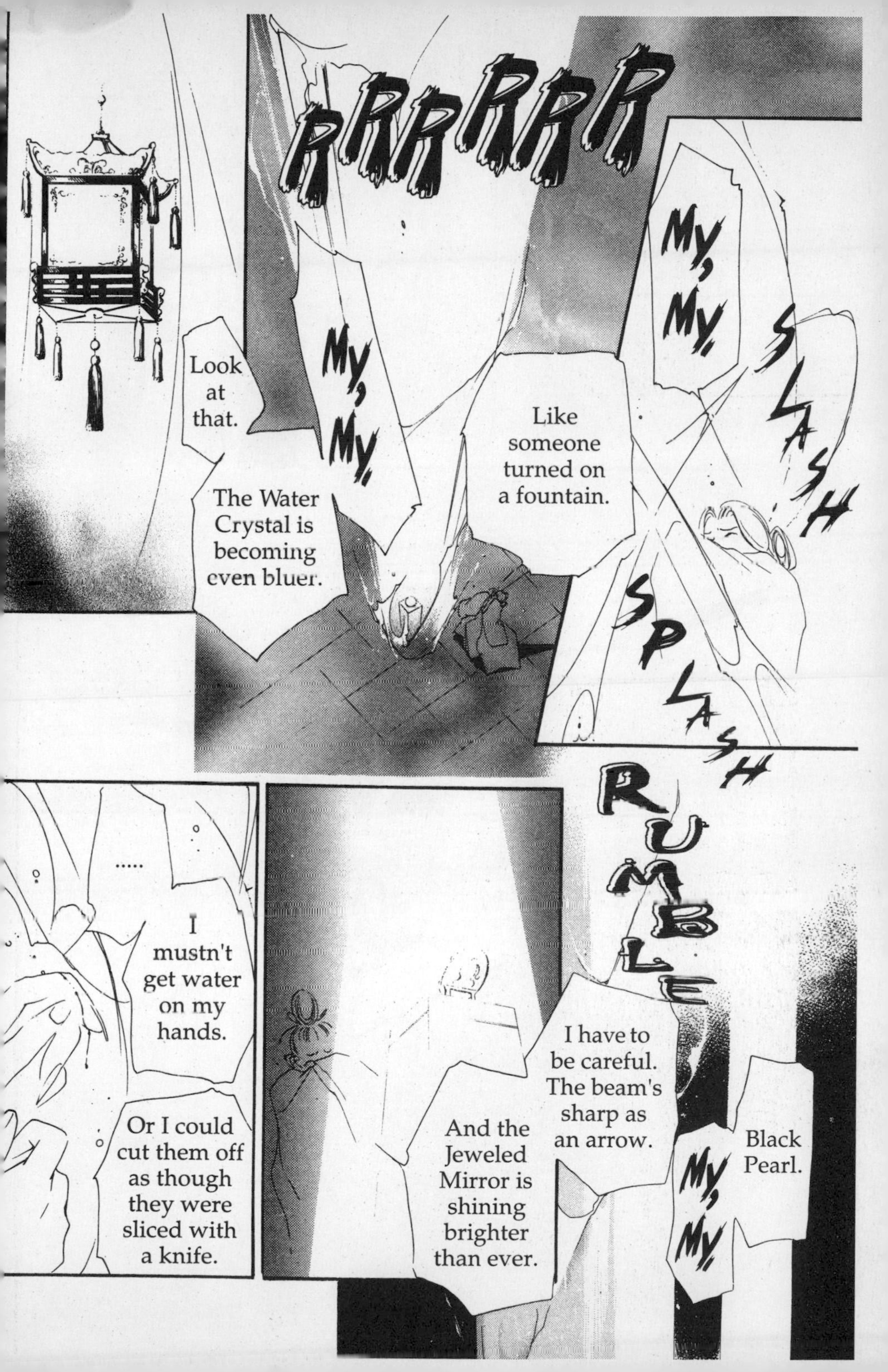
Look at that.
The Water Crystal is becoming even bluer.
RRRRRRR
My, My.
Like someone turned on a fountain.
My, My.
SLASH
SPLASH
.....
I mustn't get water on my hands.
Or I could cut them off as though they were sliced with a knife.
RUMBLE
And the Jeweled Mirror is shining brighter than ever.
I have to be careful. The beam's sharp as an arrow.
Black Pearl.
My, My.

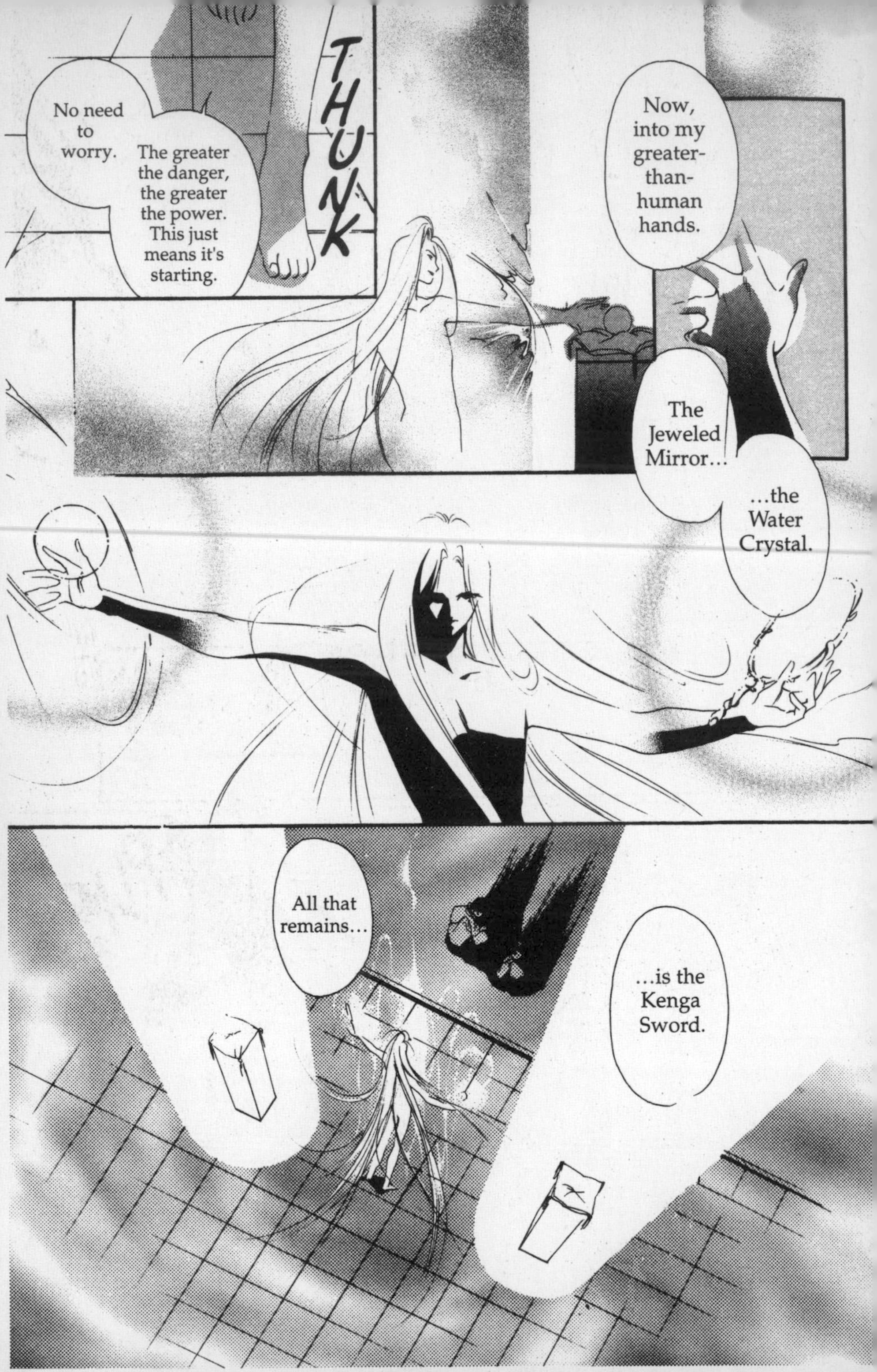
No need to worry.
The greater the danger, the greater the power. This just means it's starting.
THUNK
Now, into my greater-than-human hands.
The Jeweled Mirror...
...the Water Crystal.
All that remains...
...is the Kenga Sword.

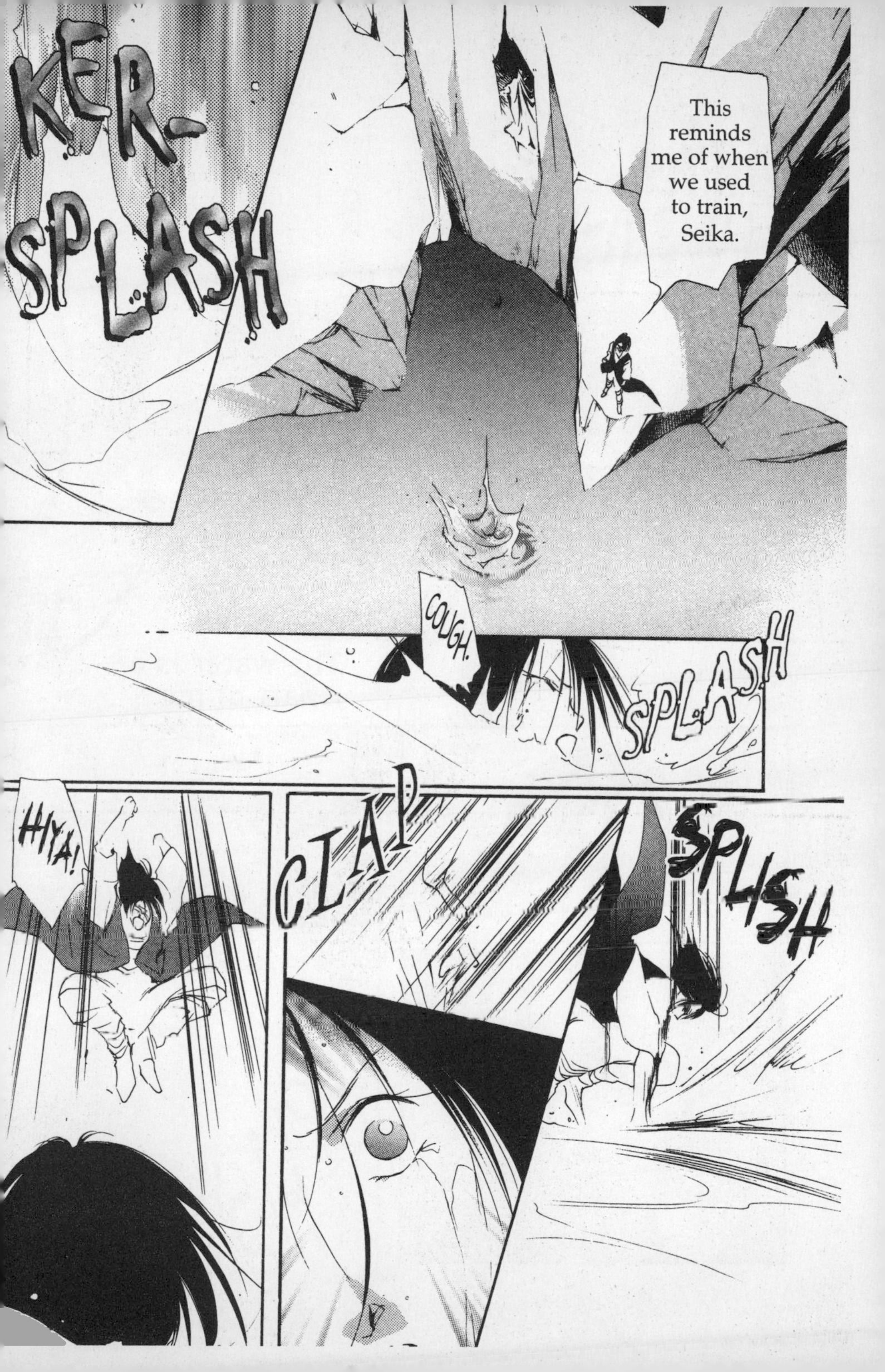
KER-SPLASH
This reminds me of when we used to train, Seika.
COUGH.
SPLASH
HIYA!
CLAP
SPLSH

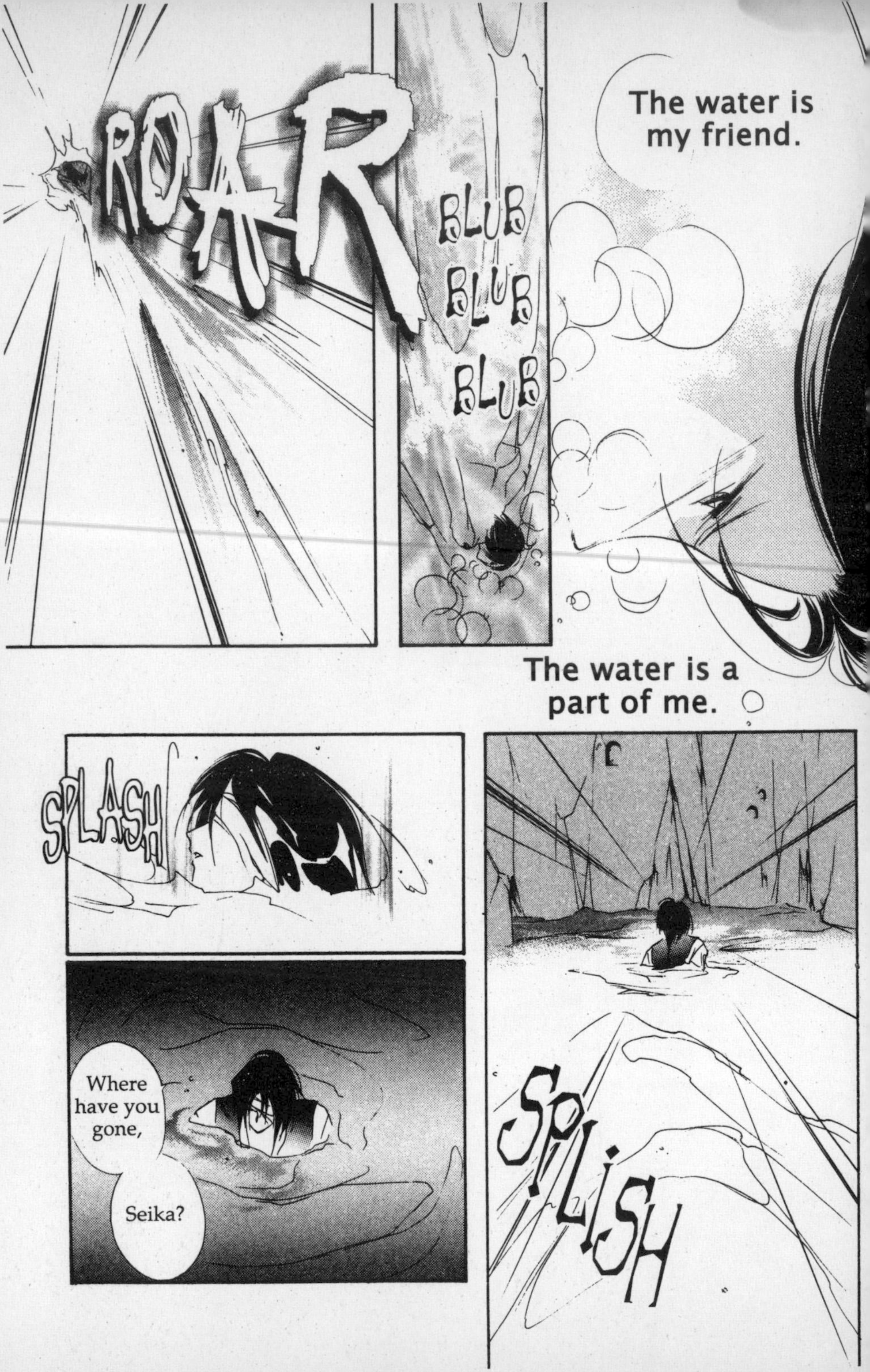
ROAR
BLUB
BLUB
BLUB
The water is my friend.
The water is a part of me.
SPLASH
Where have you gone,
Seika?
SPLISH

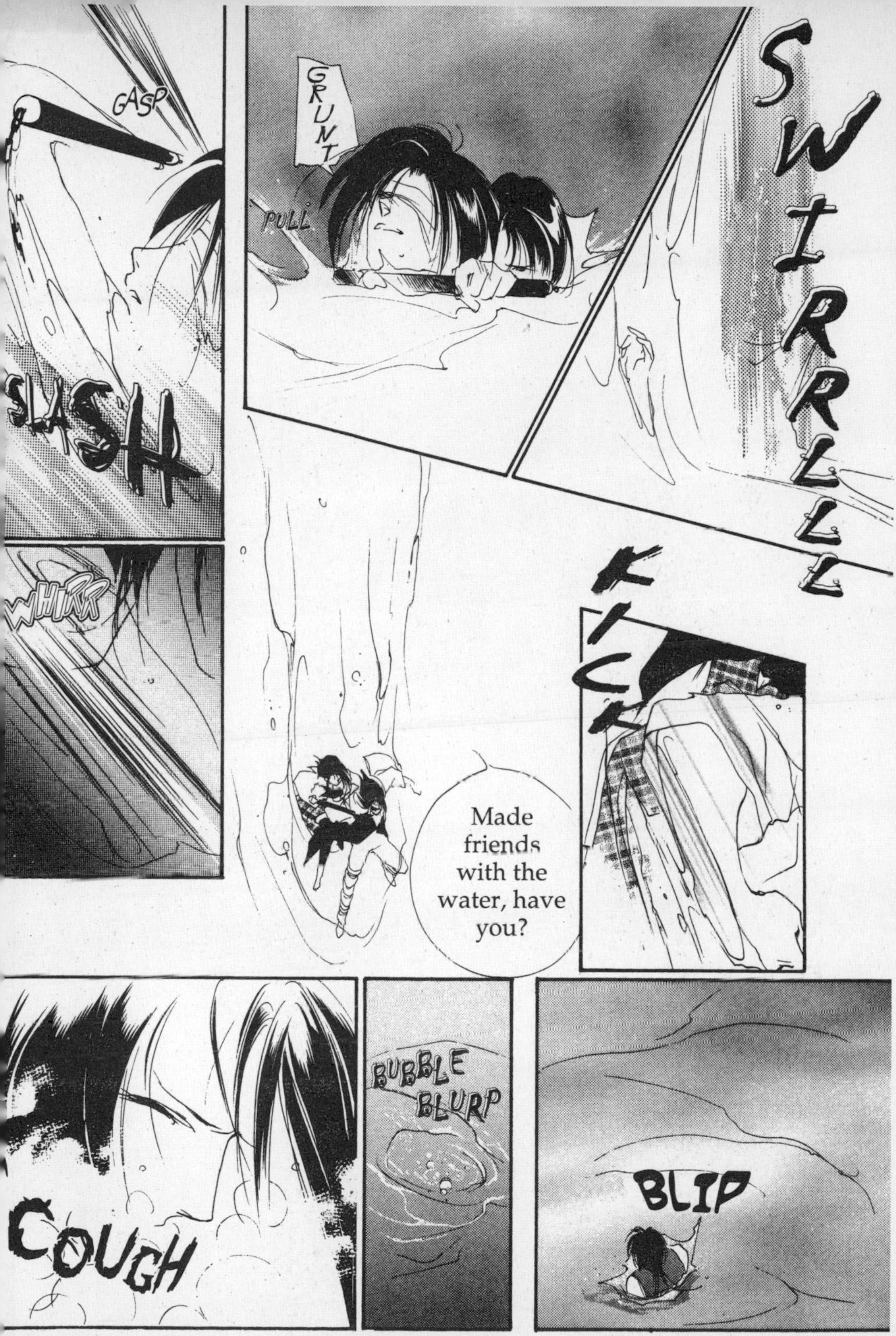
GASP
SLASH
WHIRR
GRUNT
PULL
SWIRRLLL
KICK
Made friends with the water, have you?
COUGH
BUBBLE
BLURP
BLIP

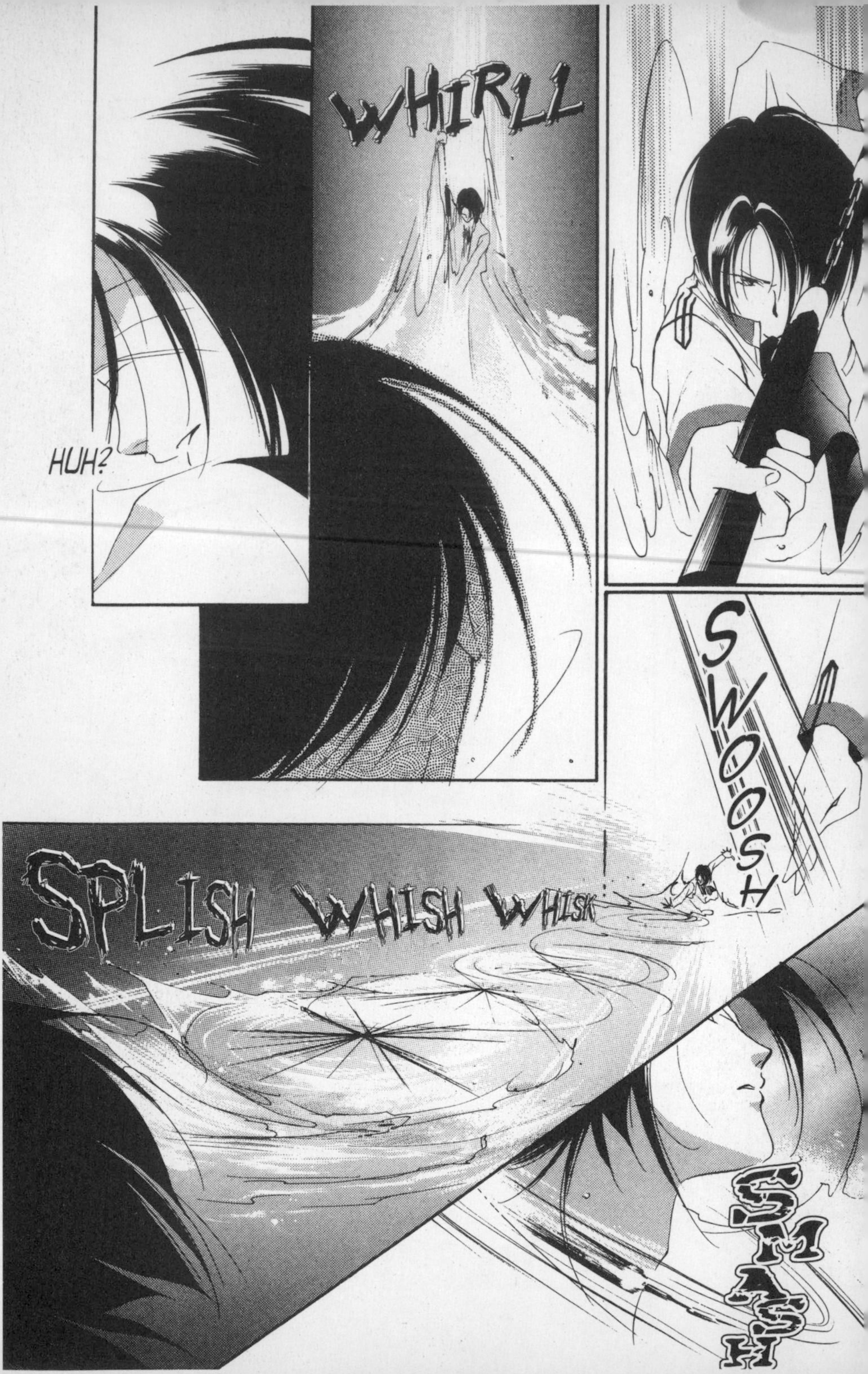
HUH?
WHIRLL
SWOOSH
SPLISH WHISH WHISK
SMASH

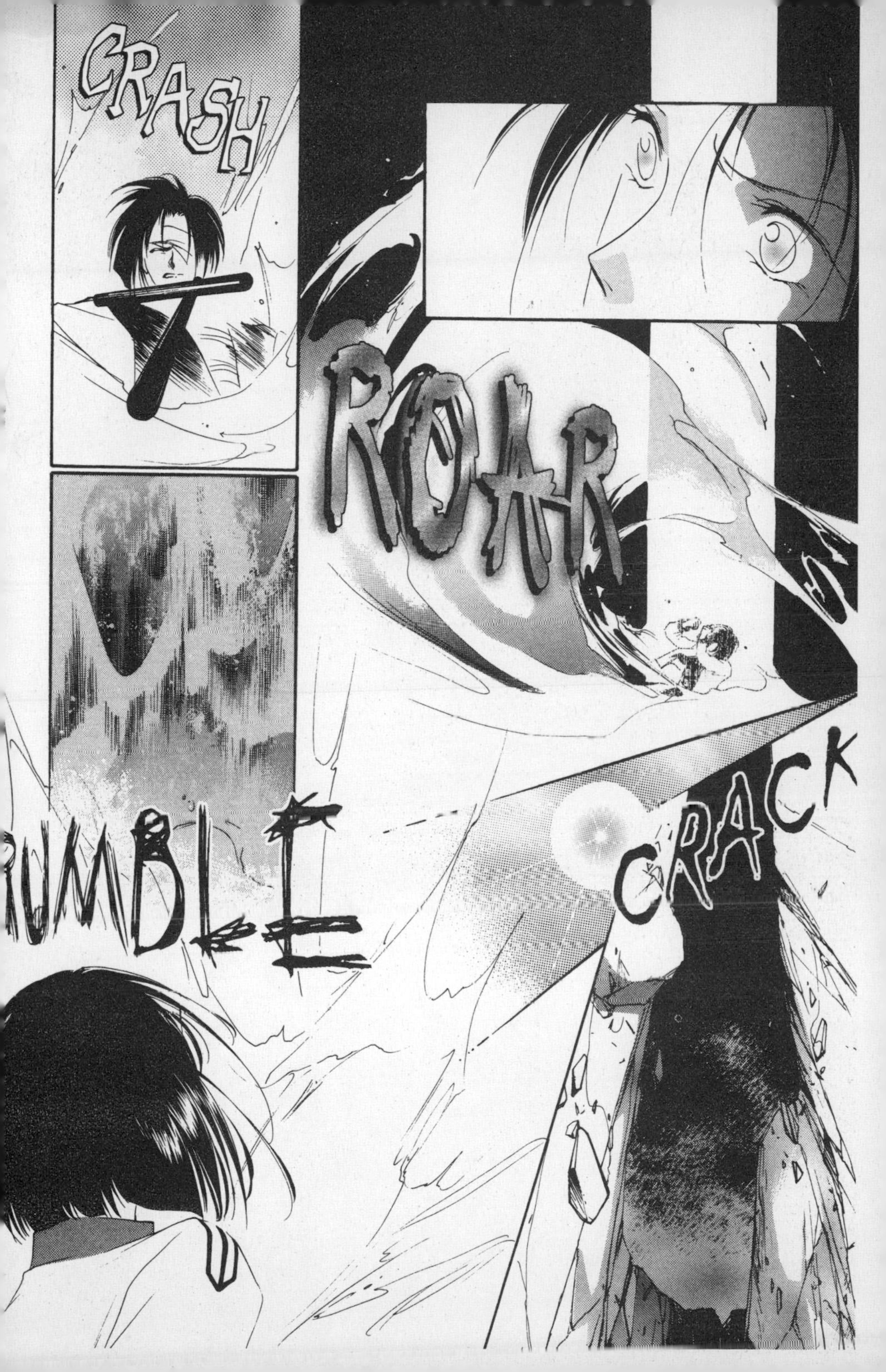
CRASH
ROAR
RUMBLE
CRACK

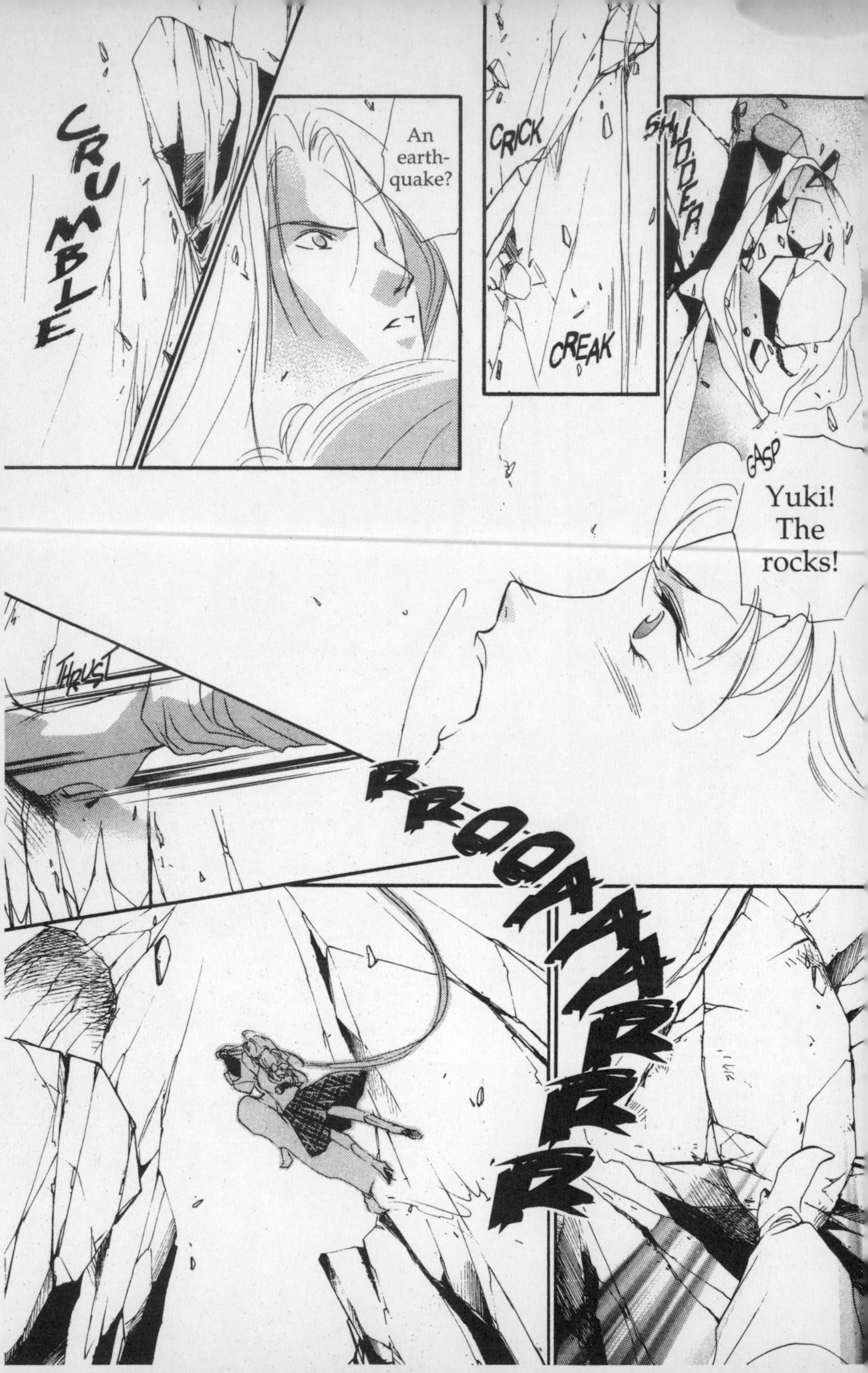
CRUMBLE
An earth-quake?
CRICK
CREAK
SHUDDER
GASP
Yuki! The rocks!
THRUST
RROOAARRRR

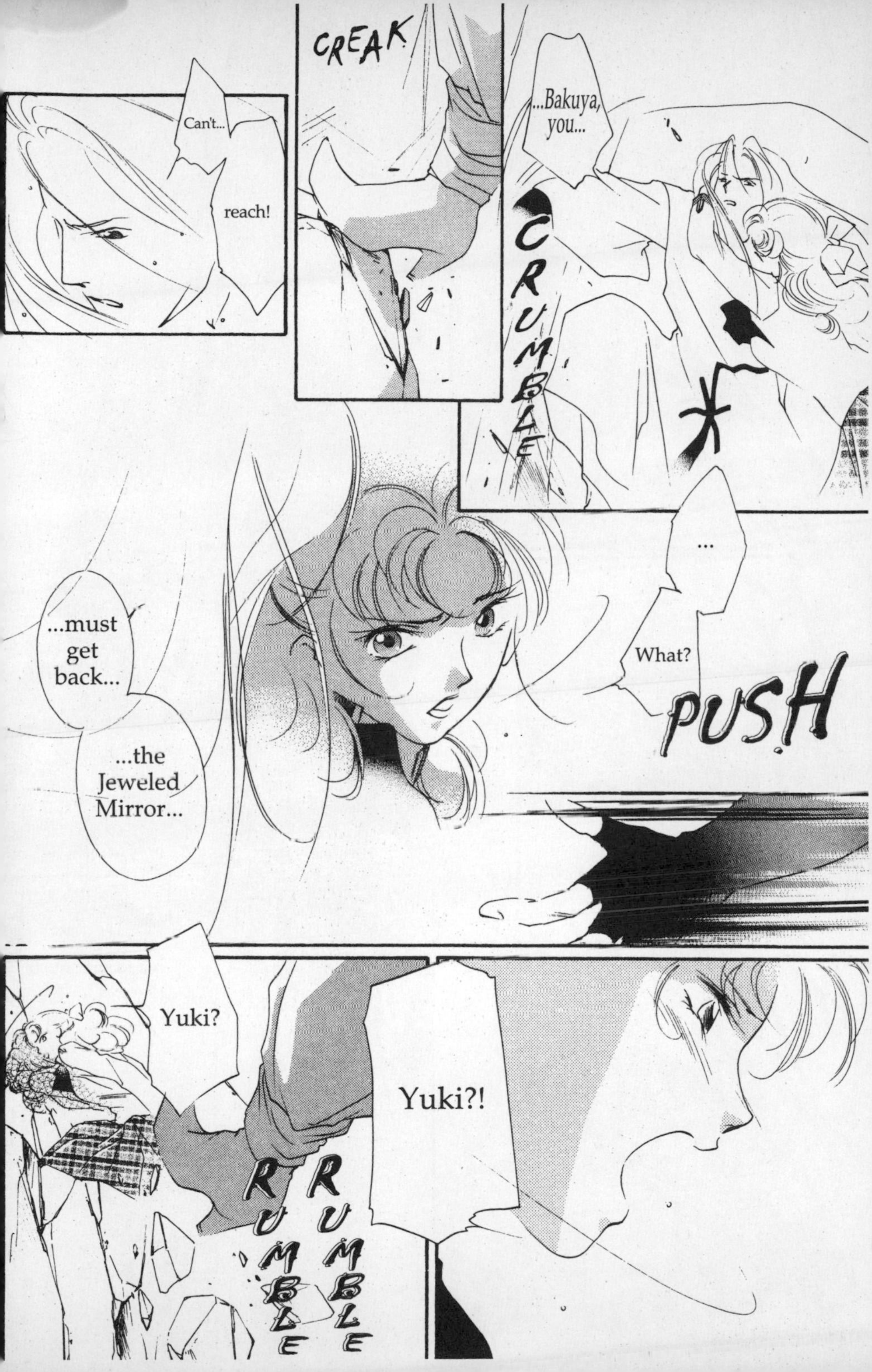
Can't...
reach!
CREAK
...Bakuya, you...
CRUMBLE
...must get back...
...the Jeweled Mirror...
...
What?
PUSH
Yuki?
RUMBLE
RUMBLE
Yuki?!

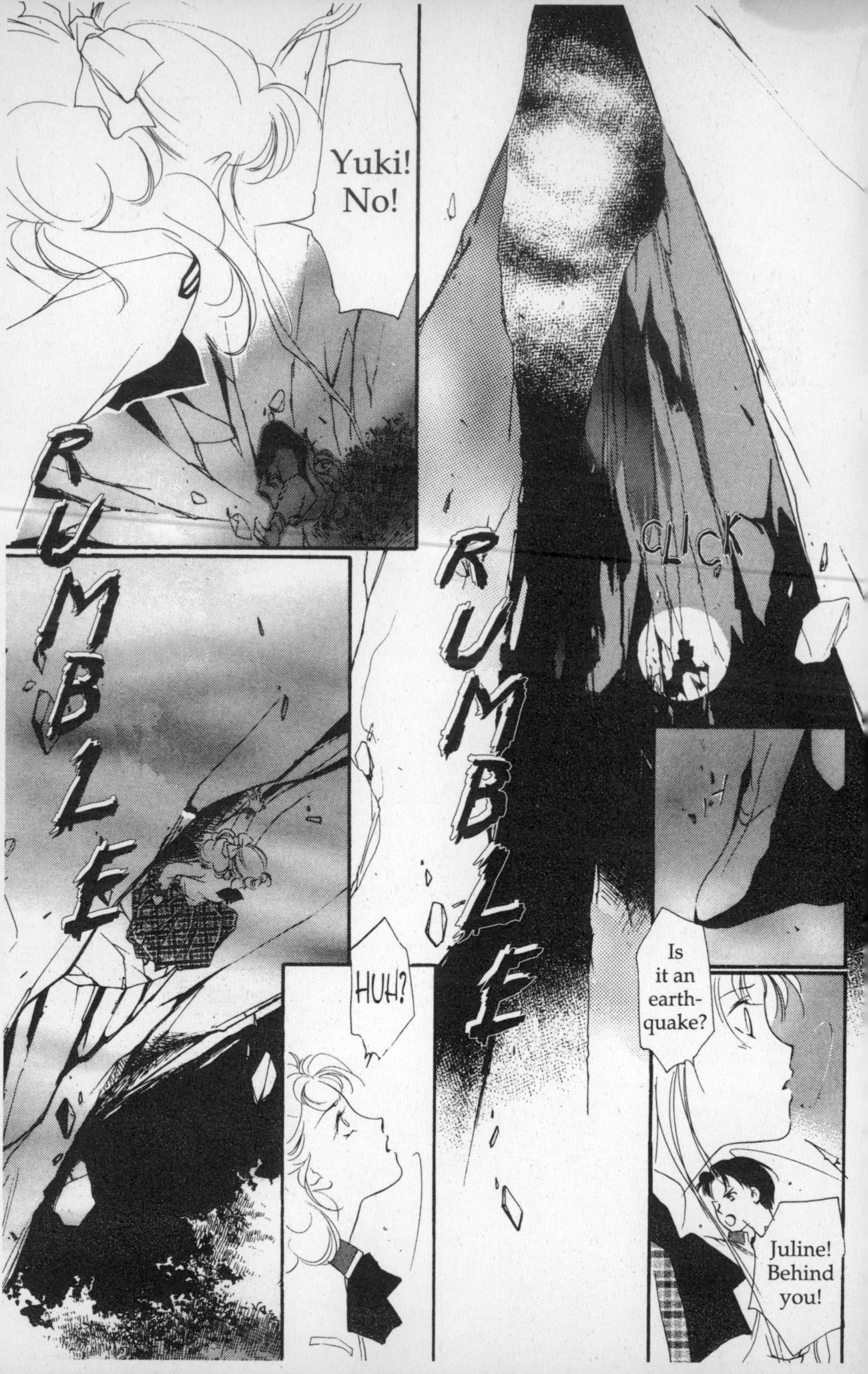
Yuki! No!
RUMBLE
RUMBLE
CLICK
HUH?
Is it an earthquake?
Juline! Behind you!

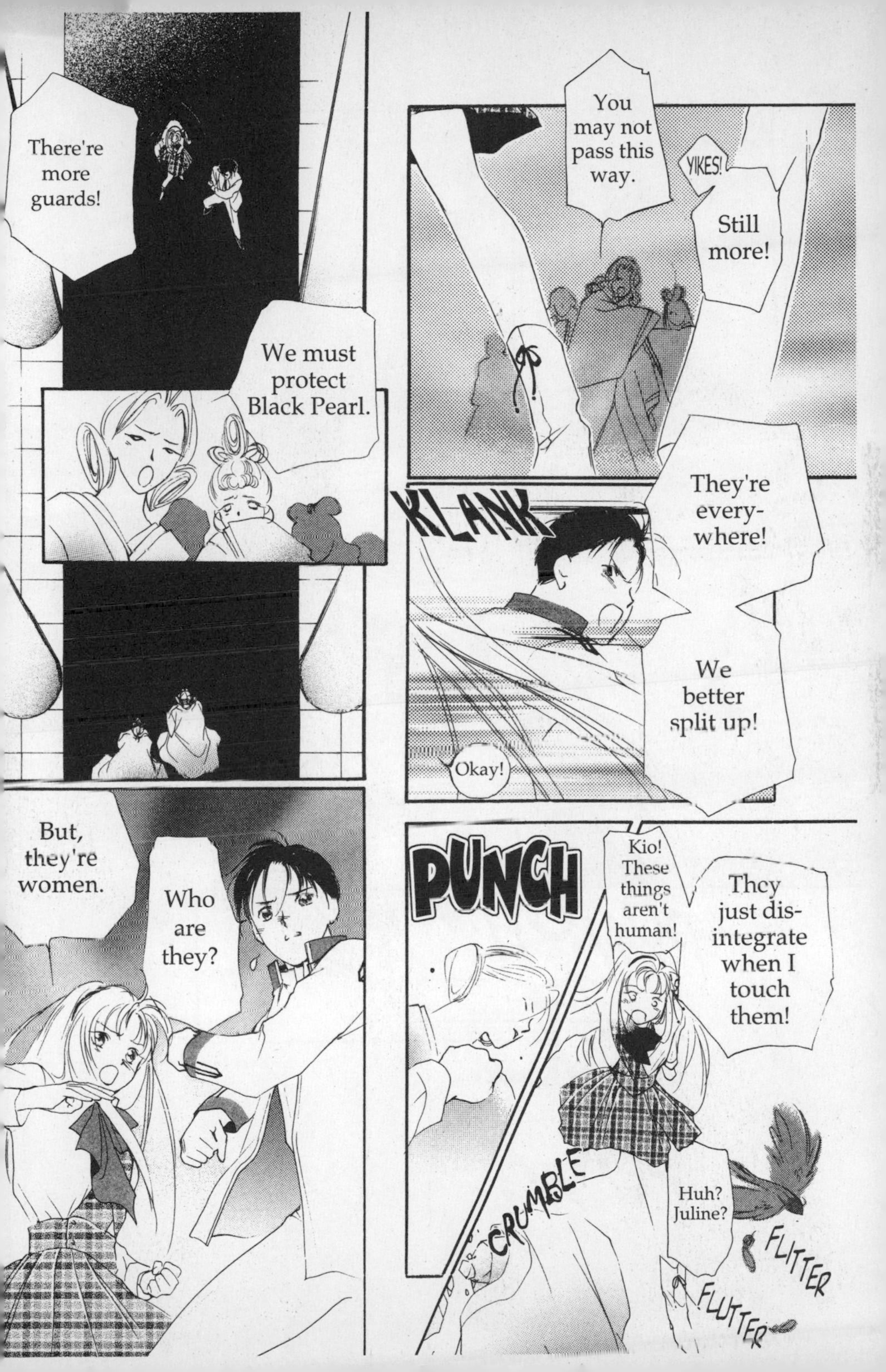
There're more guards!
We must protect Black Pearl.
You may not pass this way.
YIKES!
Still more!
KLANK
They're every-where!
We better split up!
Okay!
But, they're women.
Who are they?
PUNCH
Kio! These things aren't human!
Thcy just dis-integrate when I touch them!
CRUMBLE
Huh? Juline?
FLITTER
FLUTTER

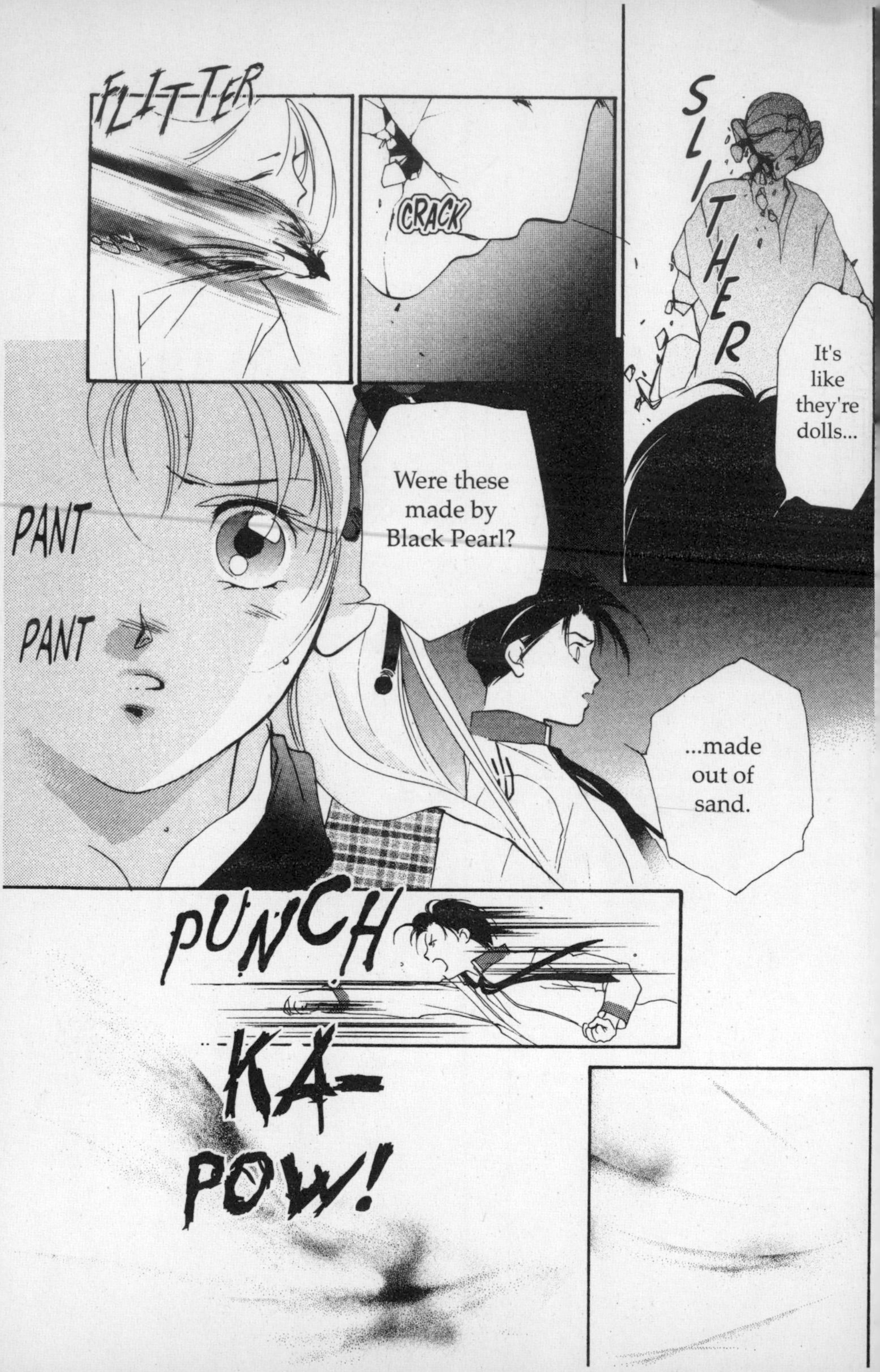
FLITTER
CRACK
SLITHER
It's like they're dolls...
PANT
PANT
Were these made by Black Pearl?
...made out of sand.
PUNCH
KA-POW!

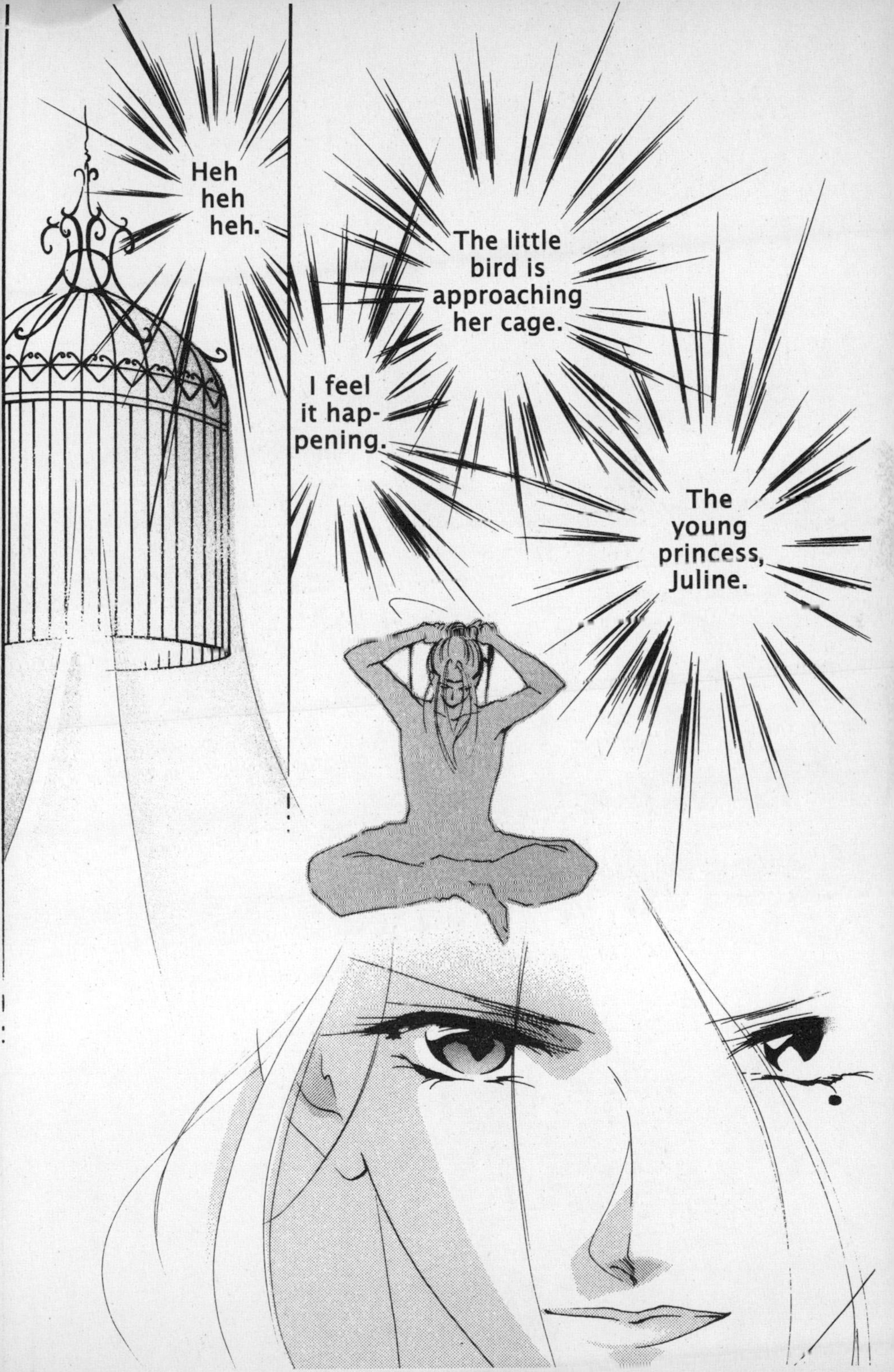
Heh heh heh.
The little bird is approaching her cage.
I feel it happening.
The young princess, Juline.

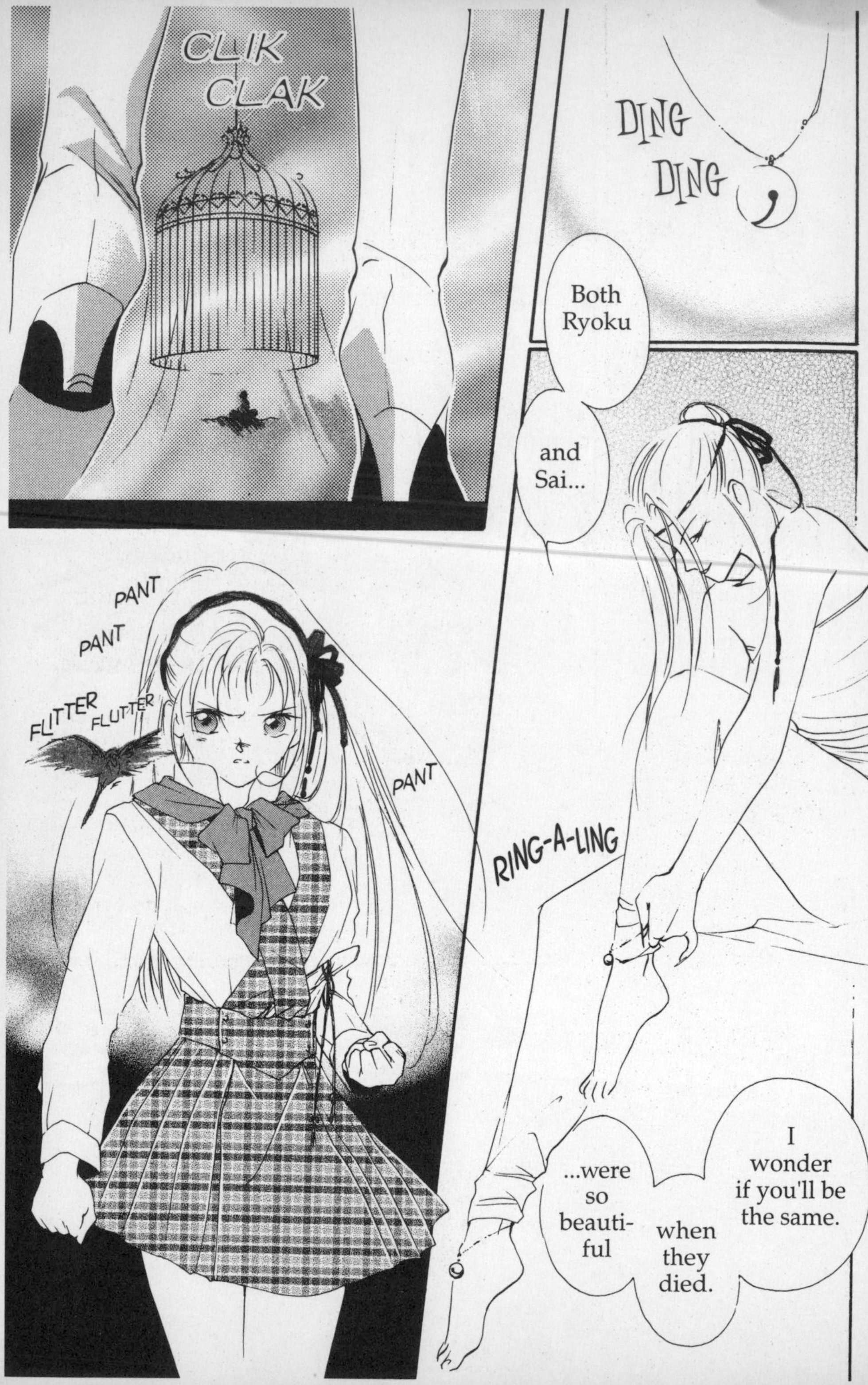
CLIK
CLAK
DING
DING
Both Ryoku
and Sai...
PANT
PANT
FLUTTER
FLUTTER
PANT
RING-A-LING
...were so beautiful
when they died.
I wonder if you'll be the same.

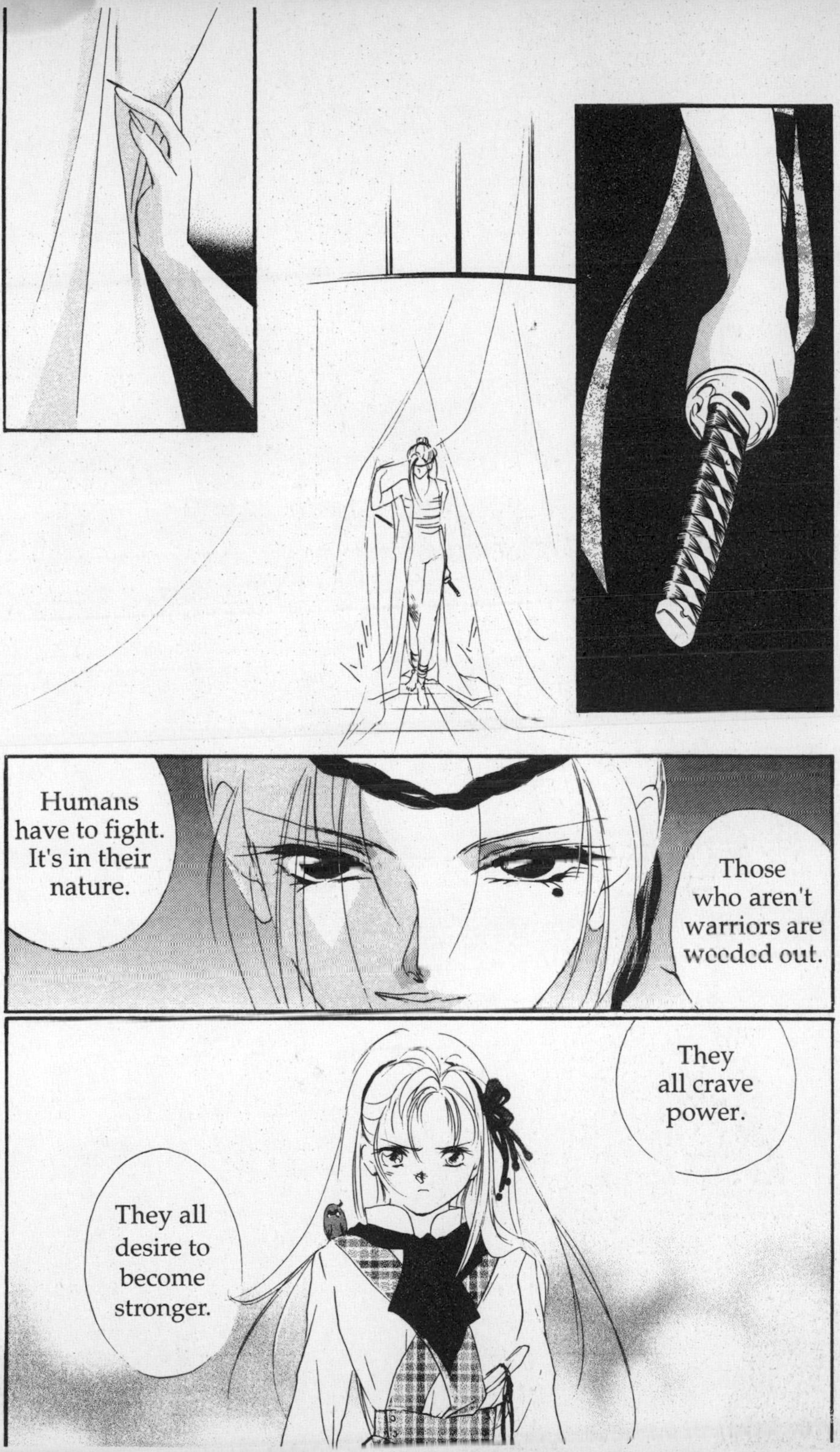
Humans have to fight. It's in their nature.
Those who aren't warriors are weeded out.
They all crave power.
They all desire to become stronger.

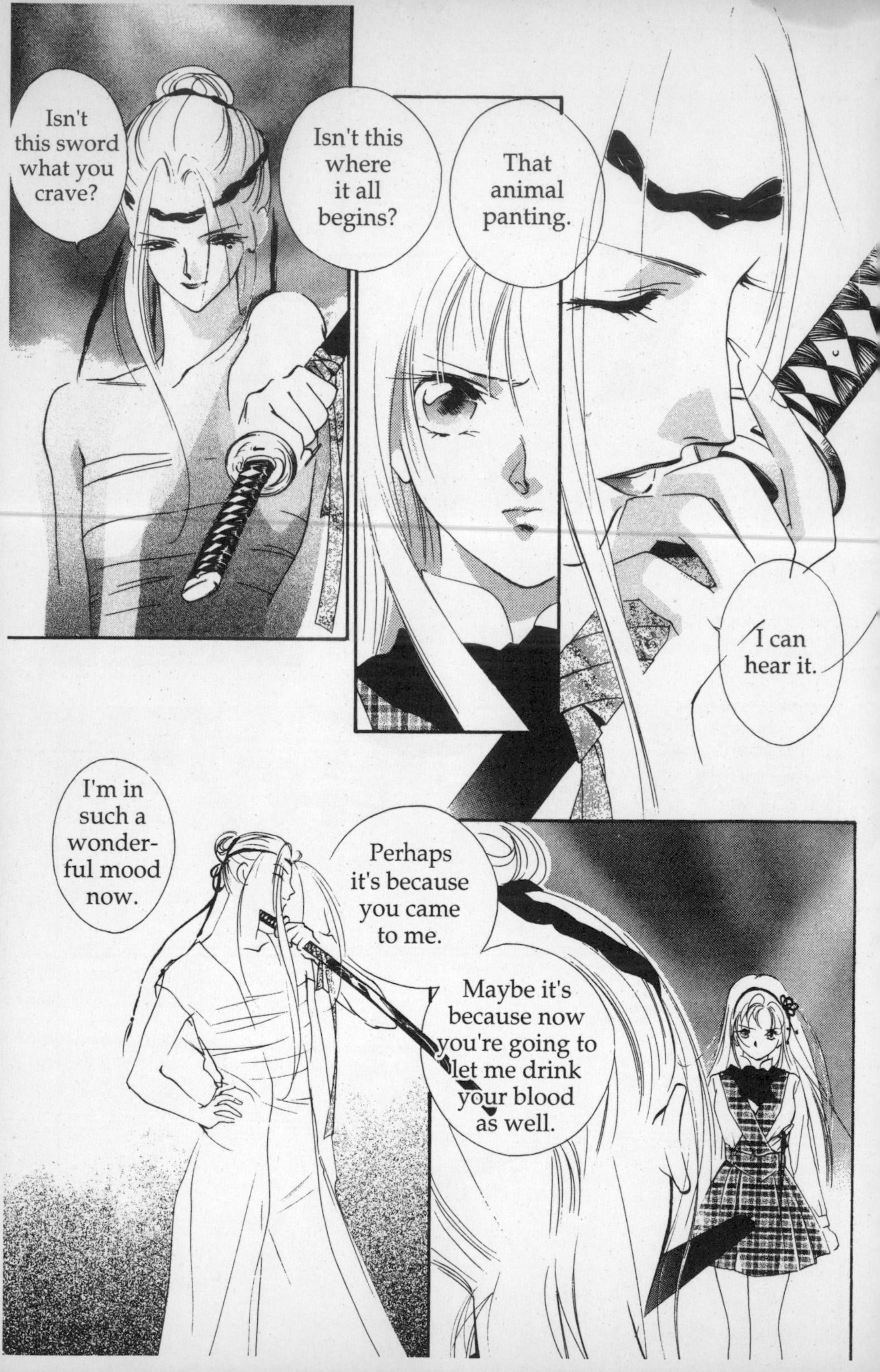
Isn't this sword what you crave?
Isn't this where it all begins?
That animal panting.
I can hear it.
I'm in such a wonder-ful mood now.
Perhaps it's because you came to me.
Maybe it's because now you're going to let me drink your blood as well.

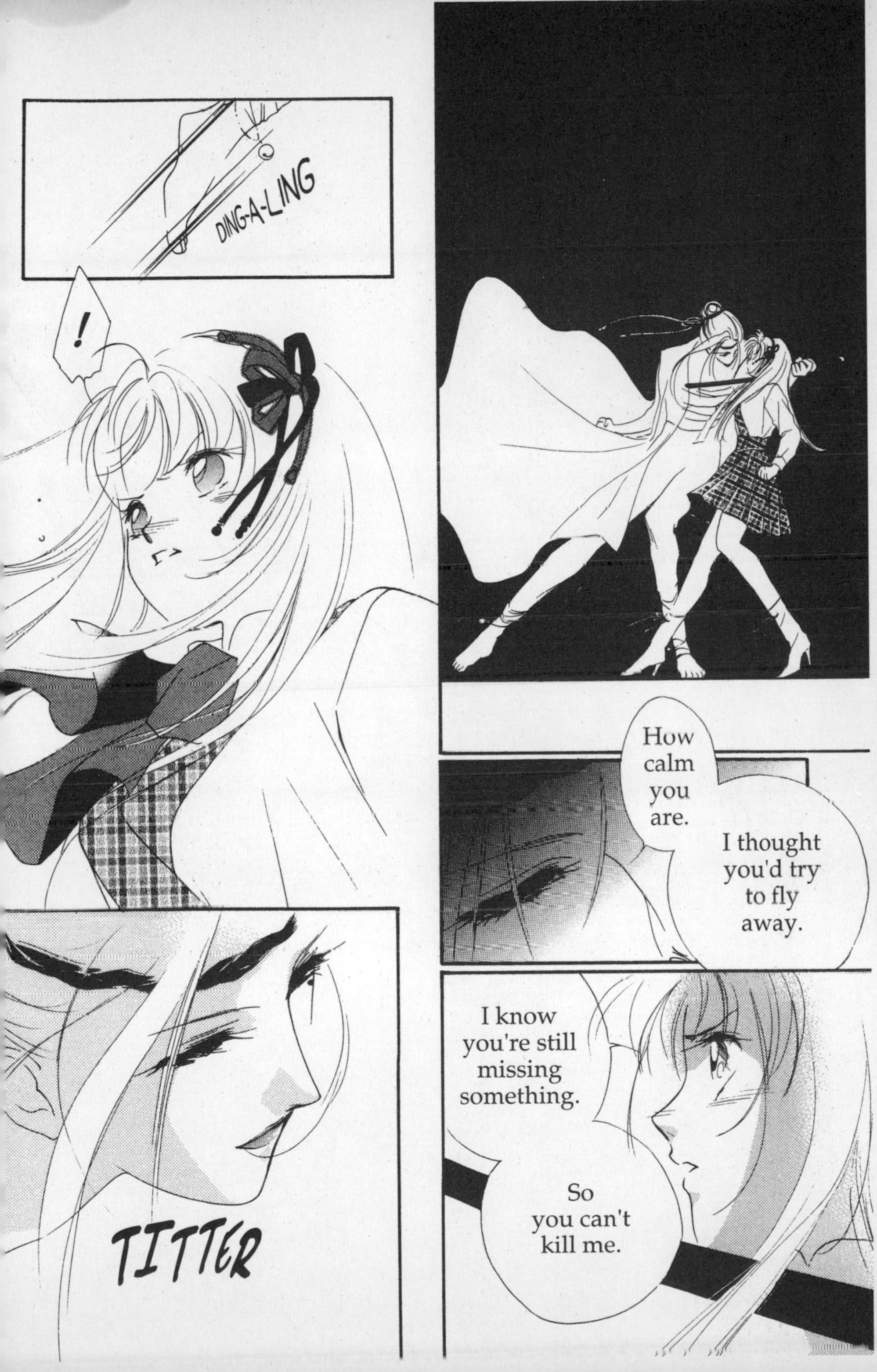
DING-A-LING
!
TITTER
How calm you are.
I thought you'd try to fly away.
I know you're still missing something.
So you can't kill me.

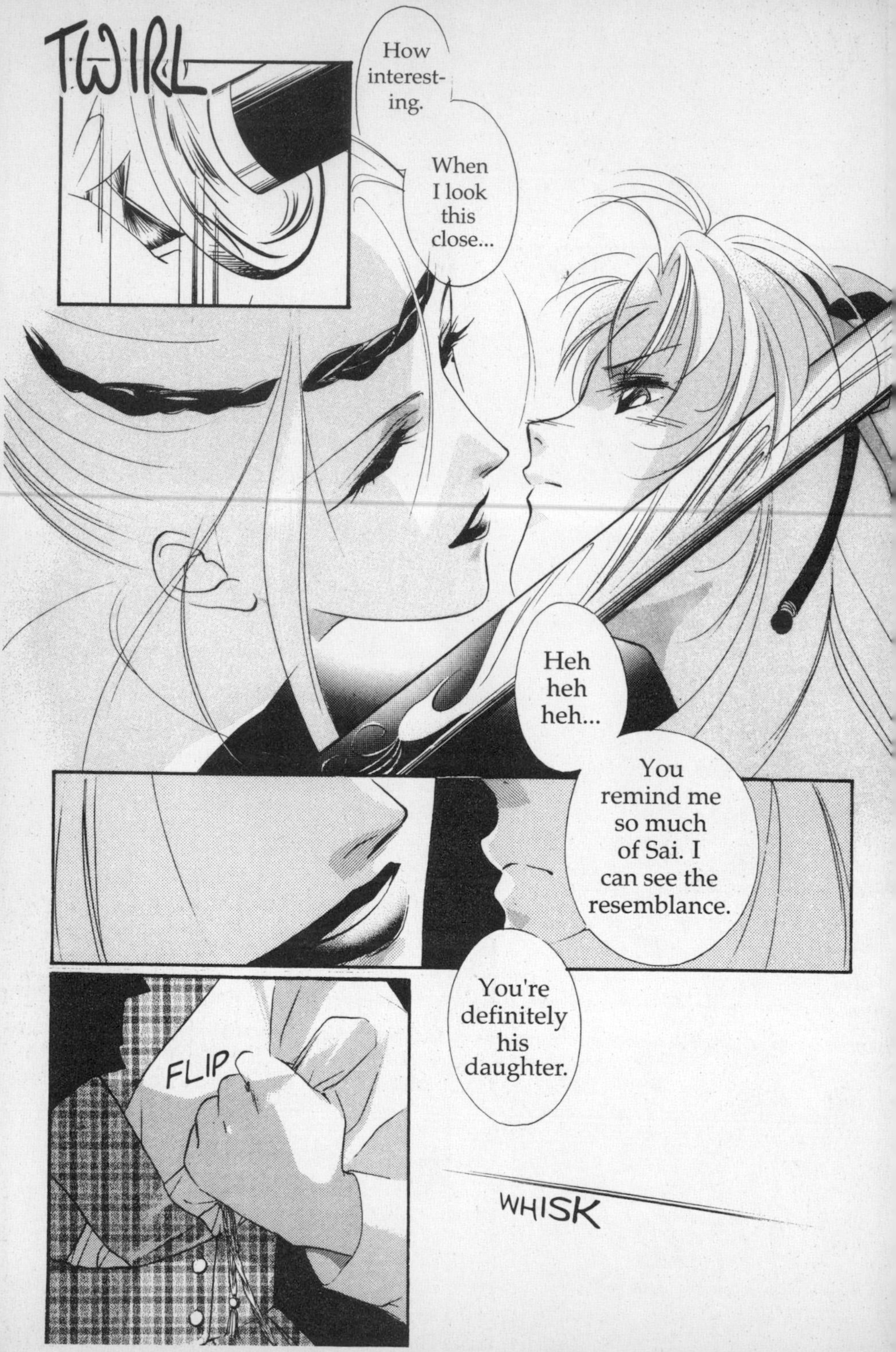
TWIRL
How interesting.
When I look this close...
Heh heh heh...
You remind me so much of Sai. I can see the resemblance.
You're definitely his daughter.
FLIP
WHISK

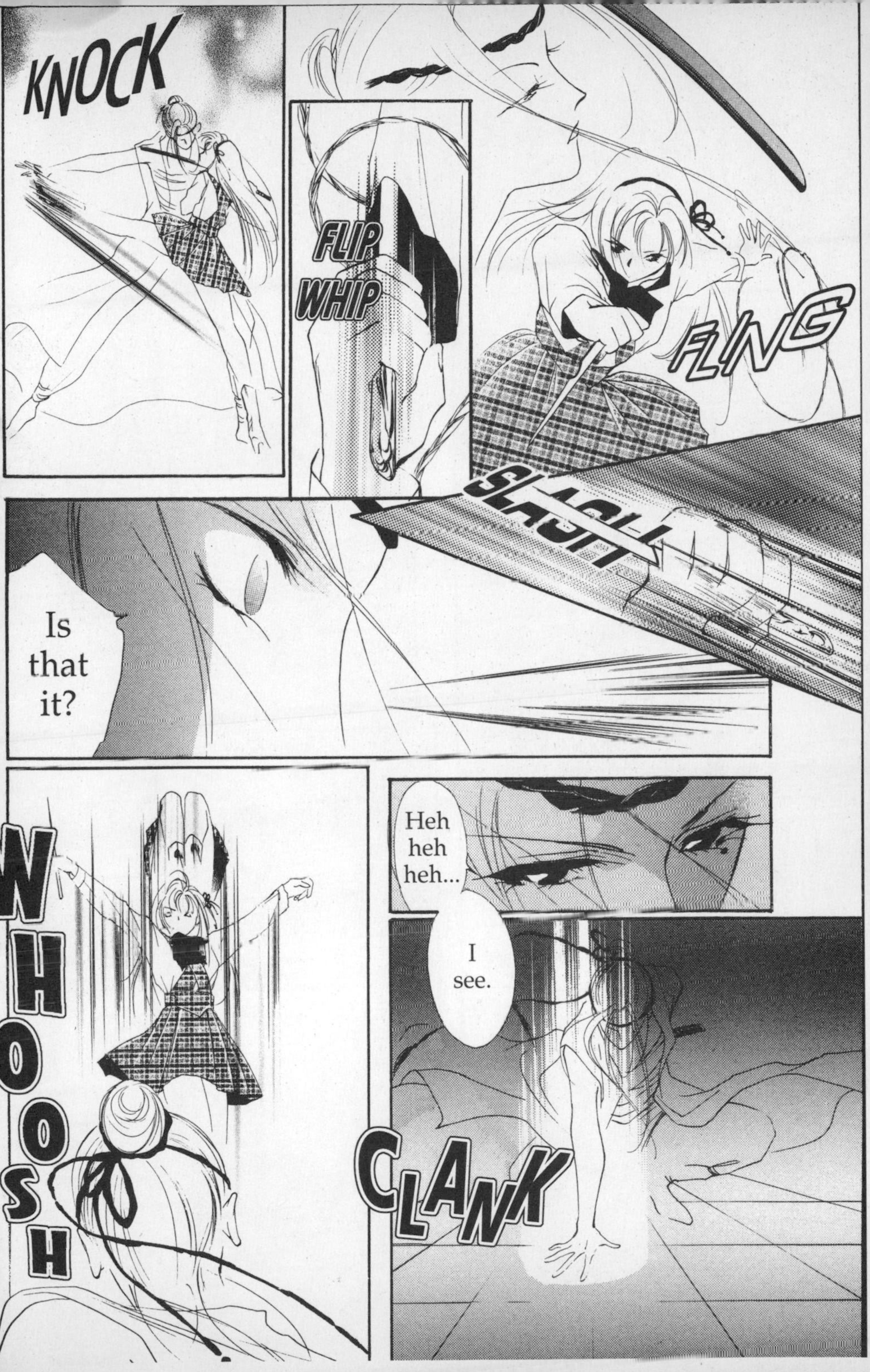
KNOCK
FLIP
WHIP
FLING
SLASH
Is that it?
WHOOSH
Heh heh heh...
I see.
CLANK

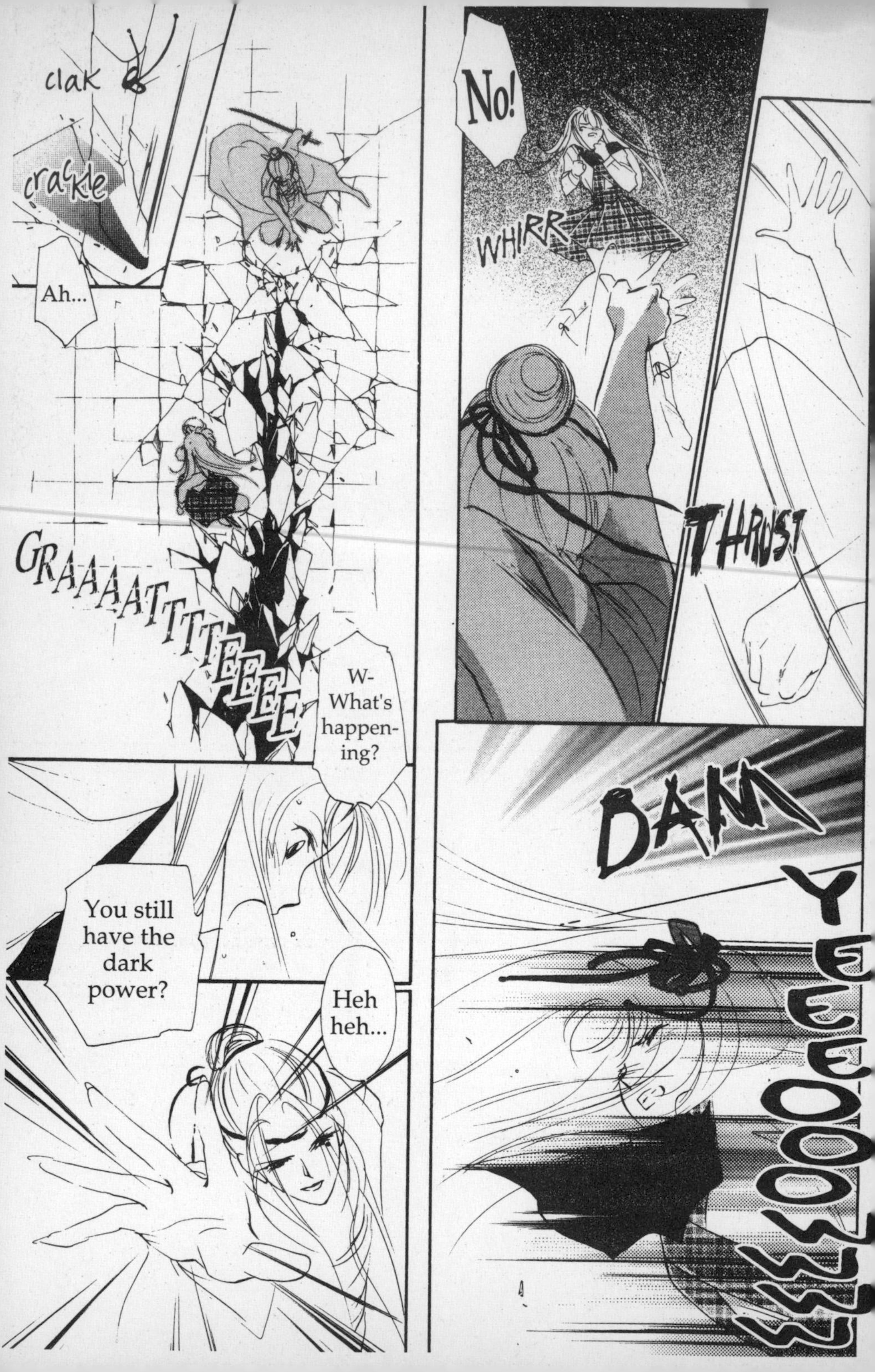
clak
crackle
Ah...
GRAAAATTTTEEEEE
W-What's happen-ing?
You still have the dark power?
Heh heh...
No!
WHIRR
THRUST
DAM
YEEEOOOWWW

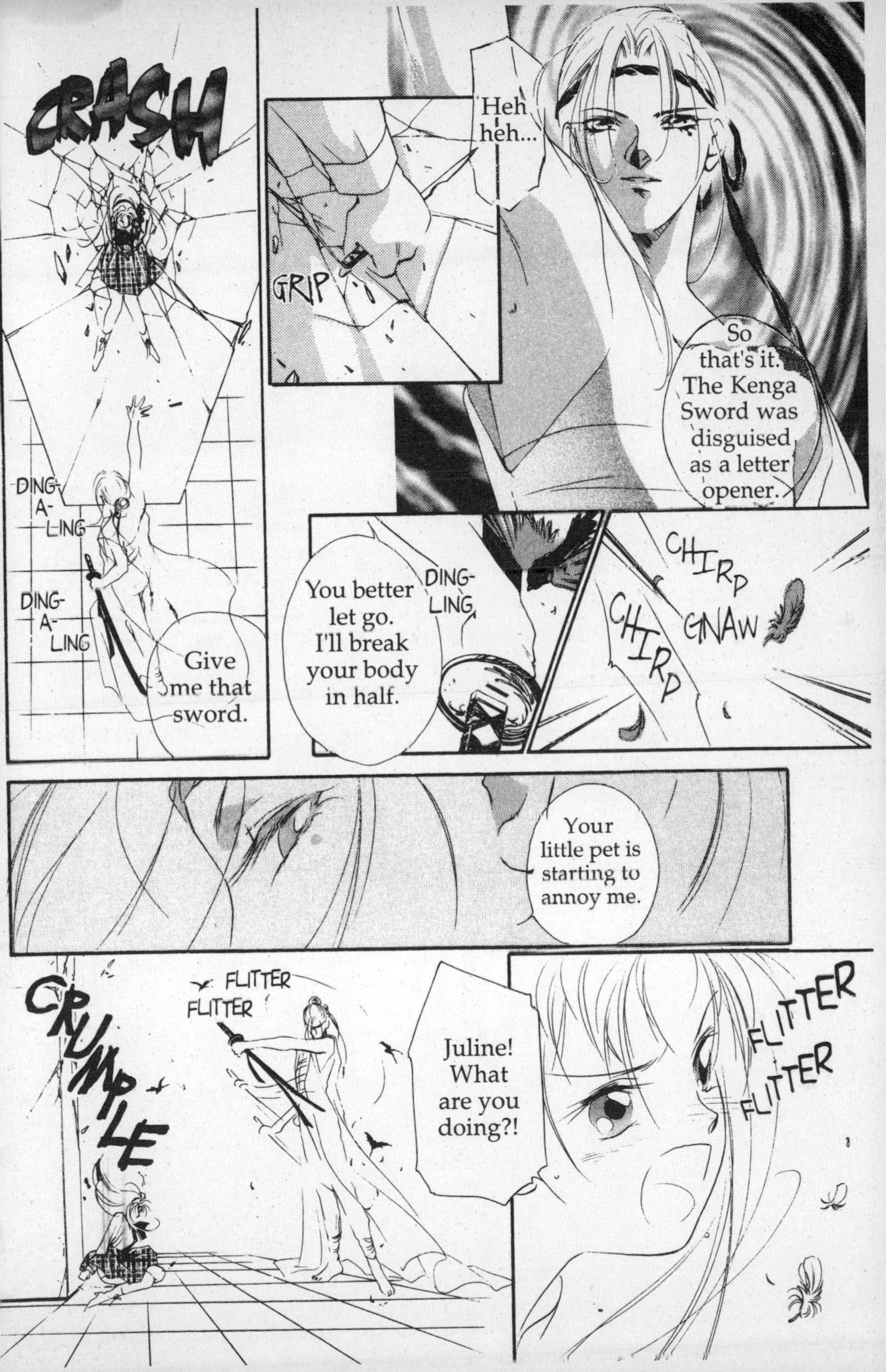
CRASH
DING-A-LING
DING-A-LING
Give me that sword.
GRIP
Heh heh...
So that's it. The Kenga Sword was disguised as a letter opener.
You better let go. I'll break your body in half.
DING-LING
CHIRP
CHIRP
GNAW
Your little pet is starting to annoy me.
CRUMPLE
FLITTER FLITTER
Juline! What are you doing?!
FLITTER FLITTER

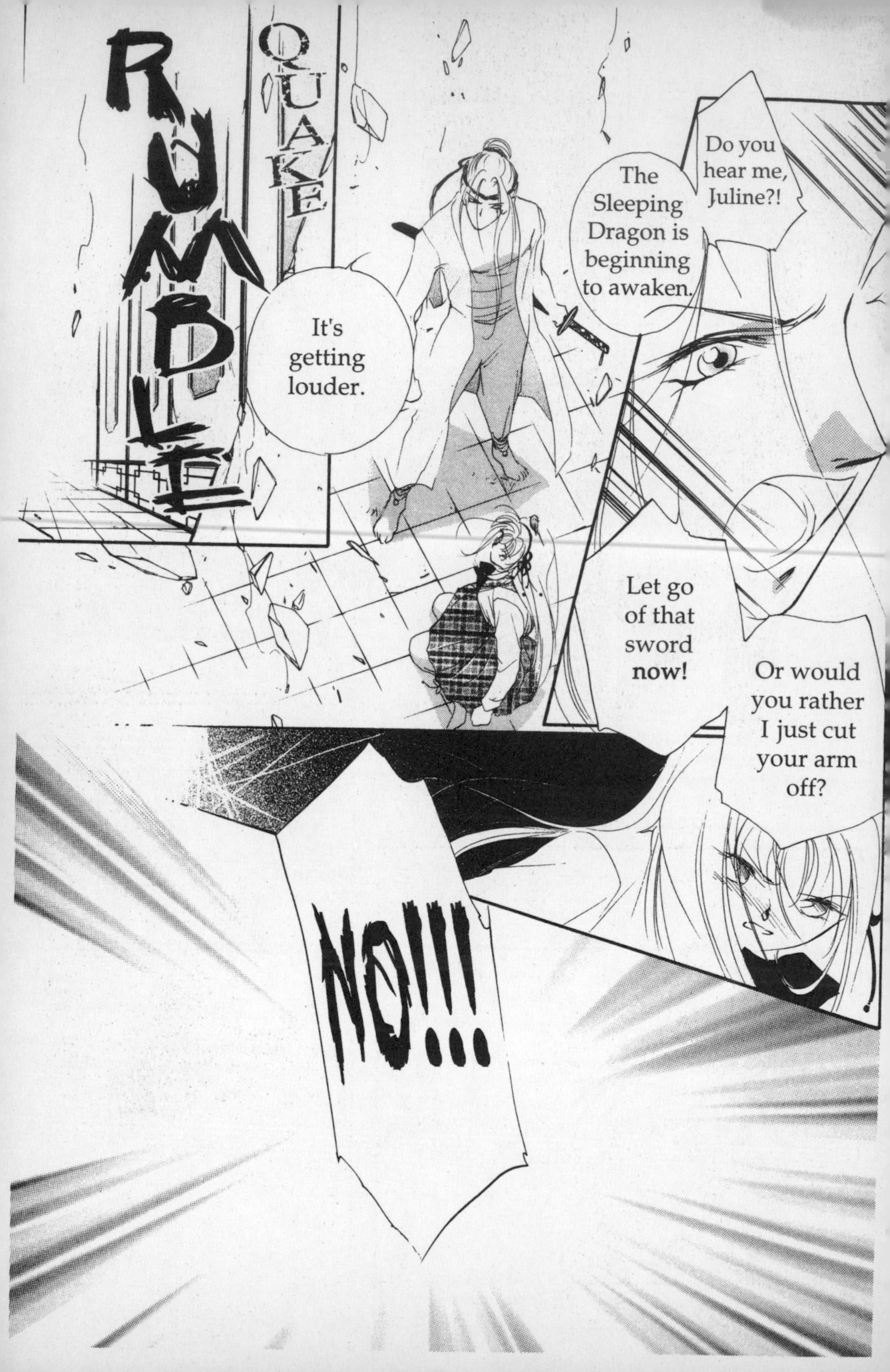
RUMBLE
QUAKE
It's getting louder.
The Sleeping Dragon is beginning to awaken.
Do you hear me, Juline?!
Let go of that sword **now!**
Or would you rather I just cut your arm off?
NO!!!...

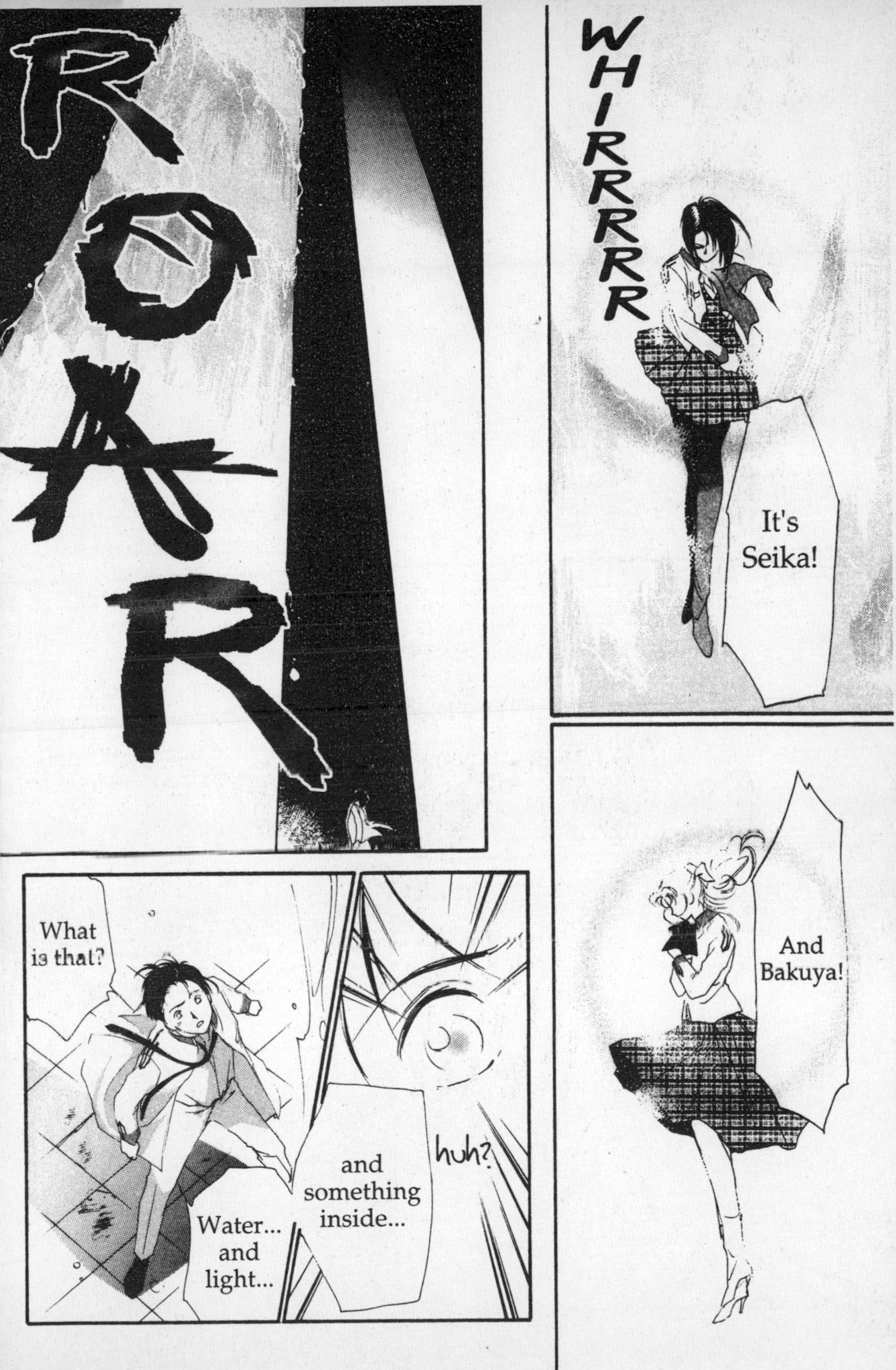
ROAR
WHIRRRRR
It's Seika!
What is that?
Water... and light...
and something inside...
huh?
And Bakuya!

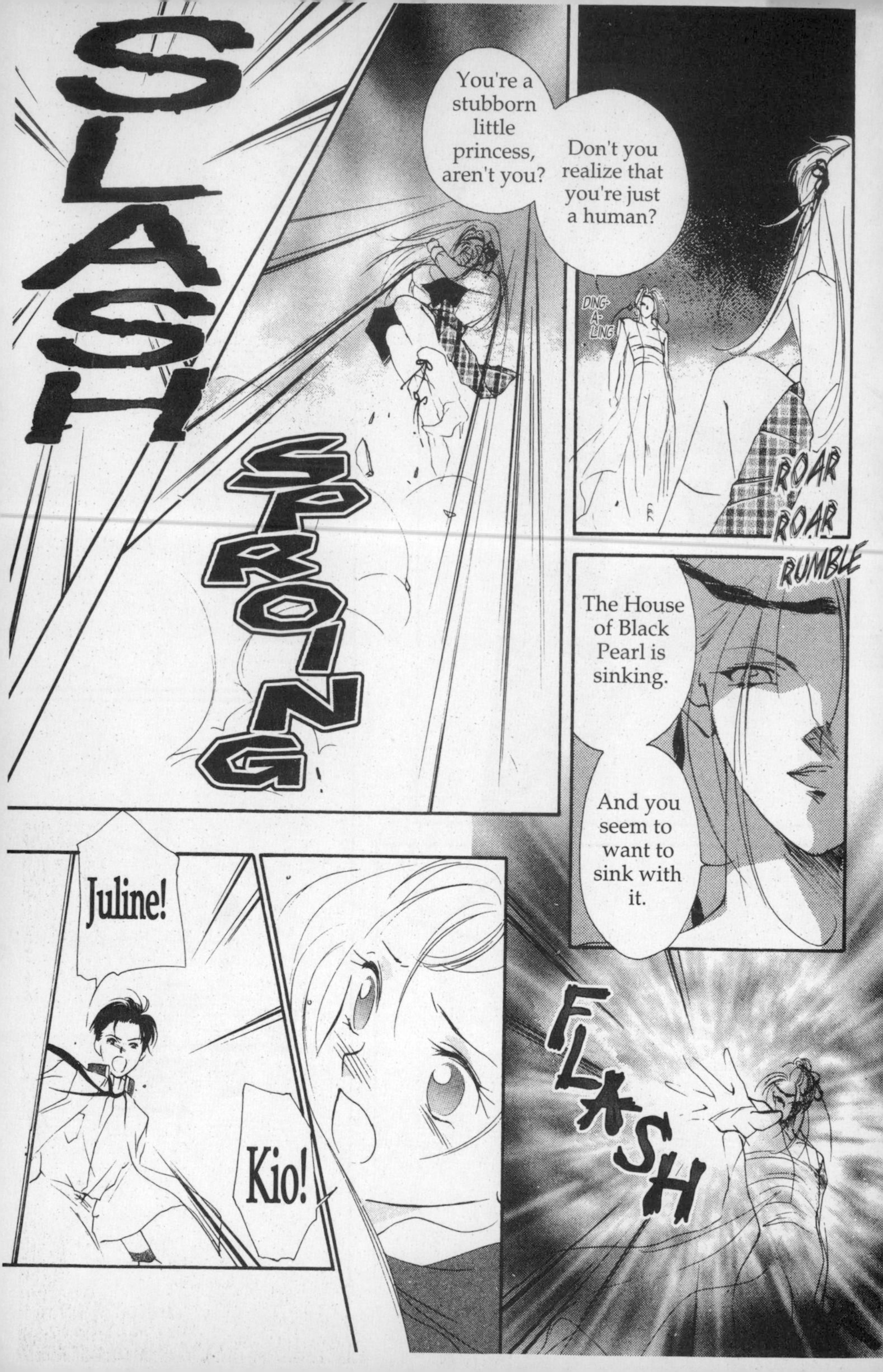
SLASH
SPROING
You're a stubborn little princess, aren't you?
Don't you realize that you're just a human?
DING-A-LING
ROAR
ROAR
RUMBLE
The House of Black Pearl is sinking.
And you seem to want to sink with it.
Juline!
Kio!
FLASH

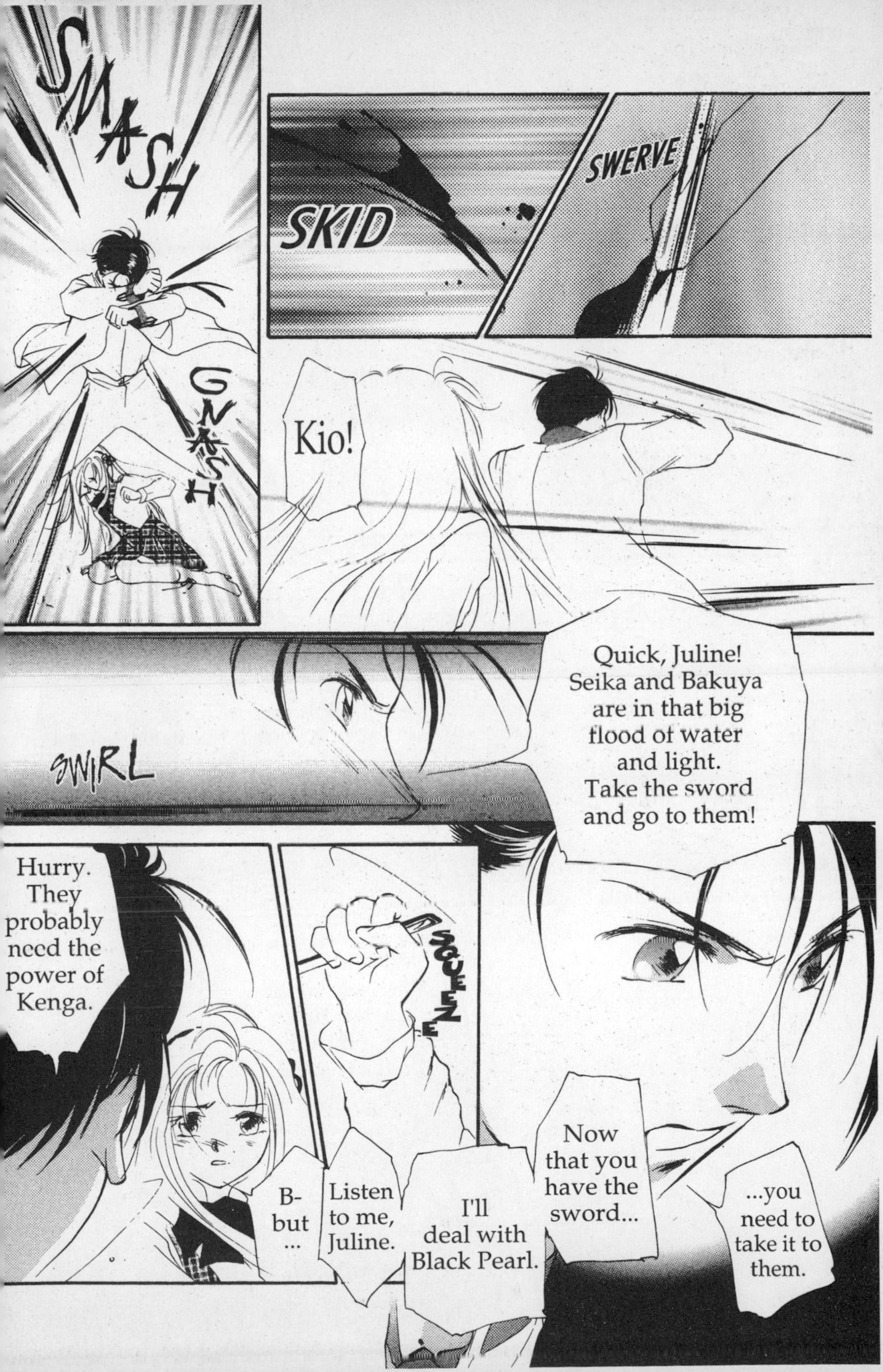

SMASH
GNASH
SKID
SWERVE
Kio!
SWIRL
Quick, Juline! Seika and Bakuya are in that big flood of water and light. Take the sword and go to them!
Hurry. They probably need the power of Kenga.
SQUEEZE
B-but ...
Listen to me, Juline.
I'll deal with Black Pearl.
Now that you have the sword...
...you need to take it to them.

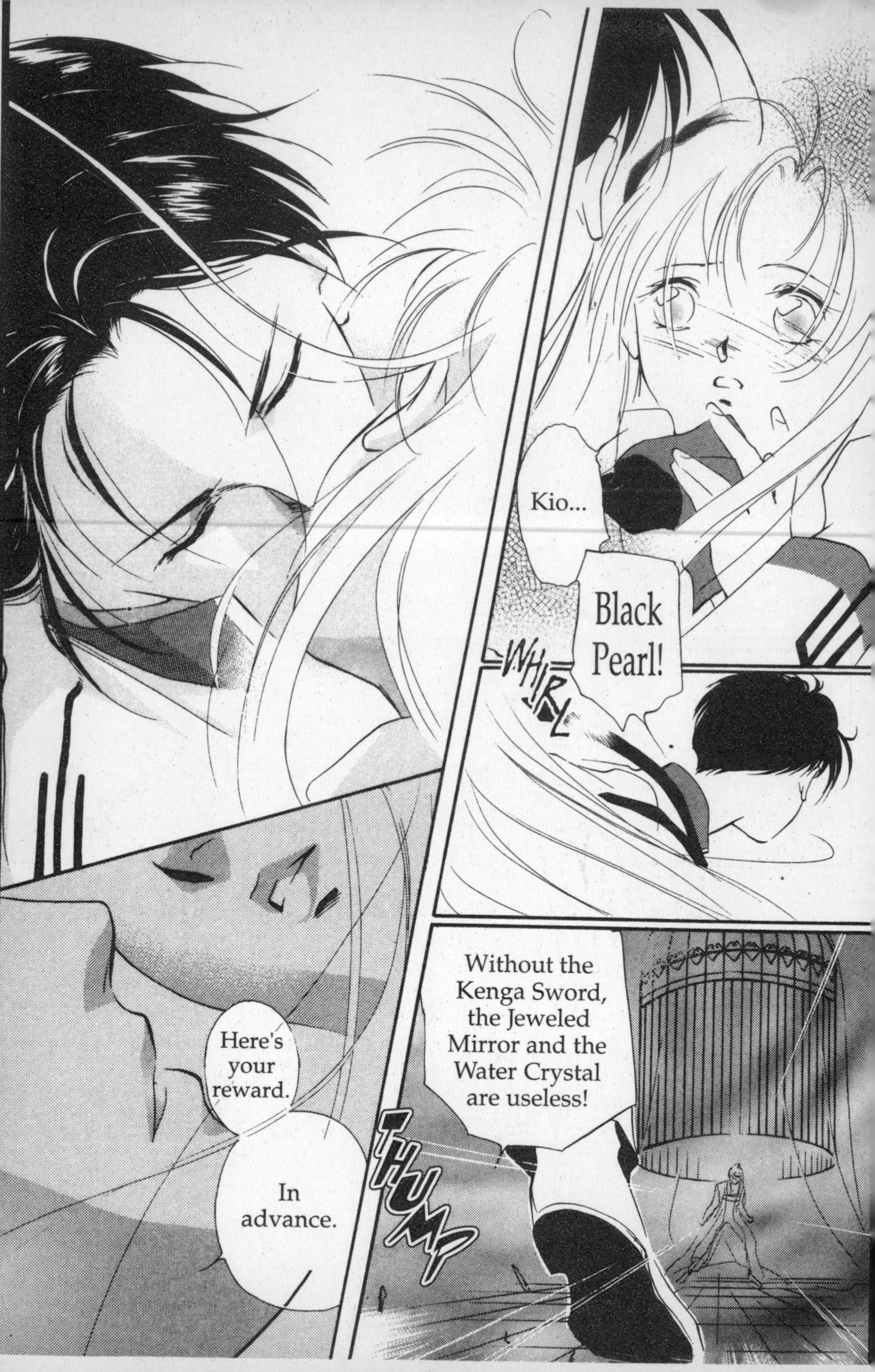
Kio...
Black Pearl!
WHIRL
Here's your reward.
In advance.
Without the Kenga Sword, the Jeweled Mirror and the Water Crystal are useless!
THUMP

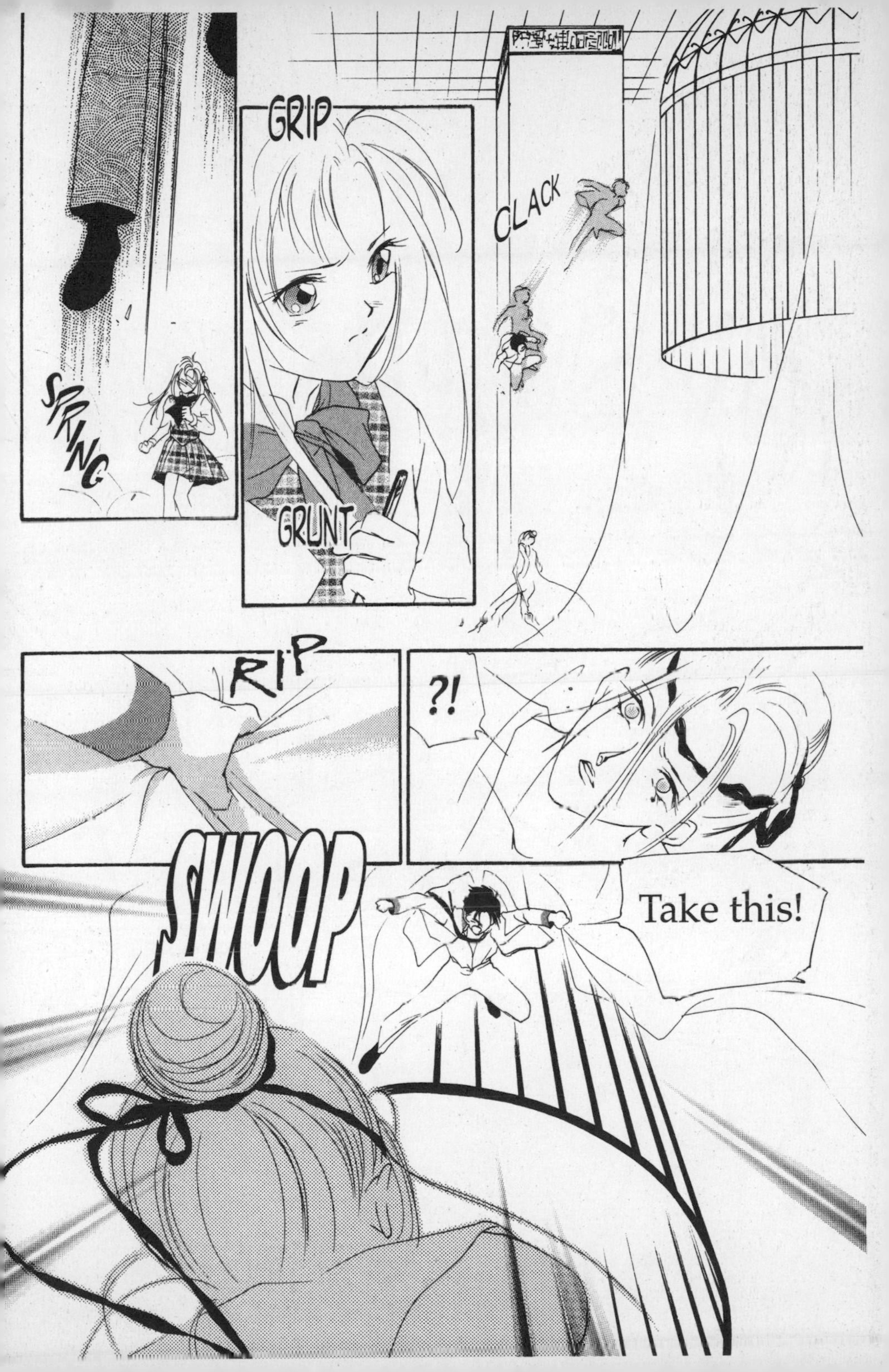
SPRING
GRIP
GRUNT
CLACK
RIP
?!
SWOOP
Take this!

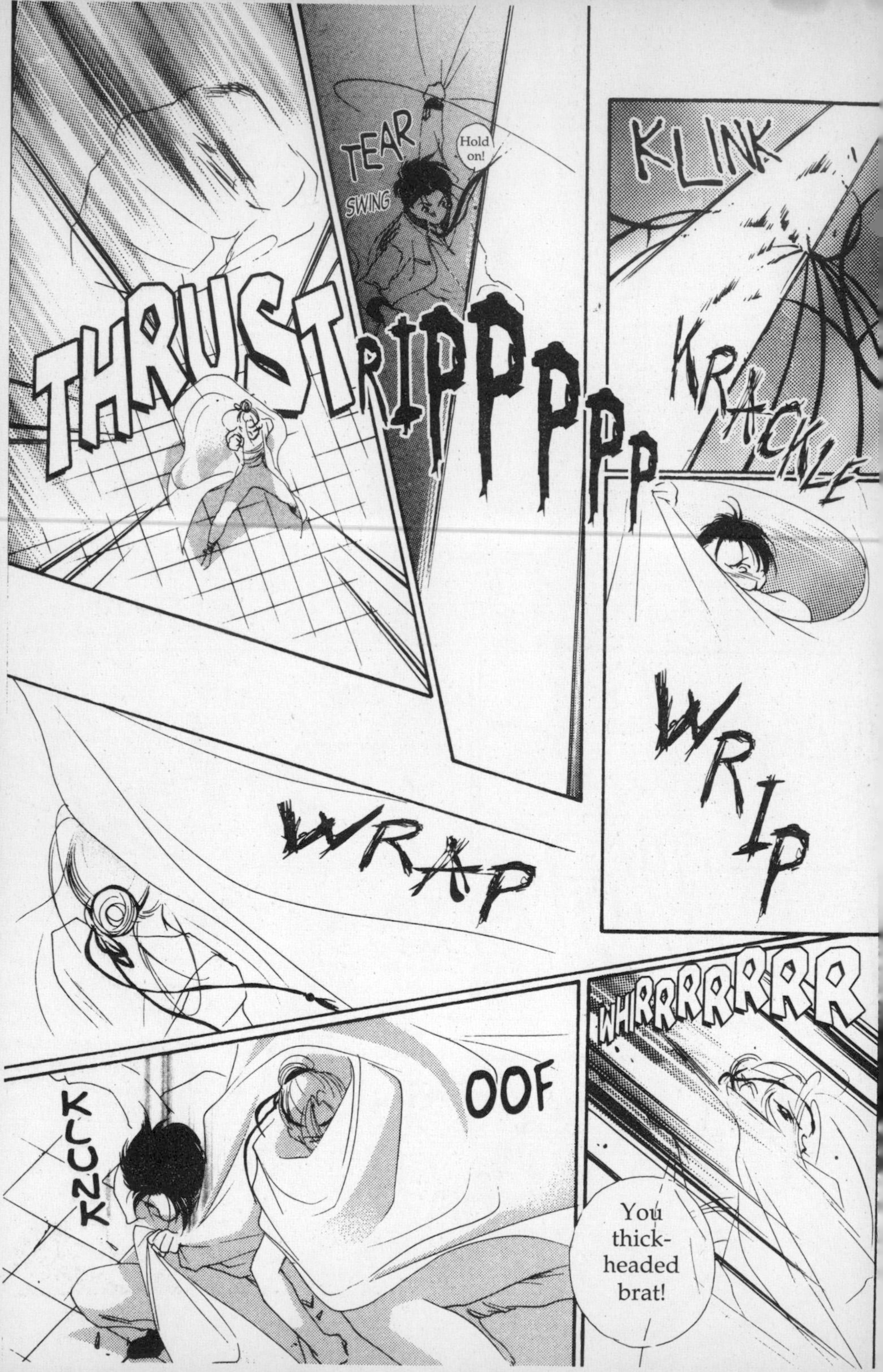
THRUST
TEAR
Hold on!
SWING
RIPPPPP
KLINK
KRACKLE
WRIP
WRAP
KLUNK
OOF
WHIRRRRRRR
You thick-headed brat!

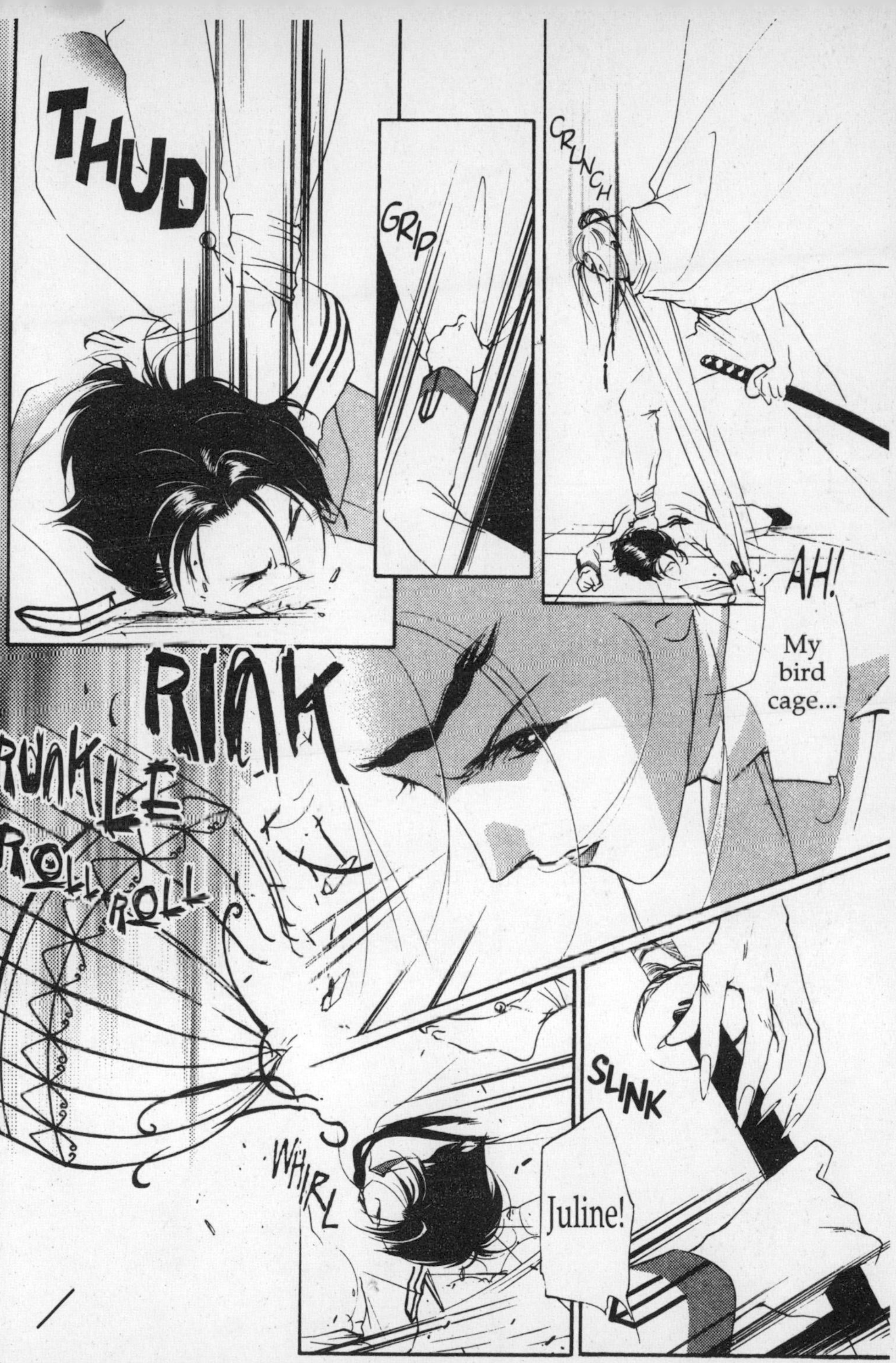
THUD
GRIP
CRUNCH
AH!
My bird cage...
RINK
RUNKLE
ROLL ROLL
WHIRL
SLINK
Juline!

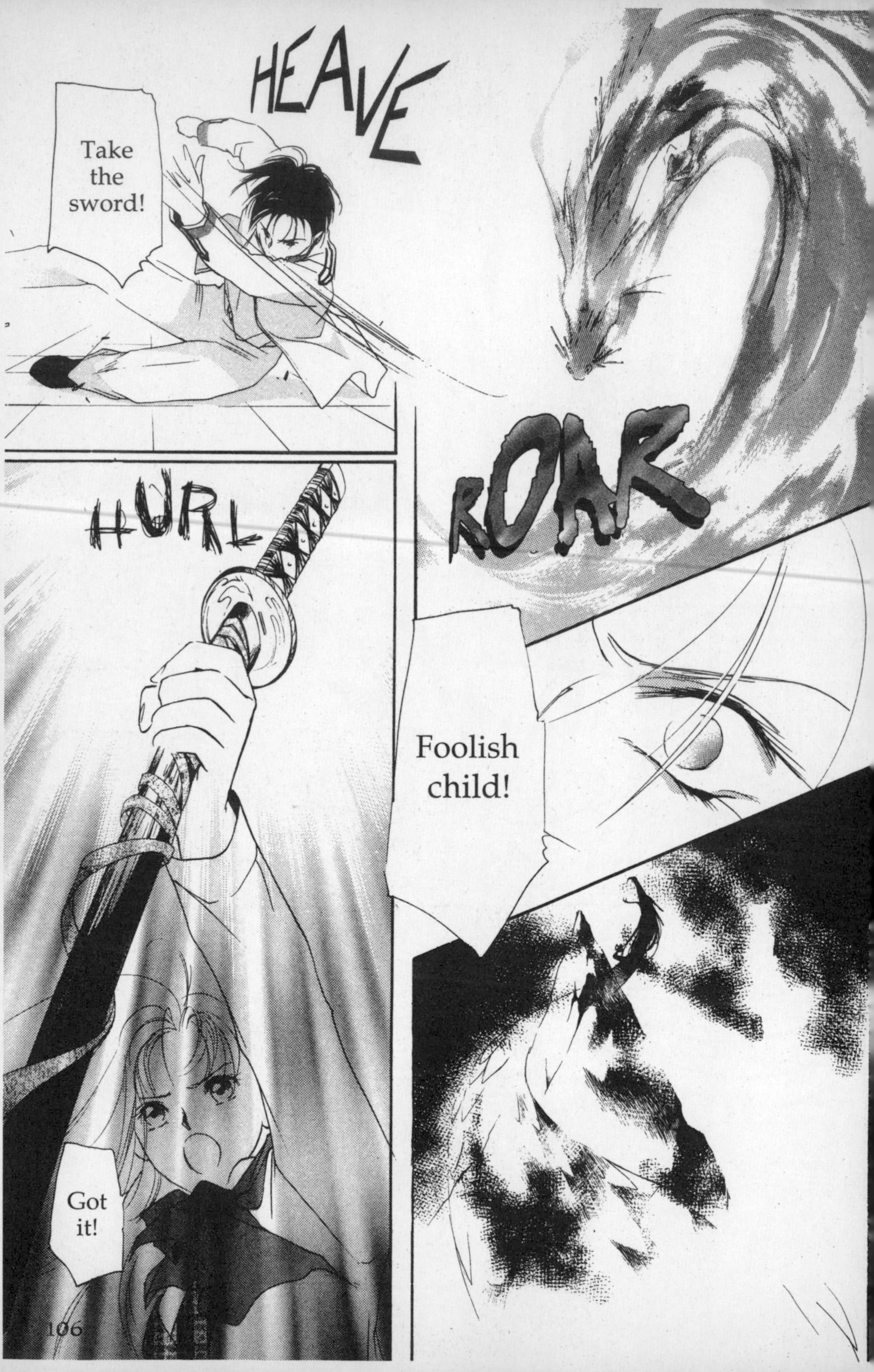
HEAVE
Take the sword!
ROAR
HURL
Got it!
Foolish child!

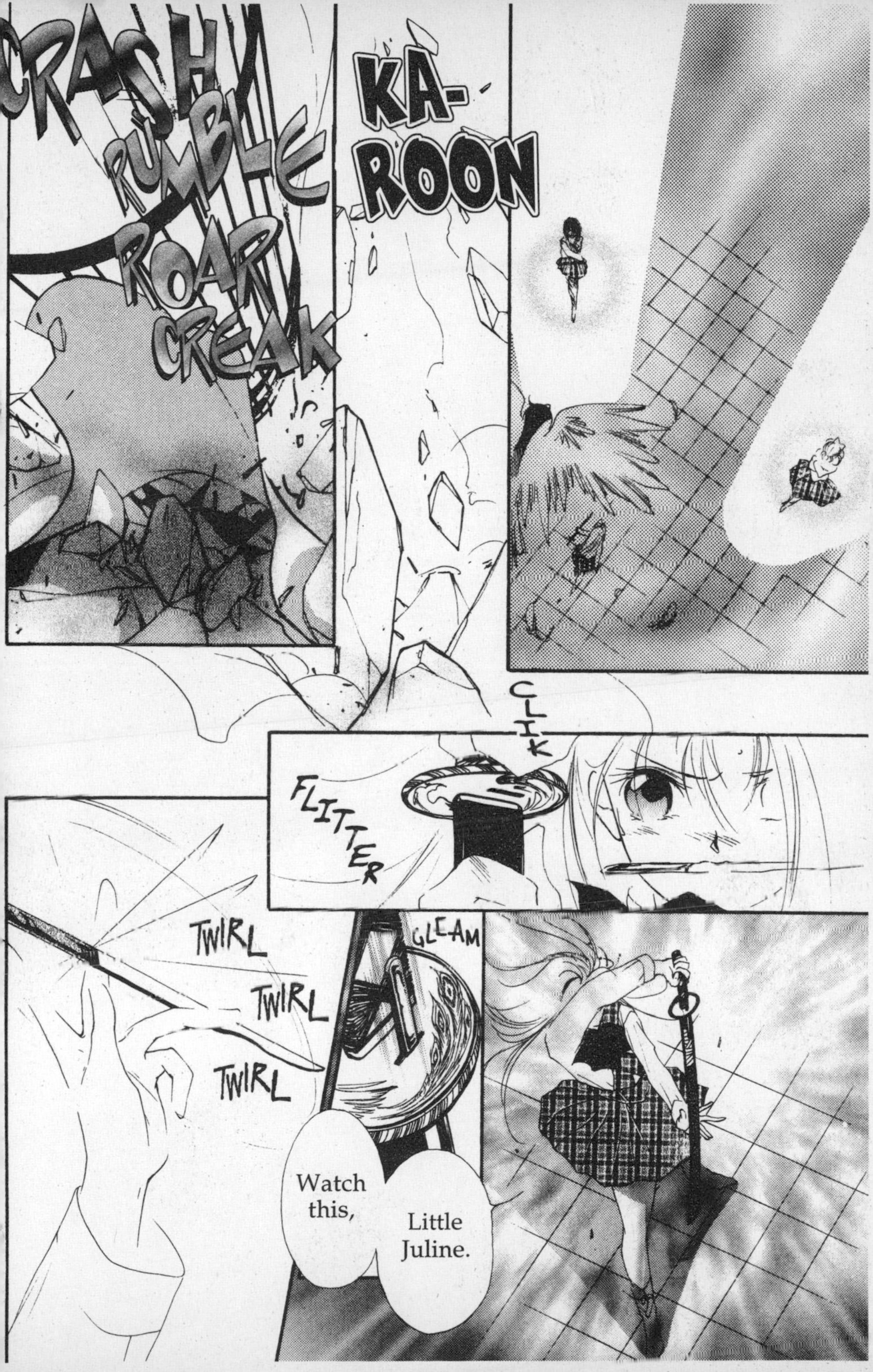
CRASH
RUMBLE
ROAR
CREAK
KA-ROON
CLIK
FLITTER
TWIRL
TWIRL
TWIRL
GLEAM
Watch this,
Little Juline.

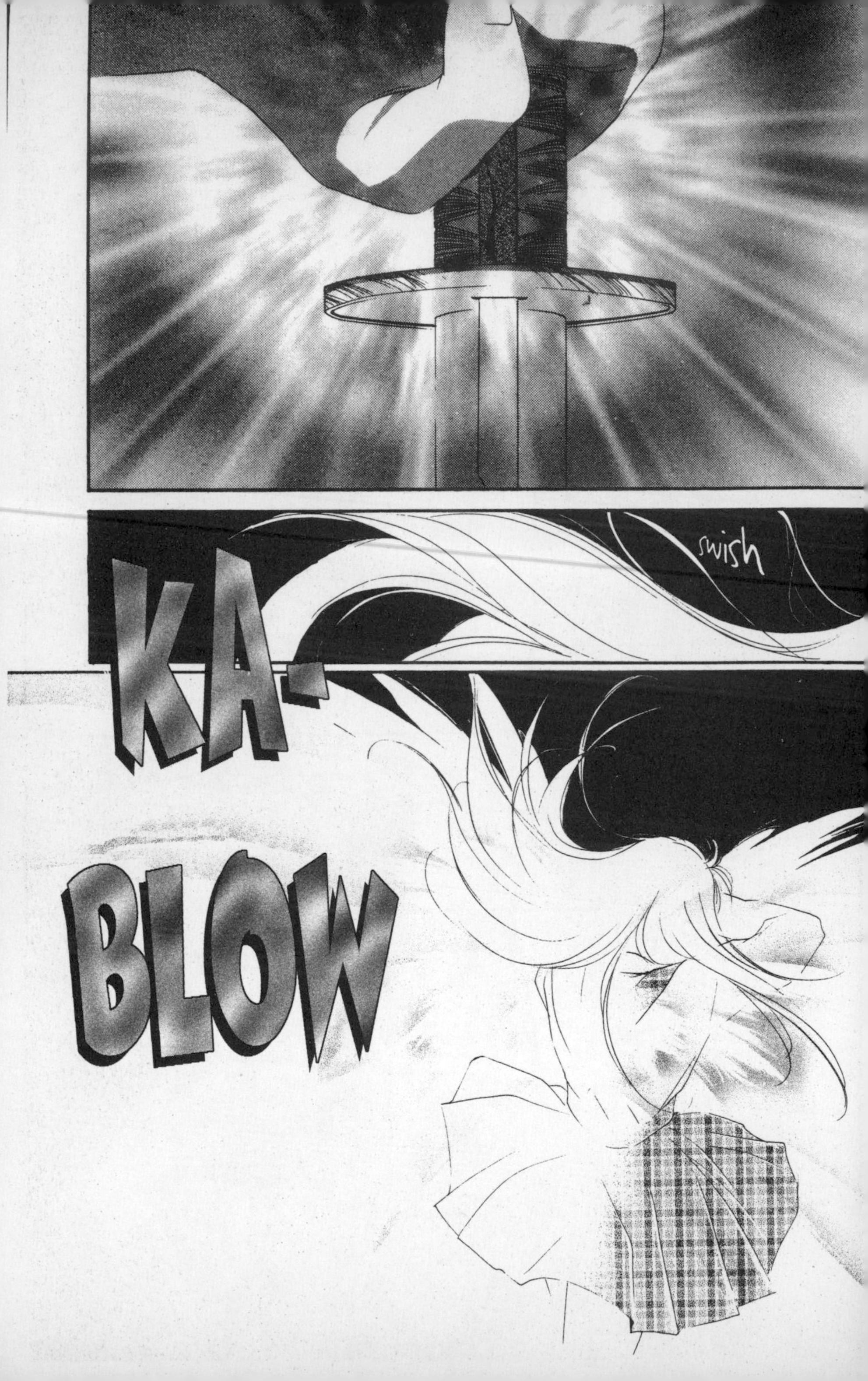
swish
KA-
BLOW

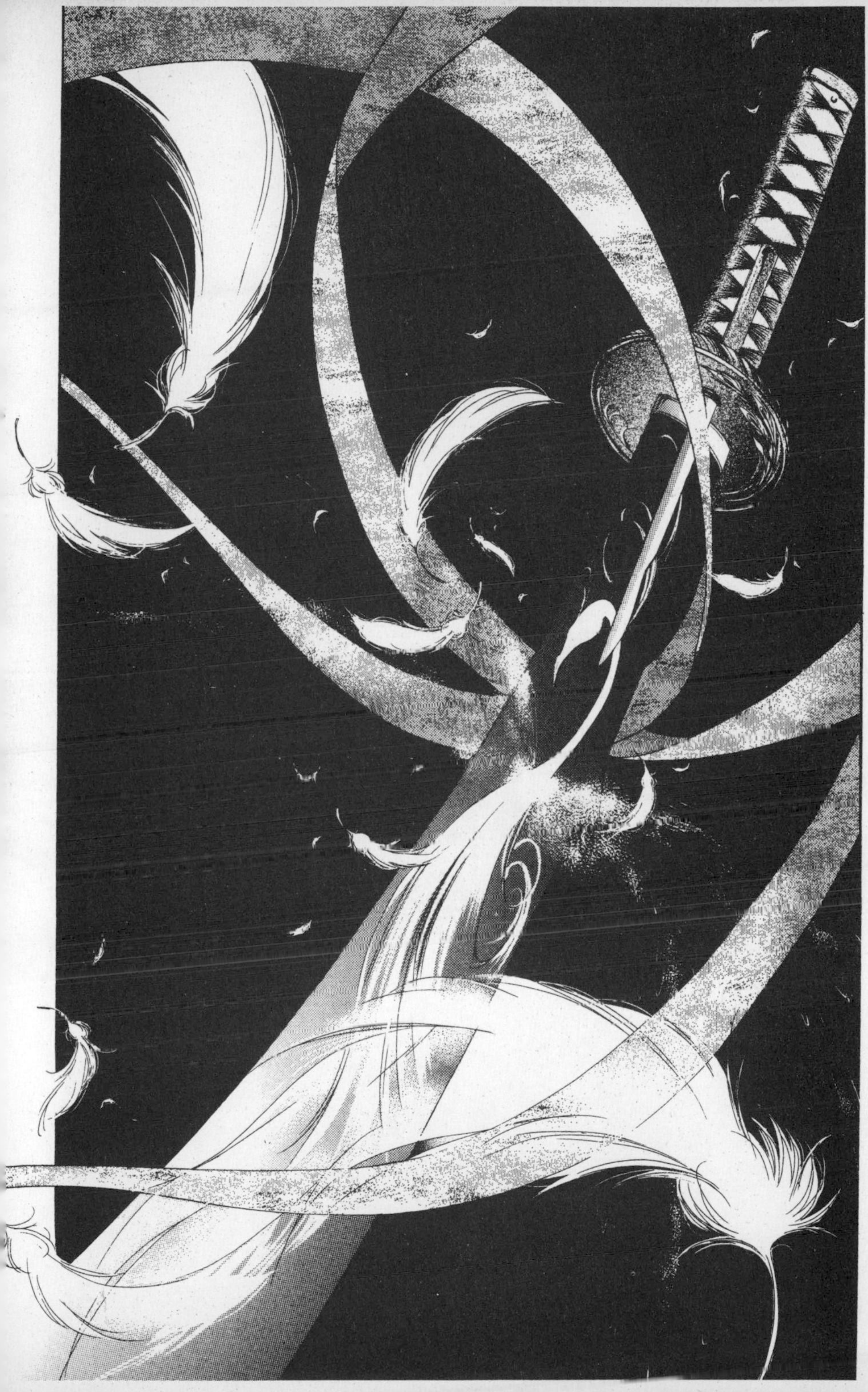

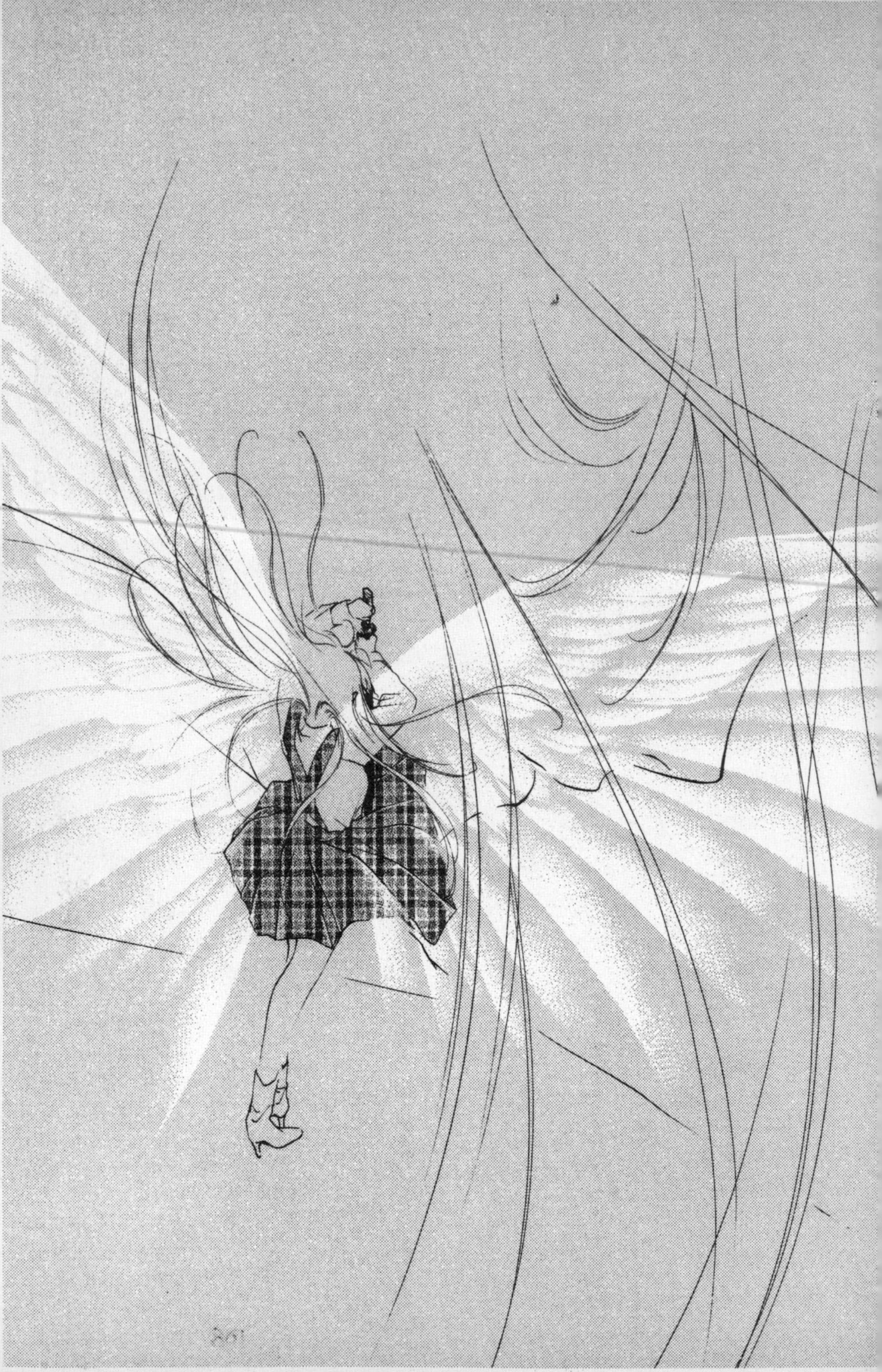

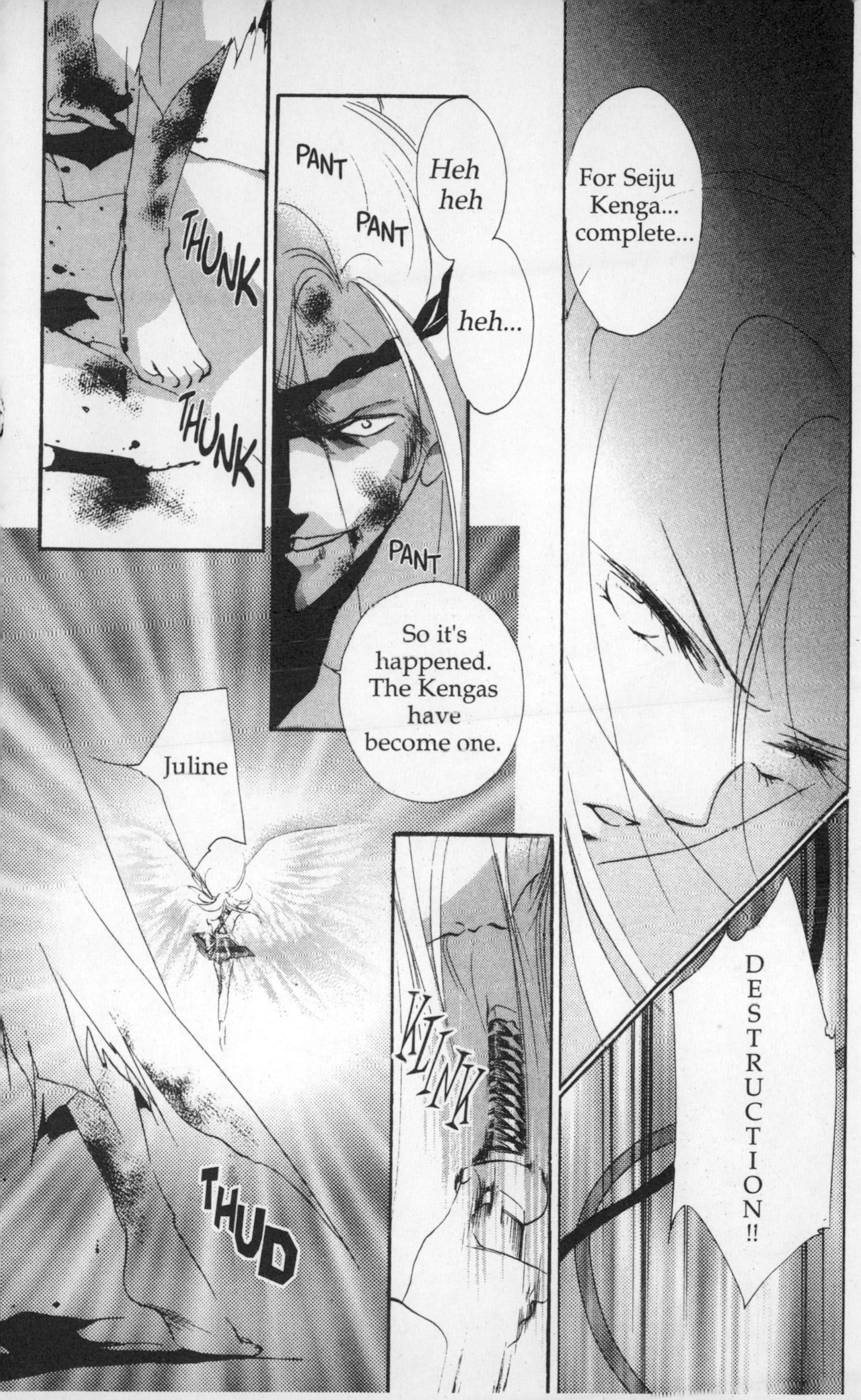
THUNK
THUNK
PANT
Heh heh
PANT
heh...
PANT
So it's happened. The Kengas have become one.
Juline
THUD
KLINK
For Seiju Kenga... complete...
DESTRUCTION!!

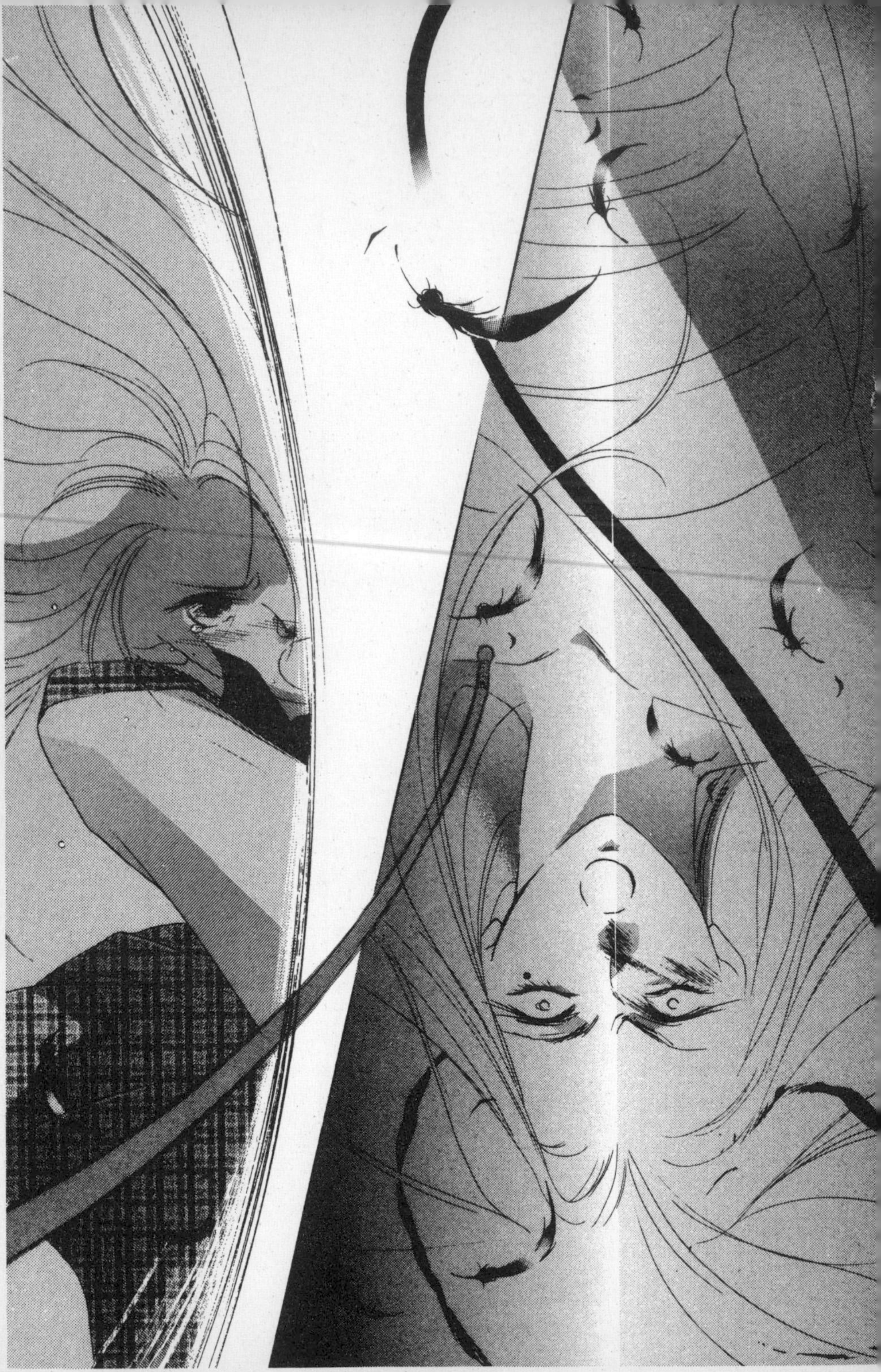

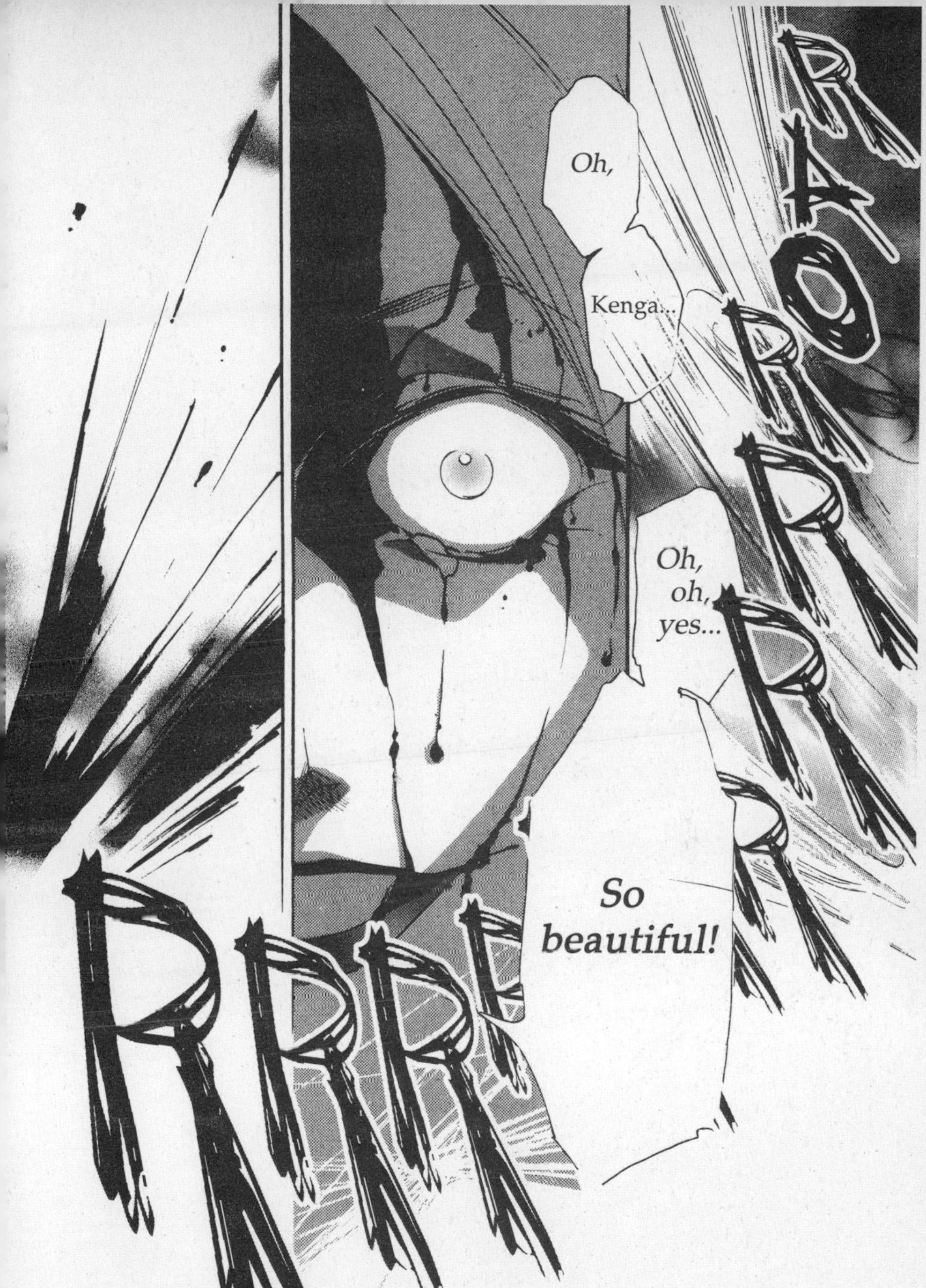
Oh,
Kenga...
RAORRRR
Oh, oh, yes...
So beautiful!
RRRR

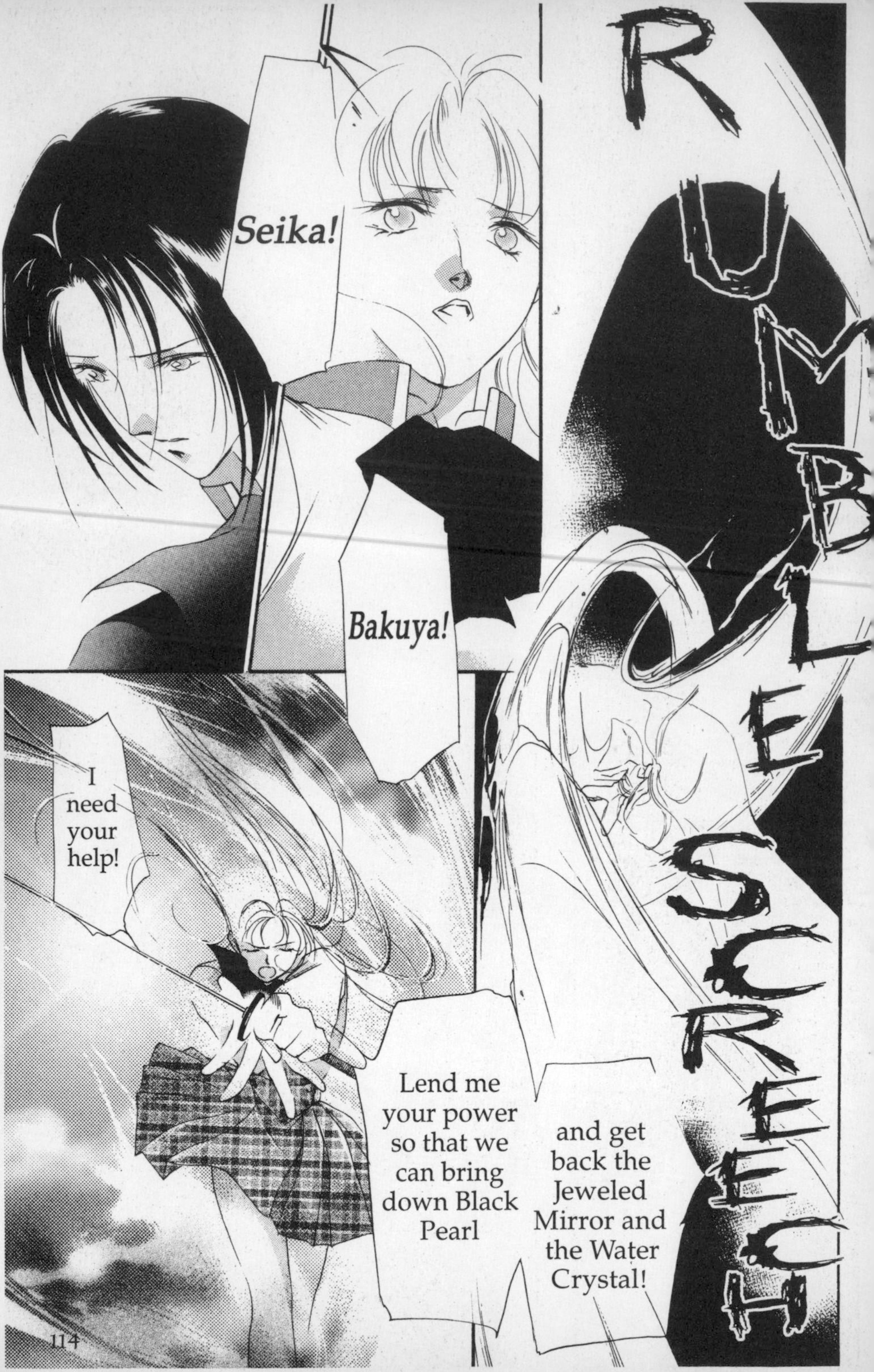
Seika!
Bakuya!
RUMBLE
SCREECH
I need your help!
Lend me your power so that we can bring down Black Pearl
and get back the Jeweled Mirror and the Water Crystal!

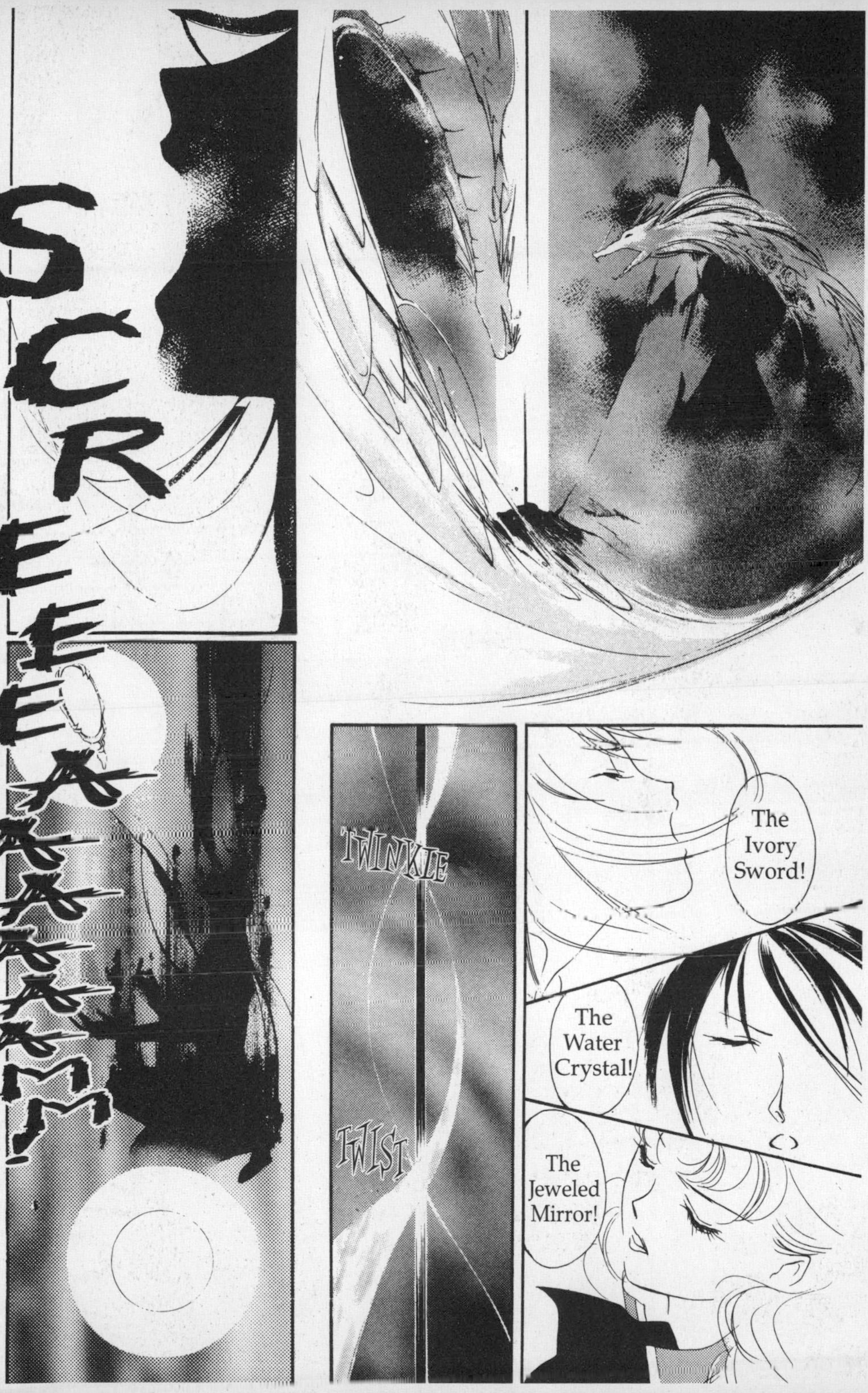
SCREEEAAAAAAM!
TWINKLE
TWIST
The Ivory Sword!
The Water Crystal!
The Jeweled Mirror!

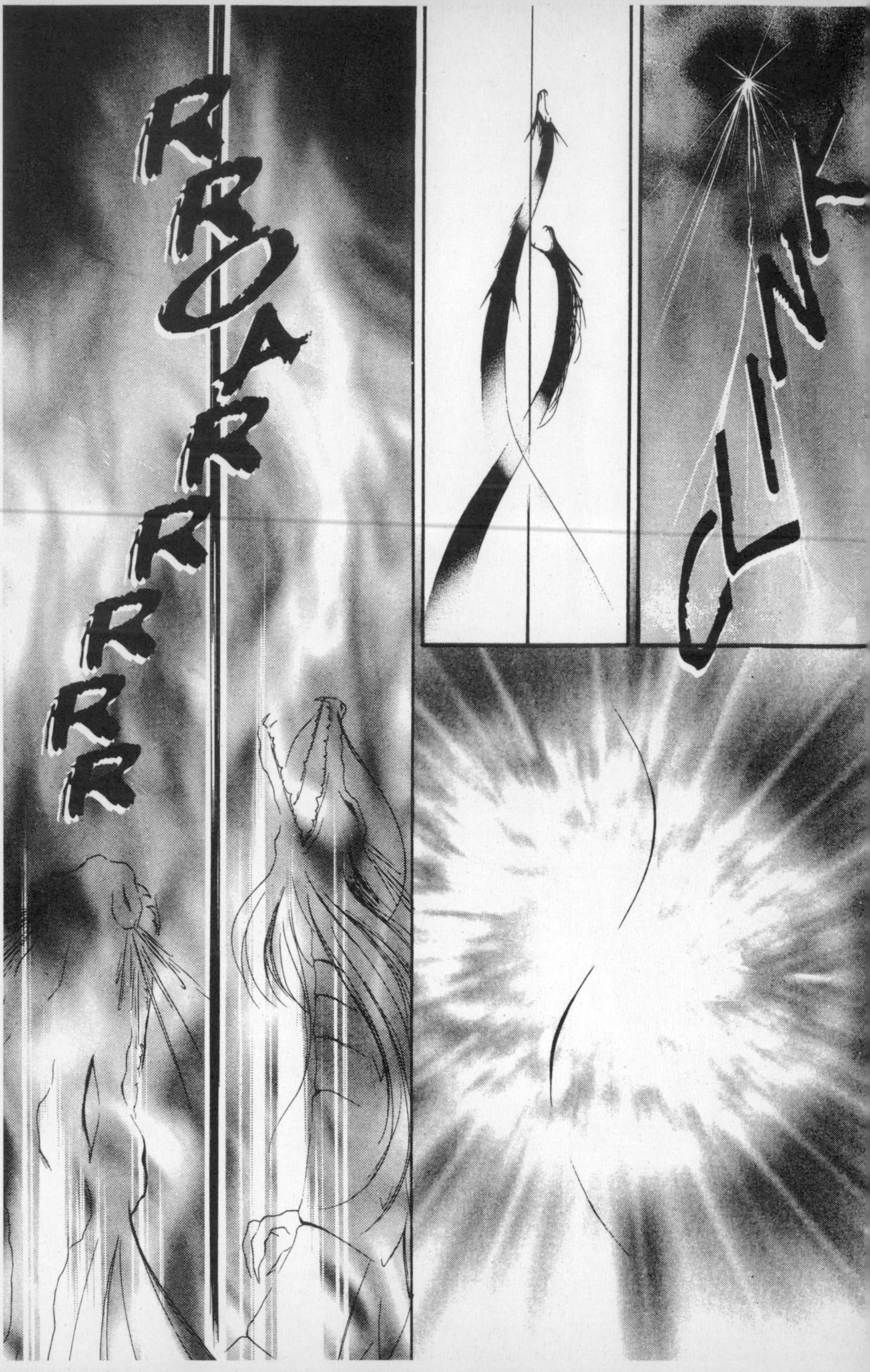
RROARRRRRR
CLINK

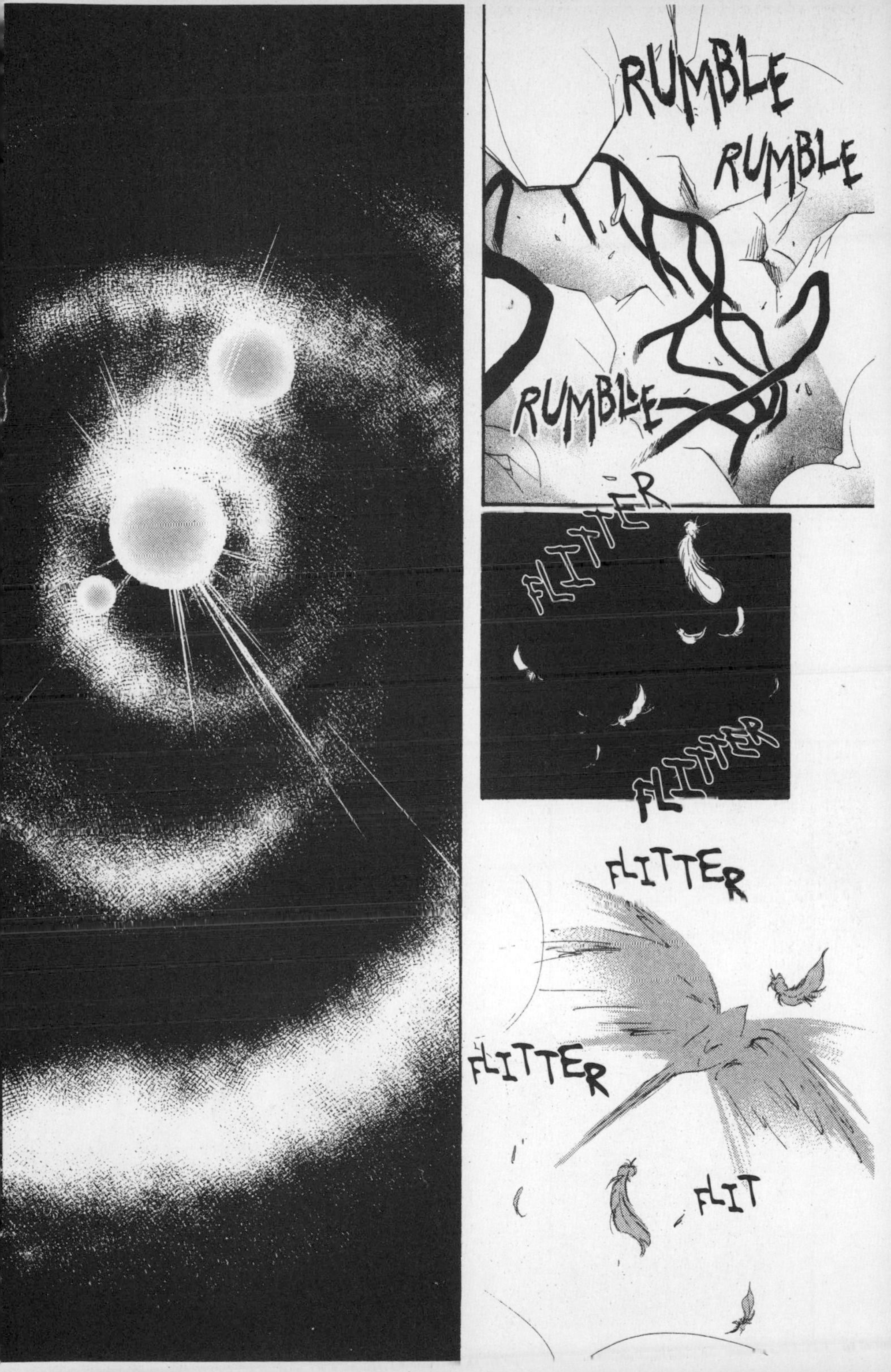
RUMBLE
RUMBLE
RUMBLE
FLITTER
FLITTER
FLITTER
FLITTER
FLIT

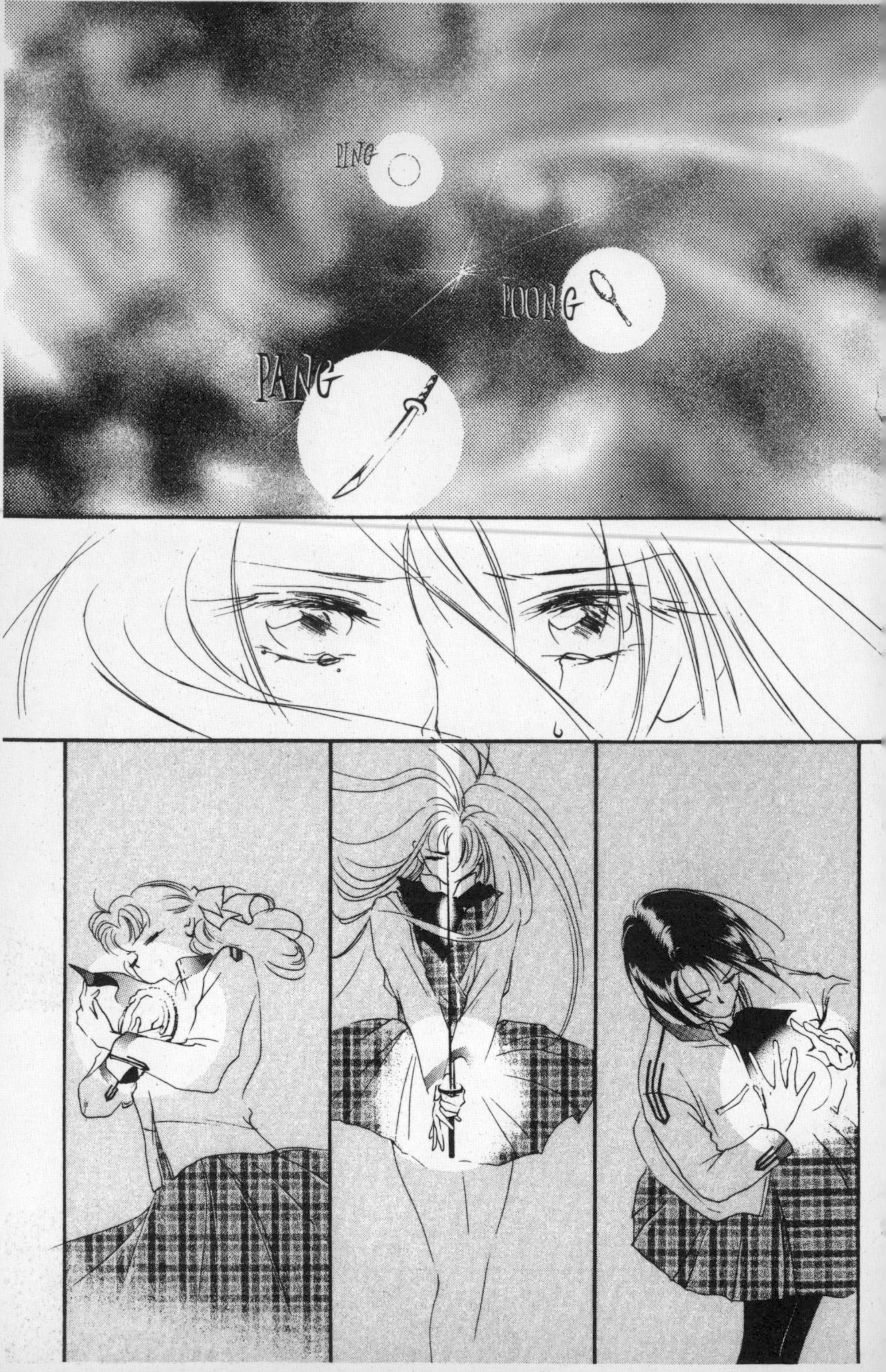
PING
POONG
PANG

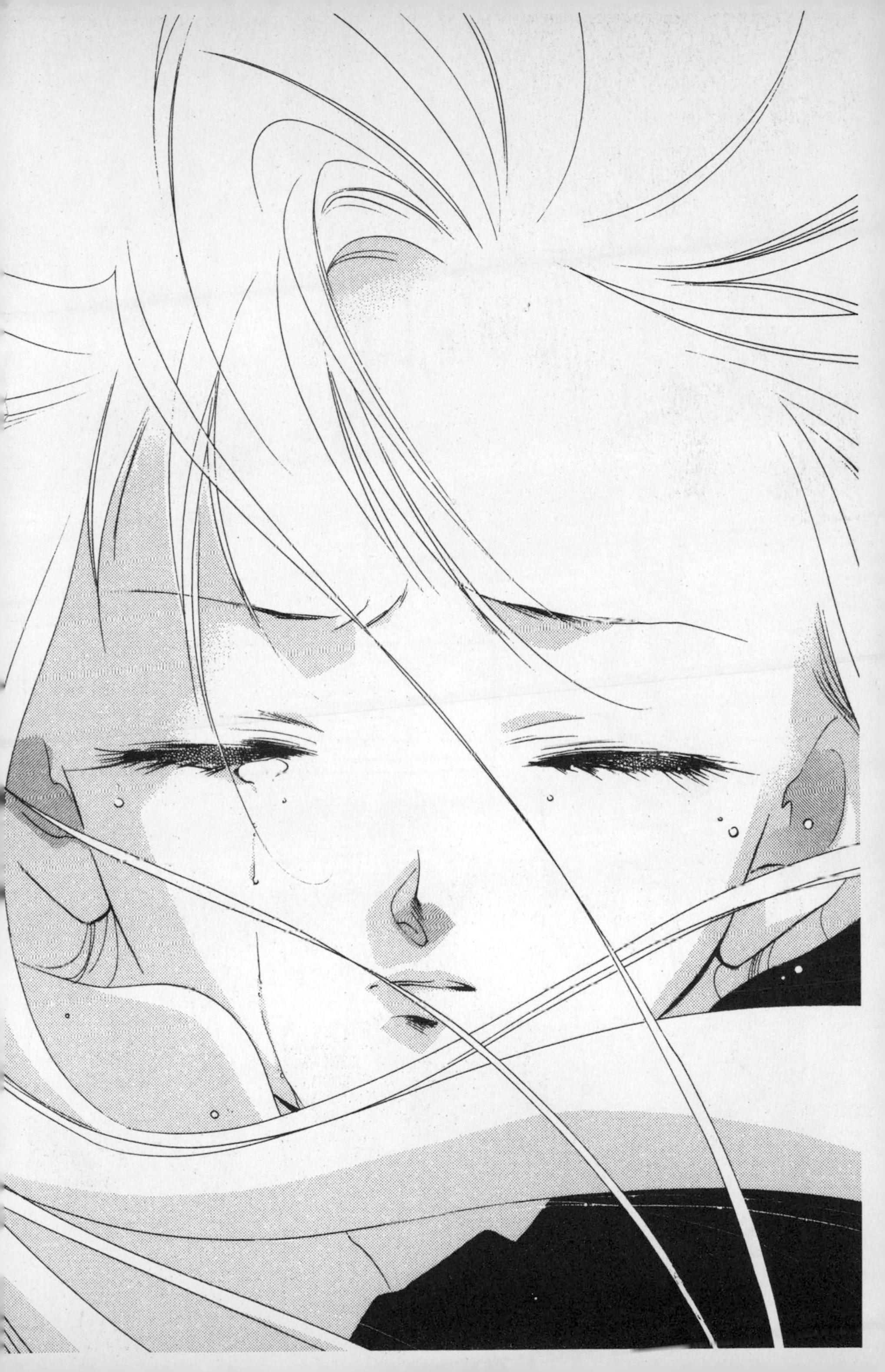

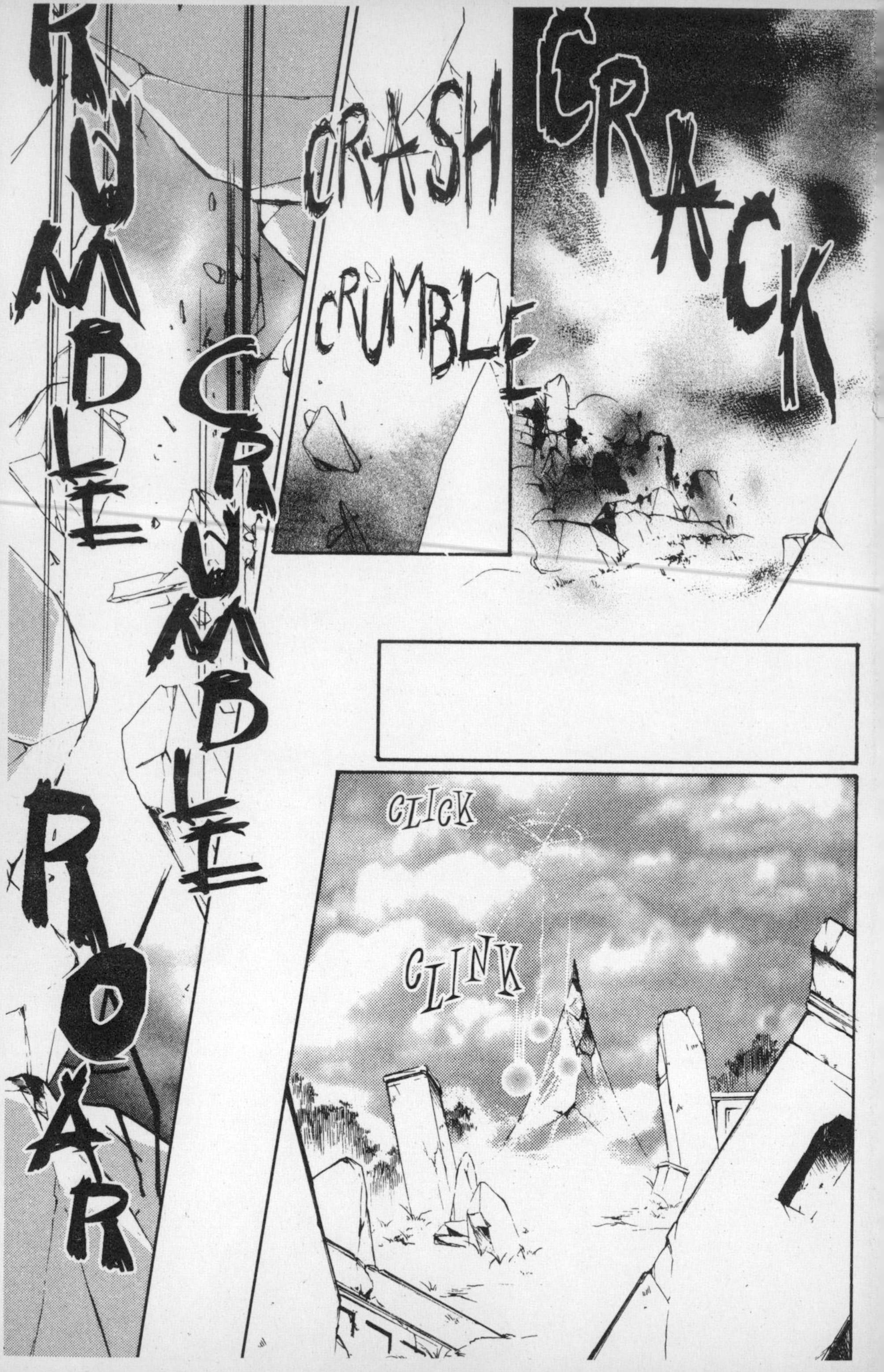
RUMBLE
CRUMBLE
ROAR
CRASH
CRUMBLE
CRACK
CLICK
CLINK

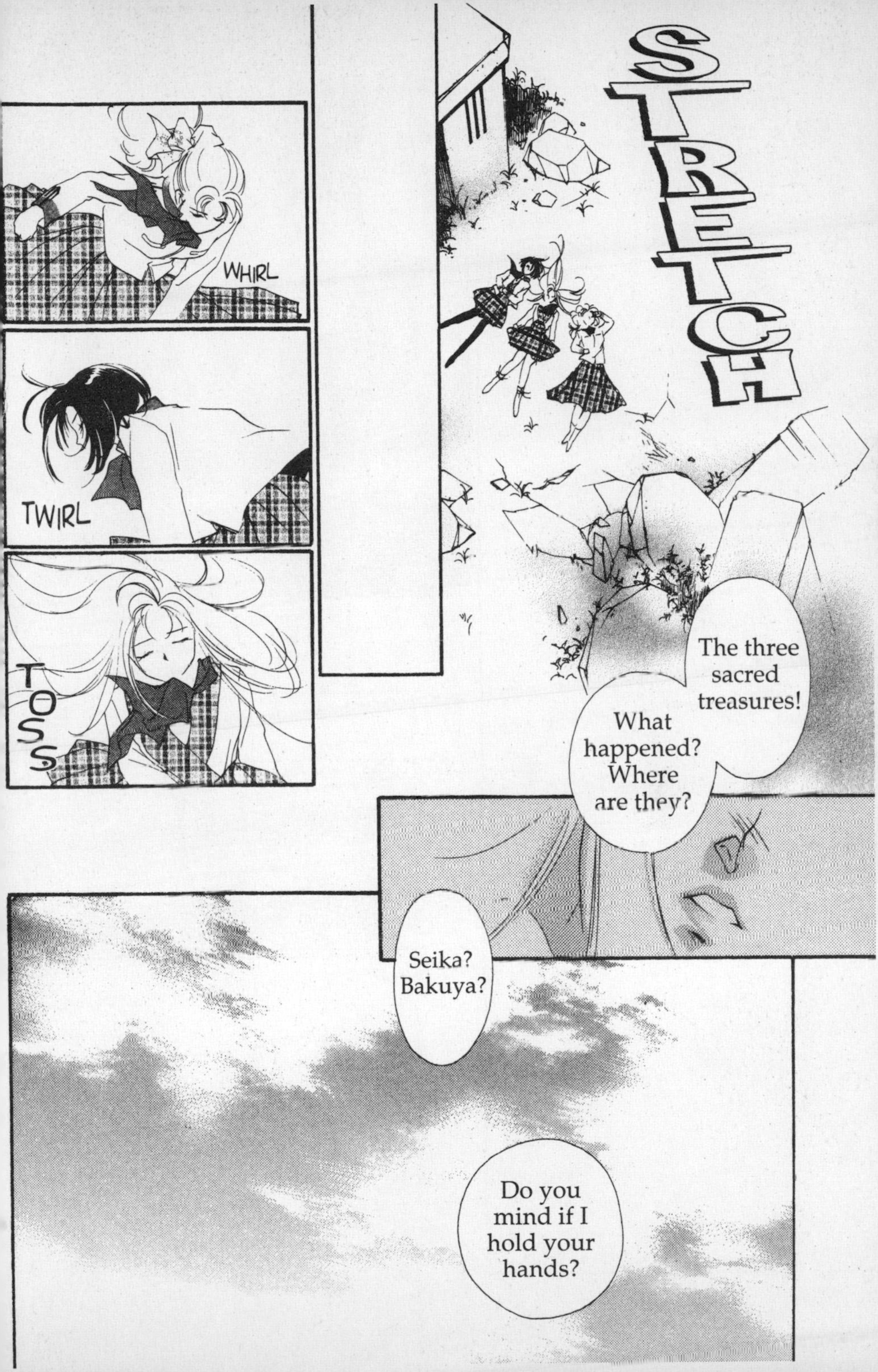
WHIRL
TWIRL
TOSS
STRETCH
The three sacred treasures!
What happened? Where are they?
Seika? Bakuya?
Do you mind if I hold your hands?

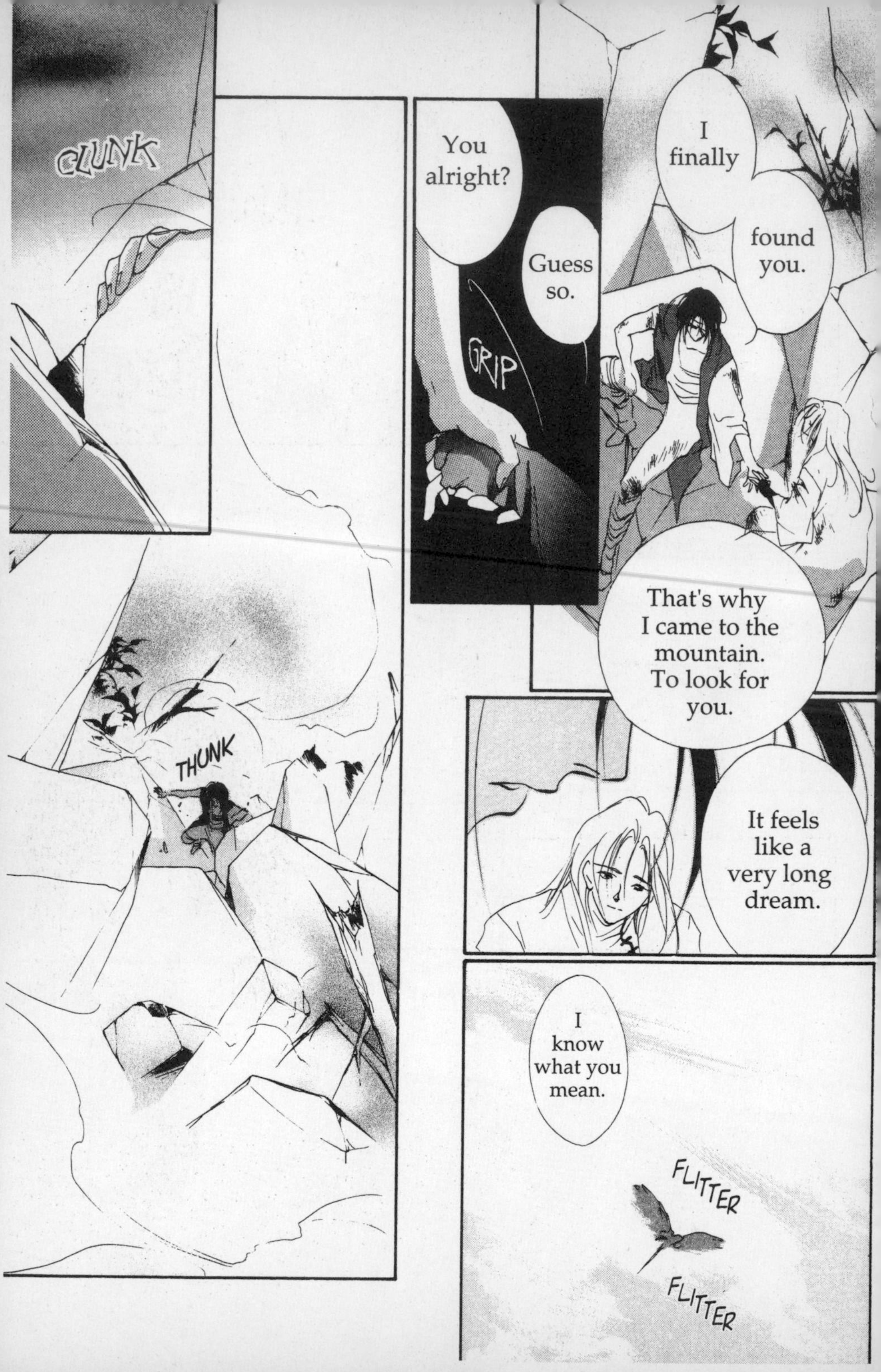
CLUNK
THUNK
You alright?
Guess so.
GRIP
I finally found you.
That's why I came to the mountain. To look for you.
It feels like a very long dream.
I know what you mean.
FLITTER
FLITTER

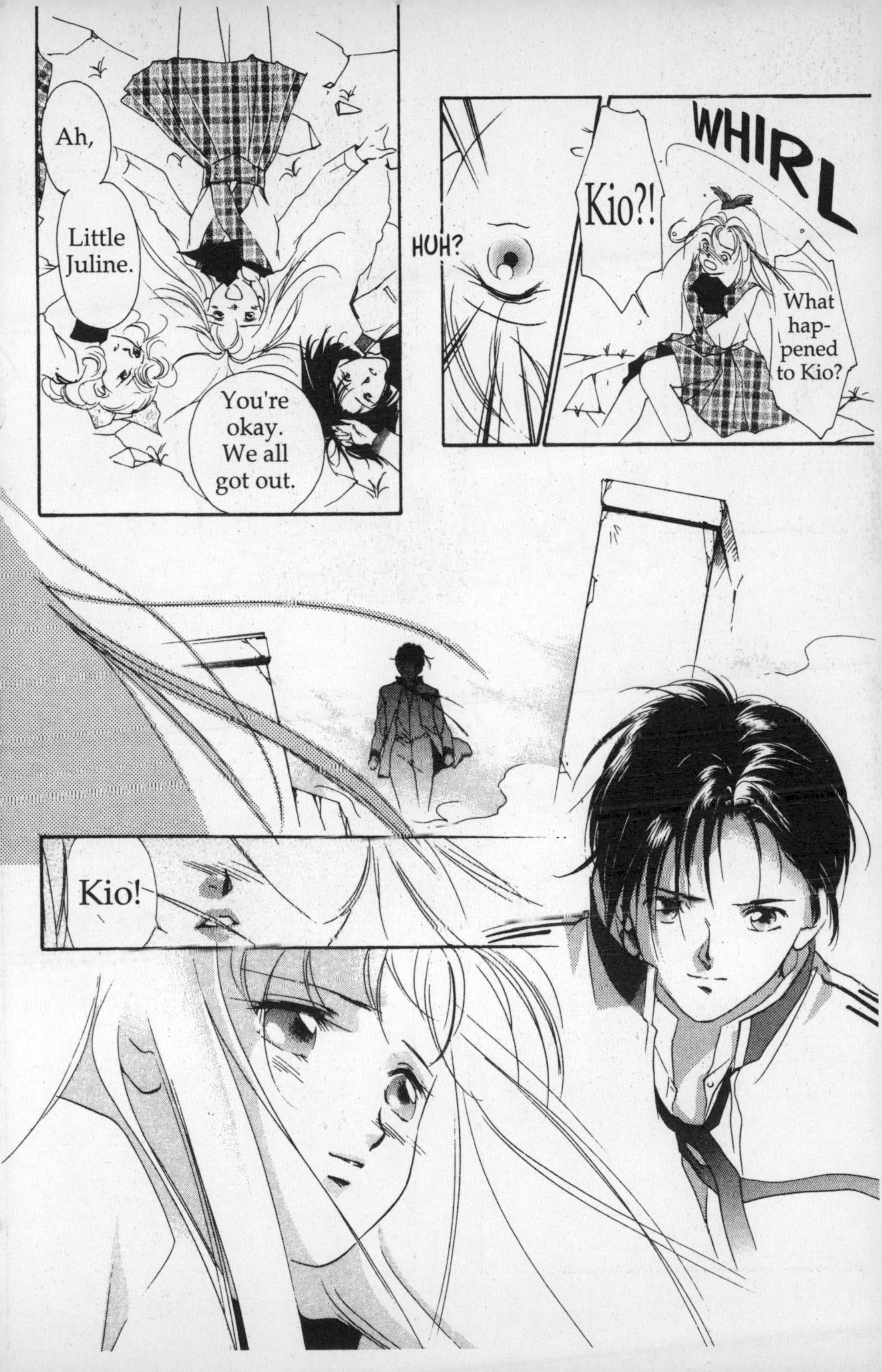
Ah,
Little Juline.
You're okay. We all got out.
HUH?
Kio?!
WHIRL
What hap-pened to Kio?
Kio!

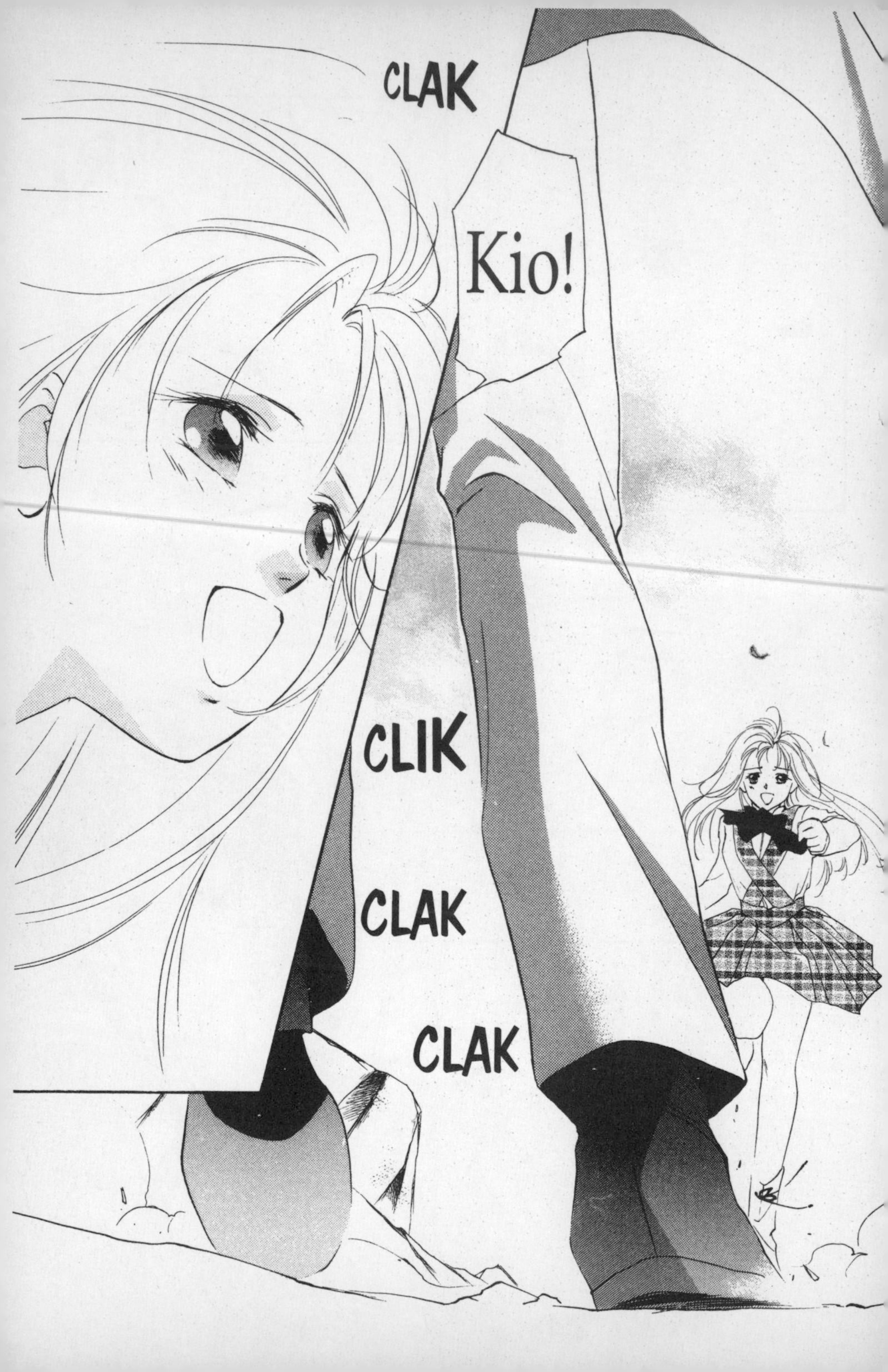
CLAK
Kio!
CLIK
CLAK
CLAK

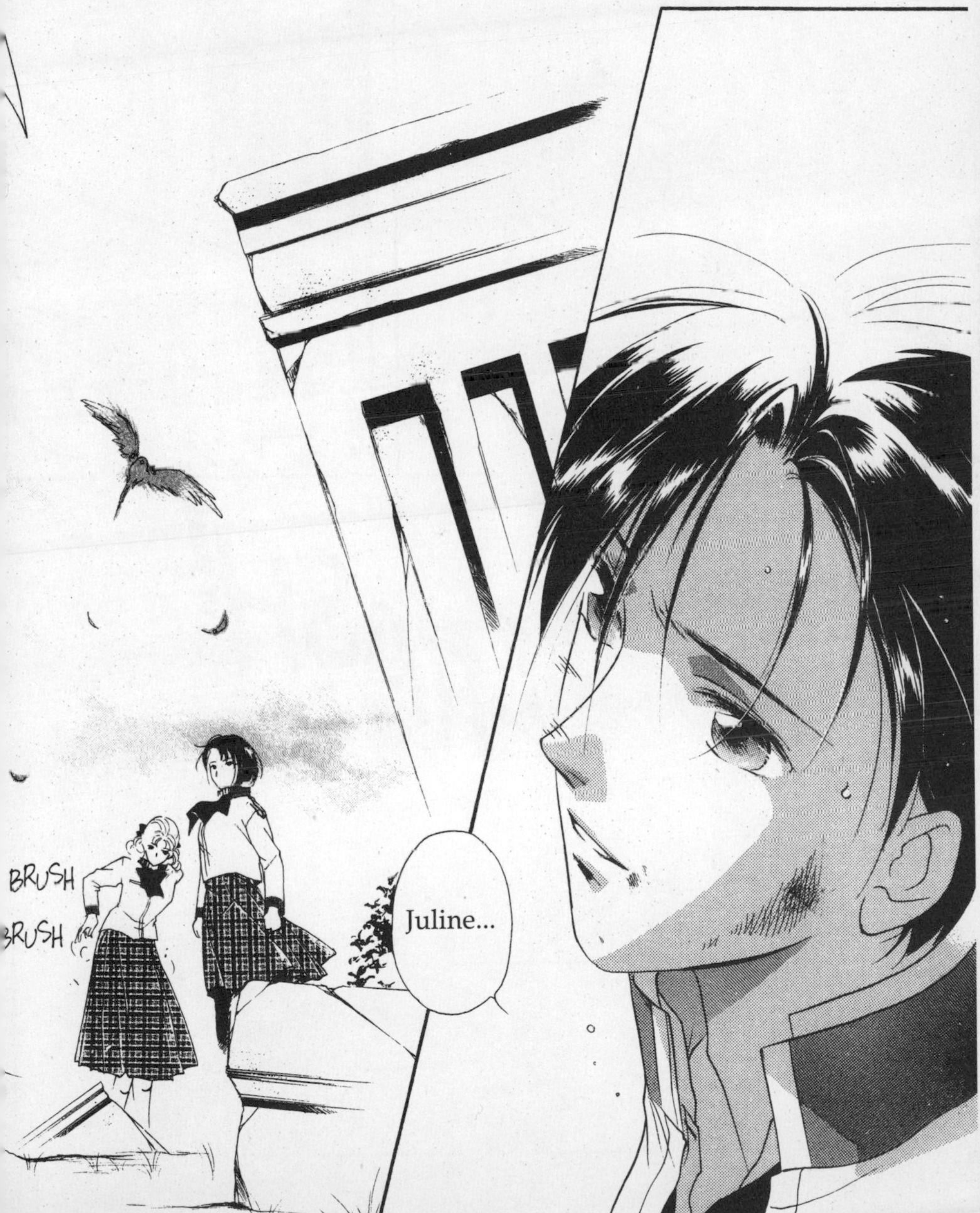
BRUSH
BRUSH
Juline...

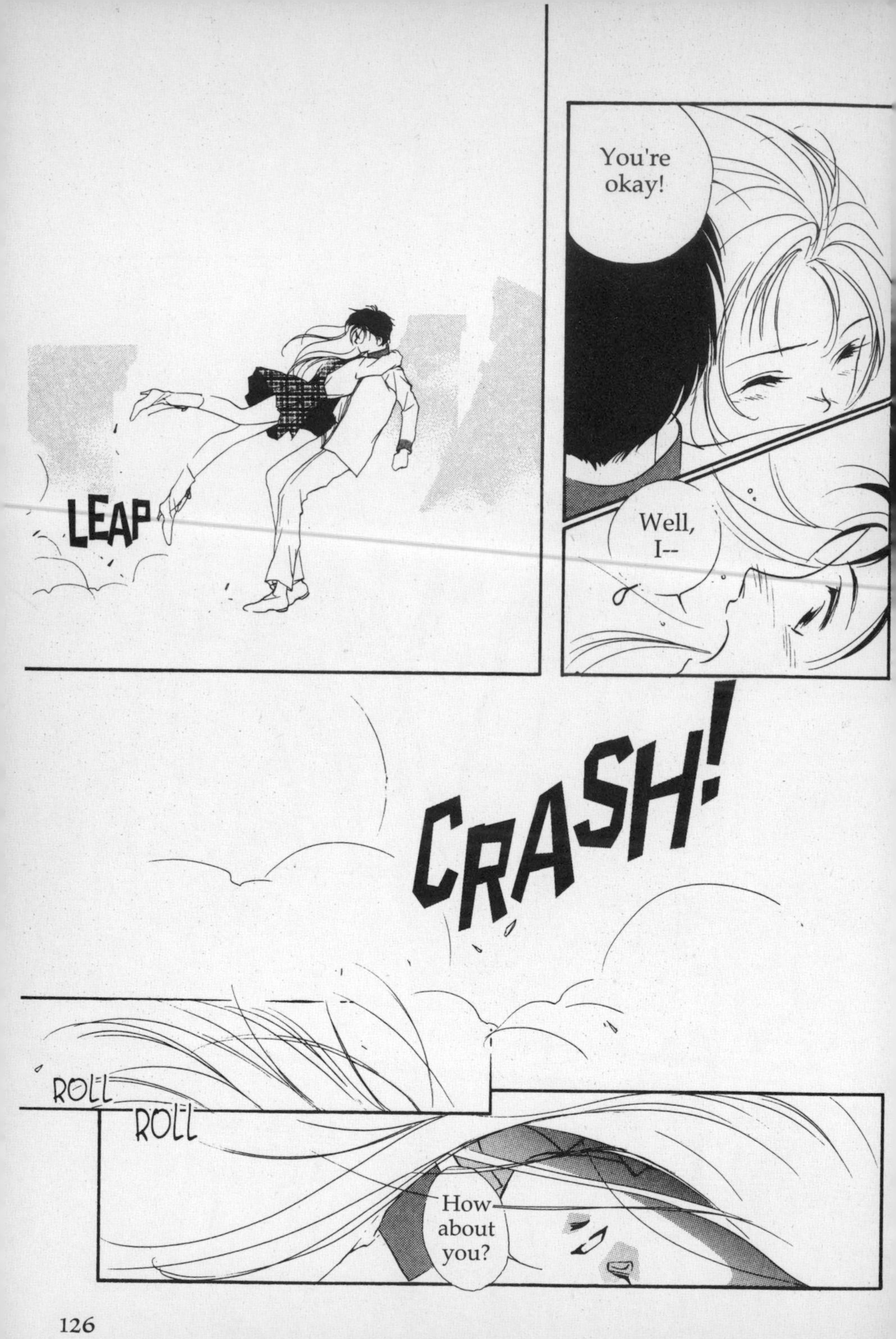
LEAP
You're okay!
Well, I--
CRASH!
ROLL ROLL
How about you?

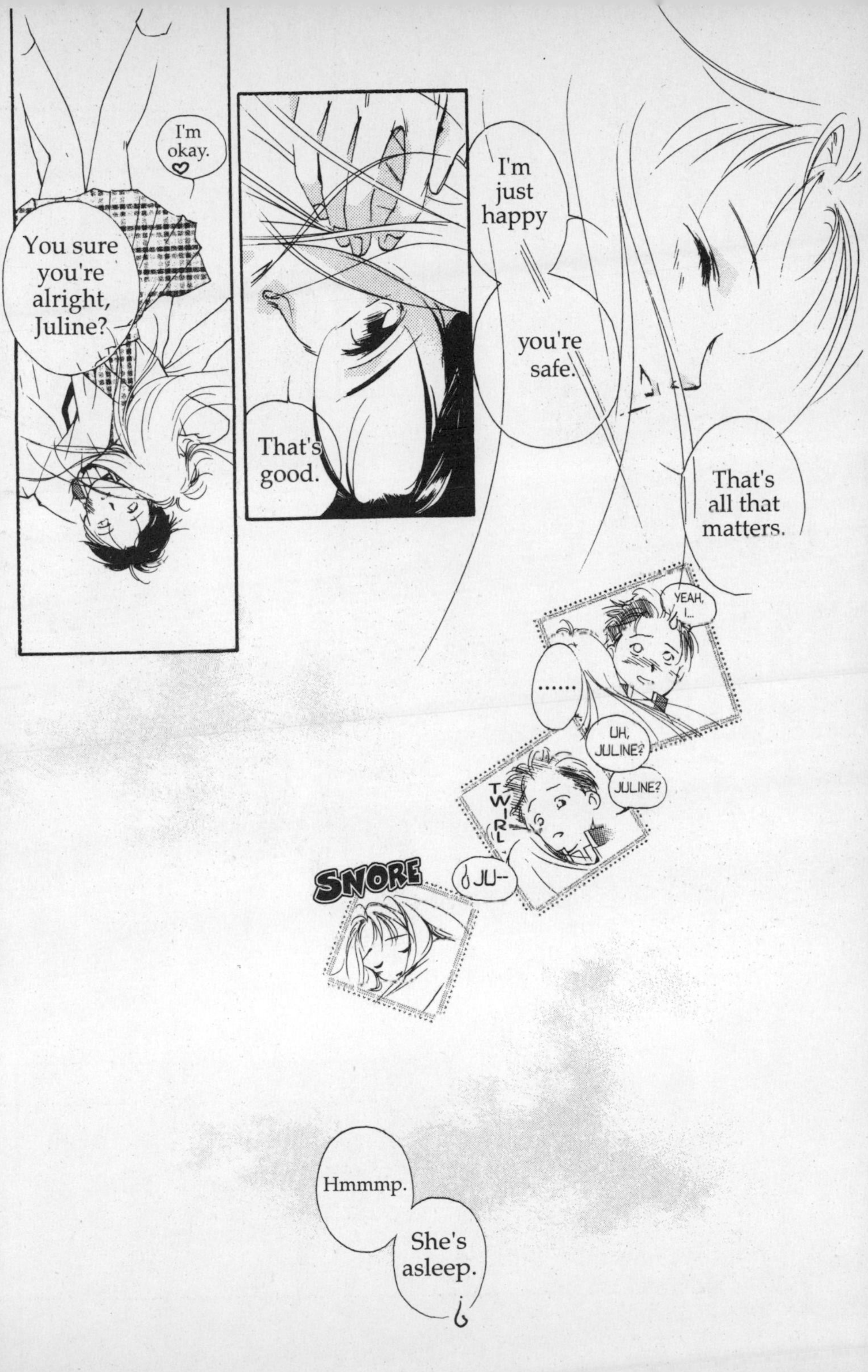
I'm okay.
You sure you're alright, Juline?
That's good.
I'm just happy
you're safe.
That's all that matters.
YEAH, I...
......
UH, JULINE?
JULINE?
TWIRL
JU--
SNORE
Hmmmp.
She's asleep.

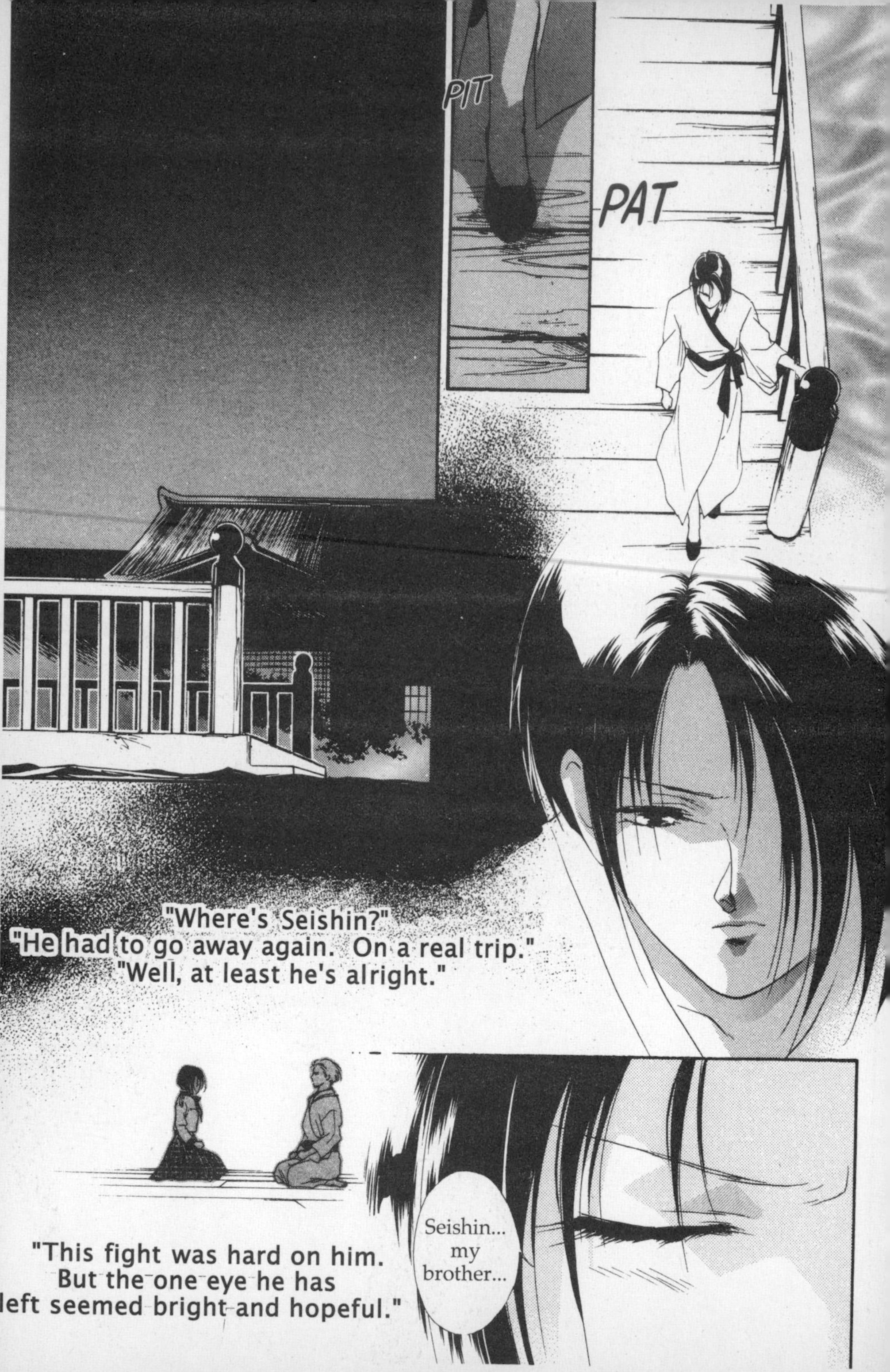
PIT
PAT
"Where's Seishin?"
"He had to go away again. On a real trip."
"Well, at least he's alright."
"This fight was hard on him. But the one eye he has left seemed bright and hopeful."
Seishin... my brother...

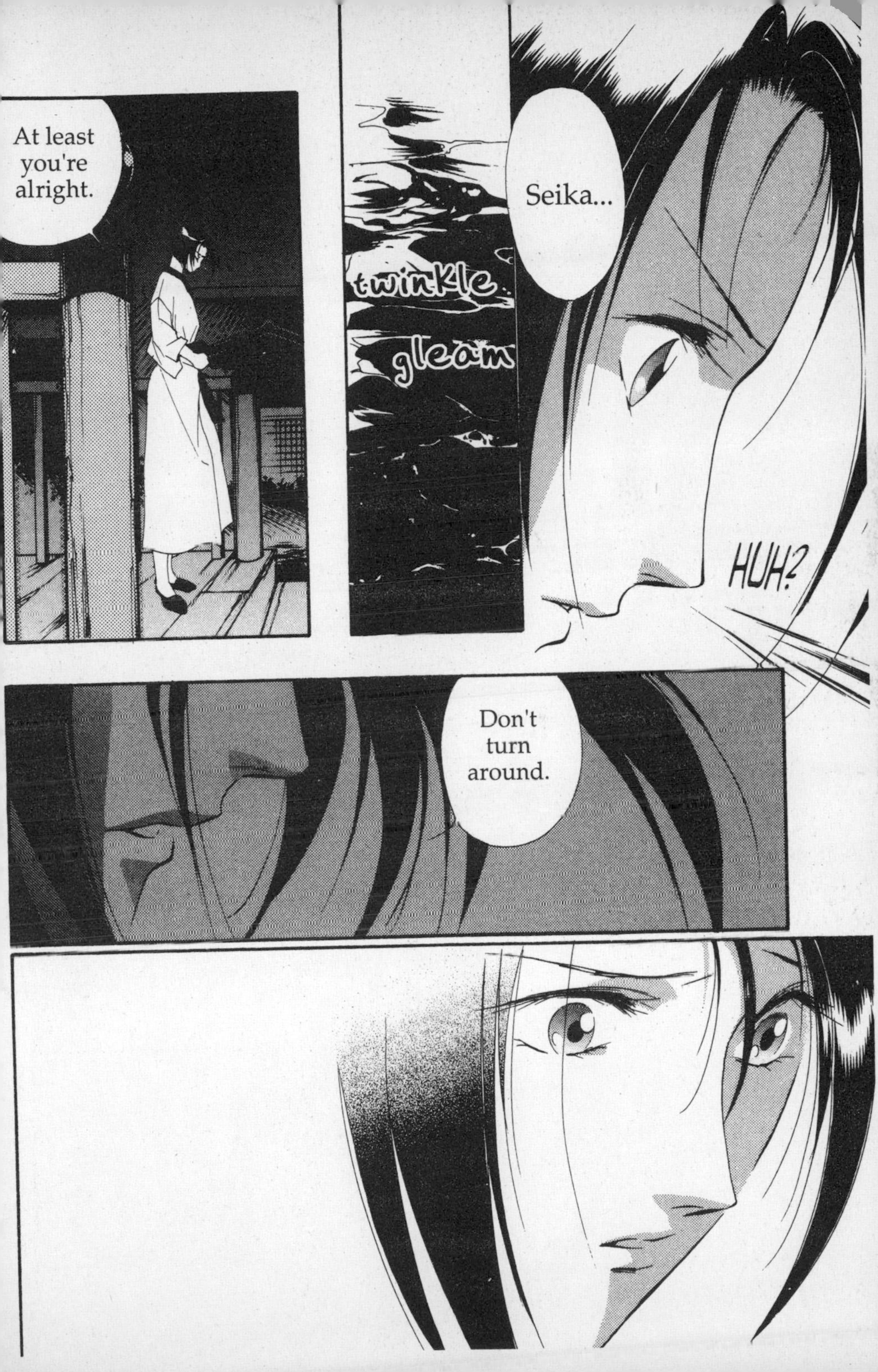
At least you're alright.
twinkle
gleam
Seika...
HUH?
Don't turn around.

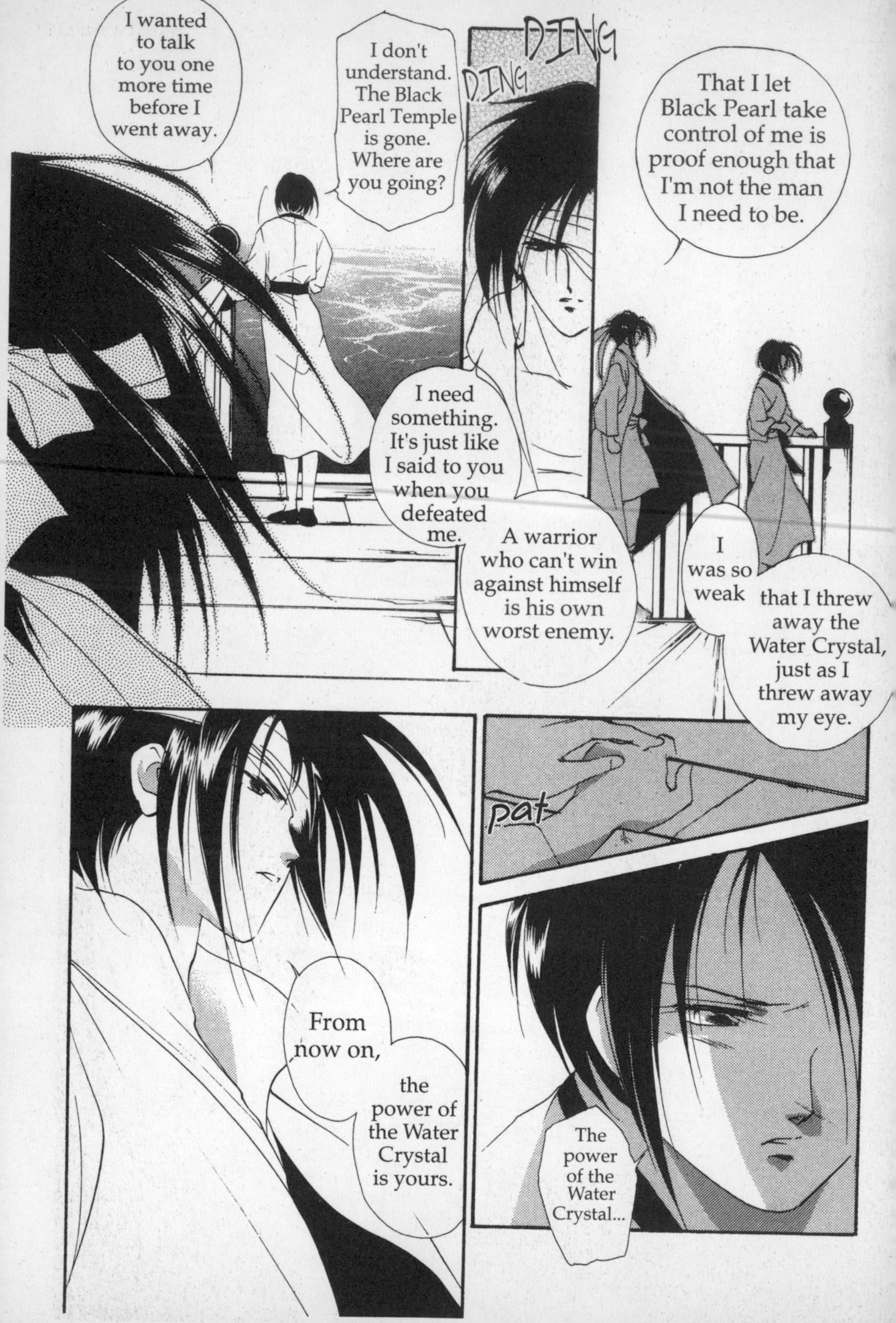
I wanted to talk to you one more time before I went away.
I don't understand. The Black Pearl Temple is gone. Where are you going?
DING DING
I need something. It's just like I said to you when you defeated me.
A warrior who can't win against himself is his own worst enemy.
That I let Black Pearl take control of me is proof enough that I'm not the man I need to be.
I was so weak
that I threw away the Water Crystal, just as I threw away my eye.
From now on,
the power of the Water Crystal is yours.
pat
The power of the Water Crystal...

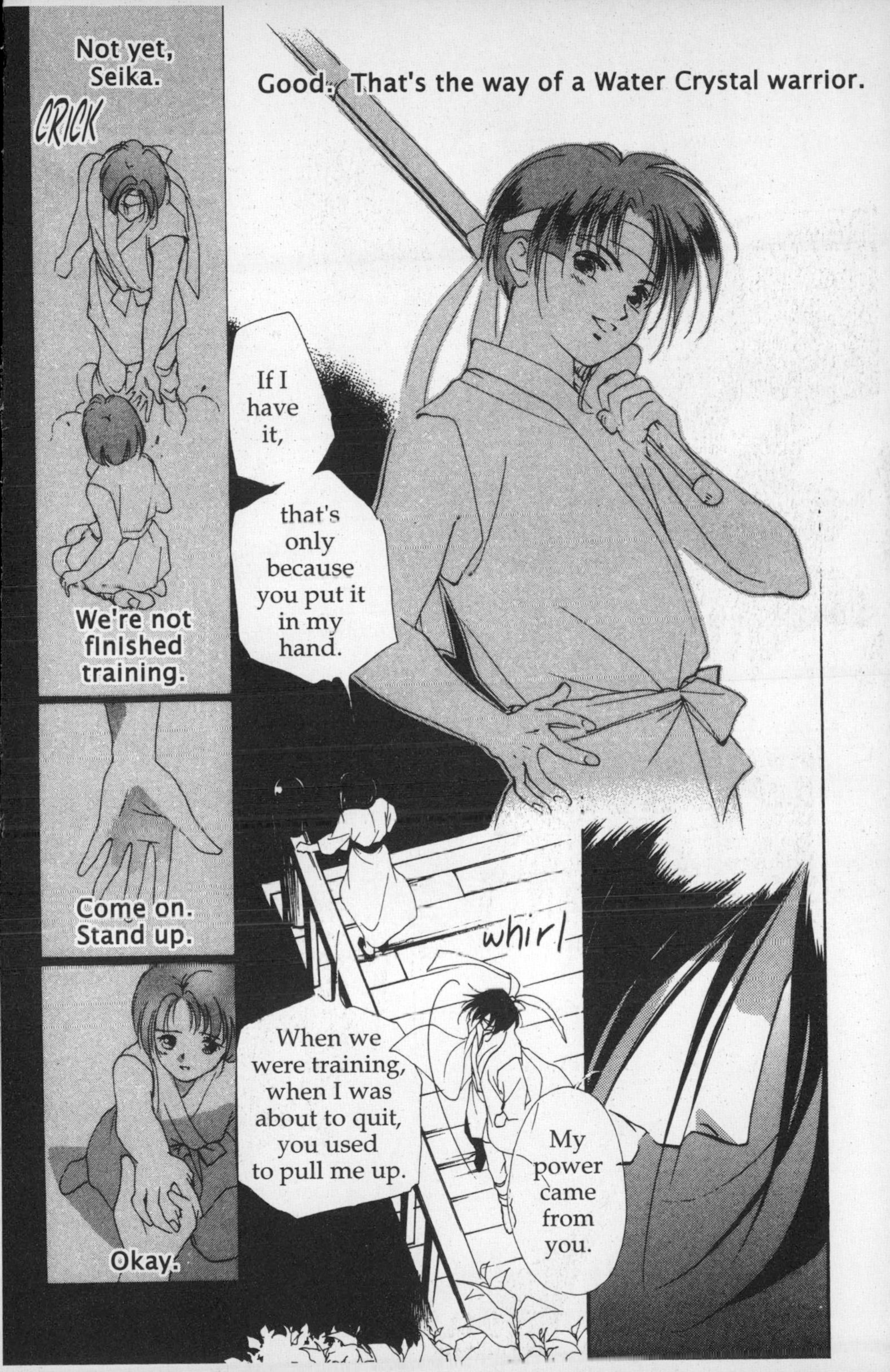
Not yet, Seika.
CRICK
We're not finished training.
Come on. Stand up.
Okay.
Good. That's the way of a Water Crystal warrior.
If I have it,
that's only because you put it in my hand.
whirl
When we were training, when I was about to quit, you used to pull me up.
My power came from you.

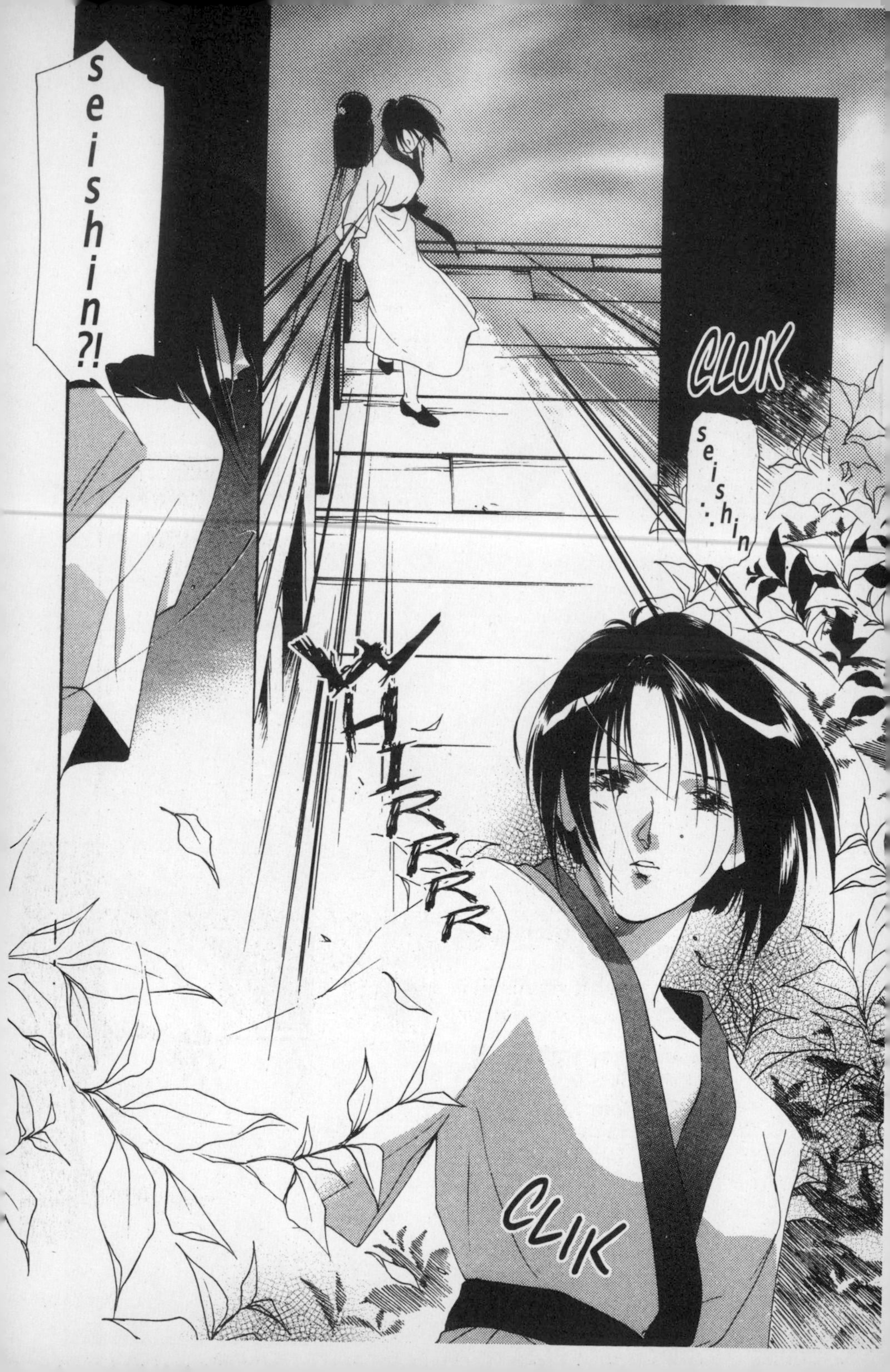
seishin?!
CLUK
seishin...
WHIRRRR
CLIK

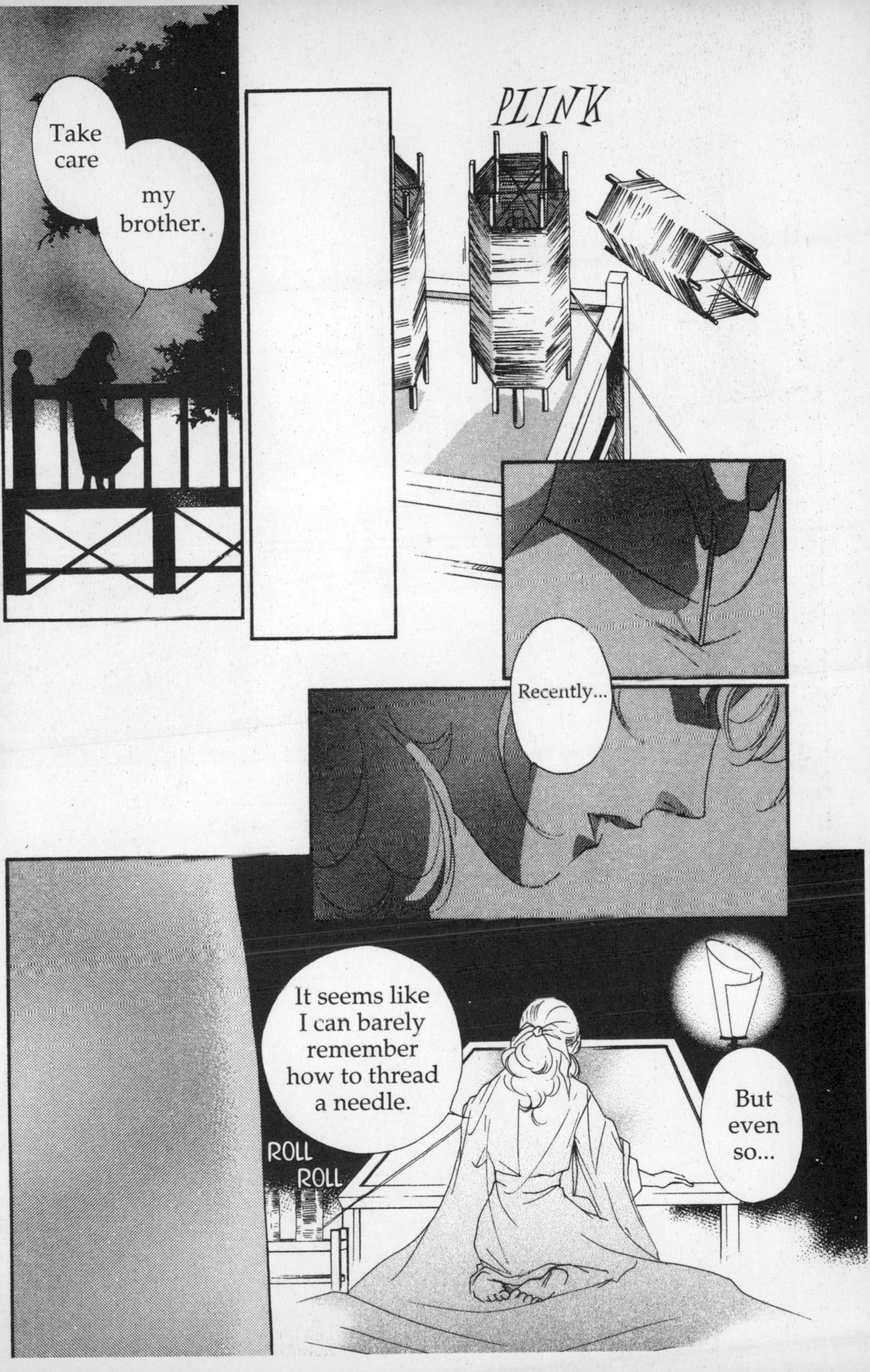
PLINK
Take care my brother.
Recently...
It seems like I can barely remember how to thread a needle.
But even so...
ROLL ROLL

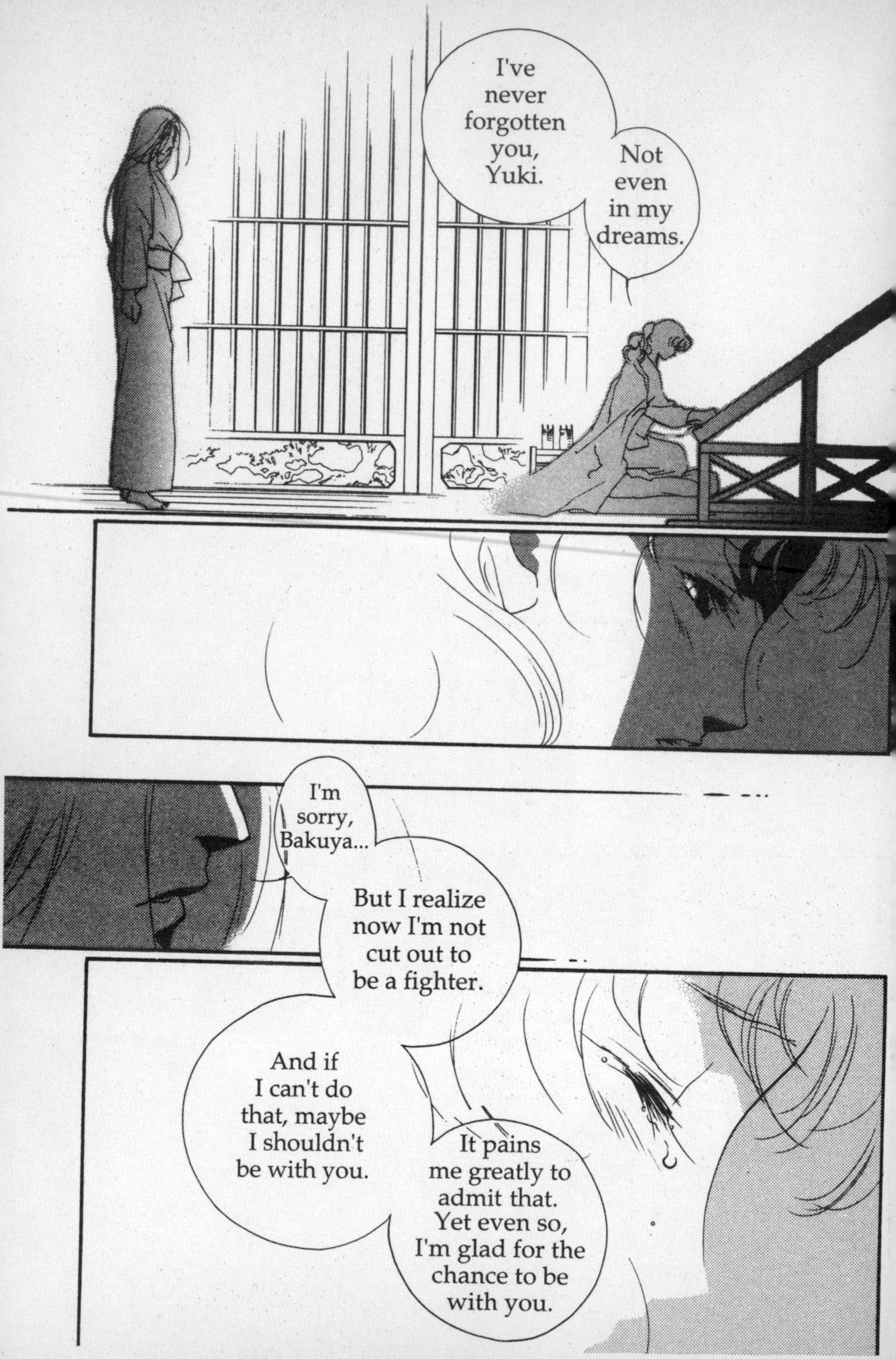
I've never forgotten you, Yuki.
Not even in my dreams.
I'm sorry, Bakuya...
But I realize now I'm not cut out to be a fighter.
And if I can't do that, maybe I shouldn't be with you.
It pains me greatly to admit that. Yet even so, I'm glad for the chance to be with you.

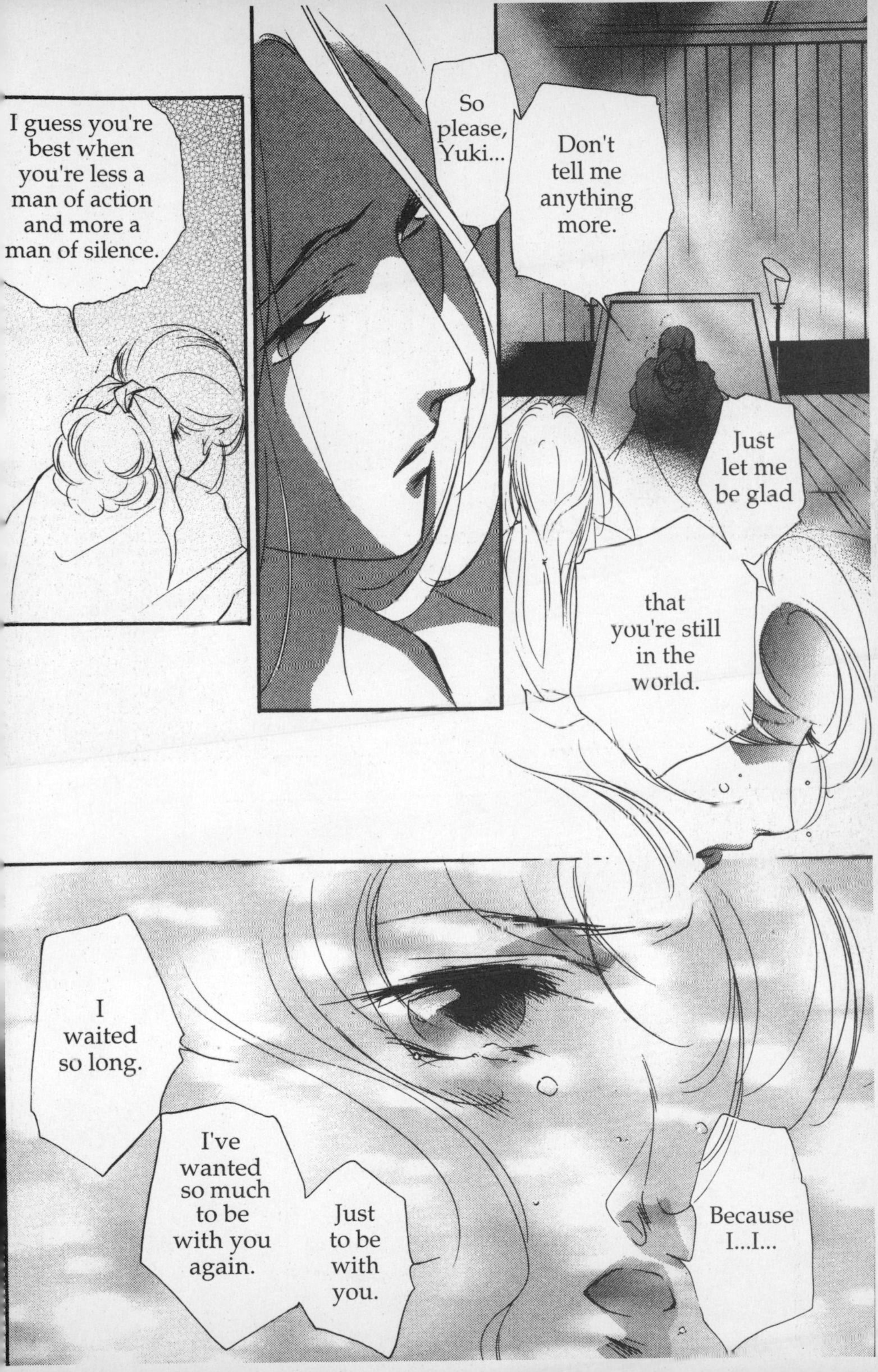
I guess you're best when you're less a man of action and more a man of silence.
So please, Yuki...
Don't tell me anything more.
Just let me be glad
that you're still in the world.
I waited so long.
I've wanted so much to be with you again.
Just to be with you.
Because I...I...

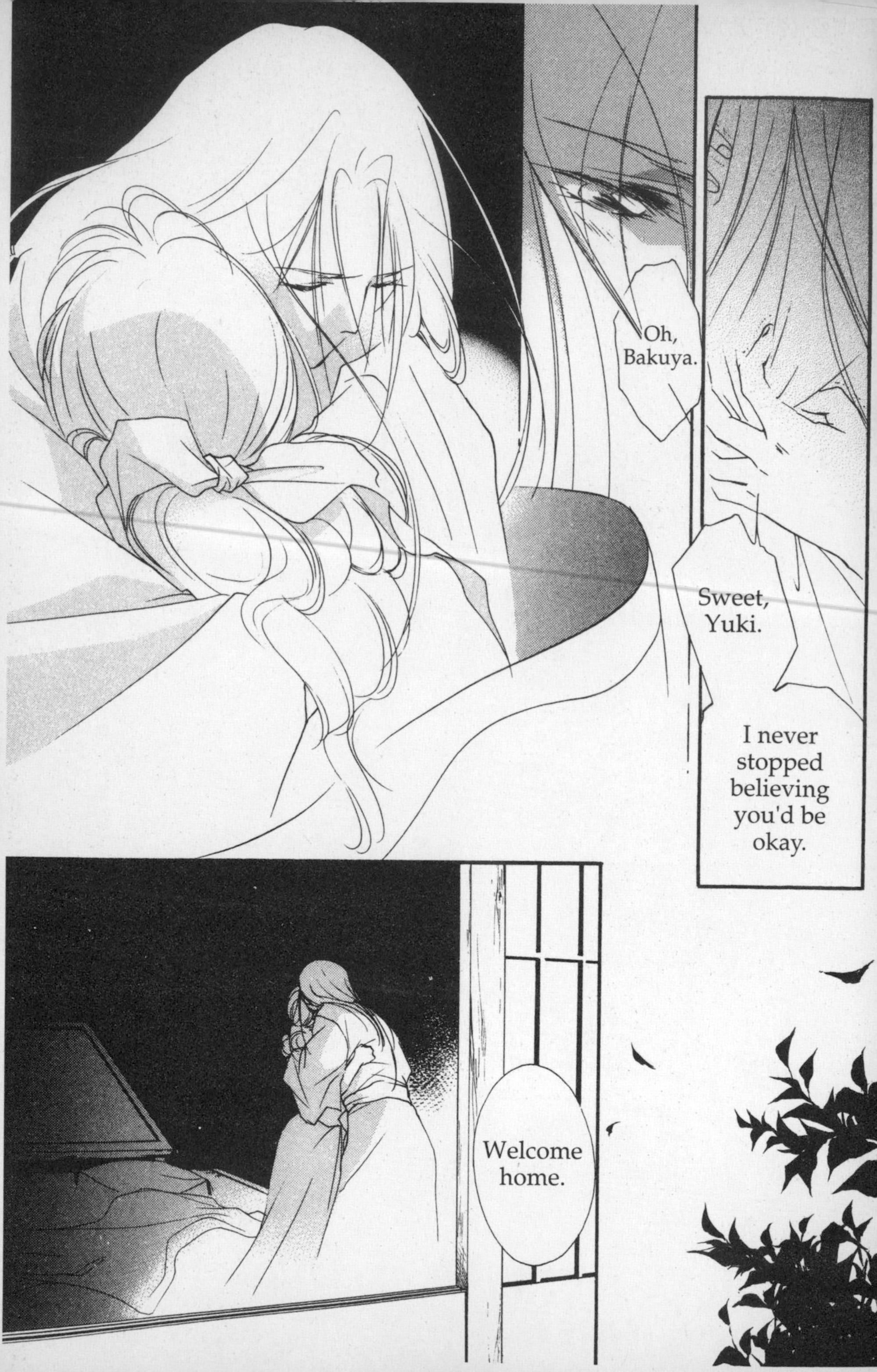
Oh, Bakuya.
Sweet, Yuki.
I never stopped believing you'd be okay.
Welcome home.

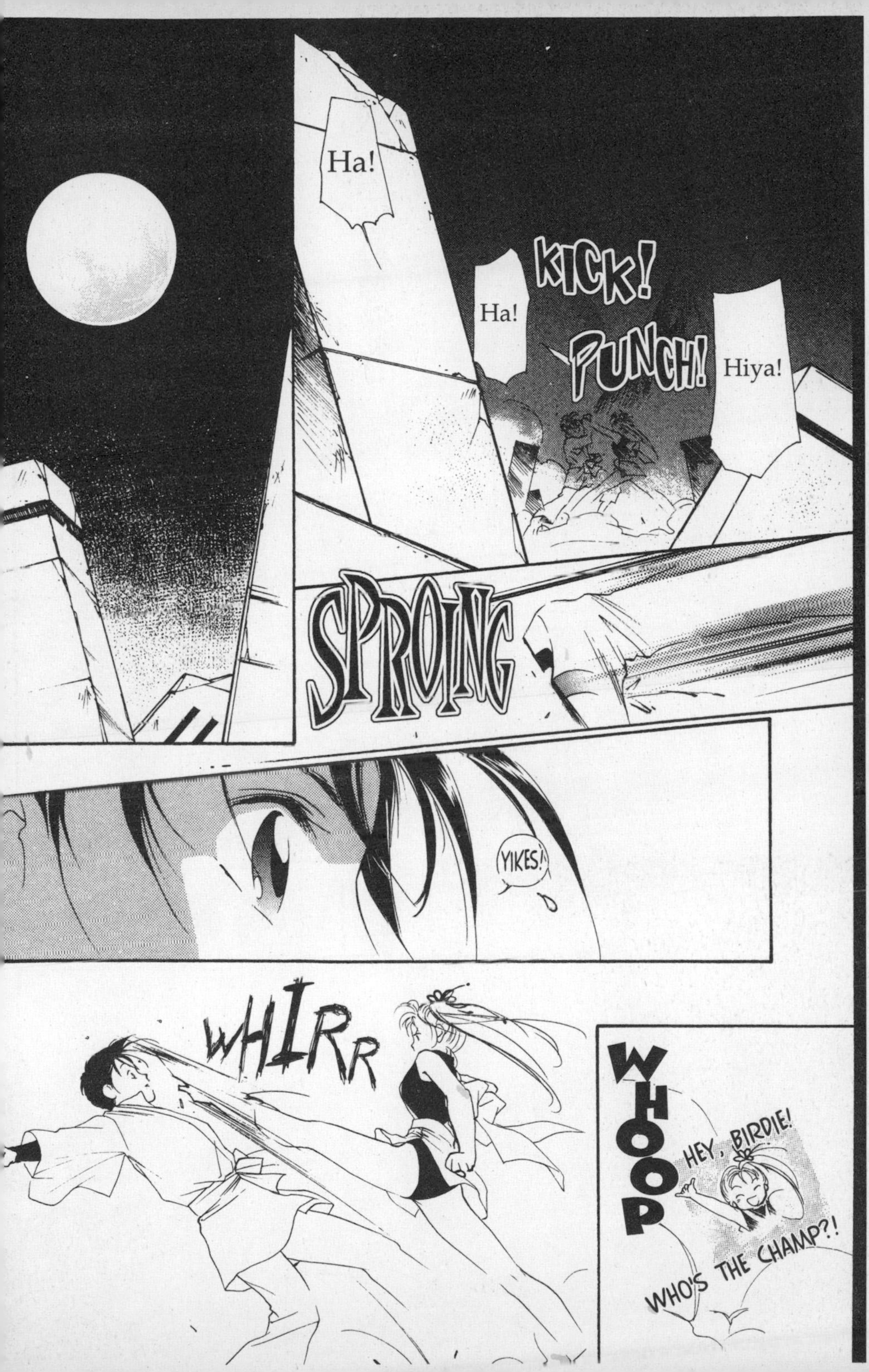
Ha!
Ha!
KICK!
PUNCH!
Hiya!
SPROING
YIKES!
WHIRR
WHOOP
HEY, BIRDIE!
WHO'S THE CHAMP?!

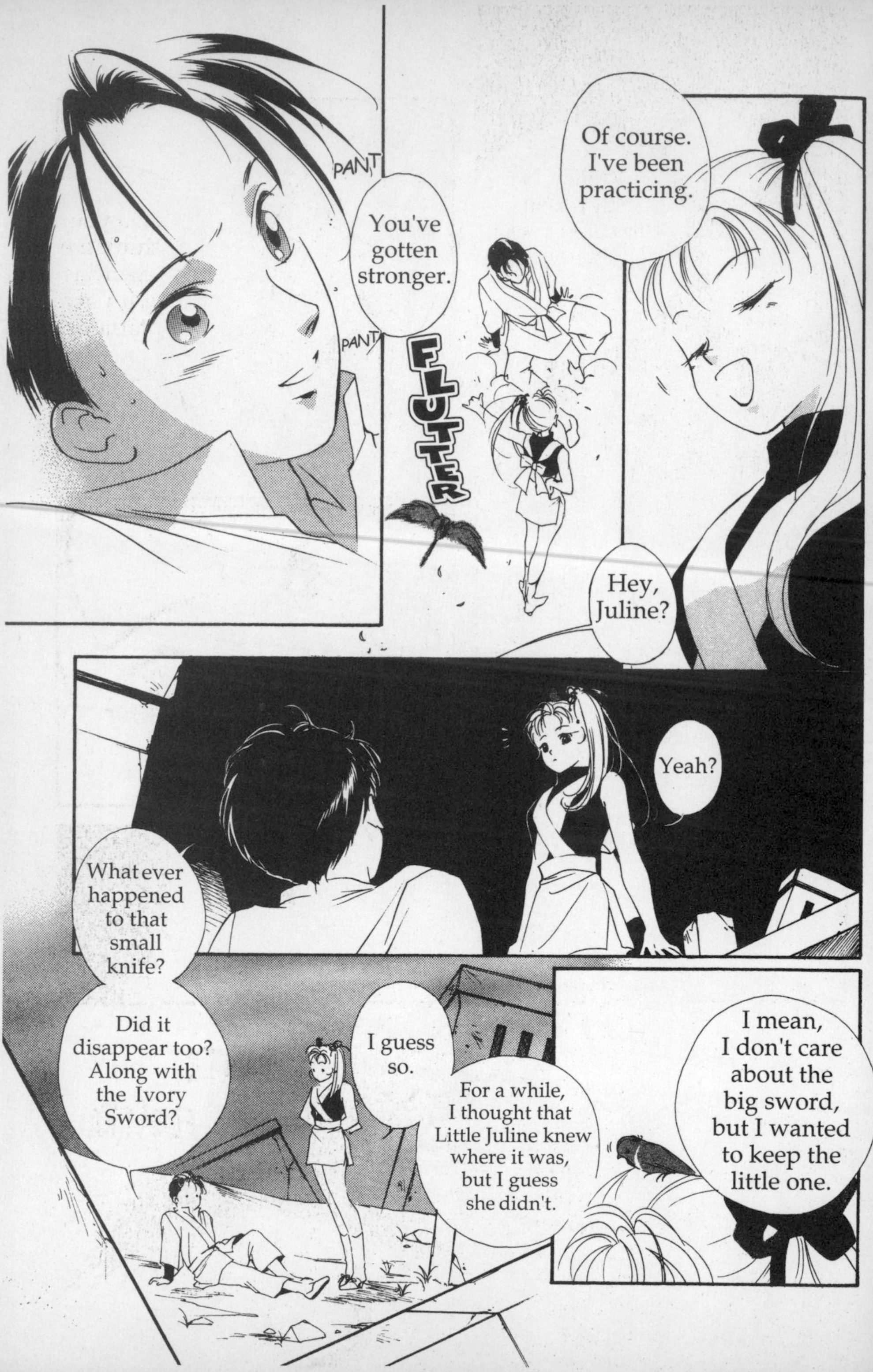
PANT
PANT
You've gotten stronger.
FLUTTER
Of course. I've been practicing.
Hey, Juline?
Yeah?
What ever happened to that small knife?
Did it disappear too? Along with the Ivory Sword?
I guess so.
For a while, I thought that Little Juline knew where it was, but I guess she didn't.
I mean, I don't care about the big sword, but I wanted to keep the little one.

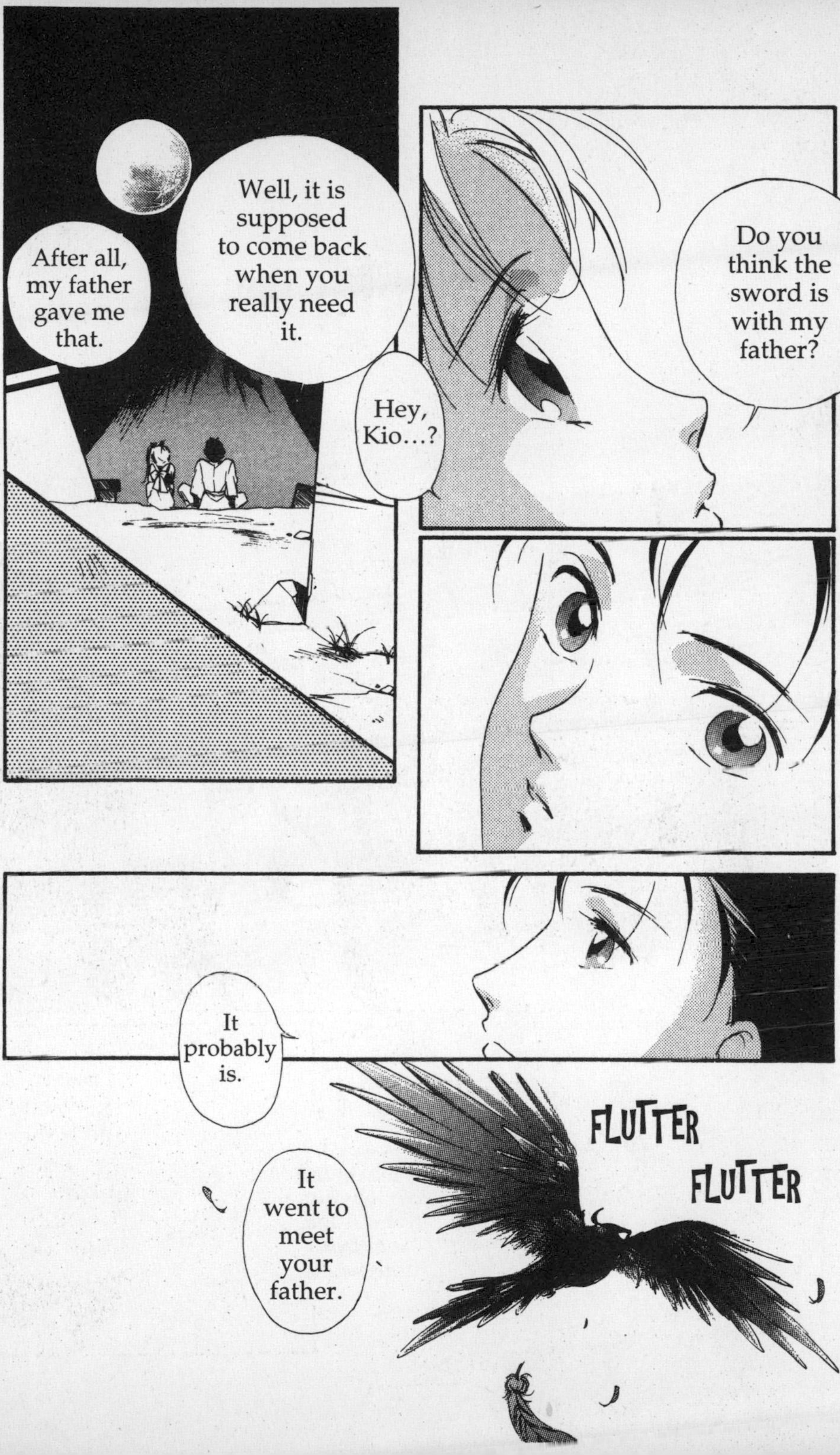
After all, my father gave me that.
Well, it is supposed to come back when you really need it.
Hey, Kio…?
Do you think the sword is with my father?
It probably is.
It went to meet your father.
FLUTTER
FLUTTER

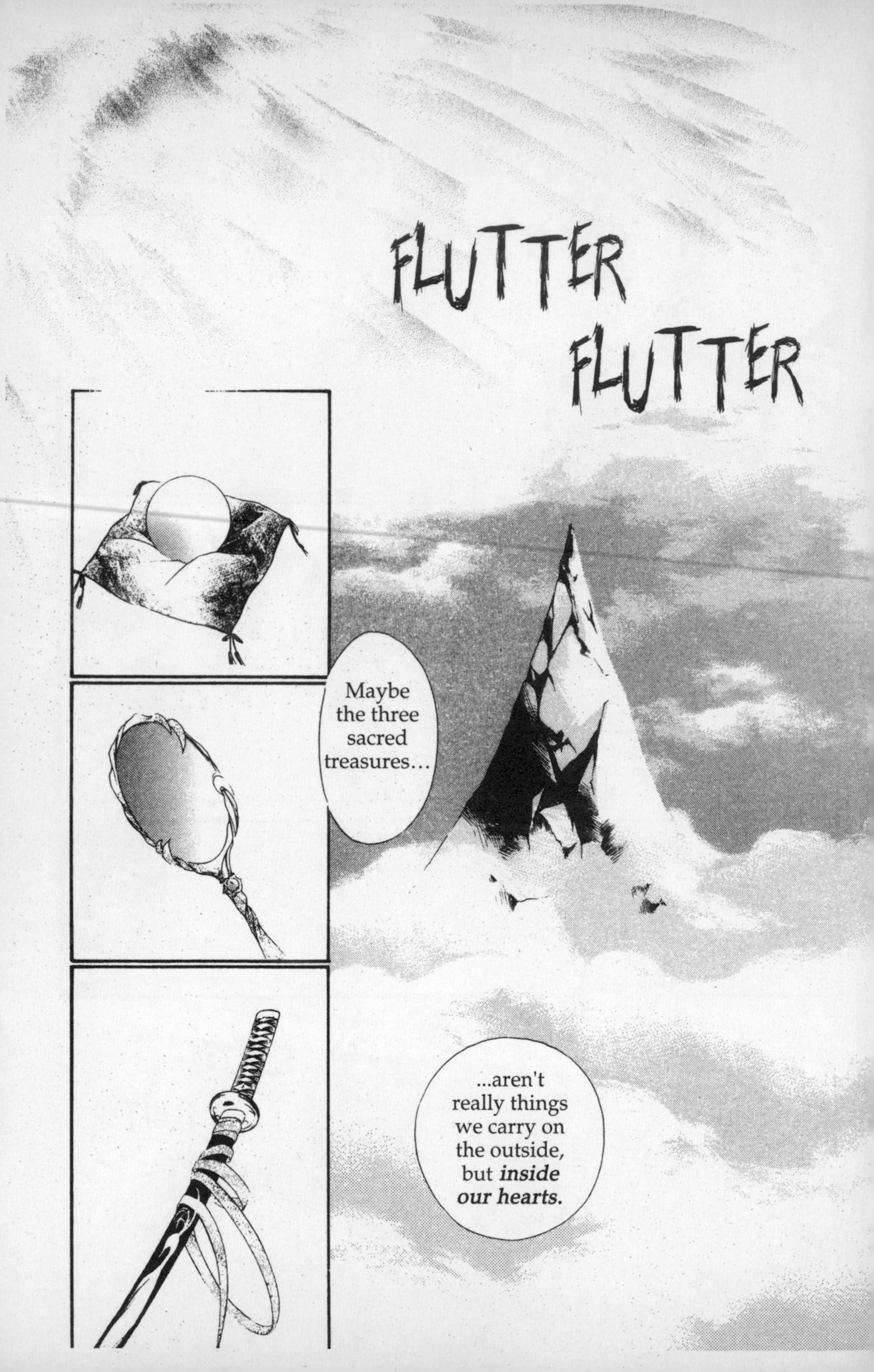

FLUTTER
FLUTTER

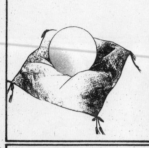

Maybe the three sacred treasures...

...aren't really things we carry on the outside, but *inside our hearts.*

Father, are you also with Ryoku, wherever you are?

I don't understand just what it is, but I feel like both of you have given me something very important.

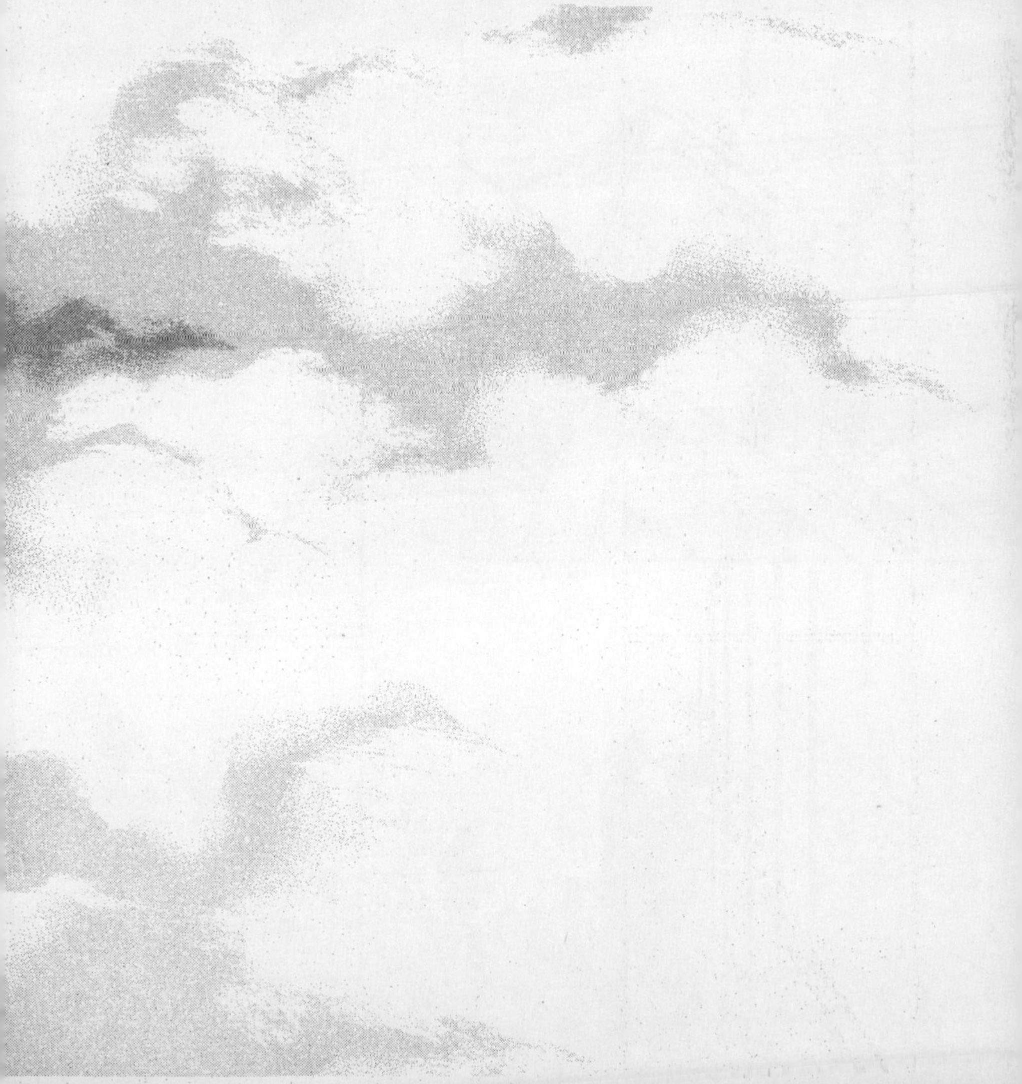

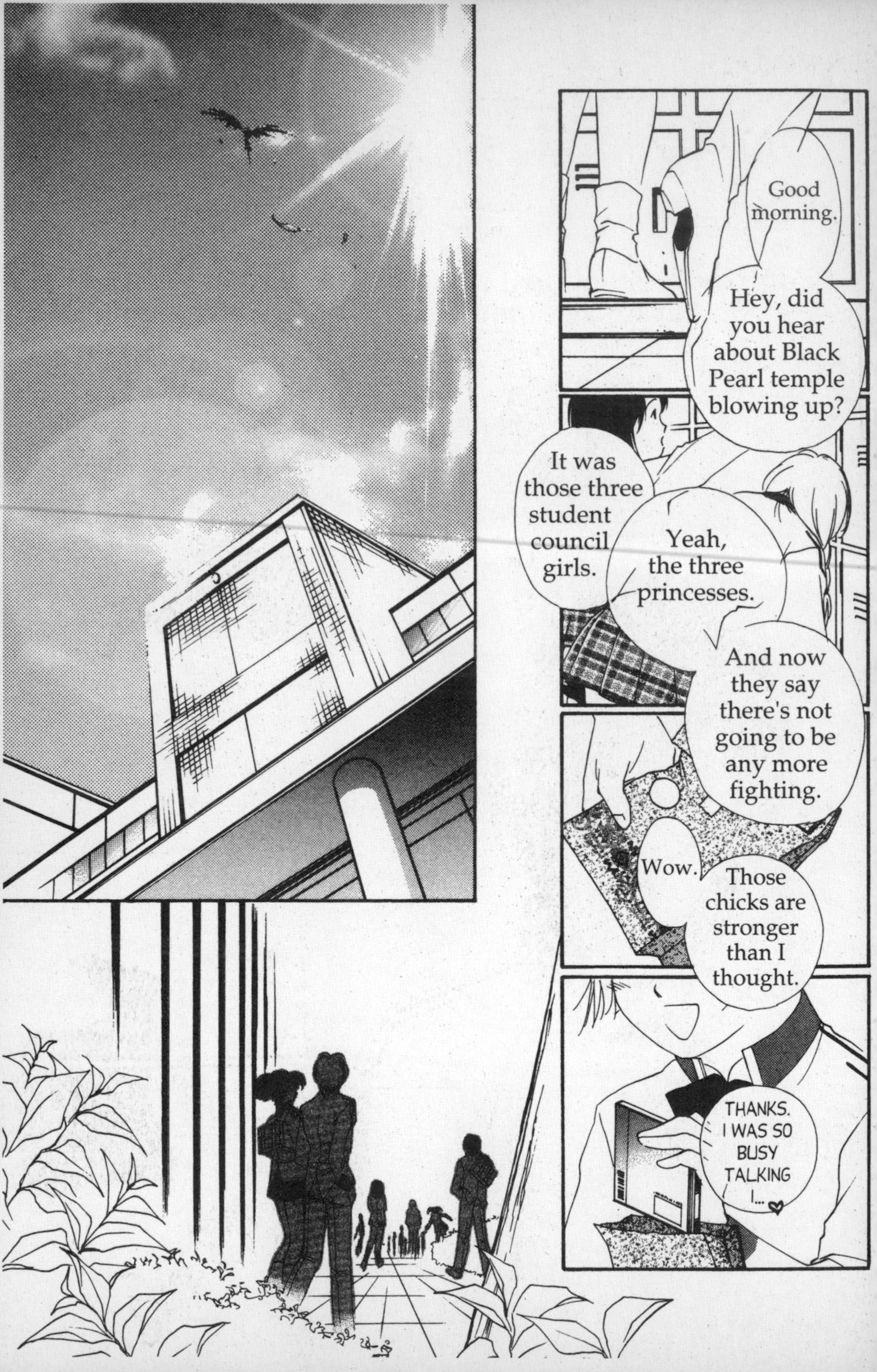
Good morning.
Hey, did you hear about Black Pearl temple blowing up?
It was those three student council girls.
Yeah, the three princesses.
And now they say there's not going to be any more fighting.
Wow.
Those chicks are stronger than I thought.
THANKS. I WAS SO BUSY TALKING I...♡

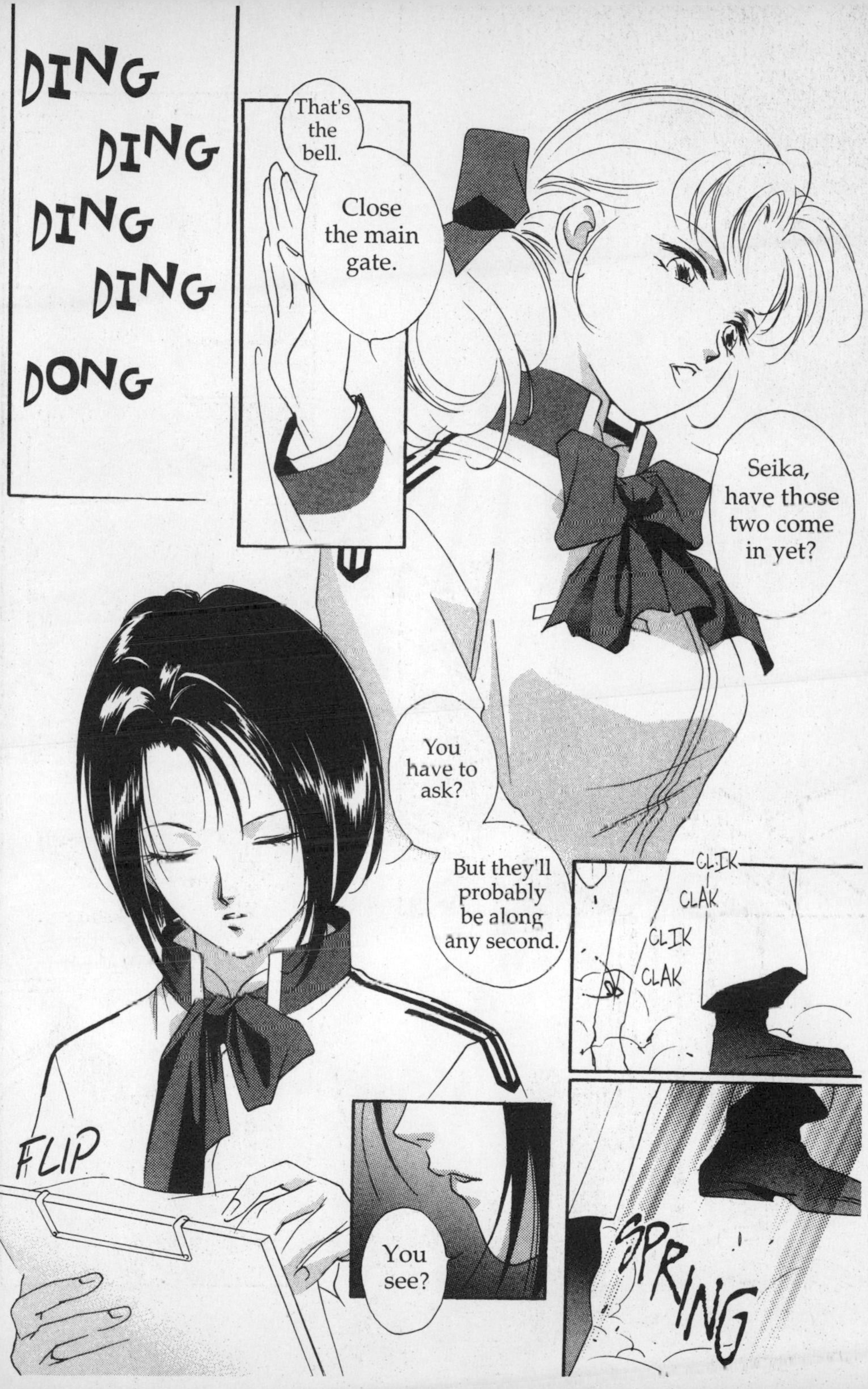
DING DING DING DING DONG
That's the bell.
Close the main gate.
Seika, have those two come in yet?
You have to ask?
But they'll probably be along any second.
CLIK CLAK CLIK CLAK
FLIP
You see?
SPRING

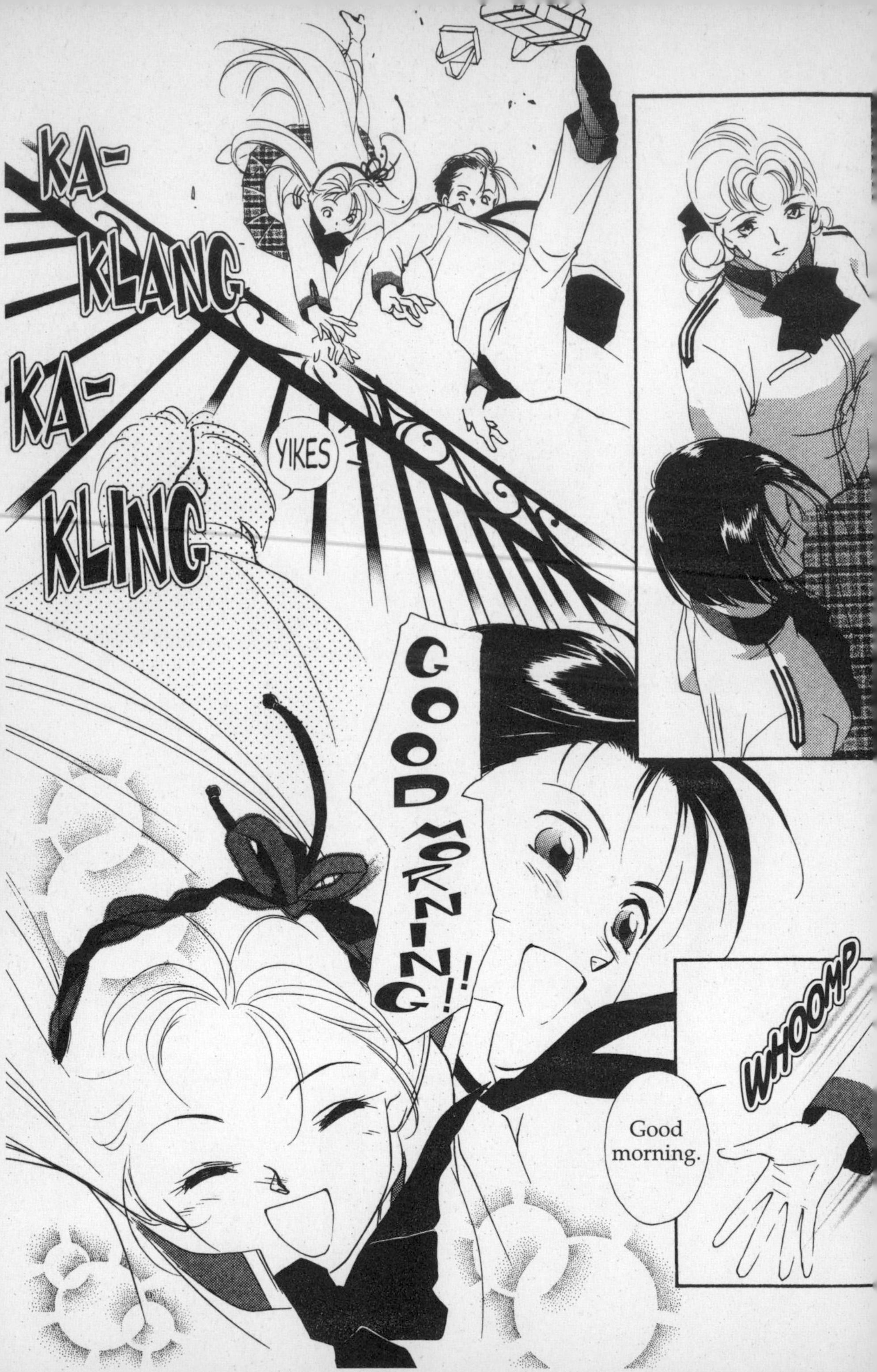
KA-KLANG
KA-KLING
YIKES
GOOD MORNING!!
WHOOMP
Good morning.

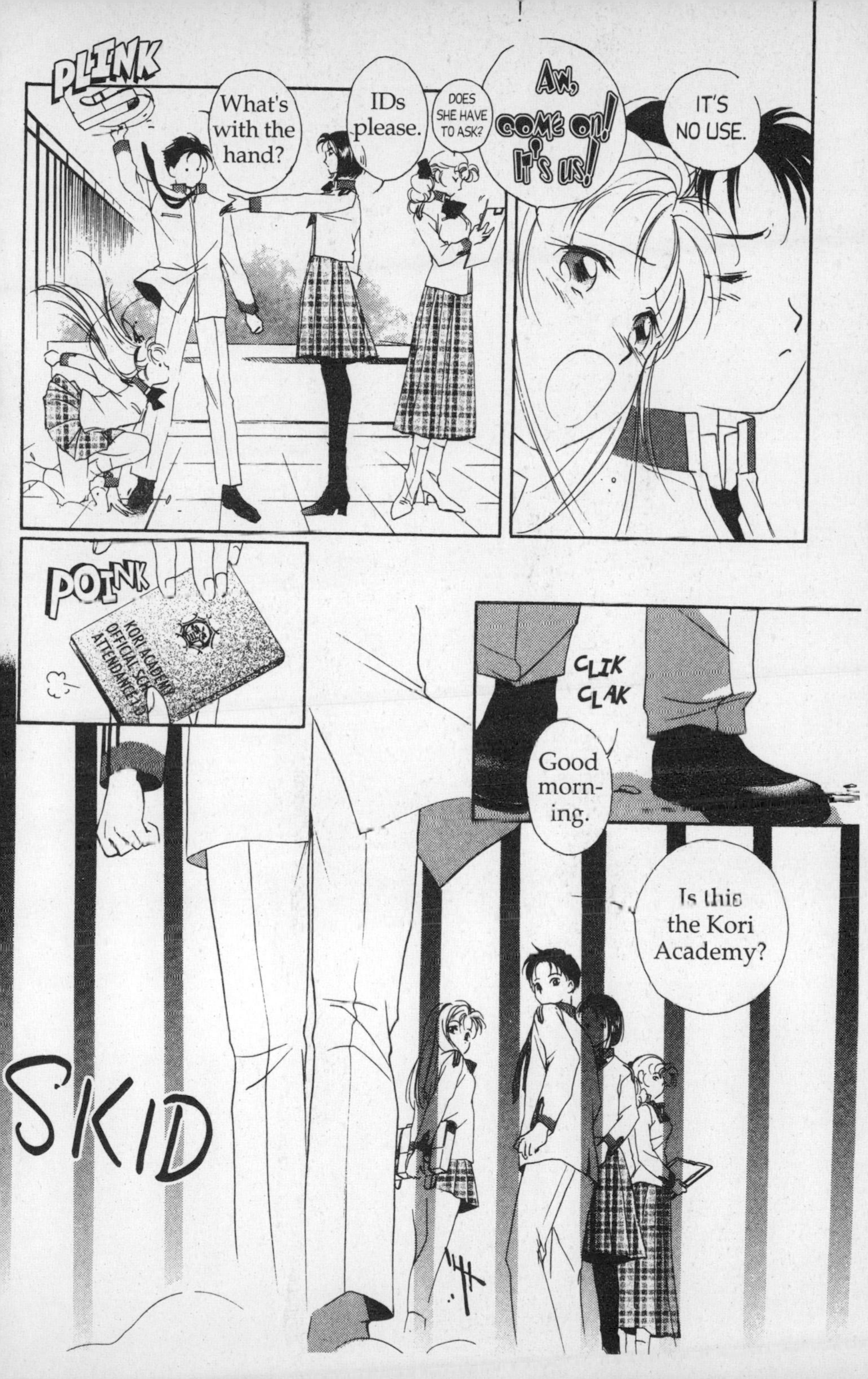
PLINK
What's with the hand?
IDs please.
DOES SHE HAVE TO ASK?
Aw, come on! It's us!
IT'S NO USE.
POINK
KORI ACADEMY
OFFICIAL
CLIK CLAK
Good morning.
SKID
Is this the Kori Academy?

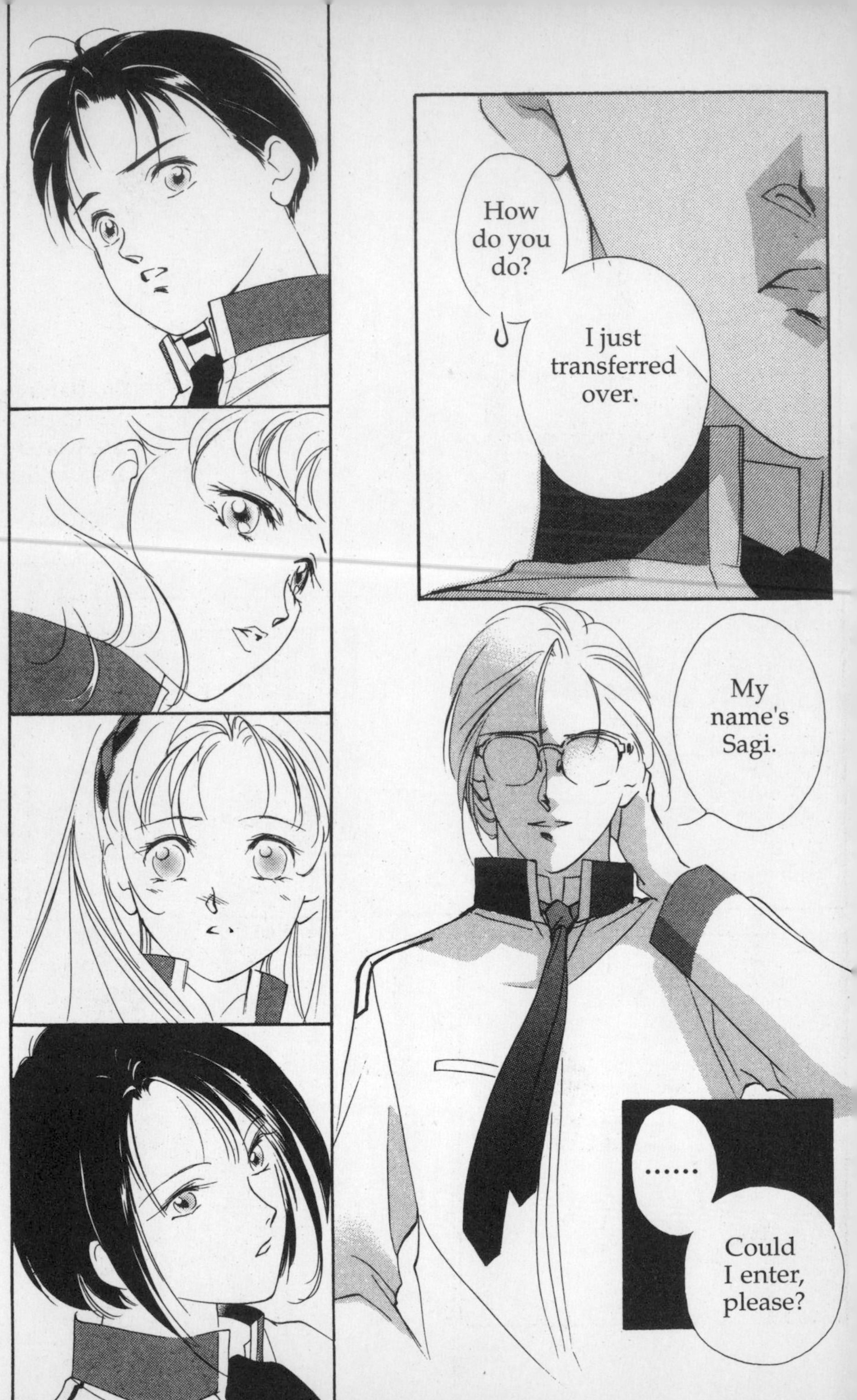
How do you do?
I just transferred over.
My name's Sagi.
......
Could I enter, please?

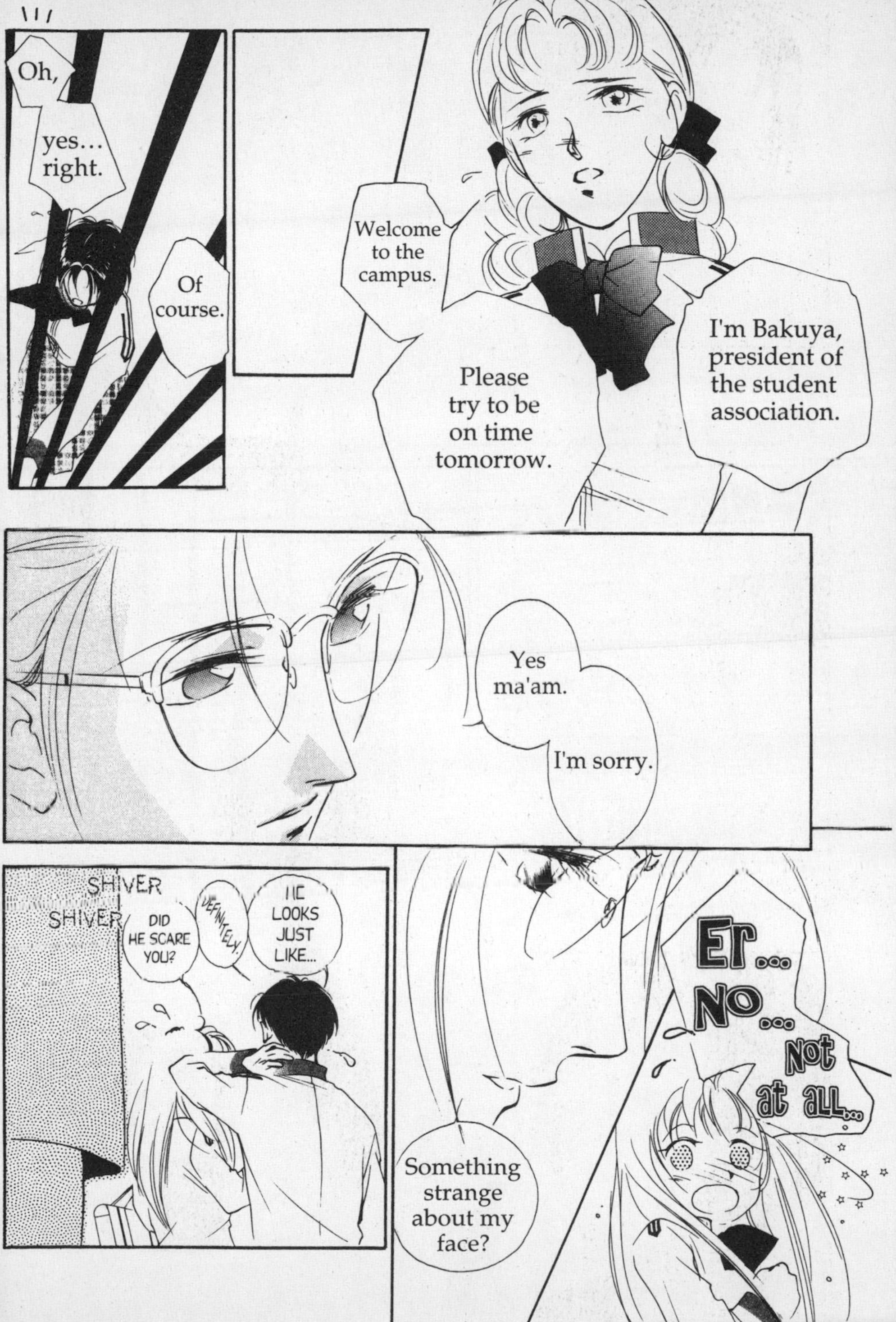
Oh,
yes... right.
Of course.
Welcome to the campus.
I'm Bakuya, president of the student association.
Please try to be on time tomorrow.
Yes ma'am.
I'm sorry.
SHIVER SHIVER
DID HE SCARE YOU?
DEFINITELY.
HE LOOKS JUST LIKE...
Something strange about my face?
Er... No... Not at all...

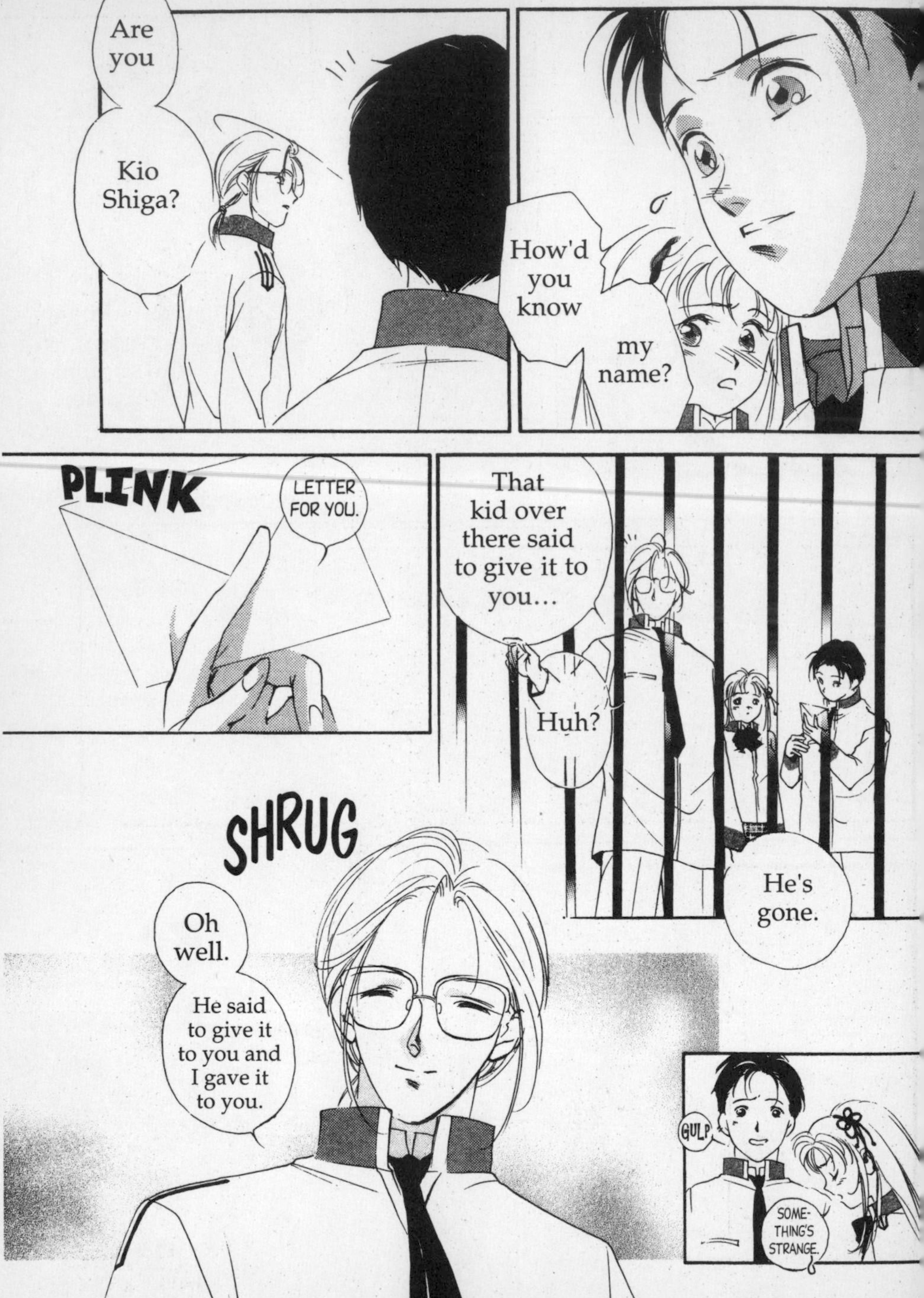
Are you
Kio Shiga?
How'd you know
my name?
PLINK
LETTER FOR YOU.
That kid over there said to give it to you...
Huh?
He's gone.
SHRUG
Oh well.
He said to give it to you and I gave it to you.
GULP
SOME-THING'S STRANGE.

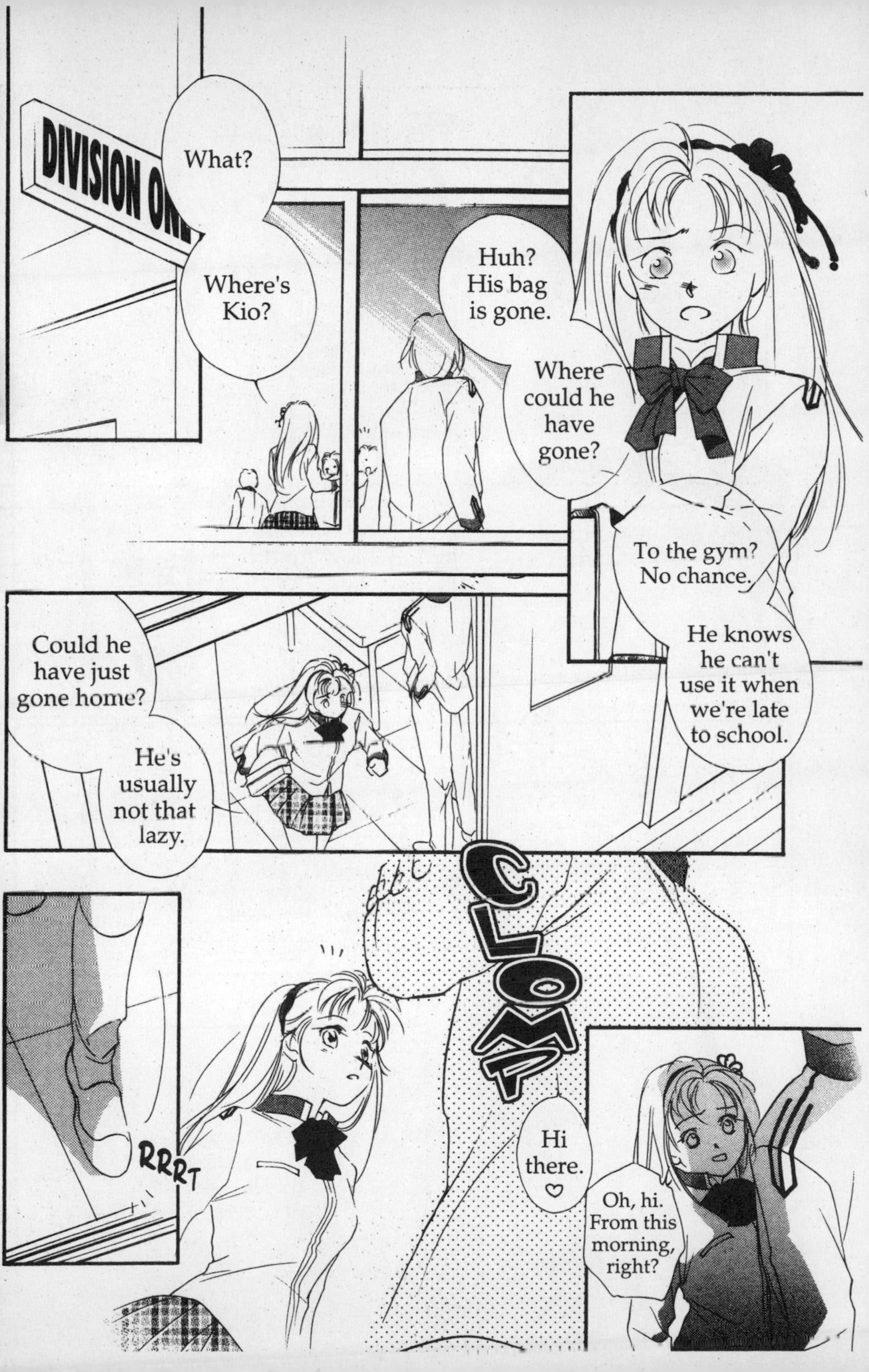
DIVISION ONE
What?
Where's Kio?
Huh? His bag is gone.
Where could he have gone?
To the gym? No chance.
He knows he can't use it when we're late to school.
Could he have just gone home?
He's usually not that lazy.
RRRT
CLOMP
Hi there. ♡
Oh, hi. From this morning, right?

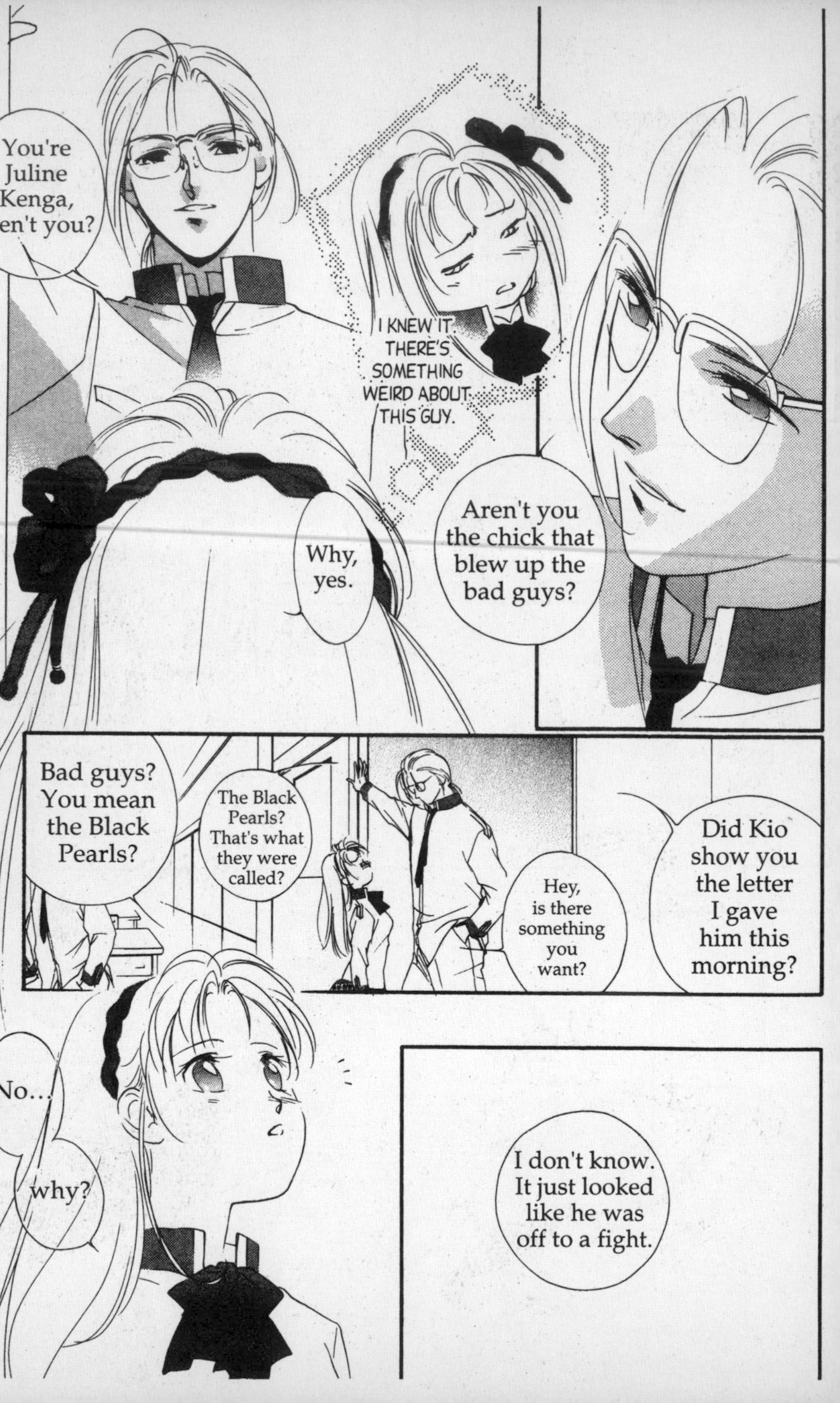

You're Juline Kenga, aren't you?
I KNEW IT. THERE'S SOMETHING WEIRD ABOUT THIS GUY.
Why, yes.
Aren't you the chick that blew up the bad guys?
Bad guys? You mean the Black Pearls?
The Black Pearls? That's what they were called?
Hey, is there something you want?
Did Kio show you the letter I gave him this morning?
No...
why?
I don't know. It just looked like he was off to a fight.

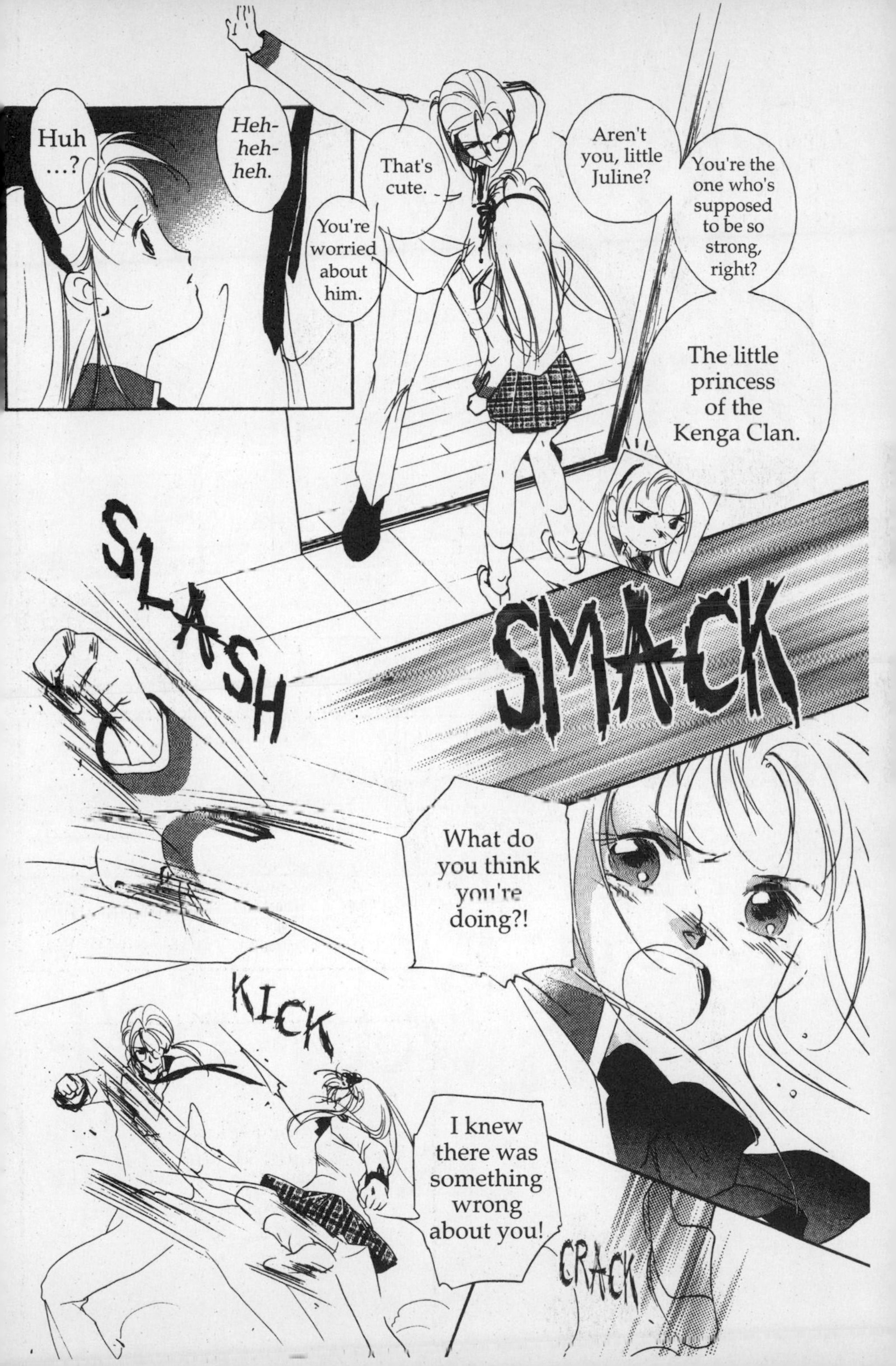
Huh ...?
Heh-heh-heh.
That's cute.
You're worried about him.
Aren't you, little Juline?
You're the one who's supposed to be so strong, right?
The little princess of the Kenga Clan.
SLASH
SMACK
What do you think you're doing?!
KICK
I knew there was something wrong about you!
CRACK

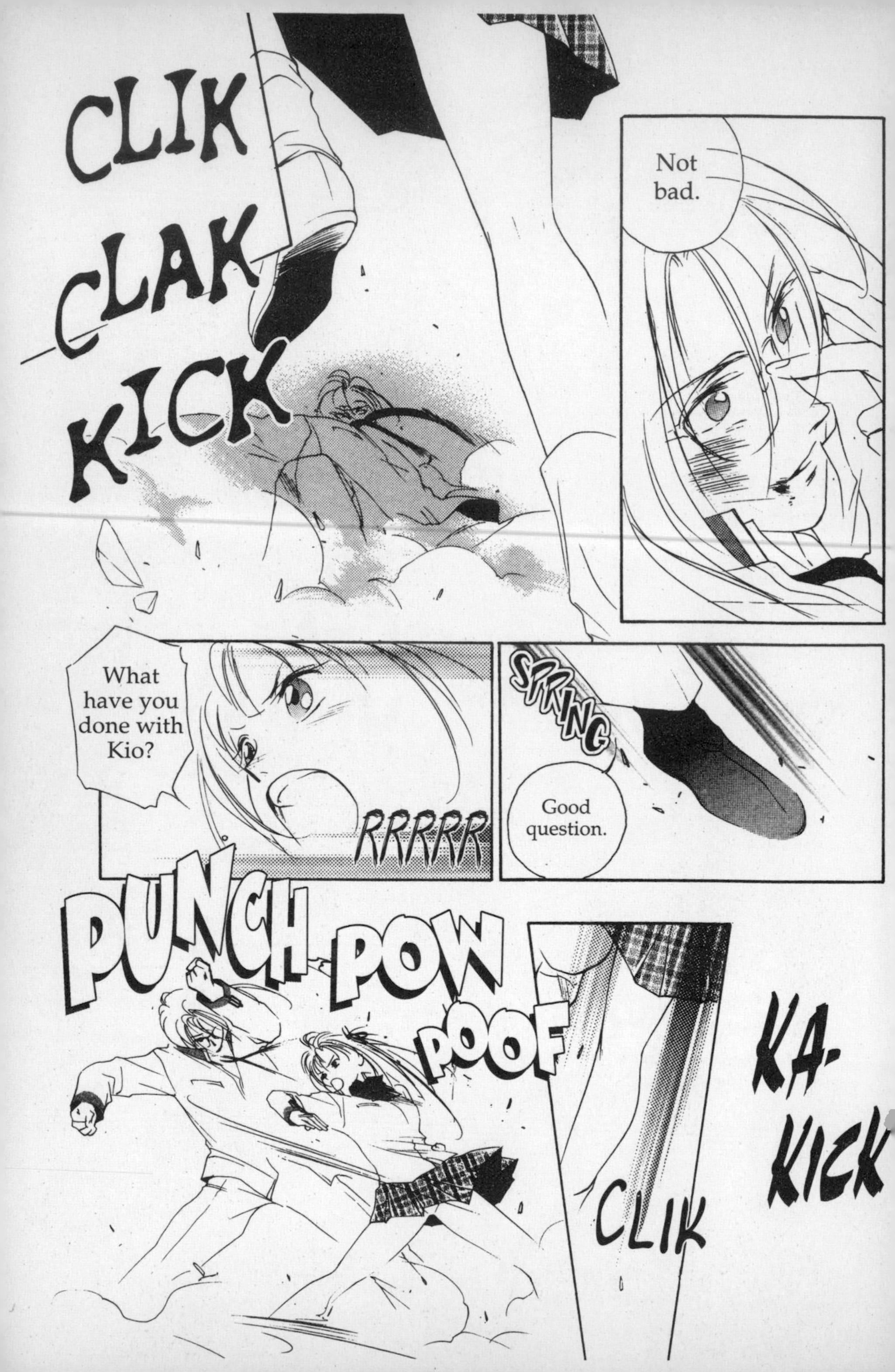
CLIK
CLAK
KICK
Not bad.
What have you done with Kio?
RRRRRR
SPRING
Good question.
PUNCH
POW
POOF
CLIK
KA-KICK

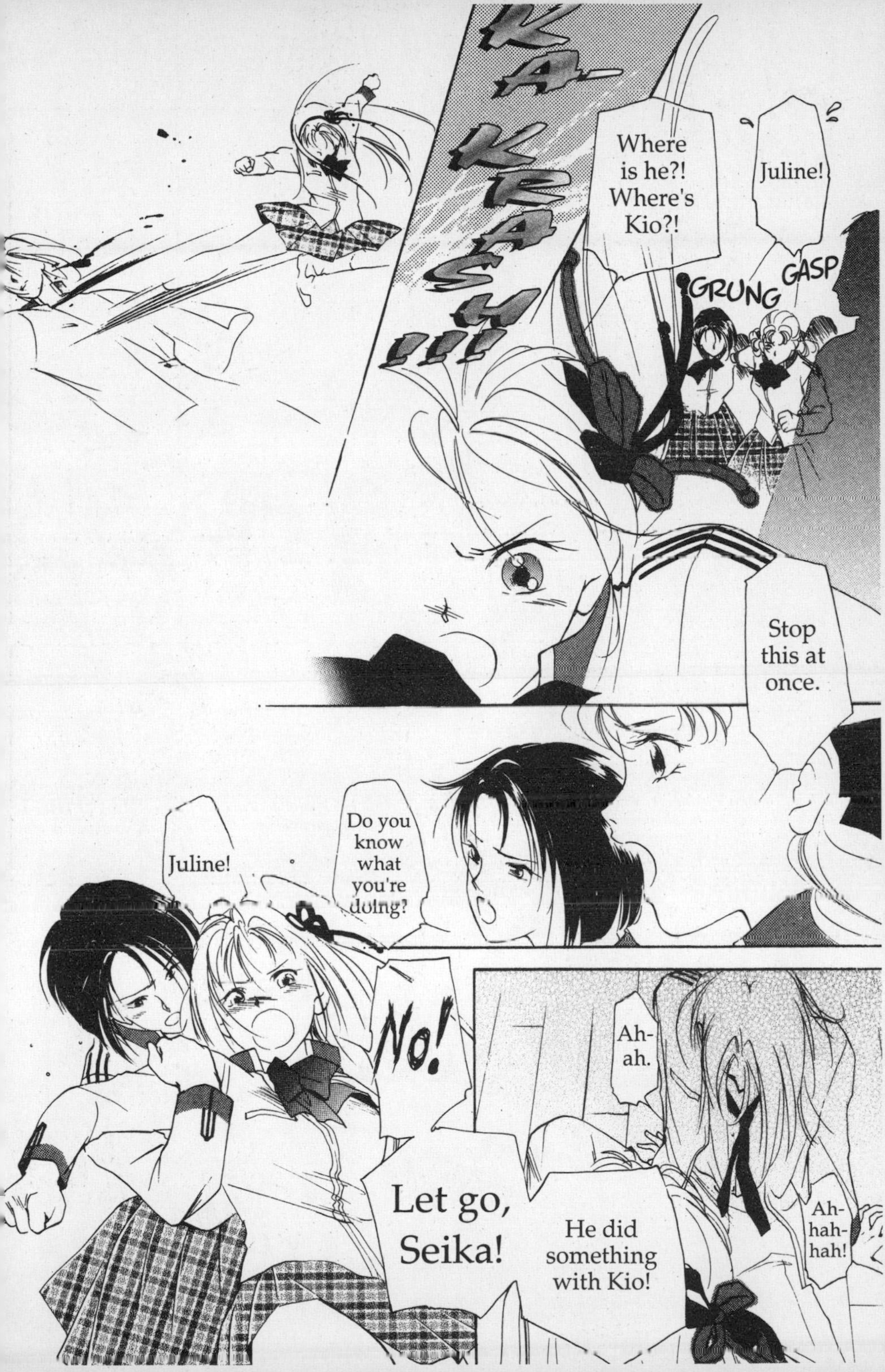
KA-KRASH!!!
Where is he?! Where's Kio?!
Juline!
GRUNG
GASP
Stop this at once.
Juline!
Do you know what you're doing?
No!
Let go, Seika!
He did something with Kio!
Ah-ah.
Ah-hah-hah!

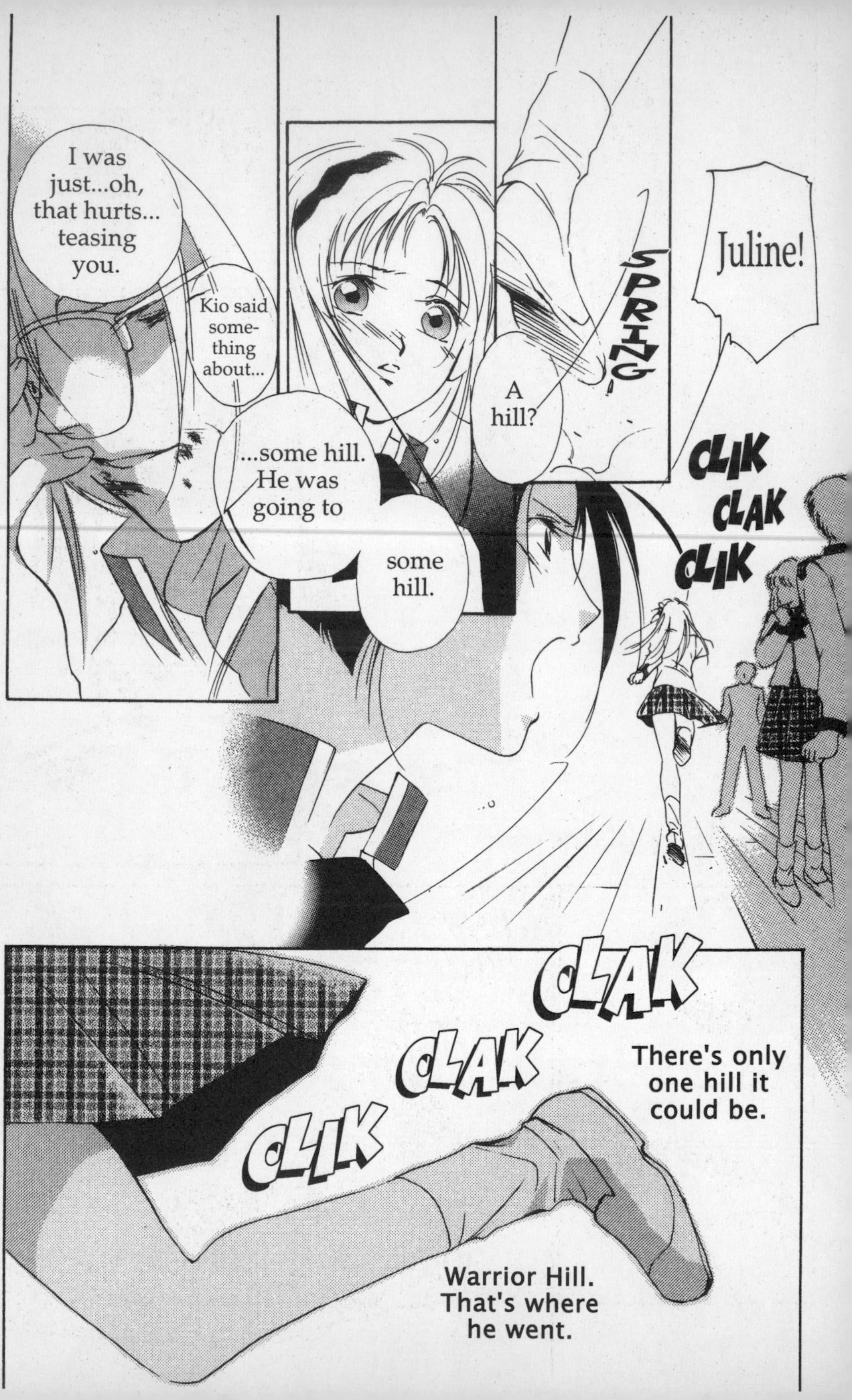
I was just...oh, that hurts... teasing you.
Kio said some-thing about...
...some hill. He was going to
some hill.
A hill?
SPRING
Juline!
CLIK
CLAK
CLIK
CLIK
CLAK
CLAK
There's only one hill it could be.
Warrior Hill. That's where he went.

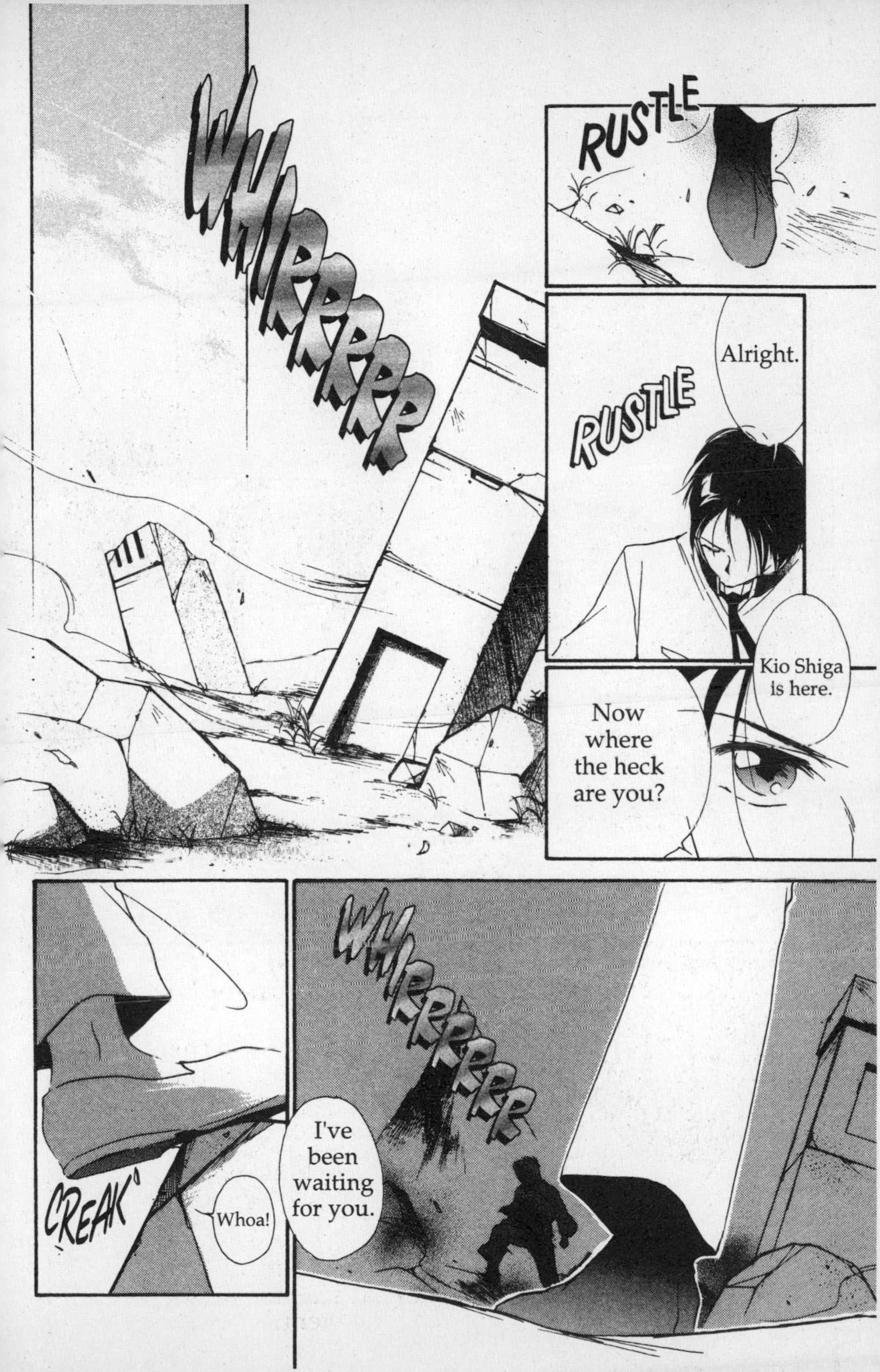
WHIRRRRR
RUSTLE
RUSTLE
Alright.
Kio Shiga is here.
Now where the heck are you?
CREAK
Whoa!
WHIRRRRR
I've been waiting for you.

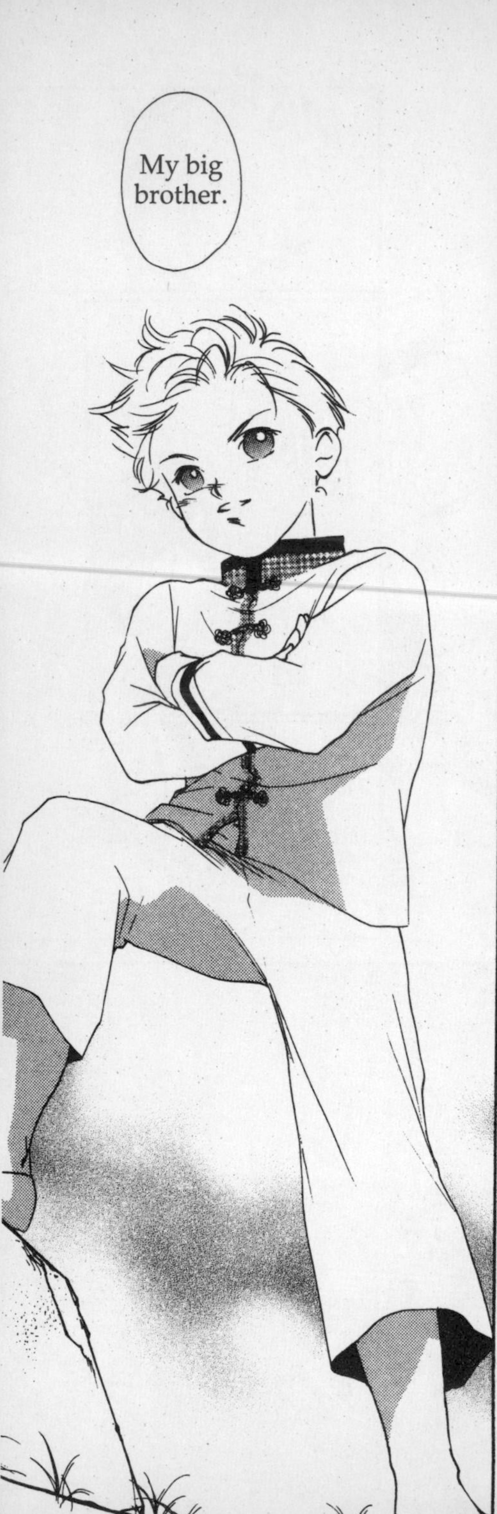
My big brother.

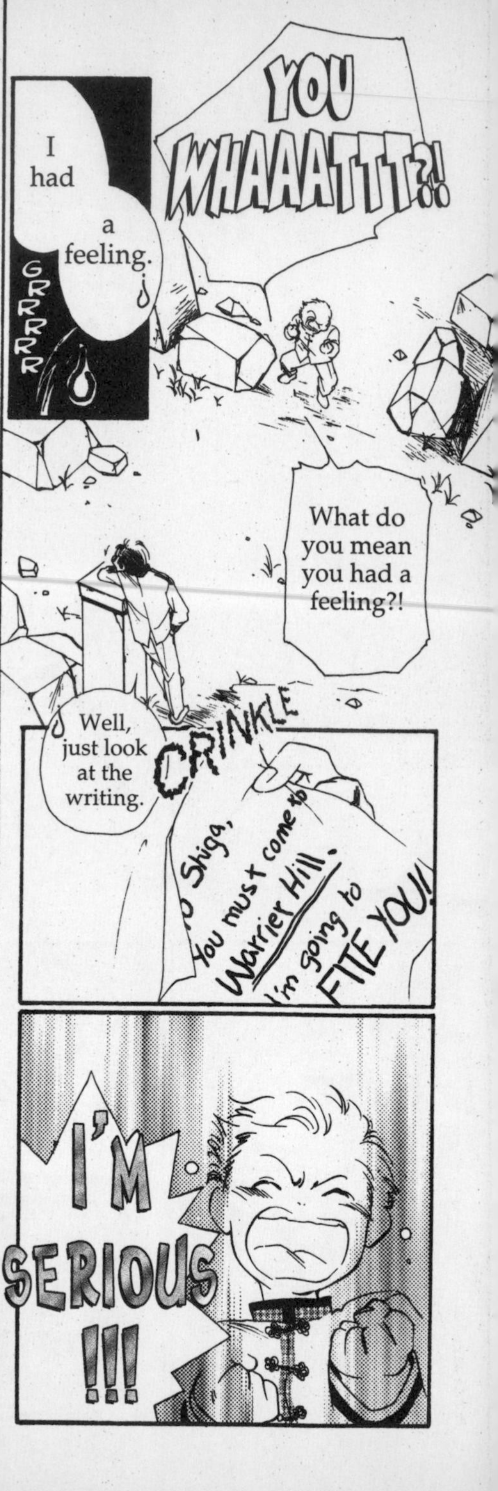
I had a feeling.
GRRRRR
YOU WHAAAATTT?!
What do you mean you had a feeling?!
Well, just look at the writing.
CRINKLE
o Shiga,
You must come to Warrier Hill.
I'm going to FITE YOU!
I'M SERIOUS!!!

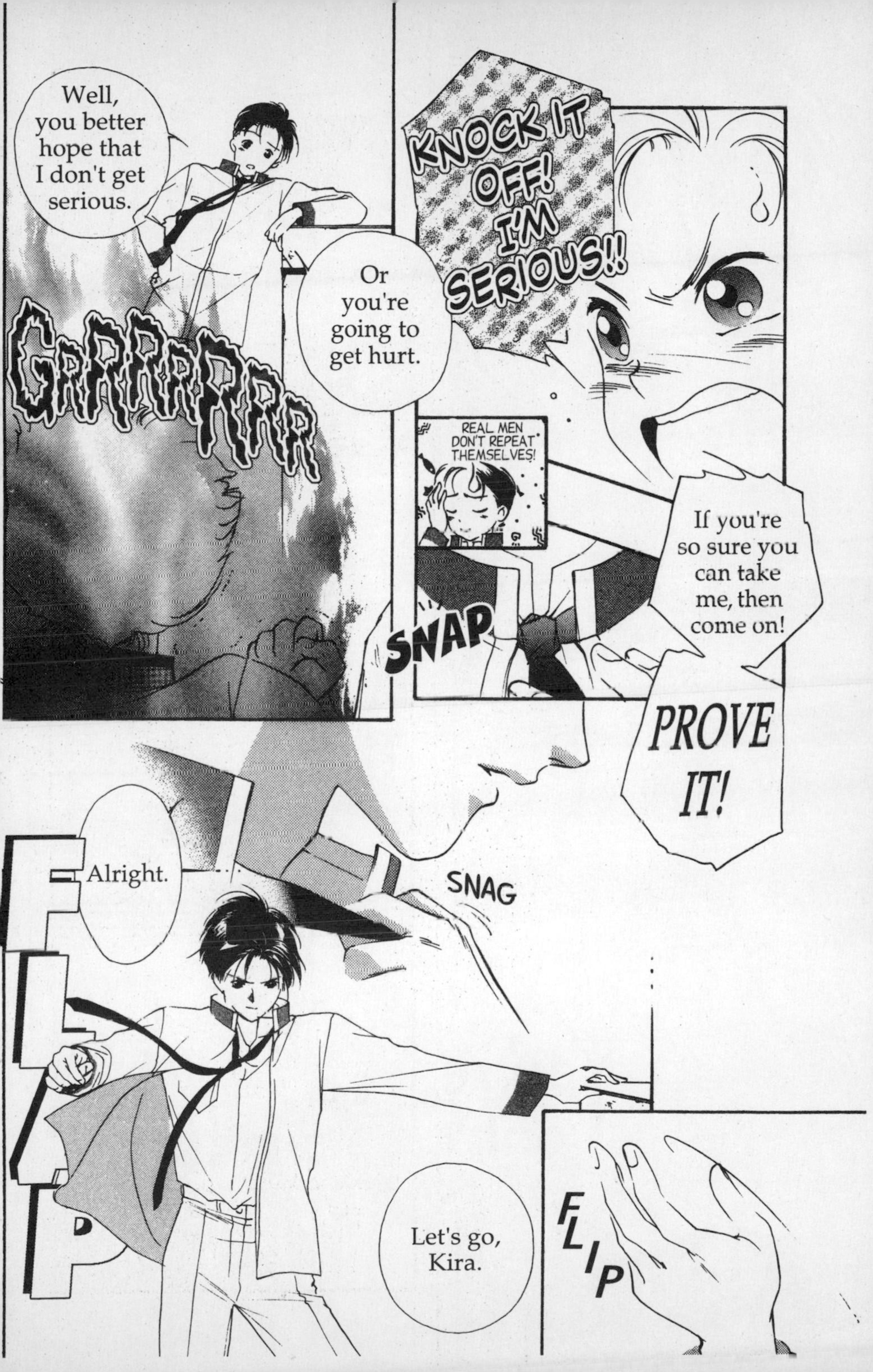

Well, you better hope that I don't get serious.
Or you're going to get hurt.
GRRRRRRR
KNOCK IT OFF! I'M SERIOUS!!
REAL MEN DON'T REPEAT THEMSELVES!
SNAP
If you're so sure you can take me, then come on!
PROVE IT!
Alright.
SNAG
Let's go, Kira.
FLIP

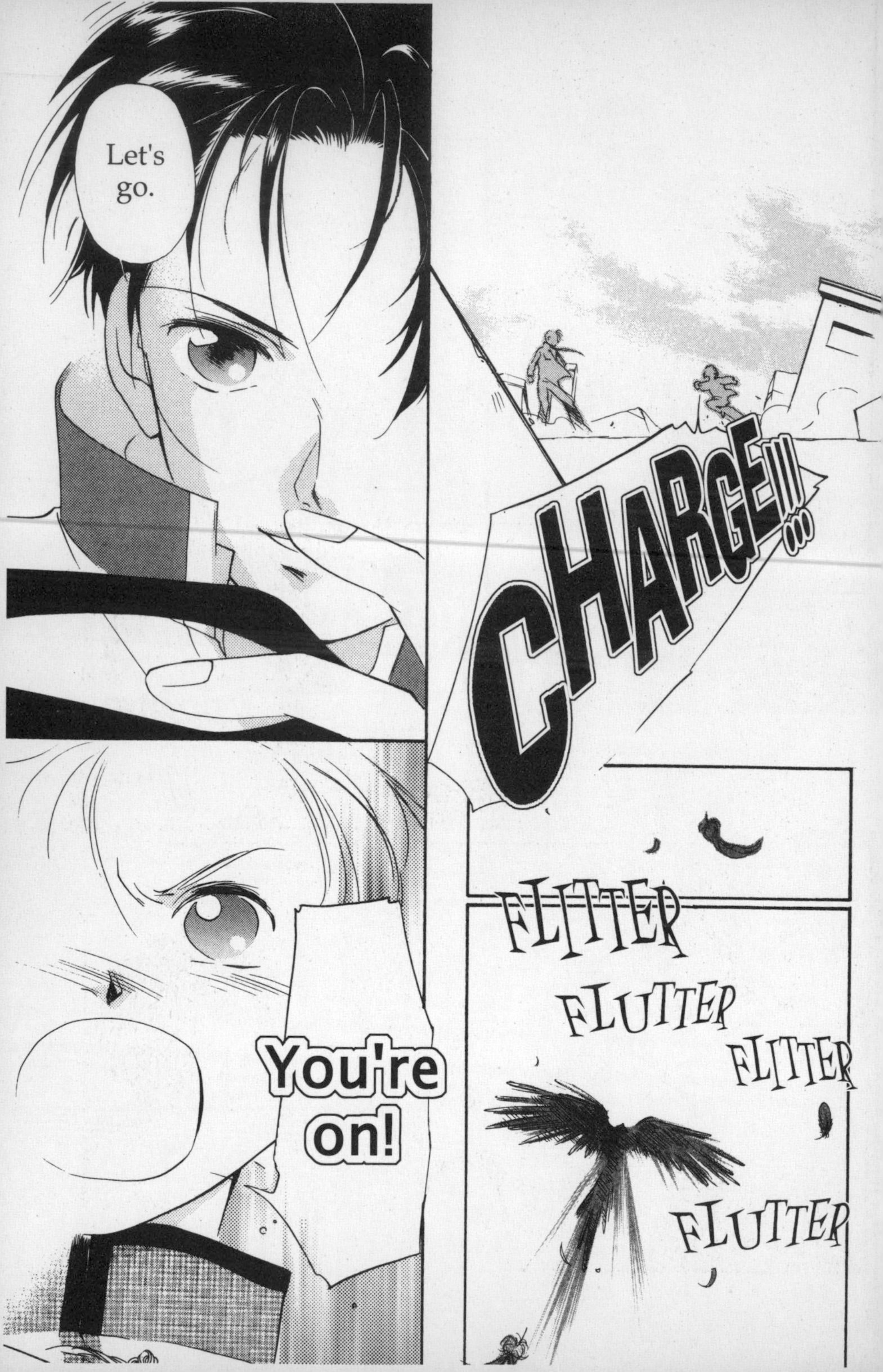
Let's go.
You're on!
CHARGE!!
FLITTER
FLUTTER
FLITTER
FLUTTER

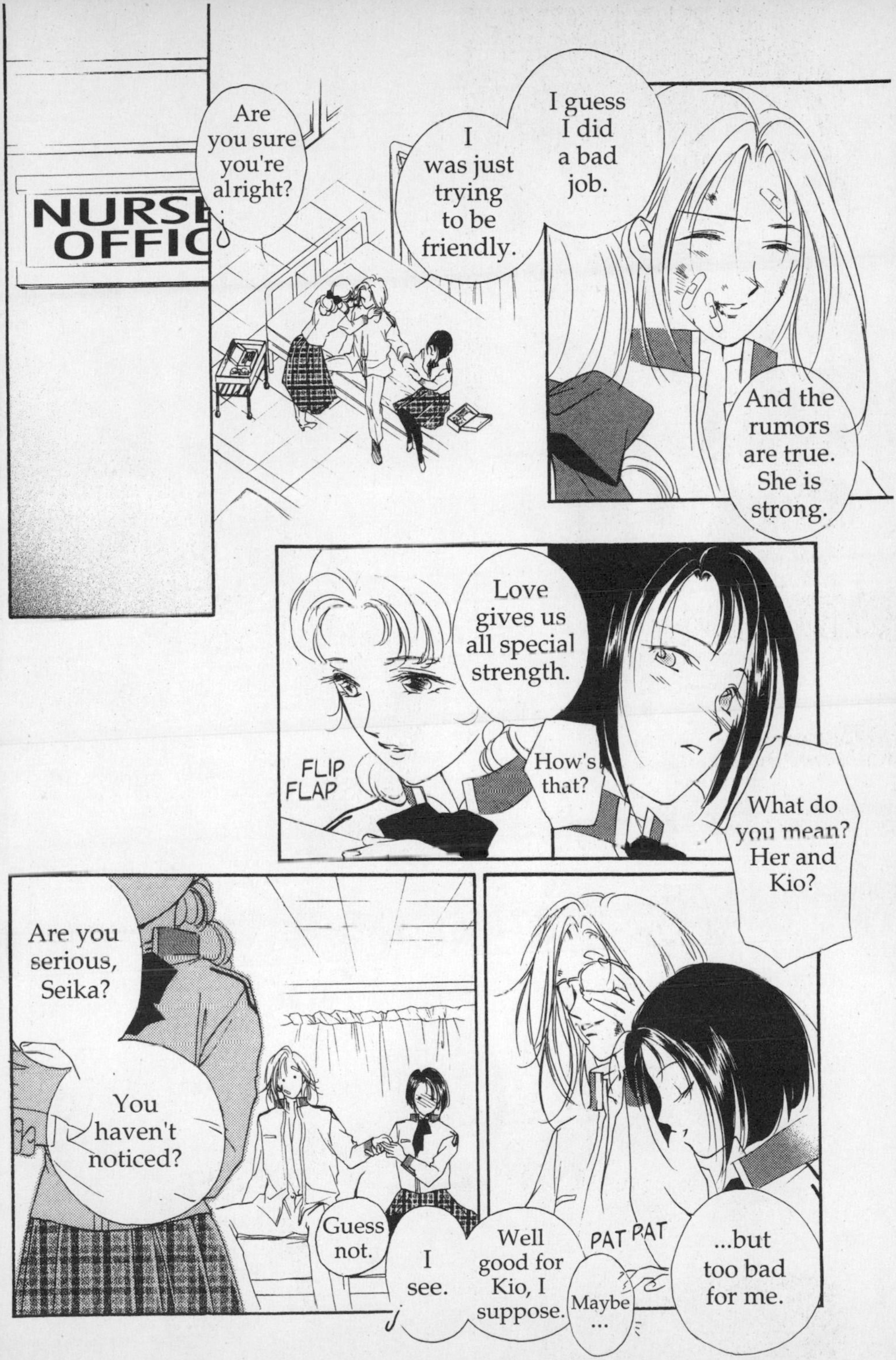
NURSE OFFIC
Are you sure you're alright?
I was just trying to be friendly.
I guess I did a bad job.
And the rumors are true. She is strong.
Love gives us all special strength.
FLIP FLAP
How's that?
What do you mean? Her and Kio?
Are you serious, Seika?
You haven't noticed?
Guess not.
I see.
Well good for Kio, I suppose.
PAT PAT
Maybe...
...but too bad for me.

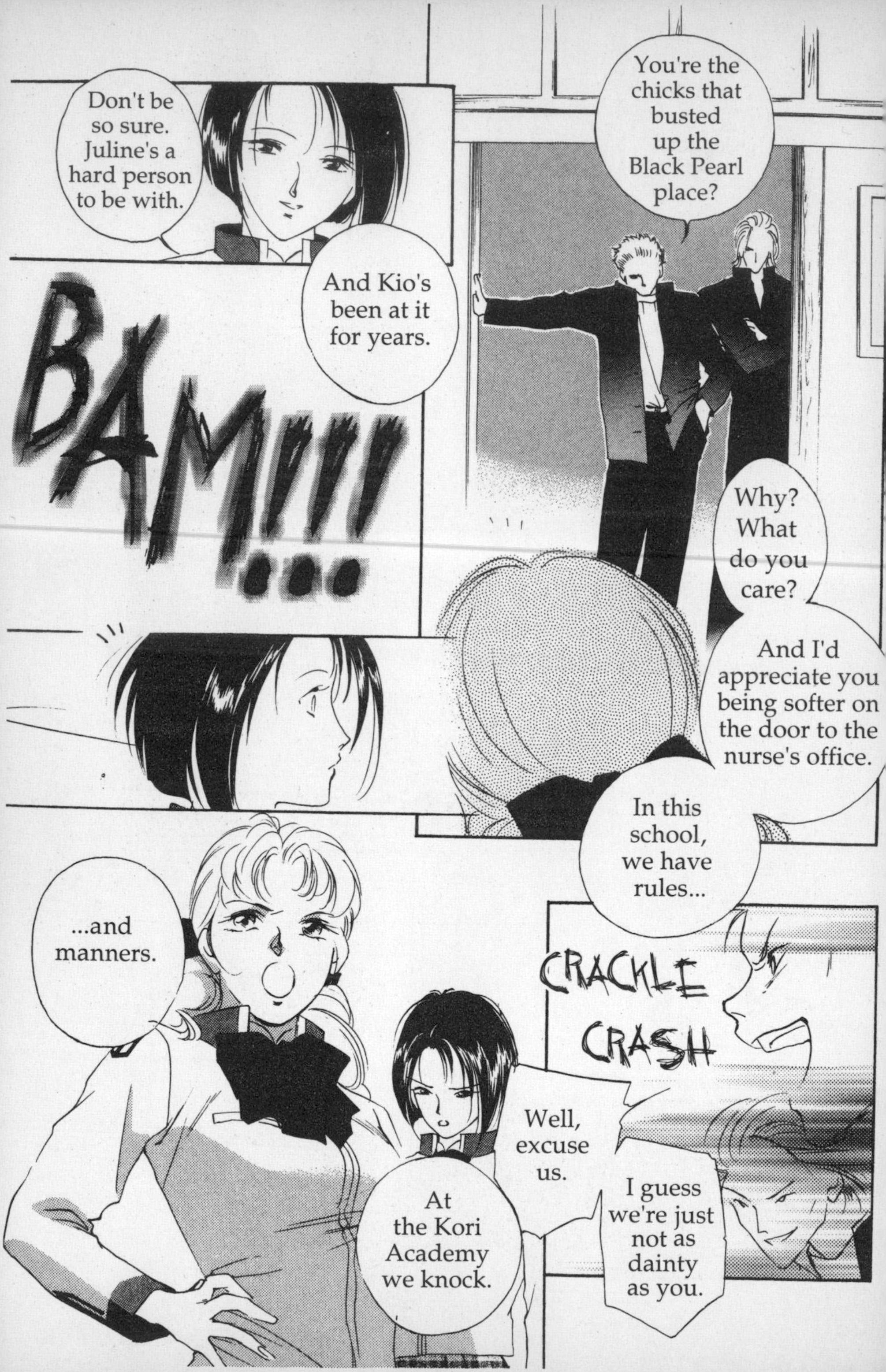
Don't be so sure. Juline's a hard person to be with.
And Kio's been at it for years.
BAM!!!...
You're the chicks that busted up the Black Pearl place?
Why? What do you care?
And I'd appreciate you being softer on the door to the nurse's office.
In this school, we have rules...
...and manners.
At the Kori Academy we knock.
CRACKLE CRASH
Well, excuse us.
I guess we're just not as dainty as you.

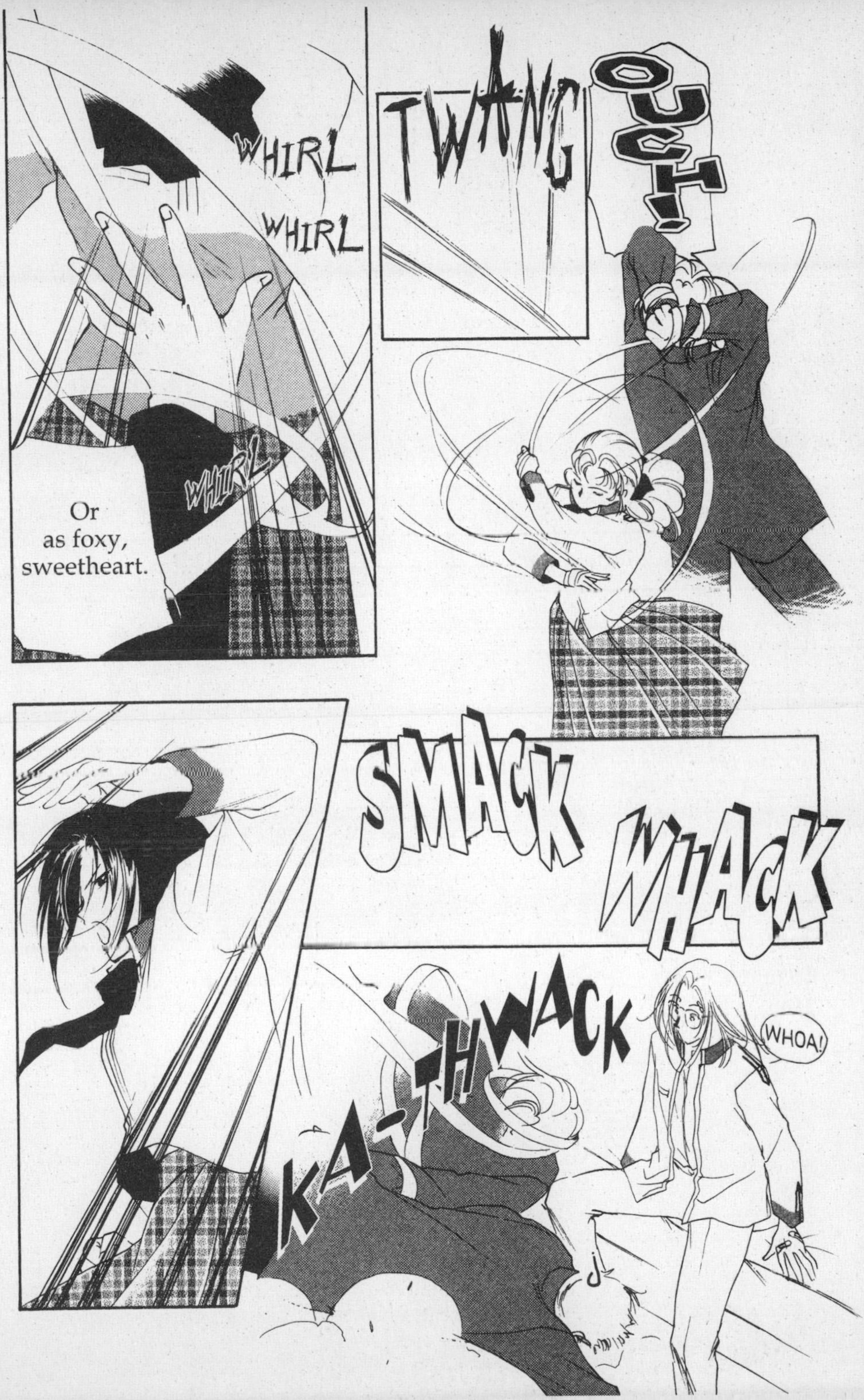
WHIRL
WHIRL
WHIRL
Or as foxy, sweetheart.
TWANG
OUCH!
SMACK
WHACK
KA-THWACK
WHOA!

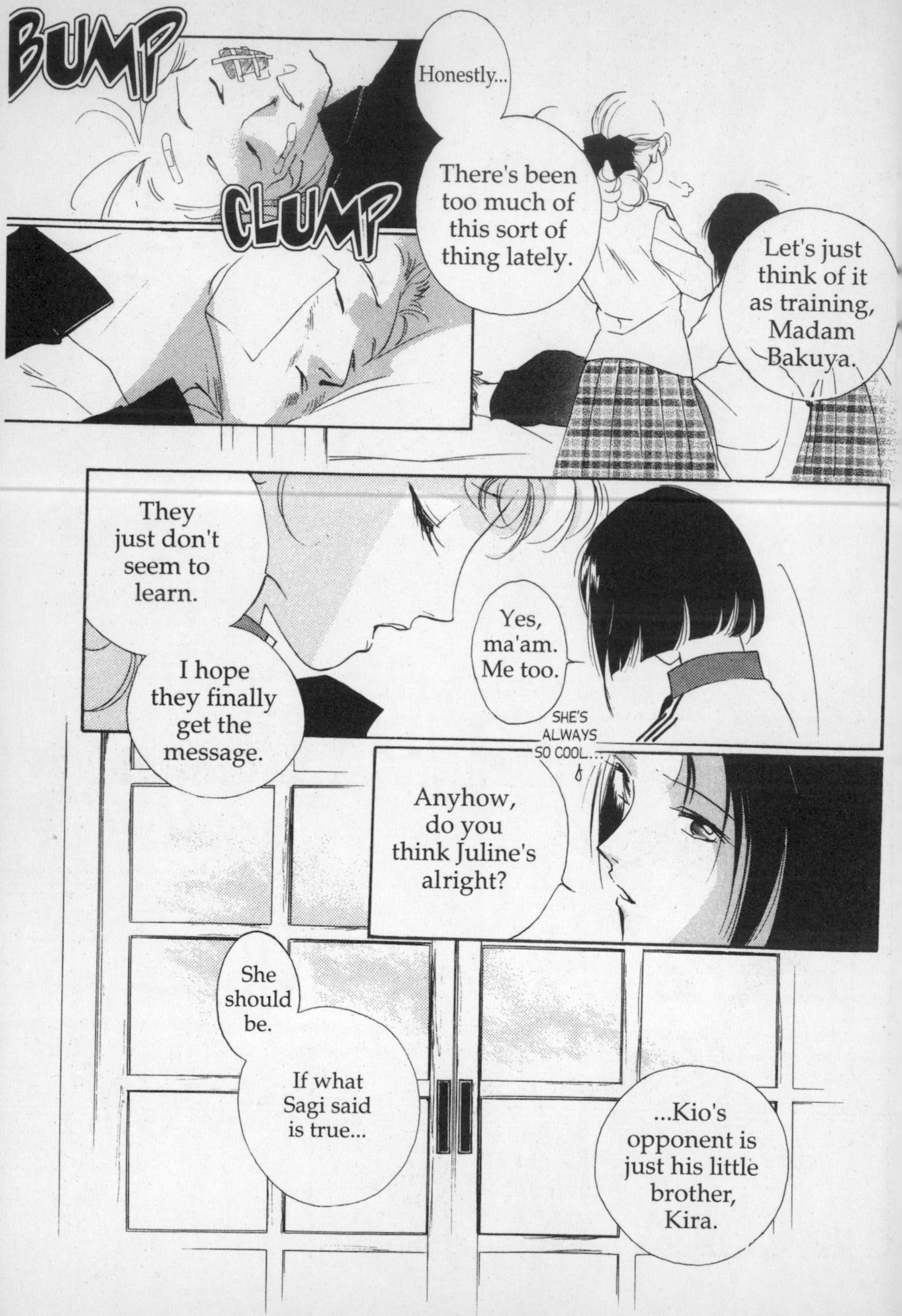
BUMP
CLUMP
Honestly...
There's been too much of this sort of thing lately.
Let's just think of it as training, Madam Bakuya.
They just don't seem to learn.
I hope they finally get the message.
Yes, ma'am. Me too.
SHE'S ALWAYS SO COOL...
Anyhow, do you think Juline's alright?
She should be.
If what Sagi said is true...
...Kio's opponent is just his little brother, Kira.

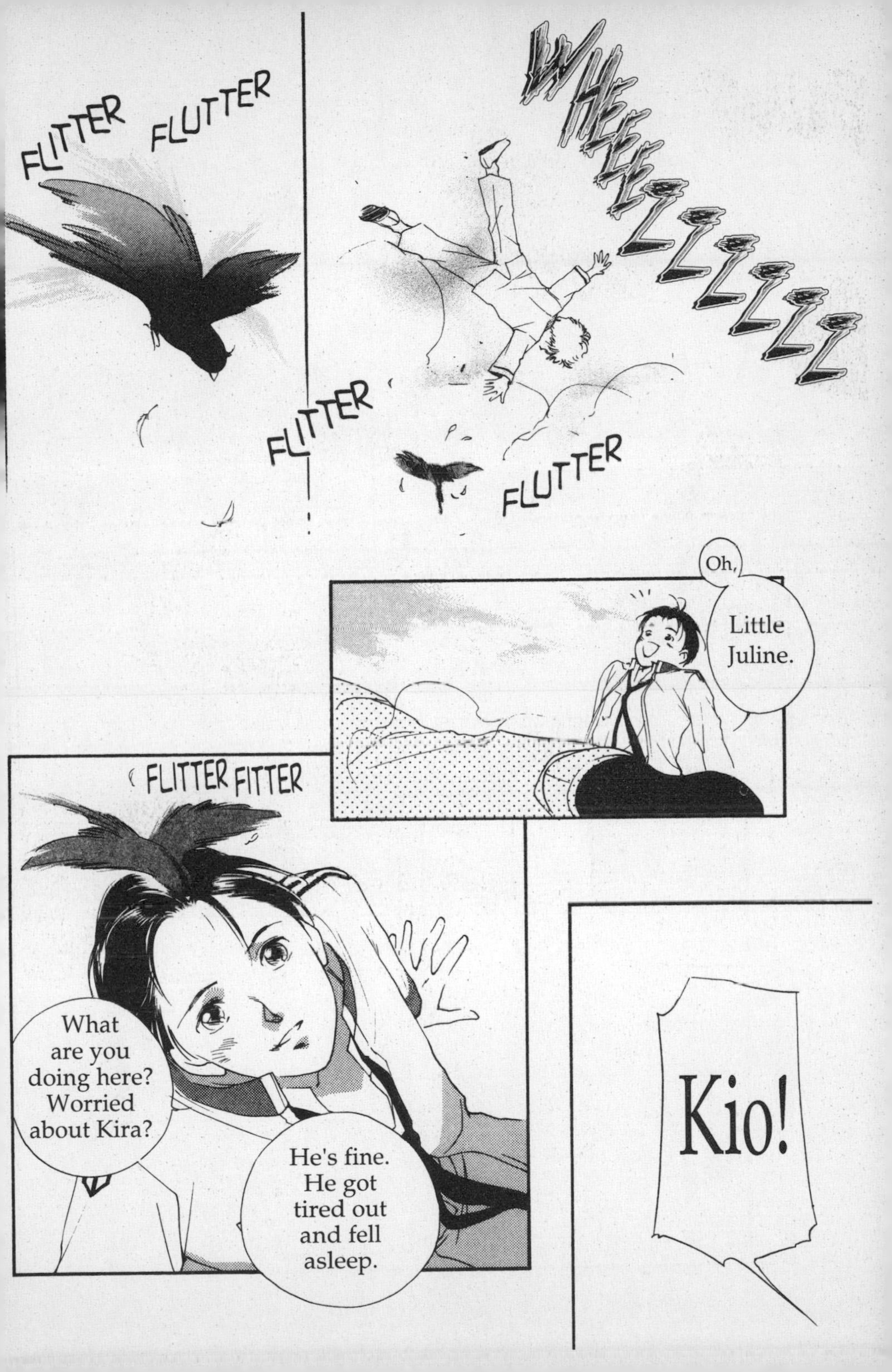
FLITTER
FLUTTER
WHEEEZZZZZZ
FLITTER
FLUTTER
Oh,
Little Juline.
FLITTER FITTER
What are you doing here? Worried about Kira?
He's fine. He got tired out and fell asleep.
Kio!

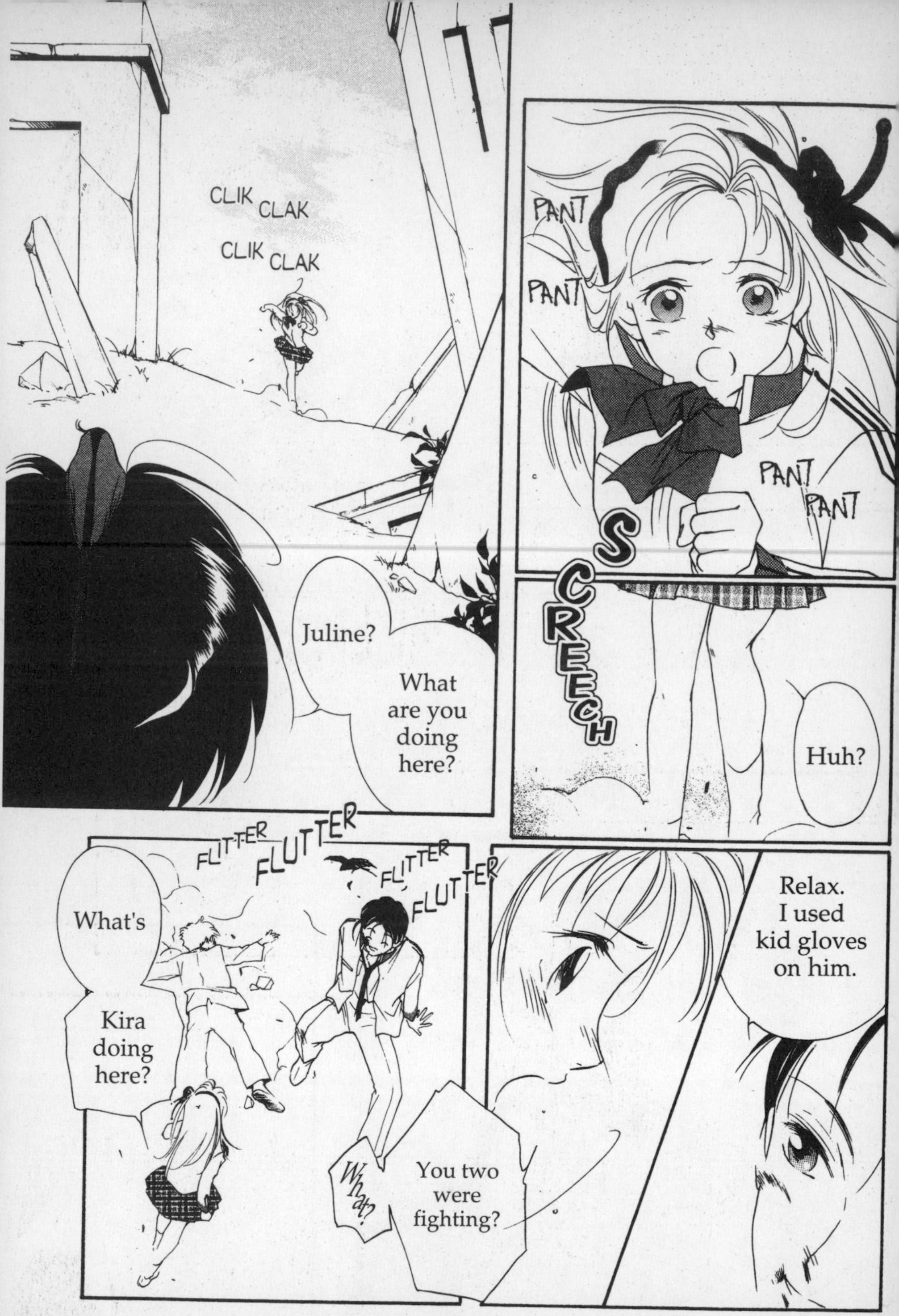
CLIK CLAK
CLIK CLAK
Juline?
What are you doing here?
PANT
PANT
PANT
PANT
SCREECH
Huh?
FLITTER
FLUTTER
FLITTER
FLUTTER
What's Kira doing here?
What?
You two were fighting?
Relax. I used kid gloves on him.

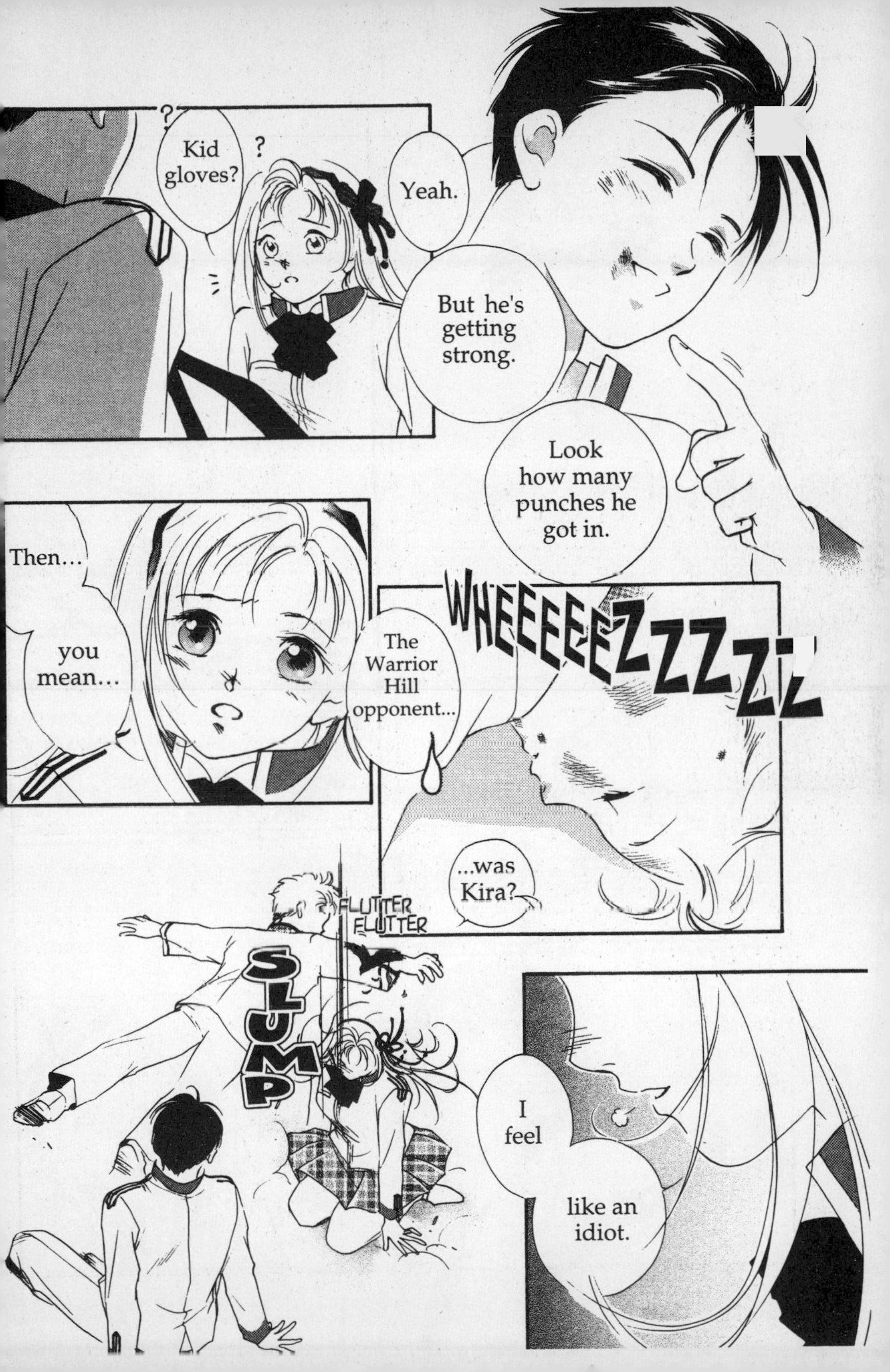
?
Kid gloves?
?
Yeah.
But he's getting strong.
Look how many punches he got in.
Then...
you mean...
The Warrior Hill opponent...
WHEEEEEZZZZZ
...was Kira?
FLUTTER FLUTTER
SLUMP
I feel
like an idiot.

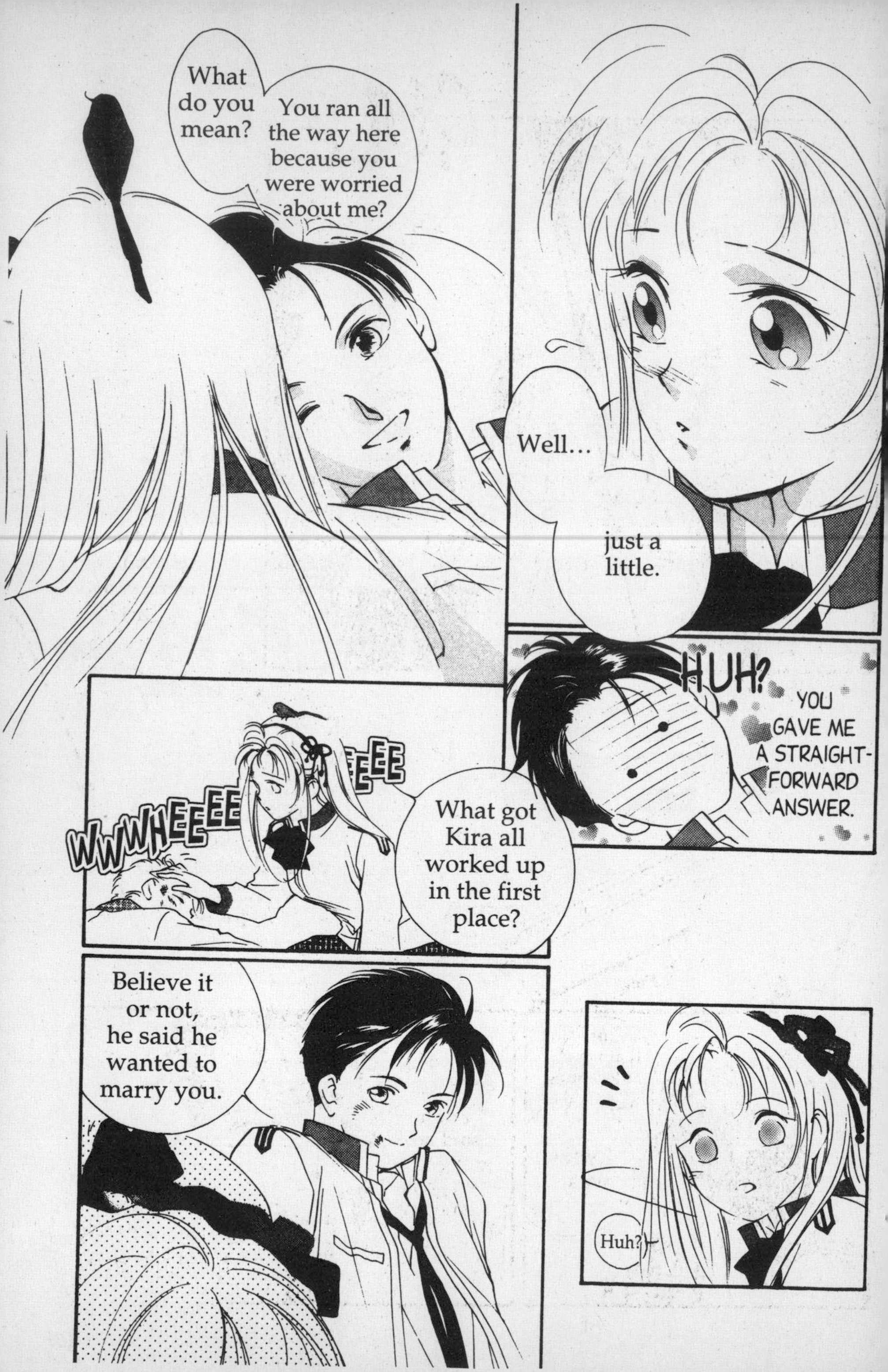
What do you mean?
You ran all the way here because you were worried about me?
Well…
just a little.
HUH?
YOU GAVE ME A STRAIGHT-FORWARD ANSWER.
WWWHEEEEE
EEEE
What got Kira all worked up in the first place?
Believe it or not, he said he wanted to marry you.
Huh?

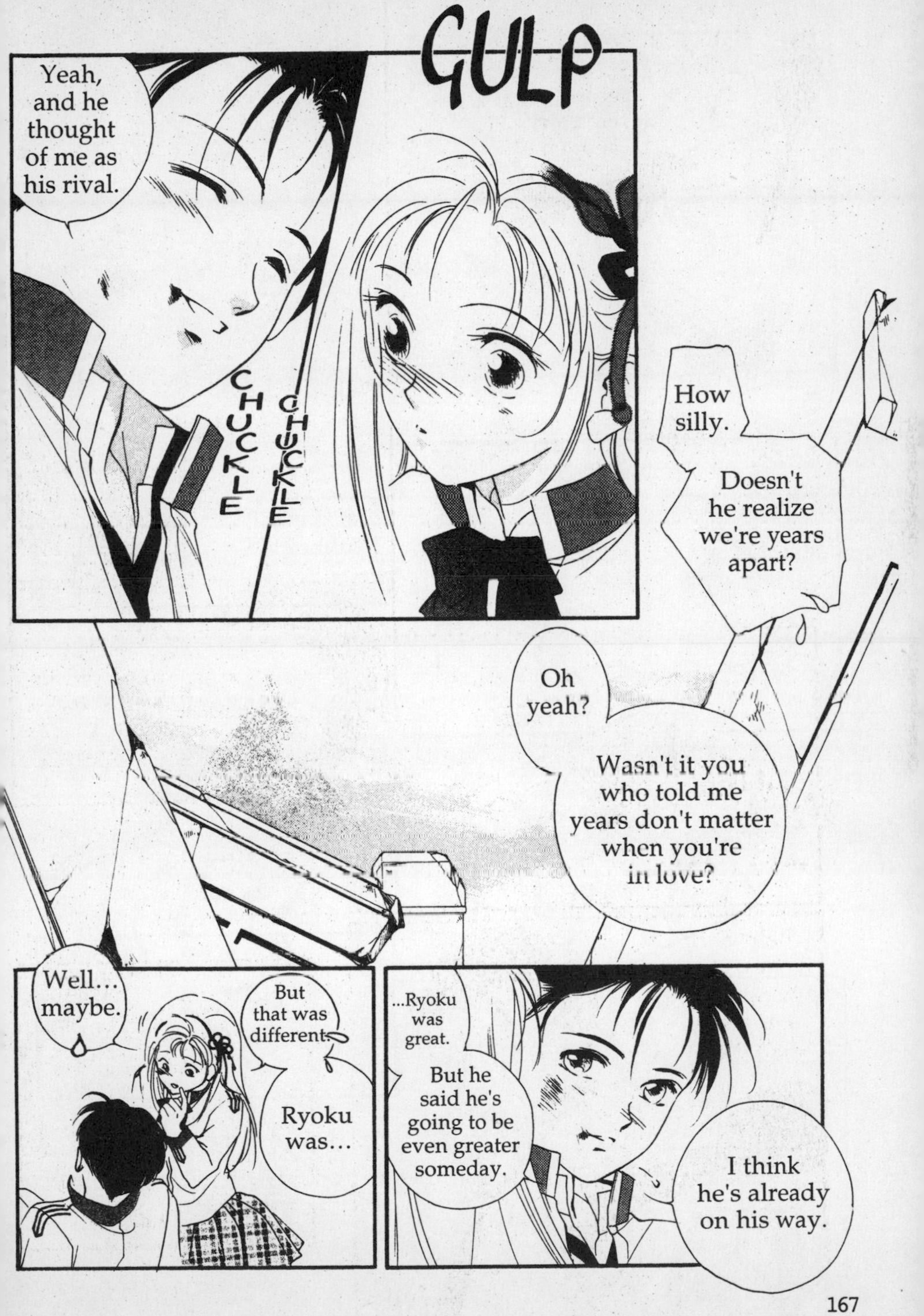
GULP
Yeah, and he thought of me as his rival.
CHUCKLE CHUCKLE
How silly.
Doesn't he realize we're years apart?
Oh yeah?
Wasn't it you who told me years don't matter when you're in love?
Well... maybe.
But that was different.
Ryoku was...
...Ryoku was great.
But he said he's going to be even greater someday.
I think he's already on his way.

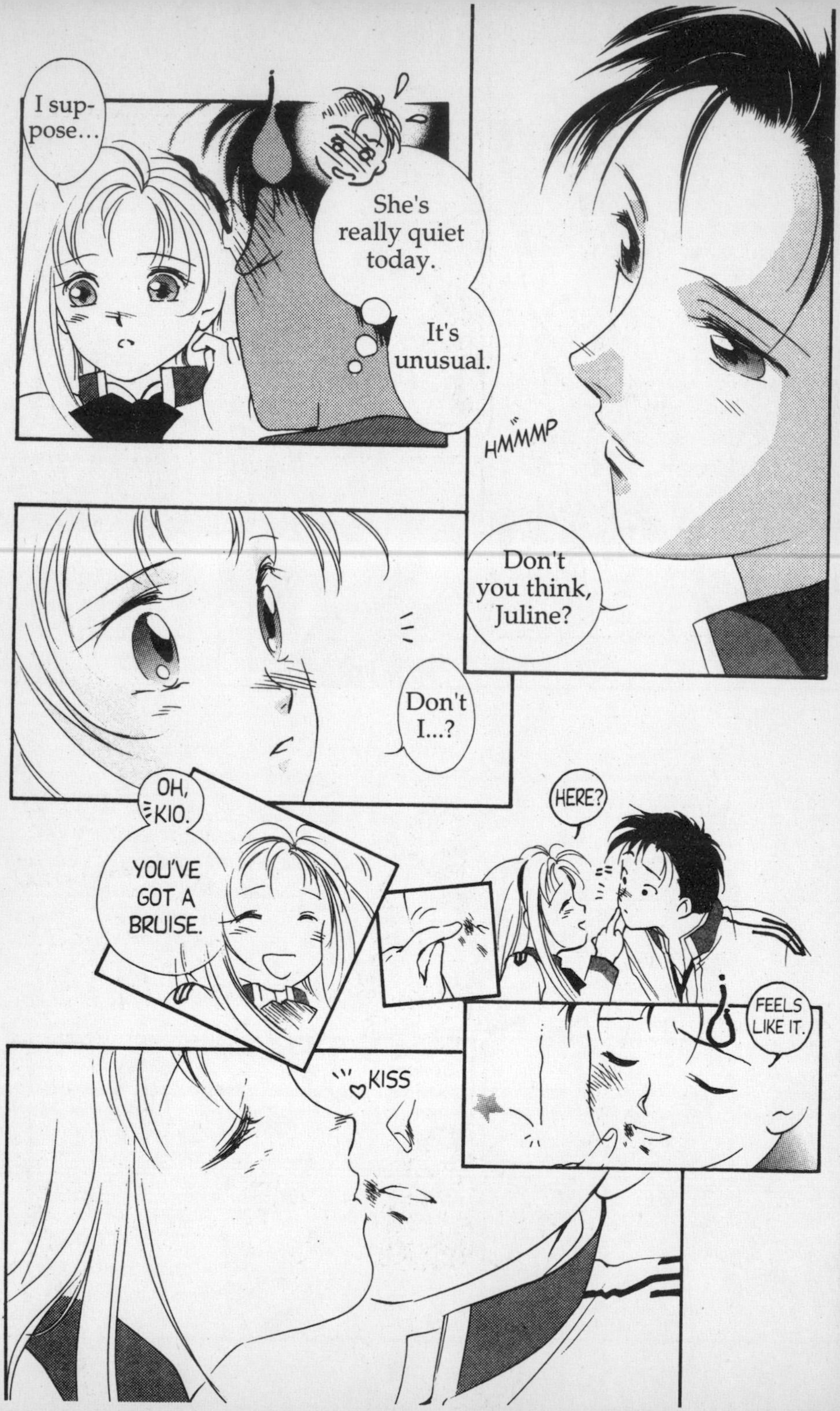
I sup-
pose...
She's really quiet today.
It's unusual.
Don't I...?
HMMMP
Don't you think, Juline?
OH, KIO.
YOU'VE GOT A BRUISE.
HERE?
FEELS LIKE IT.
KISS

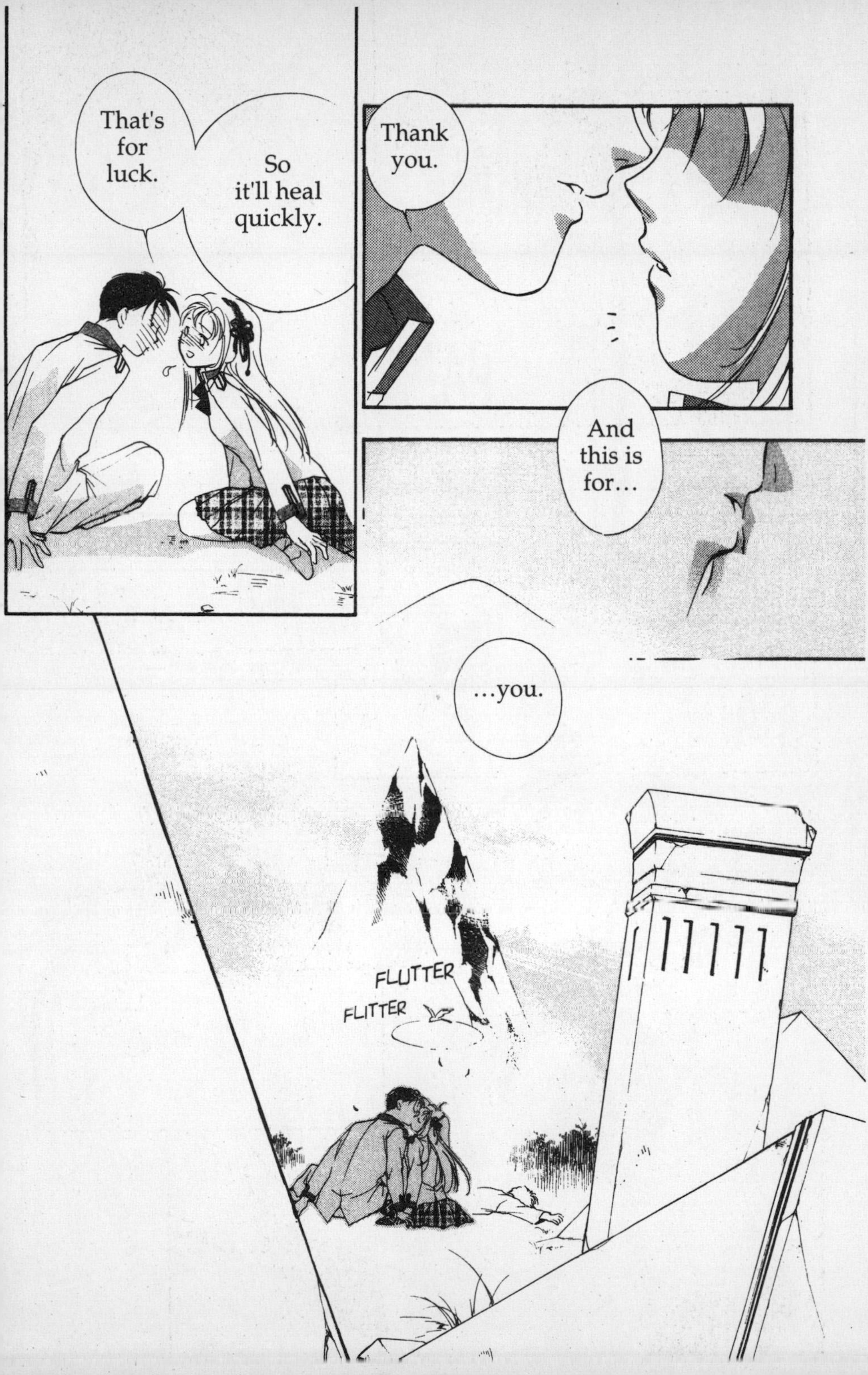
That's for luck.
So it'll heal quickly.
Thank you.
And this is for…
…you.
FLUTTER
FLITTER

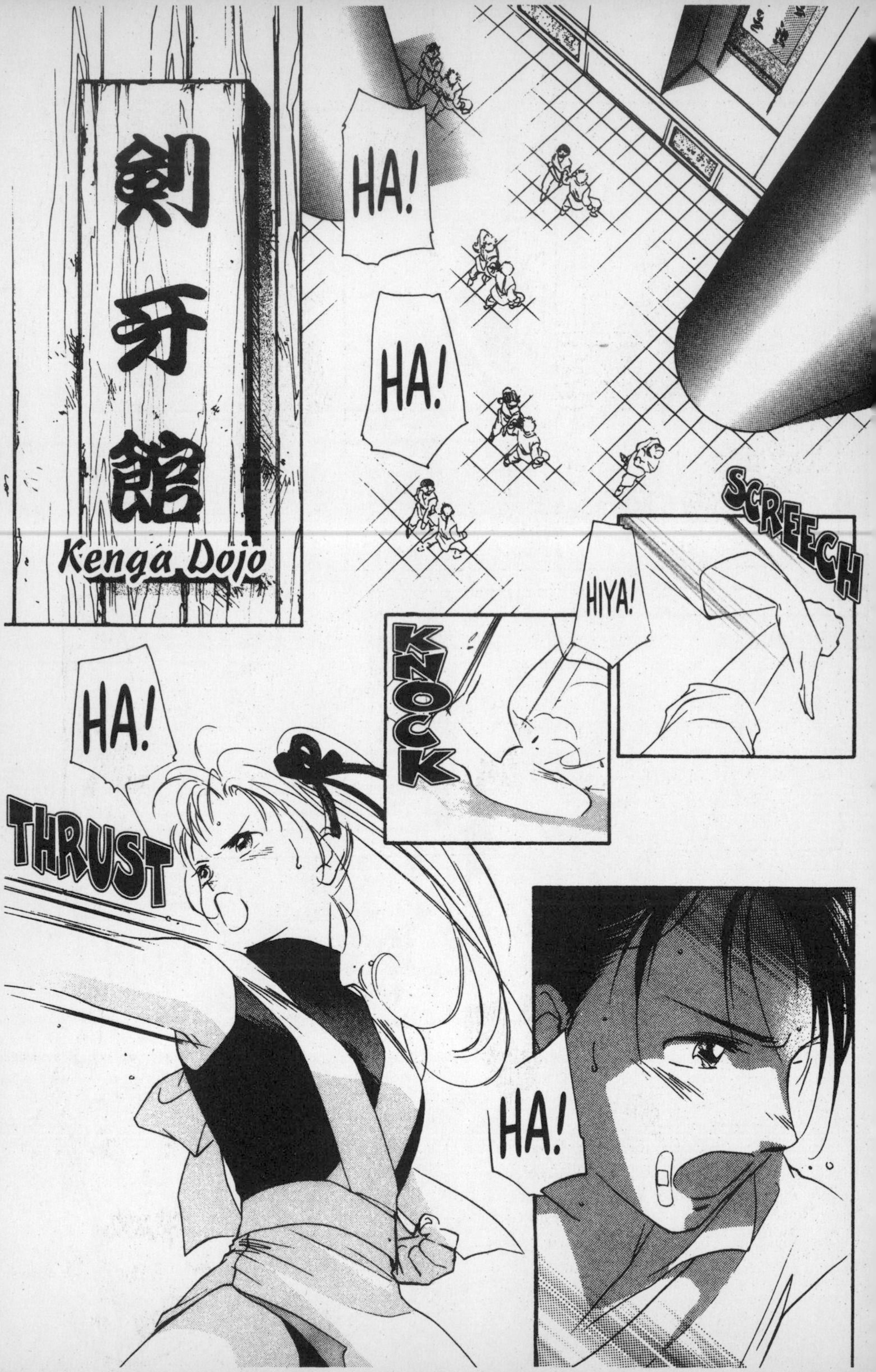

剣牙館
Kenga Dojo
HA!
HA!
HA!
THRUST
KNOCK
HIYA!
SCREECH
HA!

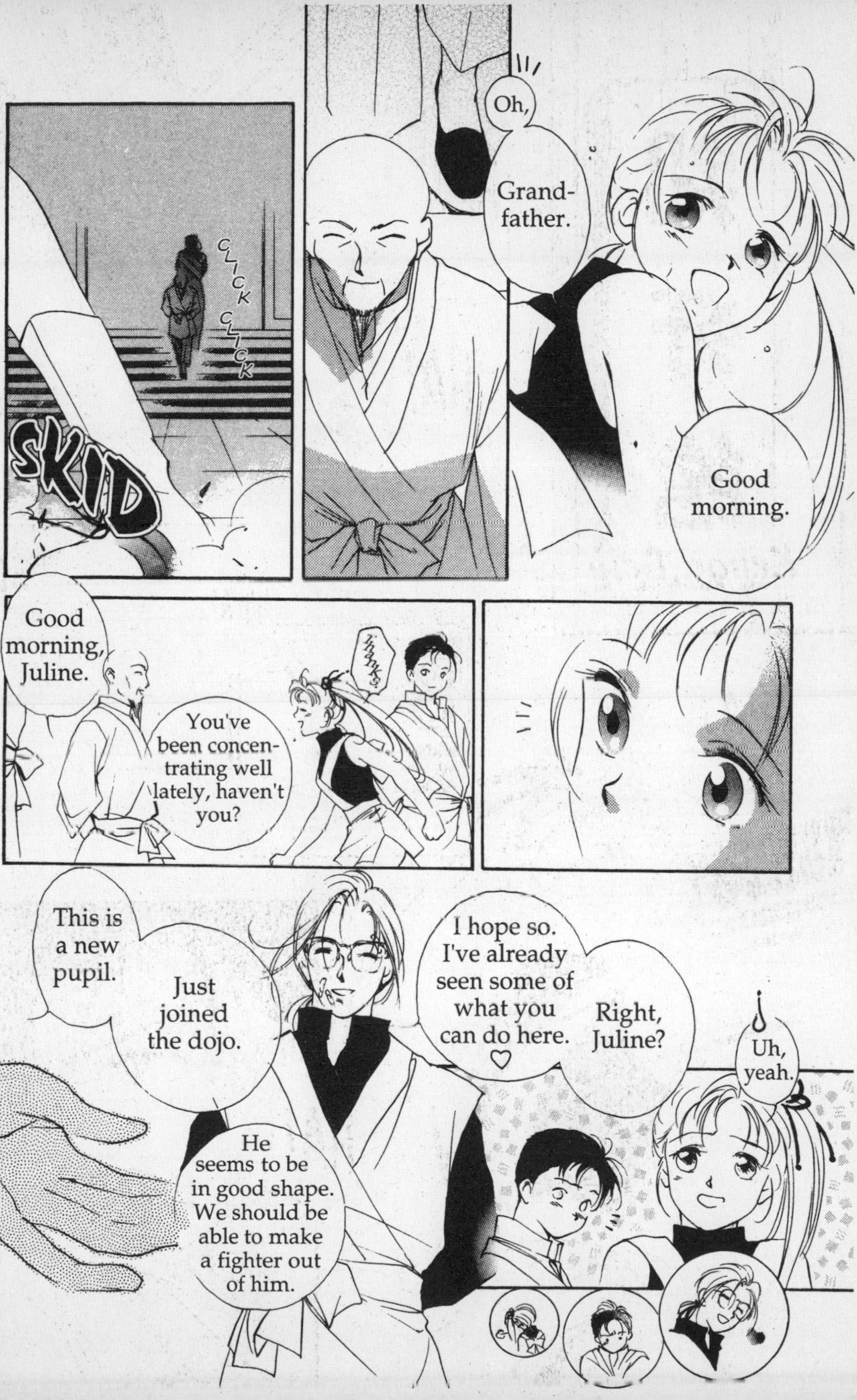
CLICK
CLICK
SKID
Oh,
Grandfather.
Good morning.
Good morning, Juline.
You've been concentrating well lately, haven't you?
This is a new pupil.
Just joined the dojo.
He seems to be in good shape. We should be able to make a fighter out of him.
I hope so. I've already seen some of what you can do here. ♡
Right, Juline?
Uh, yeah.

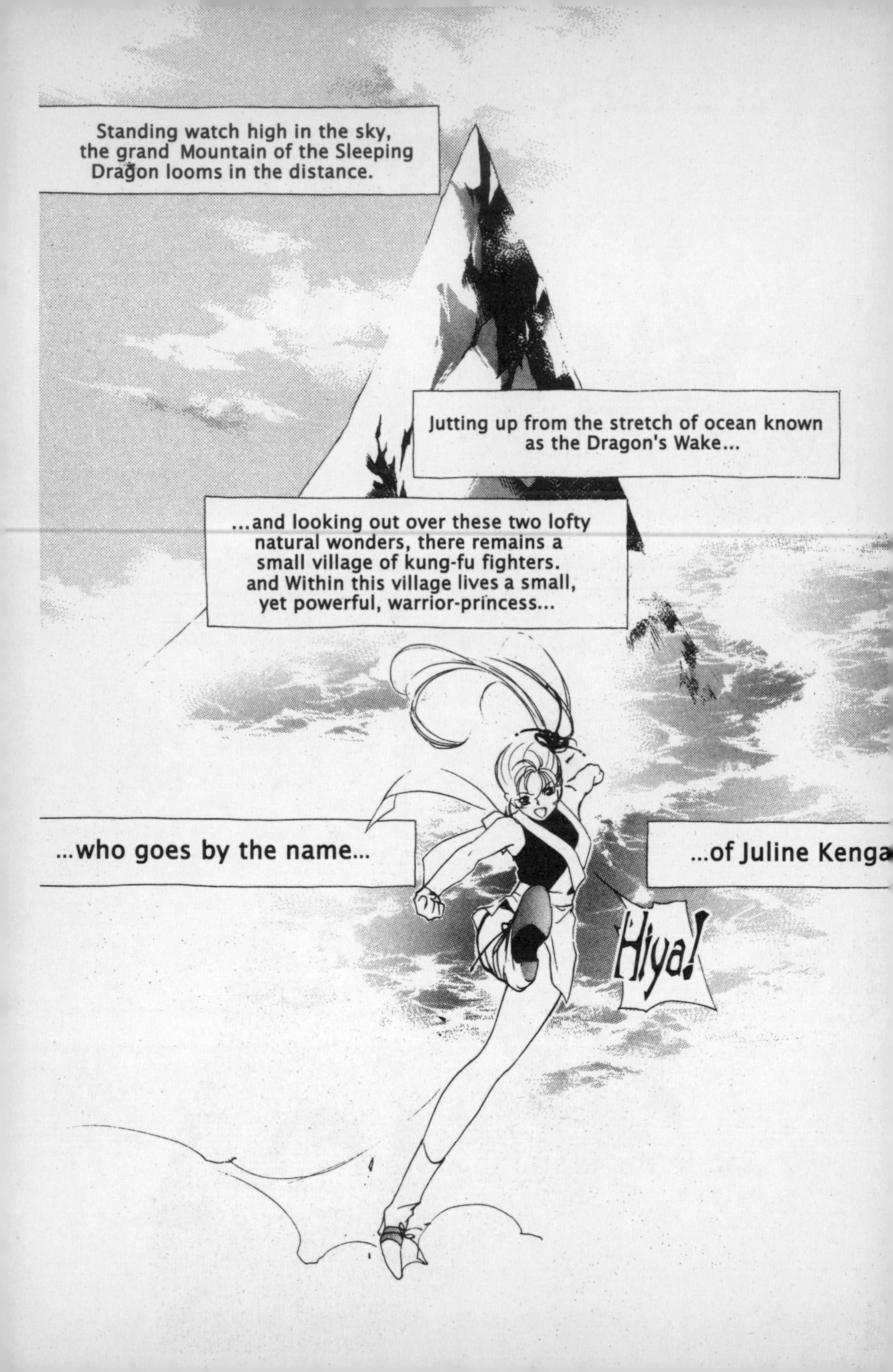
Standing watch high in the sky, the grand Mountain of the Sleeping Dragon looms in the distance.
Jutting up from the stretch of ocean known as the Dragon's Wake...
...and looking out over these two lofty natural wonders, there remains a small village of kung-fu fighters. and Within this village lives a small, yet powerful, warrior-princess...
...who goes by the name...
...of Juline Kenga
Hiya!

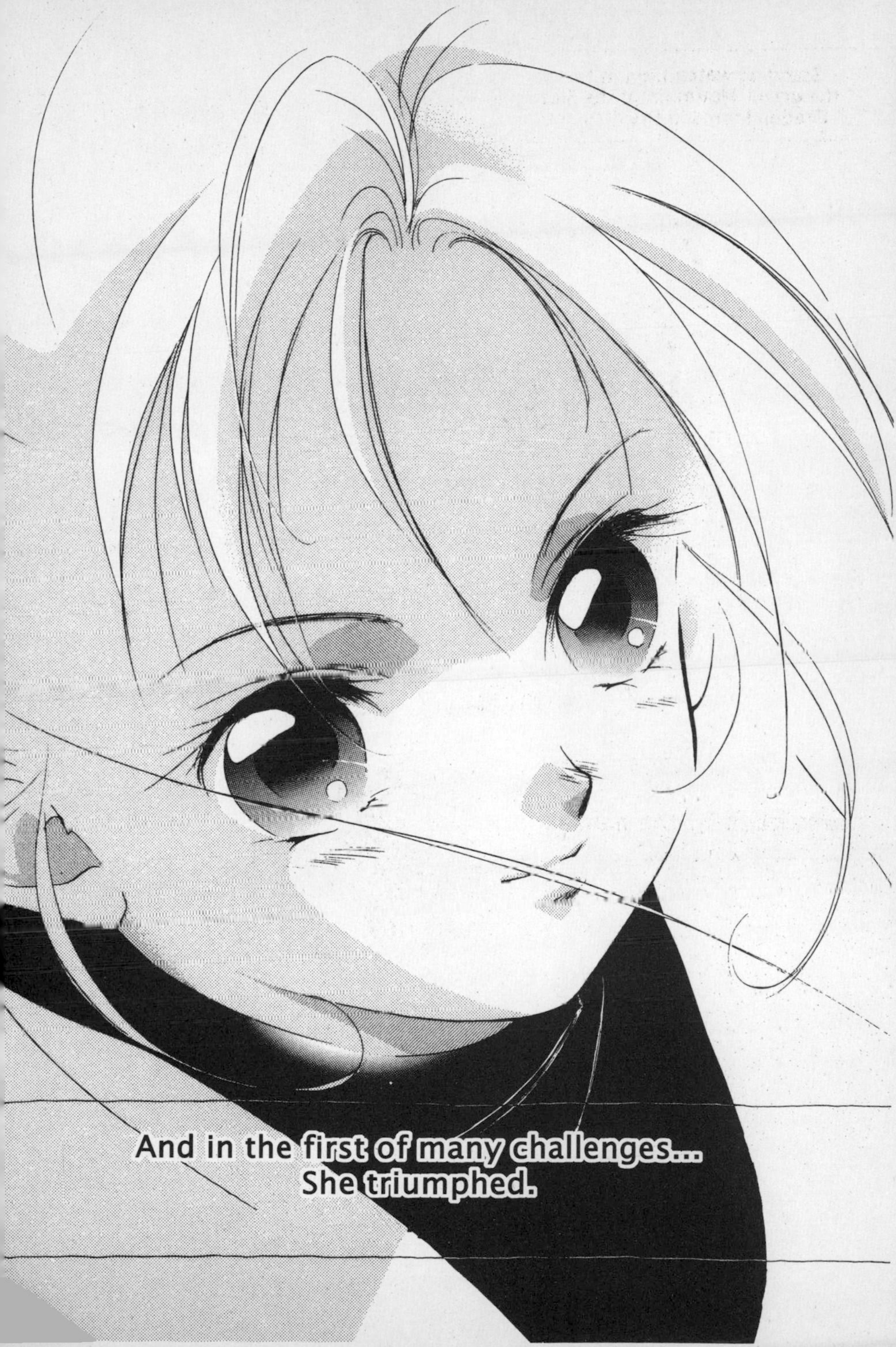
And in the first of many challenges...
She triumphed.

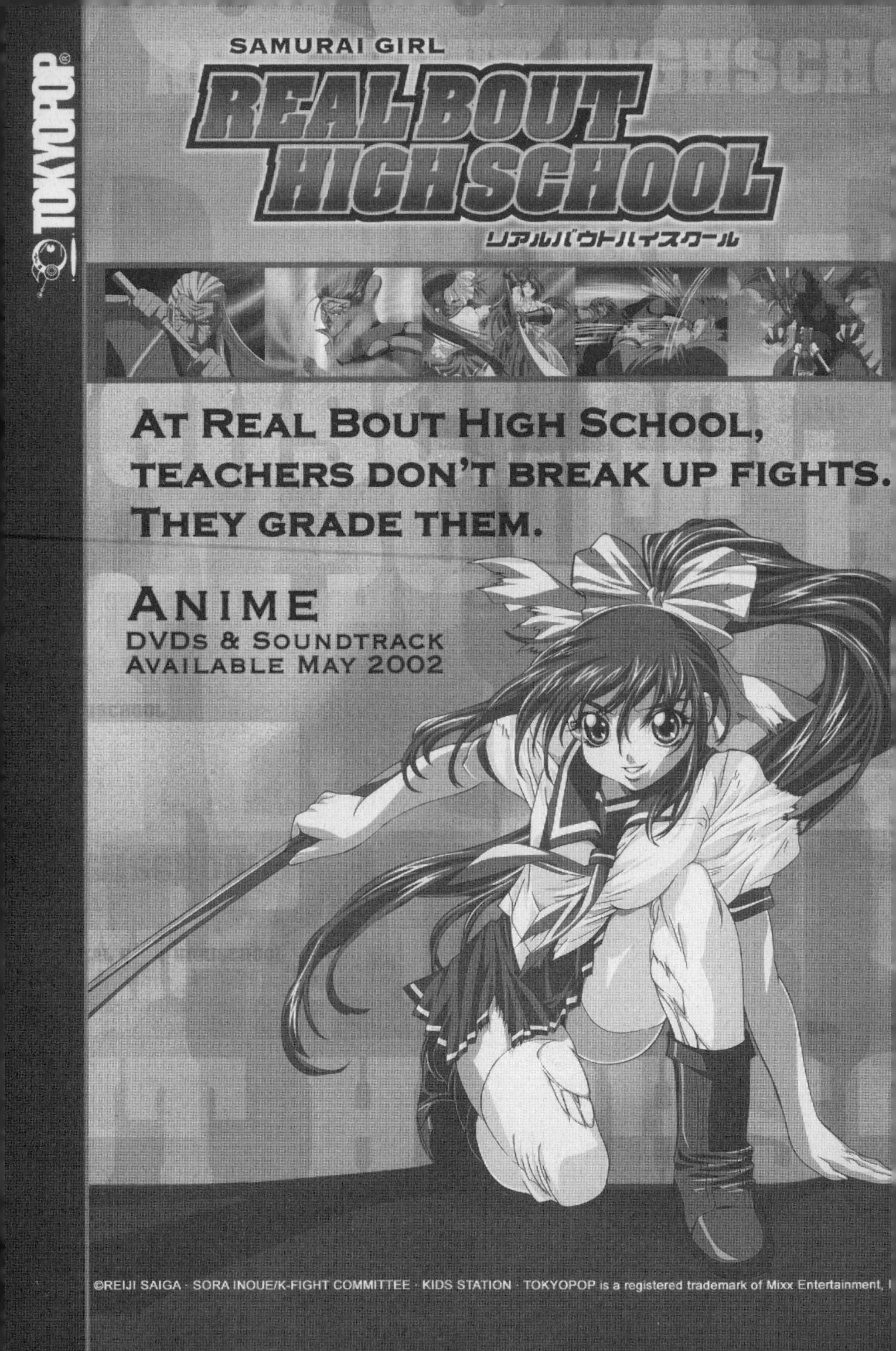

A Bad Boy Can Change
A Good Girl Forever.

Graphic Novels On Sale
April 2002!